FOREVER YOUNG

FOREVER YOUNG

A MEMOIR

Hayley Mills

WEIDENFELD & NICOLSON

First published in Great Britain in 2021 by Weidenfeld & Nicolson
an imprint of The Orion Publishing Group Ltd
Carmelite House, 50 Victoria Embankment
London EC4Y 0DZ

An Hachette UK Company

1 3 5 7 9 10 8 6 4 2

A CIP catalogue record for this book is
available from the British Library.

ISBN (Hardback) 978 1 4746 1936 3
ISBN (Export Trade Paperback) 978 1 4746 1937 0
ISBN (eBook) 978 1 4746 1939 4
ISBN (Audio) 978 1 4746 1940 0

Typeset by Input Data Services Ltd, Somerset

Printed in Great Britain by Clays Ltd, Elcograf S.p.A.

MIX
Paper from
responsible sources
FSC® C104740

www.weidenfeldandnicolson.co.uk
www.orionbooks.co.uk

For my grandchildren, with love

Introduction

For years I had been thinking about writing some sort of memoir but, for so many reasons, all my attempts had died on the vine. A short but life-changing bout with cancer in 2009 coupled with endless vacillation, hesitation and, to be honest, my lifelong struggle to be organised had left me with little more than a stack of dog-eared old exercise books, which was frustrating to say the least. I wanted to go back and remember, to make some sense of it all, not only for myself but also for my children who I felt deserved some clarity. After all, it was they who had borne the brunt, as well as reaped the benefits, of my unusual childhood.

Then in 2016 I was invited back to The Walt Disney Studios by a charismatic character called Howard Green – the Vice President of Studio Communications. We had a convivial lunch with some friends: the great songwriter and fellow Disney Legend Richard Sherman was there with his wife Elizabeth; Arlene Ludwig who had been head of publicity back in the day; and also some new friends, Michael Giaimo and Chris Buck, the brilliant co-creators of the global phenomenon that is *Frozen*.

After lunch they took me to the Animation Building, a place I'd visited many times as a child, where Walt's private office used to be. It is well known that on the day Walt left his office for the hospital, and for some considerable time after he died, nothing was changed or moved, apart from a bit of regular tidying by his secretaries. Everything was left almost exactly how it was when he walked out of the door for the last time, never to return. Eventually of course, it all had to be packed away, but not before every single inch of the office, and every object and article in it, was painstakingly inventoried and photographed, and then meticulously packed away in boxes and stored under the care of the Walt Disney Archives. One day, a smart young woman (now Director of the Archives) named Rebecca Cline had the inspired idea of restoring it to its original condition and turning it into a permanent exhibit. Which is exactly what they did – much like the Art Department would have done for the movie *Saving Mr. Banks*, only this time they had Walt's real materials – reconstructing everything down to the smallest, most precise detail. So, as you can imagine, I approached his office with some trepidation. I hadn't been back since I was eighteen and didn't know how I was going to feel.

But when I walked through that door all my initial concerns fell away, as did the years, and I was literally sent back in time . . . First you entered the outer office, where his smiling secretary always sat at a small brown desk on the left. On the wall directly in front of you, on rows of glass shelves, gleaming under the lights, were just some of the Oscars® he'd won over the years. In total, there were thirty-two of them. Each one representing years of work, each one imbued with his genius, and each one collected by Walt himself via the Academy Awards.

Straight ahead was the door to Walt's office. I opened it, stepped inside. It felt like a waking dream. Everything was unchanged, exactly as I'd remembered it. As if Walt had just stepped out of the room and would be back at any minute. This was a simple and comfortable space: a sofa, some armchairs, not at all the office of a movie mogul designed to impress. Walt's office was a place to work and think, to meet and talk. The more I walked around, the more came back to me. On his desk, little objects, papers and letters in the tray; photographs of his two girls, Diane and Sharon, his wife Lillian. A pen left on a pad with scribbled notes. Had he written to me sitting there at that desk?

And there was the baby grand, where the wonderful Sherman Brothers – Robert and Richard – used to play for Walt. I remember them both sitting there like it was yesterday, performing the song they'd written for me to sing in *The Parent Trap*. It was the first song they'd ever composed for a movie.

There was the little kitchenette with a bar and stools that had fascinated me as a child, fully equipped, every cupboard stocked with food and small bottles of Coca-Cola – all circa 1960.

And as I looked around, I became aware of the California sunlight streaming through the window, filling the room with shimmering, dancing beams of light. It was like returning to the Magician's study, a kind of sacred space.

Afterwards, Howard Green and Rebecca Cline kindly took me to The Walt Disney Archives and gave me access to this remarkable historical department, which is typically reserved for internal Company research only. Of course, all my files were there too, relating to the six films I had made for Disney, and I was given unrestricted access to these. As I went through box after box, I marvelled at how every single scrap of information had been preserved, recorded and carefully filed away. Press releases, interviews, in-house memoranda; all the letters that I had written to Walt (many of which had had to be typed out since my scribbling at that time was excruciating and often incomprehensible), and, of course, all Walt's letters to me. I was struck by how sweet they were, how personal, generous and loving. There were also letters between Walt and my parents, correspondence I was aware of but had never read, revealing tensions and disagreements about my career, much of which was a revelation to me. I was swept up by memories, so many came flooding back: the golden years of my childhood, the films I made, and of Walt Disney, the man.

Earlier that day, at lunch, Michael Giaimo had turned to me with his sweet smile, and said, 'So come on, Hayley, tell us ... What was he like?' The table hushed, they waited for my reply.

And then it hit me – of the hundreds of people now working at Disney, most had never known him, hadn't even met him. But I had. Walt Disney had been a kind of surrogate father to me through my teenage years, and the Studios had been my extended American family. For better or for worse, I'd literally grown up in Disneyland.

And that was it. The penny dropped. Not a bolt of lightning exactly, but the missing piece of jigsaw puzzle that I needed to write this book. For while this is the story of my childhood, and of course my career, it is also about a time which has now passed into history – when Hollywood was still 'Tinseltown' and the great Walt Disney was at his zenith, ruling over what was, at least in his own head, still a family business.

Flashback

The long shimmering line of black limousines inched their way forward. Cadillacs and Lincolns, all with their uniformed chauffeurs, seemed to glide towards the bright lights and the huge expectant crowd. It was a stifling hot California afternoon. Palm trees stood motionless under a cloudless sky as the leading car, a dark blue, shark-finned Cadillac, pulled up and the buzzing crowds began shoving and pushing forward, eager to get a better view. The passenger door swung open, two small feet, clad in white satin with diamond buckles, were placed delicately, side by side, upon the thick red carpet. The fans strained closer, the cameras flashed, and the owner of these two little feet finally revealed herself. Wearing a dazzling white dress with beautifully embroidered flowers tumbling down a long skirt, Elizabeth Taylor emerged like a goddess, sparkling with diamonds, smiling and radiant, at her most glorious.

The fans gasped and cheered as she moved like a queen into the barrage of exploding lights. The date was 17 April 1961 (the day before my birthday) at the Santa Monica Civic Auditorium – the 33rd Academy Awards. A glittering, glamorous, star-studded evening that would be etched in my mind's eye for the rest of my life – but for all the wrong reasons . . .

Hollywood royalty was turning out in force. These were the glory days when all the big stars still lived in Tinseltown, in the great mansions of Rodeo Drive, on Benedict Canyon and Laurel Canyon. When the Brown Derby restaurant on Wilshire

Boulevard and the Polo Lounge at the Beverly Hills Hotel were still bustling with the Bad and the Beautiful, glamorous stars, famous faces, writers and directors, movers and shakers, before they later dispersed all over the world, and before the new kid on the block, television, claimed the town, watered it down and changed it all for ever. But that was yet to come. This warm evening in 1961 belonged to old Hollywood when it was still the world capital of the Motion Picture Industry. The stars were out and everyone who was anyone was there: Spencer Tracy, Katharine Hepburn, Alfred Hitchcock, Yul Brynner, Jimmy Stewart, John Wayne, the legendary Greer Garson, evoking the charm and dignity of a bygone era; the beautiful Eva Marie Saint and Deborah Kerr, the sultry Gina Lollobrigida, the exquisite Janet Leigh with her husband Tony Curtis.

The anticipation in the great auditorium was intoxicating. As the stars settled down in their seats, a sharply dressed man in a dapper tuxedo walked out on stage: the evening's presenter, Bob Hope, by now already an Academy institution. With his dry wit and deadpan delivery he instantly held them all in the palm of his hand. And yet, behind the smiles and careless laughter of this illustrious congregation – silent prayers. All the hopes, ambitions and dreams of so many people. To win an Oscar has always meant so much: recognition and acceptance – and, in an insecure business, also the guarantee of more work. Bestowed by one's peers, it is the highest accolade. To win an Oscar is to have a little piece of immortality.

The 33rd Academy Awards saw the crowning of Billy Wilder's *The Apartment*, which won five Oscars, including Best Film, Best Screenplay and Best Director. A sweetly shy Billy Wilder collected his award from Audrey Hepburn, enchantingly fawn-like in Givenchy with long white gloves.

The Apartment's Shirley MacLaine was nominated for Best Actress, but she lost to Elizabeth Taylor who played a call girl in the film *Butterfield 8*. She walked slowly up to the stage to collect her Oscar, carefully escorted by her new husband Eddie Fisher; she was suffering severe pain from a recent back injury.

Jack Lemmon had also been nominated for *The Apartment*. This was his second consecutive nomination for Best Actor. The year before he'd been nominated for another Billy Wilder film, *Some Like It Hot* – surely tonight it would be his. In the end, it turned out he lost. Again. Even to this day, it seems comedy performances are not appreciated in the same way as dramatic roles. That night was no different; Burt Lancaster won for his dramatic role as the fiery preacher in *Elmer Gantry*. He walked up to the stage, looking like an image carved into Mount Rushmore, while Jack remained in his seat applauding generously.

The evening was not long by today's standards, speeches were brief and to the point – some even left you wanting more (Billy Wilder: 'Thank you so much, you lovely discerning people. Thank you.'). Peter Ustinov bounded up to the stage to collect Best Supporting Actor for *Spartacus*, sporting a distinctly Bolshevik-looking beard, which many people remarked on as being incredibly brave – or slightly reckless – considering Senator McCarthy's witch-hunt was still a bitter taste.

And then came the Honorary Oscars. Gary Cooper, one of the most charming, romantic and charismatic actors of all time, was given a lifetime achievement award; the wonderful Stan Laurel was awarded for 'Creative pioneering in the field of cinema comedy' . . . and then – a newcomer. A miniature statuette was awarded for Best Juvenile performance, an Oscar not given since 1954. The very first winner of this award had been Shirley Temple in 1935, when she was a tiny tot, aged six. Bob Hope stepped aside and with a great fanfare Miss Temple herself appeared on stage to present the award. At thirty-three years old, with her sweet face and charming smile, she still looked exactly like the young star who had sung and danced her way into the hearts of America.

'Charles Boyer invests in Real Estate,' she announced. 'Fred MacMurray has cattle. And John Mills has daughters.' An appreciative chuckle echoed in the auditorium. 'The Academy tonight presents an Oscar to a young actress who has brought grace and talent to the screen: the star of Walt Disney's *Pollyanna* – Miss Hayley Mills.'

The audience burst into warm applause. Shirley Temple beamed merrily at the camera while so many famous pairs of hands clapped together in celebration . . .

I was only fourteen at the time. One day shy of my fifteenth birthday. I want to tell you how it was the most amazing night of my life, or at least one of the most memorable, but I'm afraid I can't – because I wasn't there. Not only was I absent, I wasn't even conscious of it taking place. I was thousands of miles away in England, fast asleep, in a freezing cold boarding school dormitory, totally unaware of the honour being bestowed.

The fact that I slept through the 33rd Academy Awards would prove strangely prophetic. Looking back with the hindsight that time has given me, I can see how, for so much of my childhood career, I was like a passenger, passively 'sleepwalking' through so many incredible experiences, never completely aware or in control of my life. To say I went 'through the looking glass' and 'down the rabbit hole' would be putting it mildly. At the age of twelve my life was tipped on its head and I was plunged, literally, into Wonderland, often feeling very much like Lewis Carroll's bewildered Alice.

Perhaps that's just how it is to grow up. One minute you're free and innocent, full of the joys of life, and then suddenly you're struggling to make sense of anything. I had some amazing luck and good fortune, but it all came at a price. The sole purpose of every young girl should be to become a happy, strong and well-adjusted woman, but growing up is tough at the best of times, let alone when a multimillion-dollar career depends on you remaining a child. Writing about it sixty years on, I wonder whether this book is perhaps my first real chance to understand and take ownership of the strange and remarkable things that happened to me – and to that young girl who went through the looking glass.

CHAPTER ONE

First Act

Hayley is a boy's name. My maternal grandfather was Francis Hayley Bell but everyone always called him Hayley. The Bells came from Scotland, and at some point in the family history, the name Hayley was added.

Before I was born my mother was certain that she was going to have a boy. He would have red hair and green eyes, the image of her adored father who had died in London during the Blitz. Like him, he would be brave and adventurous, a writer and a dreamer, and she would call him Hayley.

Then I arrived, which must have been a bit of a disappointment – but they called me Hayley anyway.

One of my earliest memories is of standing on the balcony of our house in Chelsea with my sister Juliet, or Bunch, as we called her. It's a cold November morning and we are watching my mother being lifted out of an ambulance onto a stretcher. My father is holding a small bundle, wrapped in a white shawl trailing down to the ground, somebody else is wheeling an oxygen tank . . . The bundle is my brother, Jonathan. The flame-haired boy she has longed for, who would indeed grow up to be, in many ways, just like my grandfather Francis Hayley.

It was years before I understood how desperately she had

wanted to have a boy, not only to give my father a son, but, in some unconscious way, to bring her father back; for he had always said that if there was a 'way back' he would find it. Francis had spent most of his life in China. He was a soldier, a writer, 'officially' working for the British government, unofficially operating as a British spy. He spoke many Chinese dialects and had gone deeply into Eastern culture, becoming something of a Buddhist – hence his belief in reincarnation. During the pregnancy my mother was consumed with anxiety and nearly lost the baby due to terrible asthma attacks. After Jonathan was born the asthma went away and never came back.

So there were three of us kids: Bunchy, who was seven years old, three-year-old me, and now Jonathan had arrived, making me the middle one.

Our home at 98 Cheney Walk was a tall London house with lots of stairs. The nursery was at the top and our windows over-looked the Thames where the great barges moved slowly up and down the river. Every day we went for a walk along Chelsea Embankment with Nanny in her grey uniform, and Jonathan in his capacious pram, his wispy red hair sticking out from under his bonnet; Bunchy and I in our matching blue coats with dark velvet collars, and Hamlet the golden cocker spaniel at our heels. Bunchy always wanted to be a ballerina. She already looked like one, with her corn silk hair pushed back off her face with an Alice band, and her quick light movements. She'd dance ahead of me and I was always trying to catch up. She never stopped talking and was terribly pretty. She reminded me of a yellow daffodil. From the beginning I adored her.

London always seemed to be dark and wintry. It was as if the years of war had drained the colour from everything; food was still rationed, blackout curtains still hung thick and heavy, lights were turned out as soon as you left a room. So much was black: black cars, black taxis, black bowler hats and umbrellas, shiny black shoes. Everyone wore raincoats and hats and gloves. The bright red double-decker buses and the scarlet letter boxes were the only splash of vibrant colour in a monochrome world. Across the river you could see Battersea Power Station belching thick smoke. When you bent down to smell a flower in the garden you came up with a black nose.

I was a very ordinary, happy-go-lucky child with no great ambitions. Tagging along with Mummy and Daddy and my older sister, squabbling with my younger brother. Daddy seemed always to be working. His name was John Mills, a well-known actor, already a movie star by the time I was born, and my mother, Mary Hayley Bell, was a successful playwright, so I don't suppose you could call it an ordinary childhood – but it was a childhood. This is before everything was turned upside down, of course. Until I was twelve, I had no expectations of being an actress or a performer of any kind. I don't think I even thought about it, not once. I was just a carefree little girl who was supposed to have been a boy.

Our lives were very ordered and spent mostly with Nanny in the nursery. She was employed to look after us, to cook breakfast, lunch and tea in the nursery, and then, after she'd bathed us all, she would take us downstairs in our dressing gowns to spend some time with Mummy and Daddy – before saying goodnight. We'd often see some of their friends down there, having drinks and smoking cigarettes, and I remember being enveloped in their perfume as they bent down to say goodnight.

When Bunchy was nine she was sent away to a boarding school in Camberley, a ballet academy called Elmhurst, where I would eventually go. I missed her terribly when she went away, but she left Stanley with me. Stanley was her white mouse, named after our parents' esteemed solicitor Stanley Passmore, who would one day cast a great shadow over all our finances. I had a mouse too, called Elsie. Elsie and Stanley were married, so they had to stay together; they did everything together, even escaped out of our pockets together in the ladies clothing department in Fortnum &

Mason, causing pandemonium. Women shrieked, wrapped their skirts round their legs and jumped onto chairs. The manager had to be called in. Stanley and Elsie were finally found swinging happily on some clothes hangers.

You could say my parents were restless souls. Daddy was always seeking a new experience, he flung his arms wide to embrace life with total confidence and optimism. To quote J.M. Barrie, 'He was youth, he was joy, he was the little bird that had just broken out of the egg' – he *was* Peter Pan, really. Peter Pan without his dark side, I never saw any evidence of that. He adored what he did until the day he died at ninety-seven and never lost his love and enthusiasm for the business or the people in it. He was a true Piscean and had no enemies. People couldn't resist him. From his early life, as the son of a schoolteacher in a small village in Suffolk, to the top of his profession as an actor, his great gaiety and charm and youthful spirit carried him through. But his greatest love of all was my mother Mary Hayley Bell. Born in Shanghai, she had spent the first twelve years of her life in China; which is where my parents first met when my father was travelling the Far East with a shoestring theatre company, euphoniously named 'The Quaints'. The eldest of five children, Mummy was smart and beautiful, with thick shining copper-coloured hair, enormous green eyes and an Irish wit. She had a barbed tongue and a wicked sense of humour, which could be hysterically funny or downright cruel depending on her moods, which were unpredictable. Growing up wild and carefree, riding her pony bareback along the bund in Shanghai and Macau, she wasn't prepared for life in a cold English boarding school, which was an inevitability for many of these 'outcastes of the East', as Kipling called them. When Mummy was twelve, she and her younger sister Winnifred were sent to school in England and wouldn't see their family for a year. Whatever complexities she may have had as a child, I think this forced exile affected her deeply. She was a romantic spirit with a deep Celtic melancholy, which she struggled with her whole life and tried to express in her writing. Mummy was interested in all sorts of ideas and concepts, from the Enlightenment to Esoterica. She became friends with a famous astrologer from the *Daily Express*, who came to the house one day and, having drawn up our birth charts, gravely predicted that Hayley would 'never have children' and Juliet would 'never be legally married' – both turned out to be wrong. She must have been having an off day.

My parents moved house constantly. Daddy was always looking for the next phase of his life. By the time I left home at twenty I had lived in eight different houses. Mummy had a brilliant way of making a house beautiful and elegant, a welcoming home full of flowers and warmth. My parents' intense devotion to each other was the source of our security. We were all loved, there was no doubt about that, but their relationship came first. It was their world, we just fitted into it; that was simply how things were supposed to be.

Sometimes we would be taken to the studios or to the theatre where Daddy was working. On one occasion he was rehearsing a play in the West End – *Angel*, written by my mother – when, just before breakfast, Nanny gave in her notice, saying she wanted to be an air stewardess and had to catch the 9.30 train. So Mummy bundled Bunch and me into the back of the car and we all drove off to Wyndham's theatre. While Bunch played happily in the stalls, climbing on the red seats and chatting rather too loudly to herself, I was put in the charge of an understudy actor. This arrangement was all working fine until my mother suddenly noticed, to her horror, that the understudy was now on stage and her two-year-old daughter was nowhere to be seen. They hunted high and low, for well over an hour, until I was finally discovered just up the street in a neighbouring theatre, The Albery, sitting contentedly on the stage doorkeeper's lap, having sardines levelled into my mouth on the back of a knife. Neither the doorkeeper nor I seemed the least bit concerned.

I loved going to the film studios. When Daddy was filming near us, he would sometimes take me with him; he'd tie me to his waist with a leading rein, and we'd ride on his Lambretta. Once I was there I would be free to wander off and explore the studios, to chat to the chippies and the sparks, to play on the sets that weren't being used. From the very first I loved that world; the smell of wood shavings and paint, of Dettol in the corridors; the dark, silent sets. Everything was real and yet it wasn't: doors that seemed perfectly normal, but led nowhere; the props on a mantelpiece, the books on a shelf; all part of another, imaginary world. Then when the bright lights were turned on and the crew and actors arrived, everything came alive, everything became real. I would watch my father preparing to shoot a scene; check his mark on the floor, find his light, then clear his throat, lick his lips and sweep his eyelashes up with his finger and thumb; a make-up girl darts in to smooth down an invisible hair. He would clear his throat again.

'Quiet please!'

The bell rings, the red light is switched on.

'Action!' He steps forward towards the camera, hits the mark without looking for it . . . Or not. He says something wry, a murmur of laughter from behind the camera, and the process starts again.

I used to live in my own world of make-believe. My games would go on all day, pretending I was somebody else even when I was called in to tea, to have a bath and get ready for bed. I think it was probably a great advantage being the middle child – they tend not to get quite so much attention. Too much attention can be as bad as too little. My elder sister was bright and articulate, breaking new ground and challenging my parents constantly, while my younger brother was my mother's pride and joy, which left me more space to get on with my own things without too much interference. Their nickname for me was 'Bags' – I've never been entirely sure why. I was the clumsy one. Basically, I was regarded as a bit of a joke. I made people laugh and that was OK. I wasn't particularly pretty, I had big teeth and a nose someone once described as a lump of putty. I'd never have an aquiline nose like my mother's, I knew that for a fact. Daddy used to shoot hundreds of feet of home movies and we'd all sit on the floor shrieking with laughter and sending each other up. Bunch was always very generous in her observations.

When I was ten years old, I followed Bunch to boarding school. She was in the Senior House so I didn't see that much of her, but, as she was a school prefect, I bathed in her reflected glory. She was hugely popular and lots of Juniors had 'pashies' on her. However, when I arrived on the scene the housemistress, Miss Dodson, was not impressed and went out of her way to keep me in my place. One night, soon after I had arrived, I was in the kitchen, having taken out the dirty plates, and was just on my way back into the House dining room, when I heard my name. Miss Dodson was addressing the room.

'. . . just because she's John Mills's daughter doesn't make her any better than anybody else. And if I catch anyone "sucking up" to her, there will be trouble.'

I didn't understand what she meant. I took a deep breath, entered, and was rooted to the spot as fifty pairs of eyes turned to look at me.

I was given a wide berth for quite some time after that. Nobody would talk to me.

Miss Dodson was short and fat, her clothes were all too tight, her nose was like a beak, and with her glasses reflecting the light she looked like a little fat owl. After all these years, I harbour no resentment towards Miss Dodson whatsoever, but I have to say – she used to dribble into the porridge when she was serving breakfast.

School life wasn't all bad, of course. In prep one night, I saw a new girl sitting at her desk at the back of the room. She was very pretty with short dark brown hair. I went up to her and asked her what her name was.

'Jane,' she said.

'My name's Hayley. Will you be my best friend?'

'Yes,' she said, and then roared with laughter. I knew I'd made a good choice. She still laughs that wonderful laugh and we've been friends ever since.

There was a small wooden chapel at Elmhurst and somehow the whole school managed to cram themselves into it every day – and twice on Sundays. It was an Anglo-Catholic institution with a rather Byronic-looking school priest called Father John. He gave wonderful sermons. Tall and thin, he had a startlingly thick thatch of black hair with a few strands of silver, a pale, almost haggard face, and large dark soulful eyes. Some of the girls were in love with him – I wasn't one of them. But he was the only male we ever saw, apart from the gardener, who must have been at least a hundred.

I remember the services in that little chapel, they had a kind of magic. The coloured cloth on the altar, Father John's vestments, the smell of incense, the choir all dressed in grey with blue veils over their hair like novice nuns. The soloist was Miss Fischer, the Head of Ballet; a striking woman with iron grey hair in a roll at the back of her head and the most sublime voice – although you never actually saw her. Just her voice would appear, emanating from the back of the choir stalls. It was ethereal, like an angel. I started to read the Bible, Mummy's Bible that she'd had as a child. It was falling apart, the pages were thin and starting to turn brown, and the print was so tiny I could hardly read it, but it all added to the sacredness and the mystery.

At the end of every term there was a show. I imagined myself dancing in point shoes wearing a beautiful dress made of gossamer but something told me that was never going to happen. I was always given the scruffy parts, usually playing boy's roles. One time I played a fairy on the top of a Christmas tree wearing a very bedraggled dress made of tulle, and waving a wonky wand. I sang a funny song, and, to my amazement and delight, everybody laughed. It was the most wonderful experience, making people laugh. It was a revelation. This left a deep impression and, looking back, it was all leading me towards acting, although I would not have believed it if you had told me.

By the time I was ten years old, we'd moved to the country, to a fourteenth-century farmhouse with four hundred acres on the Kent and Sussex border. We had a herd of beautiful Guernsey cows, pigs, chickens, ducks on a pond and a Dutch barn, and no central heating. It was really for us children to grow up in and we all adored it. That is, all except Mummy. Beautiful though the farm was, she had left her heart in a Georgian house on the top of Richmond Hill called The Wick, just outside London. Pete Townshend of The Who lives there now. Mummy was inwardly troubled and prone to dark moods, but I don't think my father quite understood why. She was a writer with a poet's soul and I'm not sure she ever really wanted to live on a farm in Sussex, however romantic it might have been. She felt cut off from life, from her friends, from the stimulation of the city. People would come down and visit, of course, for the weekend or for Sunday lunch. Friends and fellow actors like Bernard Miles, Richard and Sheila Attenborough, and Lionel Jeffries and his family who used to come often. They'd all put on Wellington boots and trudge around smoking cigarettes, talking and laughing and drinking rather a lot – always lots of drinking, always lots of laughter – and picking armfuls of bluebells that would all be dead by the time they got home. I think Lionel Jeffries was one of the funniest men I've ever met; it was difficult to eat your lunch sometimes because you were laughing so much. He was six foot three and his shiny bald head was permanently scarred by the constant bashing of his skull on our low-beamed doorways. One week, the actor, writer and director Bryan Forbes brought this beautiful girl he was going to marry. I was mesmerised by her. She had the most beautiful voice. Her name was Nanette Newman. When my parents got together with Dickie and Bryan and Lionel it became absolutely riotous. Clever, witty people with a passion for life.

For a while, we were settled. My father doing his acting, while my mother would go off and write. She had an old Romany caravan parked in a nearby field, you could see it from the house. She'd had it since before I was born and it was always to the caravan that she went when she was writing. It was green and red, and the long grasses tangled themselves around the yellow wheels; you could hear the sound of her typewriter tap, tap, tapping away during the long idle summer afternoons.

The farm was a world unto itself. I'd spend hours on my skewbald pony Annabelle, roaming all day, across the fields, into the woods, singing at the top of my voice into her feathery ears; or sitting on Daphne, my favourite cow, during milking time, reading *Dandy* and *Beano* comics. There was always a radio playing music in the cowshed to relax them. Brian, the farm manager's son, said it helped with the milk yield. Bunch was in love with Brian. In the summer, with his wavy sun-bleached hair, we thought he looked like Michelangelo's 'David' in a pair of old Levi's and rubber boots.

Jonathan was by now about seven, thin as a rail, with dark red hair falling over his mother's blue-green eyes. He'd hang out all day with the men hedging and ditching, while they ploughed long furrows into dark brown corduroy fields. We'd make hideouts in the Dutch barn, climb trees, unblock streams with sticks, wander over the hills and far away. At mealtimes we'd hear the tune 'Come to the Cook House Door, Boys' played on the trumpet (Daddy was learning it for the film *It's Great to Be Young*), and there would be a mad race back to the house to get one of Soxie's enormous meals. Soxie was our housekeeper for years and she became like family. Her real name was Nell, Nellie Hicks, and she was married to Harold the Herdsman. They lived in the cottage at the start of the drive that wound down between the high hedges and fields to the farm. I think they'd been there all their married life. We called her Soxie because, well, she literally used to wash our socks by hand – much better than any machine, she said, as it made them last longer and need less darning. Soxie was quite a small person, sturdy and round like a little cottage loaf, with all the warmth and reassuring goodness of home-baked bread. Her hair was straight, a soft sort of grey, cut in a pudding basin, parted on one side and held in place by a large black kirby grip. Her eyes were round and blue as cornflowers, and her cheeks were round too, the colour of little russet apples you'd find in the long grass. She was always smiling and her voice was soft with a sweet Sussex burr. 'Hullo my darlin',' she'd say. 'How're you today?' Like she really wanted to know. We all adored her – how could you not. Soxie had lived in Sussex all her life and until we took her to Hollywood, she'd never left it.

So my life was boarding school then back to the farm. If I close my eyes it's all still there as I left it: the cold night air, the silence, the stillness, a sudden startled bird or creature crying out in the darkness, the faint smell of earth and trees and cows and Calor gas stoves; eiderdowns, candlewick bedspreads, Viyella pyjamas and Euthymol toothpaste; the blue-and-white-striped china, jugs full of fresh milk from the dairy; Sanderson's rose-patterned sofas and armchairs, curtains with hunting scenes, and gleaming horse brasses on the beam over the fireplace; Soxie's Yorkshire pudding and her sublime Victoria sponge . . .

And then, one Sunday afternoon, everything changed.

J. Lee Thompson, a well-known film director and an old friend of my father's, came down to the farm to talk about a new movie he was planning to make called *Tiger Bay*. It was going to be a thriller: a police chief pursues a fugitive sailor who has killed his cheating girlfriend in a crime of passion. The desperate man abducts the only witness to the murder – a nine-year-old boy from the docks – and while on the run, this odd couple develop a touching friendship. The boy ends up trying to protect the man so he can escape the police. The role of the man was going to be played by a famous young German actor, Horst Buchholz, in his first English-speaking role, and Lee wanted Daddy to play the Police Superintendent leading the case.

Lee and my father talked it over as they wandered down to the new swimming pool. We had excavated it ourselves with the tractor that summer. It was always freezing and filled with tadpoles and bugs. As they sauntered down they passed me, playing with some other kids; I was messing about doing silly impersonations of TV commercials. Television was still relatively novel in those days, and, in between rescue operations retrieving struggling beetles from the water, I'd perform TV jingles, doing the voices:

> *'Murray Mints, Murray Mints,*
> *Too good to hurry mints,*
> *Why make haste when you can taste,*
> *The hint of mint in Murray Mints!'*

Lee and Daddy were puffing away on their cigarettes, discussing location filming in Cardiff, the influence of documentary-style realism in New Wave cinema . . .

> *'You'll wonder where the yellow went*
> *When you go steady with Pepsodent!*
> *Pepsodent! Pepsodent!'*

My father could see that Lee had a fresh, exciting vision for the movie: set in the vibrant, buzzing, multicultural community of Tiger Bay, photographed with all the dramatic black and white shadows of a noir thriller; it would be a thrilling police chase with a touching 'odd couple' story at its centre.

> *'Palmolive, Palmolive, smoother with olive oil,*
> *Gentlest soap of all!'*

(This one involved seductive action as if washing oneself in the bath)

But Daddy could also see a weak link. A potential for this movie not to work at all.

'A lot hangs on the child,' my father said, thinking out loud, with growing uncertainty. 'He's very central to the success of the story. Their relationship really is the heart of the film . . . You need to find him first.'

'Oh, I already have,' said Lee.

'Really?' said Daddy, at once surprised and relieved. 'That's fantastic! Where did you find him?'

'Over there!' And Lee pointed at me.

My father was speechless. And then I believe he simply laughed.

I had only just turned twelve, had never been in front of a camera, never done anything except these awful 'scruffy boys' parts at school. And to add to that – I was a girl. It was quite a leap for him to make.

A short while later, we all sat down and had lunch together.

'How would you like to be in a film, Hayley?' Lee asked me casually.

My mouth was so full of Soxie's Yorkshire pudding that I couldn't speak.

'We'd have to do a screen test first, of course, see what you look like on camera,' he said, chuckling. 'And meet Horst Buchholz. But I've got a hunch you could do it . . . What do you think?'

By this time the Yorkshire pudding had gone down.

'Oh, yes!' I said, nodding my head furiously, my voice sounding a bit strangled. 'Yes, yes I'd love to do that. Thank you.'

We all met Lee again, a few days later, for lunch at the Ritz Hotel. I could tell this meeting was important. Maybe he would change his mind? I could also sense Mummy was slightly nervous. Before becoming a writer, she'd been a struggling actress herself. She hadn't had quite the same lucky breaks that Daddy had had – like being discovered by Noël Coward, while performing *Mr Cinders* in Singapore, of all places – so she knew only too well how tough the business really was. Perhaps this meeting was pushing old buttons. Halfway across the road in Piccadilly, in front of the hotel, my mother suddenly hissed at me.

'Bend your knees!'

'What?' I stared back.

'You look too tall. Bend your knees!' she whispered and marched on.

I hunched down, bent my knees until my skirt was down to my ankles, and crossed the rest of the road, probably looking like a humpbacked dwarf who'd wet her knickers.

The Ritz was the most incredible hotel I'd ever been in: like a palace, sitting on the corner of Green Park and Piccadilly. I felt I was stepping into another world of elegance and opulence. The carpets were deep and soft, the painted ceilings soared over my head with enormous gleaming chandeliers and huge carved golden mirrors. It made you feel you should whisper. The dining room must be one of the most beautiful in the world: breathtaking views across the park to Buckingham Palace, French windows draped with heavy silk curtains, immaculate tables covered with snowy white linen and sparkling crystal, and in the middle of this glorious space, a mountain of fresh flowers. I was awestruck.

We enjoyed lunch and before long Mummy and Lee were deep in conversation about the film. I should have been listening carefully, but I was busy sticking bread sticks into the snow-white butter that matched my snow-white table napkin, so I wasn't paying too much attention. Jonathan, however, most certainly was. He was hanging on every word, looking increasingly unhappy, and glancing at this enormous watch he was wearing on his wrist. It wasn't because he was jealous of his sister being the centre of attention; it was because he was seeing the family holiday we had planned in Italy slipping away from him.

'Don't forget she peels!' he exclaimed suddenly and rather loudly.

'What?' The conversation ground to a halt.

'Hayley – she peels in the sun. Her nose, her back, her whole face. She looks awful.'

He was looking a bit desperate. My parents stifled a laugh.

'Don't worry,' Daddy said with a reassuring smile. 'We don't start shooting until September, there's plenty of time for our holiday.'

So, I did a screen test. It took place at Beaconsfield Film Studios in Buckinghamshire, owned by the British Lion Film Corporation. We started filming at 9.30 in the morning, I wore my favourite tartan shirt with a hole in the top pocket. We were all quite keen on tartan, my family. The Hayley Bells had a clan tartan – the Macmillan – so we all wore lots of it, sometimes different tartans all at the same time: tartan trousers, tartan hats, tartan shirts and waistcoats, it must have been quite an eyesore for anyone who knew anything about tartans. I was sent to the make-up department and then Lee introduced me to Horst Buchholz. He was tall and good looking, and I remember noticing how his mouth curled up at the corners as if he was about to smile. And he smiled a lot. And laughed a lot. He had a way of making me laugh too, just by looking at me. I loved his voice, his German accent fascinated me. Horst was a heart-throb in Germany. After *Tiger Bay* he went to Hollywood and starred in *The Magnificent Seven*. When I met Horst that day he was just twenty-four and I adored him on sight.

The screen test seemed to go smoothly. It had been easy for Lee to reimagine the boy's role as a girl and apparently the script hadn't needed much changing. We filmed the Superintendent's scene, in which I was questioned and cross-examined by my father; and then the dramatic confrontation in the church loft, where the little boy – now a girl, called Gillie – steals the killer's weapon and holds him at gunpoint. At the end of the morning's shoot everyone went to the Bull Hotel in Gerrards Cross for lunch and Lee happily announced that they were stuck with me. I'd got the part. Lee ordered a bottle of champagne, I had my favourite fried scampi and a Coca-Cola, and Horst's eyes twinkled away at me across the table.

Once again, the Fates had conspired: someone who was looking for a boy, had got me instead.

And Jonathan got his holiday in Italy.

Before the whirlwind surprise of *Tiger Bay*, my parents had already planned to stay with Rex Harrison and his family in Portofino. We arrived there in the pouring rain. This was an omen. We had started to drag our suitcases up a muddy track that led to their villa, which was perched on a hill overlooking the little port, when Rex suddenly appeared with his new wife Kay Kendall, two tall thin figures, laughing and waving to us from under an enormous umbrella. Both were wearing crumpled linen shirts and trousers, with old faded espadrilles on their slim brown feet. They struck me as incredibly glamorous, even in the pouring rain. Rex's previous wife had been another legendary beauty, the famous German film star Lilli Palmer – she was also my godmother, although I rarely saw her.

Kay Kendall was like no one I'd ever met. She reminded me of a beautiful Afghan hound, never making a single move or gesture that wasn't elegant. She was naturally graceful and also terribly funny. A comedienne, she had the wildest, and quite the rudest, sense of humour. It was astonishing to hear it come out of that exquisite face.

We all ate ripe figs and Charentais melon and Prosciutto sitting on the terrace in the blazing sun, gazing down over the shimmering blue Mediterranean. I also had my first taste of Italian gelato, never to be forgotten. The grownups sat around in the sun, laughing, talking, drinking copious amounts of the local Blanc de Blanc; they'd fool about on Rex's yacht and leap shrieking into the sparkling water. Unfortunately, there was a plague of jelly fish, the size of dinner plates, which were virtually invisible and left great painful welts all over your body. After lunch, when the grownups would go upstairs for a much-needed siesta, Jonathan and I would play with Rex's son, Carey. He was a little older than me, sweet and quiet and very clever. He'd spend hours in his cool shuttered room, playing army battles, which he had devised using the hundreds of bottle tops he'd collected. His father was scathing about it ('Go and play with your bottle tops!' he'd snap dismissively). Sexy Rexy, as Daddy named him, could be quite cruel. All the charm and smiles would disappear in a flash with a cutting remark. I don't think he was very interested in children.

One night Rex and my mother had a terrible row. I'm not sure what it was about – it may even have been about Carey – but it ended with us all rather ignominiously dragging our suitcases back down the hill to stay in a little *pensione* in the port. It was slightly awkward to say the least. Mummy and Rex did make up before we left; we had dinner sitting outside on the cobbles and Carey sat on the ground at Rex's feet with his chin on his father's knee.

Once the summer was over, we returned to Britain with the film now looming. Daddy and I both had lots of lines to learn. Sometimes Daddy would suggest we run through a scene while we were driving somewhere, or once, when we were walking through Mayfair in the centre of London. We were going through the police interrogation scene, when he suddenly stopped in the middle of the pavement, grabbed me roughly and shook me by the shoulders – *Shake!*

'Is this the man you saw coming out of that woman's flat, Gillie?' he shouted in my face – *Shake!*

'Is it?!' – *Shake!* 'Think Gillie, think!' – *More shakes!*

Scandalising a woman walking past us, we both grinned rather weakly at her and then beat a hasty retreat up the street before she called a policeman.

Finally, on 15 September 1958, J. Lee Thompson started filming *Tiger Bay*. I was twelve years old.

Cardiff's docks had been called Tiger Bay for so long, no one could remember how it got the name. Some believed that sailors had brought the name from California, where in San Francisco a similar quarter was known by the same title. In the days of the fast sailing ships, as British trade expanded across the world, this Welsh fishing creek in the Bristol Channel grew into the world's largest coal port. The dock area was famously infested with thugs and harpies and prostitutes of the most vicious type who operated as thieves' decoys. 'These women, as dangerous as tigers' – hence the name.* Not long after we finished filming *Tiger Bay*, the old tenement buildings were razed to the ground, the playground cemented over, and new, clean but soulless high-rise flats took their place. The thugs and harpies and prostitutes went too. But also, sadly, the name: Tiger Bay is now Bute's Bay named after the Marquis of Bute who owned the land.

When I arrived there in 1958 Tiger Bay was a vibrant, noisy, multicultural and, according to local residents, largely peaceful community filled with families and children from a myriad of different backgrounds all living together. The docks brought great ships and tankers from across the world, and with them seamen from foreign lands many of whom stayed and married and raised their families in Tiger Bay. Lee's vision for the film was to portray this diverse slice of society as honestly and vividly as he could, shooting on location, employing local extras for the scenes. I don't think it had really been done before in British cinema, certainly never in Wales. None of us knew it then, of course, but the film would soon become an important historical document of a bygone time.

The first day of filming was for the opening scene in the movie. We were on the old ramp leading down to the water, a long black stone wall with a solid iron railing. The big clock on the Pier head showed 8 a.m. It was overcast and a cold wind from the Bristol Channel ruffled the water across the bay. Under my blue duffel coat I wore Gillie's clothes, my one and only costume for the film. It had been put together by my mother in London: the dark blue

---

* David Martin, *Tiger Bay* (1946). Martin & Reid, London.

jeans, the old blue sweater with the arms cut off above the elbow (that was her idea, she cut them herself with a pair of scissors) and finally a pair of black plimsolls. That was it.

Somebody gave me a mug of hot sweet tea and I looked around at the rest of the cast. All kids. Most of the children in the scene were local except for Michael Anderson Jnr, who was already an experienced actor at thirteen. There was a local boy called Neil Sinclair, who would go on to become a celebrated historian and write books about the history of Tiger Bay, but I had never met any of them. It was a bit like a first day at school, the kids regarding each other silently as Lee Thompson explained what we were going to do.

In this scene, the children are playing a noisy game of Cowboys and Indians. Gillie wants to join in but they don't want her: she's a girl, she hasn't got a gun, just a tiny lead bomb on a string that bangs, one pitiful cap at a time. Some of the boys make fun of her and her silly bomb on a string, which they steal. She flies at one of them in a fury, pummelling his chest with her fists. I found that difficult. I didn't even know his name, he was extremely thin and bony, and he seemed so nice. I apologised to him afterwards.

After that first day, I took to filming like a duck to water. It was a small independent British film, so nobody made any sort of fuss about me on the set. I didn't seem to feel the cold; people were always rushing at me with my duffel coat, which I never wanted to put on. Nothing fazed me: singing in front of the church congregation, or to Horst in the scene in the belfry, I just did it. Helped I'm sure by those times at home I'd sung at the piano with my father for his long-suffering guests. Learning lines was easy and quick. I could never understand what took my father so long to learn his – he'd disappear into his room with his tape recorder for hours. What was he doing in there? I'd learnt mine, that was that. It was a few years before I discovered that there was actually quite a lot more to it than that. Years later when I was struggling to keep my head above the murky waters of adolescence, I yearned for the simplicity and ease of those first days.

It was wonderful to be working with my father. He always showed the most remarkable patience. We would just play the scene. He was the Police Superintendent and I was Gillie Evans, it was as simple as that. And when we finished the shot we both went back to being ourselves again. How lucky I was to work with an actor like him for my first film. When I looked into his eyes I saw the Superintendent and I knew that he saw Gillie. This really was his whole approach to acting; he'd say, 'If you believe, *they'll* believe.' That's the wonderful thing about working with good actors; it's really so simple, and anything is possible.

Some of the scenes were quite dramatic and complex for a child. Horst's character, a Polish seaman called Bronislav Korchinsky, returns to Cardiff looking for his girlfriend Anya who has changed her address without telling him. He goes searching for a house where he thinks she might be living. It's the same building that Gillie lives in. Gillie points the way and there's a brief rapport between them. Soon afterwards, Korchinsky locates Anya only to discover she's taken a lover. Hearing the two Polish lovers rowing upstairs, Gillie sneaks up and spies on them through the letter box. She watches in horror as the woman goads and threatens Korchinsky with a pistol; the couple fight, the sailor wrestles the weapon out of her hands – and in a blinding rage, he shoots her dead.

Of course, I was also incredibly lucky to have as my director Lee Thompson, the man who made such classics as *Ice Cold in Alex*, *Cape Fear* and *The Guns of Navarone*. Lee was a strong, sensitive character, who had a rare and compassionate understanding of people, which was the key to his magic as a director. He had been an actor himself in his youth, he'd written plays for the West End and screenplays for Associated British Pictures, he'd worked as an editing assistant at Elstree Studios, and also as a dialogue coach for Alfred Hitchcock. He'd even been a bantamweight boxer. During the Second World War he served in the RAF as a tail gunner in the B-29 Superfortress bombers – an unimaginably dangerous perspective from which to view combat and one which may well have helped him to appreciate the nature of suspense.

Lee knew exactly what he wanted, he shot the picture as he would edit it. I loved him and had total trust and confidence in him. He was small and slight; his hair was long and straight and hung down to his collar, slicked back behind his ears. For a man who must have witnessed all sorts of horrors in war, there was something very sweet and gentle about him. He was always smiling, he had a funny way of almost laughing every time he spoke. There was a nervous energy about him, he was never still, constantly playing with these little strips of paper torn out of old scripts and newspapers, which he called his 'twiddles'. These ended up all over the studio floor and you could use them to track his movements throughout the day.

Lee never told me how to say something, he only ever told me what was happening in the scene. He'd ask me questions – how was Gillie feeling? What did she want? Was she telling the truth? Or was she telling a lie? I understood; and if I was always humming while he was talking, he understood that too. He knew I was listening, he knew that I cared, that I wanted to do it well. And I wanted to please him too – and see his smiling face come around the camera at the end of a take.

I loved playing Gillie Evans – I think she was a bit like me. That was another tremendous bit of luck, to find a knockout part like that for my first film. First experiences have a huge impact upon our lives, upon our future, for good or bad, but Gillie was perfect. I thought if I had been born into her life, that's how I would have been. She stood on her own two feet, said what she thought, was often quite rude and was a habitual liar. She had a good sense of humour and didn't suffer fools, she was afraid of nothing, and she was tough. In the film, both the girl's parents are dead. She lives with her long-suffering aunty played by the darling Megs Jenkins. When Korchinsky meets Gillie he doesn't really treat her as a girl, but as a tough little child. She's a survivor and he rather admires that. So he steals her away into the Welsh mountains while he decides what to do. He's got to find a ship and get away. A special bond develops between them, they're rather alike, and both basically alone. By the end of the film it's almost a love story.

Looking back, it's a strange and a wonderful thing to have a strong, potent relationship, albeit in front of the camera, with a handsome grown man of twenty-four when you're only twelve years old. Normally it would never have happened, I would have just been the middle child at the table, listening to the grownups' conversation, speaking only when spoken to. But now we were playing these characters, I was involved in his life. Gillie loved Korchinsky and wanted to save him. She knew that what he had done was wrong, but she also knew he hadn't meant to do it, and that basically he was a good person. Obviously, I loved him too. I secretly hoped that one day they would make a sequel, where Gillie is all grown up and goes to meet Korchinsky when he comes out of prison; he falls in love with her and they go off and get married!

Horst was very sweet and gentle, he never seemed to get bored or irritated with me, as far as I was aware. I wouldn't have blamed him if he had, because I was terribly talkative. He made me laugh a lot, often during a scene, which Lee didn't find quite as funny as we did. He was also quite intense. His dark eyes had a penetrating quality. He had a very pretty girlfriend called Myriam Bru who was a French actress and dressed so beautifully, I thought she was *très chic*.

After the location work we moved to London. For the final day's shooting we returned to Beaconsfield Studios to shoot the climactic scene in a water tank doubling as the Bristol Channel. In the story, Korchinsky has fled on a merchant vessel but the police track him down, chasing the ship in a pilot boat, with Gillie in tow. In a tense confrontation the police board the ship and order the captain to hand him over, but Korchinsky is saved because the ship has drifted outside the 'three-mile limit', and beyond the jurisdiction of British law. Korchinsky seems to have got away with it but when Gillie falls overboard and starts to drown, he dives into the ocean to save her. They are rescued by the Superintendent in the pilot boat and Korchinsky is placed under arrest.

The scene in the water was scheduled for after lunch. People were celebrating the end of shooting a bit prematurely with a glass or two of red wine. Normally my dad was very disciplined and never drank in the middle of the day, but that day he must have made an exception. When we were at home us kids were often allowed a little wine diluted with water, so I was no stranger to drink, but on this occasion there was considerably more wine than water in my glass – or two – and by the time lunch was over I was tottering back across the lot. I looked down with interest to find that I had two right feet and two left, and I realised that I was drunk. The blow was hardly softened when I arrived at the Sound Stage. Tacked onto the great soundproof doors was a notice: 'Congratulations Horst and Myriam on your engagement' and little drawings of wedding bells.

He wasn't going to wait for me to grow up, he was going to marry Myriam. I was heartbroken.

When we finally shot the last scene in the water tank, I was flailing around so much, so drunk, and so heartbroken, I almost did drown.

For the whole time we had been filming, Lee didn't want me to watch myself on the rushes (the screenings of the previous day's shoot) which everyone else did, every day after lunch. He probably didn't want to risk me becoming self-conscious, so the first time I ever saw myself on screen was at *Tiger Bay*'s premiere in London. My parents still owned a little flat in town and I used to sleep in Daddy's dressing room. It was terribly exciting. I had a new dress made of dark blue organza with a big stiff petticoat underneath and little black lace slippers. It was the most gorgeous thing I'd ever worn and I was thrilled to bits. Everyone was dressed up. Daddy looked so handsome in his dinner jacket and Mummy was wearing her beautiful beaded grey dress; I remember being so proud to be out with them, and their friends like Laurence Olivier, all of us sitting expectantly in our cinema seats, waiting for the lights to go down . . . But when the film began and I finally saw myself, so huge up there, projected on that enormous screen, I got such a shock that I couldn't stop laughing. It was awful, I was in danger of becoming quite hysterical. My father kept kicking me sharply to shut me up; especially in those serious scenes. I thought they were the funniest of all. I suppose it was nerves, and partly embarrassment, not wanting to take myself too seriously. Laughter covers up all sorts of things. But I didn't laugh at the film's ending. It was very moving and felt like we were saying goodbye all over again.

In the 1950s the newspapers were all powerful. The notices for film and stage were of vital importance. After a first night in the West End, actors and producers would wait up until the crack of dawn to read the papers and learn their fate. In New York you would go to Sardi's on 44th Street, you'd eat and drink and generally keep yourself occupied until the *New York Times* appeared. If the notices were good the champagne came out, if they weren't everyone just slid quietly home.

The morning after the premiere for *Tiger Bay* I woke up early. A finger of sunlight found its way into the little dressing room and I could hear the porter moving the dustbins around in the courtyard below. I looked at my new blue dress hanging on the cupboard door and remembered the night before. It had been so exciting and now it was all over; the film was finished and released in the cinemas, and tomorrow I was going to go back to boarding school. Life would return to normal again. I got out of bed and eased open the squeaky door and tiptoed silently across the carpet to the kitchen and saw that the papers had been delivered; the porter had put them on the table in the hall. And then I remembered – the notices. For the first time it crossed my mind – what would they say? Would they like the film? Would they like Daddy? Horst? What would they say about ME?

I knew how important they were. Thinking about it, my parents had seemed a bit nervous – I think I'd been kidding myself that I wasn't too. So I went into the living room and opened one. I searched for the right page – the reviews were usually at the back, I knew that. Then a headline caught my eye and I caught my breath. The more I read the more shocked I became. Not because they weren't good, they were good, most of them, very good, but because of what they said about me:

'*Tiger Bay* is dominated from first to last by Hayley Mills ... who acts her father off the screen.'

I was appalled. It wasn't true. I didn't know what to do, I was terrified. I didn't want Daddy to read things like that, it was ridiculous, absurd, he'd be so hurt and upset.

He mustn't see them, I must get rid of them. I cast around frantically trying to decide what to do. The telephone rang in the hall, I heard their bedroom door open ... In a flash I'd stuffed all the papers underneath the sofa as far as they would go. Then I heard my father's voice.

'Have the papers arrived yet?' he called. 'Has anyone seen the papers?'

I hid behind the living-room door, staring down at my bare feet and chewing my nails. I was still in my pyjamas. Slowly I opened the door and peered out – no one there – I fled back to my room and got dressed. Maybe they'd give up and forget about the papers and go off and do something else.

Katy, my parents' secretary, arrived to do letters with Daddy.

'That's odd!' she said. 'Everyone else's papers have been delivered.'

I was on tenterhooks all morning; then the cleaning lady arrived and she found them under the sofa while she was doing the hoovering. They all soon guessed it was me.

'Why did you do that, Bags? Why did you hide the papers?'

I chewed my nails and looked into my father's blue eyes.

'I didn't want you to see them and be upset.'

He laughed and hugged me. 'Of course I'm not upset,' he said. 'I'm proud, that's all.'

'But it's not true,' I said, 'it's just stupid.'

'Look, one day, if you ever have children of your own, they will do something wonderful and you will just be so proud of them. It's even better than when you do things yourself!'

But it didn't feel right. I was glad the reviews were good for the film, and that they'd liked me, but it was very strange and unsettling being the focus of that sort of attention, an attention that had always been my father's prerogative. No one had ever taken me seriously before. I didn't mind that, I was loved, I made them laugh, they'd even laugh at my school report, they didn't take that seriously either! But now, all of a sudden, things felt different, there'd been a shift.

Tiger Bay was a success, and so was I.

★

There was also yet another big shake-up at home, this time with Bunch. She had recently been accepted at the Royal Academy of Dramatic Art – and was all set to start – when she auditioned for a wonderful part in Peter Schaffer's first play *Five Finger Exercise*, opening in the West End at the Comedy Theatre. She got the part, the play turned out to be a big hit and she received excellent reviews. It was wonderful and we were all thrilled, especially me. Privately, I had been very anxious about the fuss over *Tiger Bay* and the effect it might have on Bunch. After all, she was the one who had always wanted to be an actress, she had known right from the start what she wanted to do – at least, once she decided she didn't want to be a prima ballerina, when she was ten. She was the star of the kids, the oldest, the trailblazer, and the thought that all the fuss about me might make her unhappy in any way was unbearable. One day, unbeknown to me, she took herself off to see *Tiger Bay* alone. She sat through the film and cried all the way through the credits, and then watched the whole film again – twice. She told me later that it could have been very difficult for her if she hadn't absolutely loved the film, and me in it. But she said she was really proud of me. And of course, this made me love her even more, and she has been a constant source of love and support ever since.

I had felt surprisingly at home in front of the camera and secretly hoped I might act again. *Tiger Bay* had performed strongly at the box office and my performance had been well received, even winning me a prestigious Silver Bear at the Berlin Film Festival, which arrived by courier; but no further jobs were offered, not even a polite enquiry. *Tiger Bay* just receded into the distance and I soon stopped thinking about it. I told myself I never expected anything more to come of it, I don't think anybody did, not really, and so . . . nothing did. My parents were probably quite relieved. It had been a wonderful experience and great fun, but now it was over. My foray into acting was a flash in the pan. If I wanted to become an actress when I was older and had left school, well, we could think again, but, in the meantime, there was my interrupted education to concentrate on . . . And so I went back to Elmhurst.

Back to school; school routine, the smell of chalk and Wright's Coal Tar Soap, boiled cabbage and mince, and unwashed hair; lessons, ballet, midnight feasts – which meant sharing each other's toothpaste and dreaming of running away when the moon was full, climbing down the iron fire escape and getting home by morning in time for breakfast – then the sound of Miss Dodson violently ringing the morning wake-up bell, and the mad dash to the loo. No one was allowed to leave their freezing dormitory after lights out; if you were taken short in the dead of night you had to use the communal chamber pot. It was an enormous thing, you had to grope about under a bed to find it, then sit there in the middle of the room, on the icy linoleum, trying desperately not to fall in. In the morning a prefect would collect the 'slops' in a metal bucket. Hardly a job that endeared one to the position.

The main event of the Christmas term, and the one thing that I really was looking forward to, was the school play, which was always a version of the Nativity. They did it every year in the little wooden chapel. Somehow the whole school managed to cram themselves in, with a few brave parents squashed up at the back. The Nativity was a beautiful play, it had a magic. The most serene-looking girl was typically cast to play Mary. I would have loved to play Mary myself but I understood I just didn't have what it takes for the part. I couldn't see myself playing Joseph or a Wise Man either, and I certainly didn't want to play a shepherd, they had nothing to do. No, the part I desperately wanted was called 'Youth'. Bunch had played this role in my first term at the school and I had been mesmerised. Youth is very romantic, she appears at the very end of the play, dressed in white, she emerges out of the darkness from the back of the chapel, and runs up the aisle until she reaches Mary and Joseph and Baby Jesus, then falls on her knees in front of them and delivers this wonderful speech about love and hope for the future. I always thought it was so moving and inspiring. And it was, in my opinion, the best role. Privately I thought I had more than a fair chance of getting it – after all, I was a professional actress, I had had some pretty good notices, and had just won a BAFTA, so . . .

That Sunday after Evensong, Father John stood up in chapel and announced who was going to be cast in the Christmas play. He went through all the parts.

'The role of Mary – Sally Anne Hendrickson; the role of Joseph – Paddy Robinson . . .'

The Wise Men, the Shepherds; no mention of me yet. Then finally . . .

'And the part of Youth will be played by . . .' I waited for my name to be read out. 'Jane Alexander.'

Jane?! My best friend. I was stunned.

I was also very glad I hadn't told anyone how much I wanted the part. I was genuinely happy for Jane, I was sure she would do it beautifully, but, really, I had fully expected to get it, especially as my sister had played it four years earlier. Now, secretly, I was so embarrassed. I could hear Miss Dodson's voice in my head: 'Just because you've made a film doesn't mean you're better than anybody else.'

I wasn't given anything to do in the Christmas play. Not even a shepherd. Nothing.

So many actors lament for roles they didn't get – the ones that got away – great parts that they would have been perfect for, which would have transformed their career. I have a few of my own. The School Nativity was my first bruising experience. I don't think I've wanted a part so much ever since.

Eventually term ended and I returned home. For some weeks now Daddy had been in Australia filming *Summer of the Seventeenth Doll* for United Artists with Ernest Borgnine and Anne Baxter. It was still going on when school finished, so we all flew out to see him and spent Christmas Day together on Bondi Beach.

Bunch had to go back early to rejoin *Five Finger Exercise* at the Comedy Theatre in London after her Christmas break. She seemed so much more grown up than me, a beautiful young woman, while I was still a buck-toothed child. I adored her and always wanted to be with her, doing what she was doing, but it must have been a bit of a bore for her. I missed her terribly; she left a bottle of perfume called Devon Violets on the dressing table, I kept it and smelt it every now and again and pretended that she was still there.

For a while, it was just Johnny and me in Australia, messing about and arguing, and pushing each other into the swimming pool. We had a maid called Angelina who was partly of Indigenous heritage; she was always warning me about not wearing my bikini top. 'You'll get breast cancer!' she'd cry. Many years later I did and I wondered if that holiday had anything to do with it.

Daddy's film finally finished and my parents threw a big party. Lots of the actors and crew came but also the England cricket team. Everyone got riotously drunk and Anne Baxter fell into the pool and lost one of her earrings, so the entire cricket team stripped off their shoes and dinner jackets and jumped into the water to help her look for it. They'd just lost the Ashes.

Daddy returned with us to England in January 1959, which seemed all the more cold and inhospitable after the baking southern hemisphere. I was just preparing myself for my imminent return to a freezing Elmhurst when my father received a call from his agent, Laurence Evans. Laurie Evans was the most influential theatrical agent in London and already a legend in his own right. A tall, imposing figure, always beautifully dressed in dark expensive suits and silk ties that complemented his pale blue eyes, with a long pale face, clean shaven except for a moustache that he always kept at the same length, just short enough to give a sharp prick when he kissed you. He had a great sense of humour and a wonderful voice, deep and sonorous, which must have lent his negotiations tremendous gravitas and power. During his long and distinguished career his clients included legends like Laurence Olivier, Ralph Richardson, Ingrid Bergman, Alec Guinness, Peggy Ashcroft, Rex Harrison, and my father, of course, who was his first client when he started as an agent at MCA. As a rule, most actors love receiving calls from their agent because it probably means there's a job. If Laurie Evans telephoned you, it was likely to be a *well-paid* job, so my father leapt up to take the call. However, on this fateful occasion, the work enquiry wasn't for my father. It was for me.

'Walt Disney is in London,' Laurie announced. 'He's casting a new picture and he wants to meet Hayley.'

CHAPTER TWO

Enter the Magician

It was a cold, damp, drizzly January afternoon. Jonathan and I sat waiting outside my parents' London apartment in the back of an old black cab, its idling engine sounding like a small tractor.

'Where *is* she?' Daddy murmured under his breath. We all peered anxiously through the fogged-up windows. My father seemed uncharacteristically tense. He was always punctual and this was an important meeting. 'What on earth is she *doing* in there?' I could tell he wasn't happy. He rolled down the window then jumped out and opened the taxi door as my mother came running down the steps from the house, her coat flying behind her in the wind, and a funny look on her face.

'Thank God, Baba . . .' he gasped in relief, then stopped suddenly, as she thrust a small struggling puppy into my arms. 'Oh no! Baba, not the puppy!' he protested hopelessly. 'This is too important! She'll pee everywhere!' But Mummy just laughed and climbed into the cab. 'She'll be fine. Just go!'

My father knew very well that if my mother had decided on something it would be very hard to change her mind, and anyway, it was too late to argue now. So that was that. Jonathan and I were delighted to have the puppy and we spent the short journey, from Berkeley Square to the Dorchester Hotel – where the man

I was going to meet was staying in the Penthouse Suite – arguing over who was going to hold her.

Suky, the puppy, was a strange sort of talisman: a white miniature Pekingese with two gleaming black eyes and a wet black nose. She was a 'sleeve Peke' – in ancient China only royalty and high-born Mandarin were allowed to own this dog, and they would carry them around in their great silken sleeves. Suky was the most adorable character, but she wasn't actually ours. She had originally been given to Vivien Leigh as a sort of breaking-up present from Laurence Olivier. Britain's theatrical First Family were close friends of Mum and Dad (and godparents to Bunch and Jonathan) but by then it was well known that, behind the scenes, Larry and Viv's famously tempestuous marriage had well and truly hit the rocks. The dazzling couple hadn't legally separated yet but were both living apart. Vivien was at home, working in the West End, while Larry was in New York, performing on Broadway in John Osborne's *The Entertainer*, in the midst of a passionate affair with his co-star, the young Joan Plowright, whom he would later marry. But ending such a long and deeply embedded romantic relationship was torturous for them both, especially for Vivien who was often ill and struggled with her bipolar disorder. No one seemed to understand this illness in those days, nor know how to treat it, other than with brutal sessions of electric shock therapy. Worrying about her constantly and racked with guilt, Larry plied Vivien with expensive gifts: a Rolls-Royce one year, a beautiful new apartment in Mayfair the next – and then Suky. But however well meant, a Pekingese puppy just wasn't practical. Vivien had only recently moved into her new apartment, and exquisitely decorated it herself, when Suky peed all over the lime green carpets. For poor Vivien, teetering perilously day-to-day on an emotional tightrope, it was all too much to cope with, so she gave the dog to us – which was fine. Our carpets weren't new and they certainly weren't lime green.

Of course, we kids couldn't appreciate just how much trouble

Vivien was in. Not really. We were just glad to have Suky bouncing around in the back of the cab. It felt comforting having her along for the meeting. Another movie maker, another hotel, only this felt quite different; not at all like meeting J. Lee Thompson at the Ritz. For a start we all knew Lee, he was an old friend; meeting Lee at the Ritz had felt more like a very glamorous family outing. Today was something else altogether.

None of us had ever met this man. Walt Disney's fame was unprecedented. He was a living legend – and not just as a maverick Hollywood mogul but as a visionary pioneer and creative genius. Even to us small kids he was a superstar, as iconic as his creation Mickey Mouse. It's incredible to think that, still to this day, most children's first film is one of Disney's. Mine was *Snow White and the Seven Dwarfs* – it was unforgettable and terrifying. Just his name alone conjured up a whole world of magic and awe.

And here we were, me and my little brother, my mum and dad, jammed into this stuffy taxi with a wriggling puppy covering us in white hair, crawling through the rain to meet the great magician.

The doorman grabbed the handle and opened the door.

'Afternoon, Mr Mills,' he said with a big grin on his face.

Everyone always seemed pleased to see my dad.

We sailed into the Dorchester's spacious lobby, past more smiles at reception; a bellboy called the lift and we began floating up to the top floor. Nobody spoke. Mummy busily tidied her hair in the mirror, whistling tunelessly through her teeth like she always did. It was her nervous tic. Even Daddy was strangely quiet. Nobody spoke. Silence. Only the sound of the lift whirring upwards and Suky snuffling through her tiny nose, desperate to get down.

Then we all got out and I was standing outside a door – 'The Harlequin Suite'. I remember very clearly looking up at a small plaque of a dancing Harlequin.

And then the door opened and a tall man was standing there wearing a pair of light grey trousers and a pale yellow cardigan; he had grey hair and a moustache. He smiled. I think for a second we all stared back with our mouths open, sharing the same thought – it was Walt Disney!

I realise now, it had been a stroke of genius for my mother to bring the puppy, because it completely deflected the attention – and the pressure – away from me. Of course, the honest truth was, everyone was quite nervous and Mummy cleverly intuited we'd need some help; Suky was our ice-breaker extraordinaire. The first few minutes after we arrived were spent on the floor of Mr Disney's suite, playing with the dog (or rushing at her with expensive magazines at the first sign of that fateful squatting position, and the potential ruin of the Dorchester's beautiful carpets). I told Walt all about Suky; how brave she was, how she had absolutely no idea what a tiny creature she was, how she loved chasing the cows at the farm, how she would often use their cow pats as stepping stones, and how sometimes a cow pat would collapse and she'd fall in – which didn't seem to bother her at all. He had laughed. And I remember, I had liked the way he laughed. There was something shy about him. Something endearing. Something that I recognised.

He took us all on a tour of the suite, which to this day must be one of the most glamorous hotel suites in London: huge rooms with high ceilings and glorious panoramic views across Hyde Park (you can check out the Harlequin Suite online now, it's still available to book at £6000 a night – breakfast included). After the tour, Walt gave Jonathan and me a small bottle of Coca-Cola each with a little straw, and the three of us went out onto the balcony to enjoy the wonderful view over the tops of the rain-sodden sycamore trees. One thing that impressed me deeply was this incredible panel board on the balcony; it was a map of the view from the penthouse, which would light up to indicate all the great landmarks of the city. We loved pressing all the buttons – Walt seemed to enjoy it as much as we did.

'I must get something like this for Disneyland,' he said as he looked down at me. 'Have you ever been to Disneyland?'

'Oh . . . no,' I said.

'Well, I hope someday you get a chance to come. I'll show you around myself.'

Jonathan and I stared back wide-eyed.

It was getting dark, in that late January afternoon sort of way, so we went back into the suite and Walt and my parents had a drink. I recall the conversation was lively; my parents were wonderful company, Daddy was a big star and good at talking to people, but he also had that special quality that drew others to him and seemed to automatically make him the centre of things. This coupled with Mummy's vitality and beauty made them an enormously attractive couple. I looked up, seeing them all talking together, aware that my charmed childhood was all down to them. For so much of my life, they led the way, the waters parted for them and I just crossed over in their wake. However, unbeknown to me (and to my parents) there was a lot more going on in this meeting than met the eye.

The windows darkened as evening fell. The atmosphere got quite merry and, I think, despite the suite's size, it started to feel a bit noisy with two kids and a manic puppy rampaging about. Then, quite suddenly, we found ourselves back out in the corridor, waiting for the lift, on a bit of a collective high. It was over.

Thinking back, I don't remember Walt talking about films, or acting, or the movie he was planning to make. I don't recall anything to do with work being discussed at all. He hadn't asked me searching questions, but whenever I spoke, I remember he had looked and listened with a smile, a nod, sometimes a little laugh. I certainly didn't feel that I had been under any particular scrutiny. It was the nicest casting meeting I've ever been to, or would ever go to. And I have Walt and my family to thank for that.

And Suky, of course.

So we got into the lift, floated back down to reception, got a cab home and talked about what we were going to have for dinner, quite unaware that I had just had one of the most important encounters of my life, with a man who was about to reshape my future – and tip my family on its head.

Soon after the Dorchester meeting, Laurie Evans came to see my parents, carrying a large Manila envelope in his hands, and he was closeted in my father's study for a long time. Usually this would have been quite normal, but in this case it felt peculiar. I sensed the conversation was all about me. Mummy went in and came out again looking oddly distracted, whistling through her teeth again, and there was a palpable mood of unease in the house. Something was up.

Walt Disney had made Laurie a remarkable offer. It was at this point my parents realised that the relaxed and affable man at the Dorchester, sipping bourbon in his woolly cardigan, was a very different creature when he donned his suit and got down to business. This man wasn't playing – and he drove a tough deal.

The Disney Studios wanted me for an exclusive seven-picture deal. That meant seven pictures for Disney, one a year, every year, for the next seven years of my life. The first film was going to be *Pollyanna* – a picture Walt had high hopes for and which was about to go into pre-production. My parents were gobsmacked. So was Laurie. Firstly, this was a huge break; second, it was an exclusive contract. Actors being signed exclusively to studios was common in the thirties and forties, but by the late fifties, with the rise of the 'super agencies' like Lew Wasserman's MCA, the studio system had been replaced by the 'star system' and these types of contracts were becoming regarded as increasingly old-fashioned. Yet this was exactly what they were offering me in 1959. Disney were building their own repertory company of young actors. Their thinking was, if the studio spent all this money launching talent they wanted exclusive rights over their investment. And it all sounds perfectly reasonable when you think of it as a 'brand', say, like nylons or cookies, but it gets harder to swallow when it's your own daughter, and a child no less.

Of course, Disney and his team presented the offer thoughtfully

and carefully. Each film I made would be tailored to keep pace
with me as I grew up . . . appropriate roles would be found to suit
my age and my stage of development . . . etc., etc. But, to use a
baseball parlance, my parents had been thrown a curve ball. They
had hoped for an opportunity for their daughter, not a professional straitjacket.

It's not that my parents weren't realistic about it, they both
appreciated this was an incredible offer, but I don't think they
were ready for it, I mean – in their own heads. To them, I was
still just Bags: a bit of a joke. They didn't really think of me as
an actress. I hadn't trained and struggled in the profession like
they had. *Tiger Bay* had been a one-off. No one had offered me
a job here in England after that film, and nobody at home was
seriously expecting that this was going to be my career for the
rest of my life. Did I even want to be an actress? Was this my
dream? My parents didn't know. I certainly didn't. 'This should
be happening to Juliet,' I thought. '*She's* the talented one. She's
the one who's serious about acting.' Likewise, Daddy had always
known he wanted to act – it was his calling. Like a priest to the
cross, he'd worshipped the stage since he was knee-high. I wasn't
driven like that. Not at all. Perhaps I lacked self-awareness – or
just ambition? Whatever the reason, I'd just never thought that
far ahead.

But a long-term Hollywood contract with Walt Disney was
now on the table and my father knew this was a very rare kind
of offer. Acting is an insecure profession, full of insecure people,
and the unpleasant truth is that there's just not enough jobs to
go around. On a good day we worry about finding work; on a
bad one we fear we'll never work again. So for any British actor,
even an established name like my father, to get the chance to
star in a Hollywood movie was (and still is) a big deal. Let alone
under exclusive contract. As Daddy knew only too well; back in
the 1940s, he had been under contract to J. Arthur Rank. The
deal had seemed like a blessing at the time. He'd produced some

memorable films, H.G. Wells's *The History of Mr Polly* being one of them. But ultimately, his contract turned out to be a double-edged sword, for while it opened up opportunities, it also excluded him from others, and in the end he was happy to be free of it. Based on that experience, my father worried that being tied to Disney, an infinitely more powerful studio than the Rank Organisation, might be too much for his twelve-year-old daughter. Was this really the best thing? He was in a terrible quandary – accepting the offer felt just as scary as turning it down.

There was no question that, ultimately, Mummy and Daddy would be the ones to make the final decision, but I suspect they felt an honest and open chat with me might help them decide. So, later in the day, my father called me into the drawing room to tell me the news.

Mummy was in there too, sitting quietly. It all felt very odd talking about money and movie contracts.

'Does this mean I don't have to go to school?' I replied, slightly embarrassed.

Daddy smiled wearily and said that unfortunately there were laws about these sorts of things and that I would almost certainly be given a personal tutor. I could see he was struggling.

'What worries us, Hail . . .' he said, searching for the right words, '. . . is what happens if at some point in the future you decide you just don't want to do acting any more. You see, you would still be bound by the terms of the contract. To make a film every year. And that would be a huge commitment for you, or rather *for us*, to make. On your behalf, I mean.'

I didn't know what to say. It all sounded fantastic and utterly unreal.

'You'll be tied up in this contract till you're twenty.'

Twenty? Just the idea of me being twenty was inconceivable! Eight years was like eight light years away. We'd all be flying around in spaceships by then.

'But, if we turn this down,' my father went on, 'we are extremely worried that one day, when you're older, you may well resent us for losing you this opportunity.'

It felt like they were talking about some other girl's life. Not mine. I pretended to nod along thoughtfully.

'Then there's Jonathan to be considered,' Daddy went on. 'Mummy can't keep going off to California to look after you and leaving your younger brother alone at home.'

Silence. I noticed him exchanging a glance with Mummy.

'And of course,' my father said, 'you will make a lot of money.'

'Will I be able to buy a pony?' I asked, rather flippantly. I already had a pony. It was the nerves talking – I was starting to feel increasingly uncomfortable.

From the look on their faces I could see they were feeling uncomfortable too. This all meant a lot to them; the money part as well. Both my parents had known hardship and struggle, but that was all long before I came along, and the concept of money meant almost nothing to me. I lived at home, in Wellington boots most of the time, I had pocket money, of course, half a crown a week, and there was my Post Office savings account for buying presents and things. I didn't need any more than that. I don't think I was spoilt; privileged certainly, but we were always grateful. My parents were doing their best to explain what was happening to me, but I couldn't appreciate the sacrifice they were going to have to make in their own lives, if I signed. And of course, I had absolutely no idea what it would mean for me personally.

'What do you think, Hayley?' Daddy asked, perhaps as a last recourse.

I took a deep breath and looked past him out of the window across the garden. I could see green fields stretching away into the distance. I knew I had to say something. Suddenly Hamlet shot out of the house, barking his head off, with Jonathan in hot pursuit. He must have seen something, a rabbit maybe? I watched them until they were out of sight, and tried to imagine the future.

'Hail?'

I blinked back into the room. 'Yes, Daddy?'

'Do you really still want to act?'

I bit my nails. I didn't know what to say. I had enjoyed making *Tiger Bay*. I cast my mind back to that whole experience, working with Lee, with Horst, filming down on the docks. Of course I enjoyed acting. Actually, I suddenly realised, I loved it.

'Will we all be together? Or will I have to do it alone?' I asked.

I noticed my mother look at my dad before she spoke. 'I can promise you, that one of us will always be with you.'

I took another breath.

'Well, then. Yes. Yes, I'd like to do it.' And with that, I jumped up from the sofa and ran off to stop Annabelle, my pony, from breaking into the kitchen.

Making decisions is so much simpler for a child. If you enjoy something, you do it. If you don't, you don't. It's so pure and innocent and completely selfish. So, as far as I was concerned, the problem was sorted. But my parents continued to agonise. Laurie was sent back to the negotiating table to petition for a one-off deal for *Pollyanna*, but the studio wouldn't hear of it. They piled on the pressure – this production was ready to go and they had another actress standing by to take my part should Laurie Evans decline! The Disney Studios knew what they wanted – and they were used to getting it.

What did my parents expect? Hollywood is a shark tank, where fame and fortunes are made, and the weak are eaten alive. Walt didn't get to where he was without being tougher and smarter and more relentless in the pursuit of his dreams than all of his competitors. So, it's fair to say, when it came to deal-making, the Mickey Mouse Club took no prisoners.

I could tell my parents were feeling the strain. On reflection, I'm sure the thing that most worried them, much more than the pressure and the expectation on me, was the impact that it would have upon their family. The truth is, there were two great loves in my father's life: his wife and his work. I honestly think if he had to choose between the two, he'd have struggled. That might sound harsh, but it illustrates how intensely devoted he was to both of them. Mummy was his life, she completed him. But so did acting. From the thrill of discovering a character, playing it for the first time in front of the cameras, or walking out onto a stage, into the light, and feeling that connection with an audience – it was a love affair. If someone, or some*thing*, makes you feel so happy and alive then *of course* you surrender your heart and devote yourself entirely. My mother's priority was to stay with Daddy. She followed him wherever he went; she wanted to be there and he wanted her. That's why, in 1938, she decided to give up acting, a career in which she had invested many years' hard labour, to become a mother and wife. She became a prolific writer, of course, but she could write wherever he was – in a hotel, or a desert, or on a glacier, or a film set.

So they had found an arrangement that worked for them. We kids lived in the shadow of their great romance. It was the bedrock and stability of our life. We were moulded to fit in with their lives, not the other way around. The other way around was unthinkable! Absurd! And yet that is precisely what was on the cards. If their twelve-year-old daughter was going off to make movies in 'Horrorwood', as Mummy called it, she would have to travel with me – and this would split them up.

A few days later they told me it was all over, the deal had stalled and my parents had walked away. The decisive moment, which I only discovered much later, arose from a casual acquaintance of my parents – a man called David Kilmuir, the then Lord Chamberlain (and Rex Harrison's brother-in-law) – who dropped a bomb on their dinner party by declaring that there was a law in England that no child under the age of fourteen could leave the country for gain. This was a rude shock to Disney and Laurie, both of whom had somehow yet to be alerted to this glaring legality; but for my parents it all came as a huge relief, because now they didn't have to make the decision. The Law had made it for them. The deal was off. Normally a grand agent like Laurie Evans would have swatted aside such trifling legal issues – all lawyers relish finding ingenious loopholes in the law – but my parents had had enough stress and worry, and I think they just wanted the whole thing to go away . . . Except it didn't.

Unbeknown to my parents, this deal already had quite a backstory, beginning with *Pollyanna*'s creative originator, David Swift. Before making *Pollyanna*, David had worked mostly on Disney's animation teams, but he'd been looking for an opportunity to direct live-action and had hit on a smart idea to remake – or, to use the modern parlance, 'reboot' – Eleanor H. Porter's classic novel about the little girl with a 'glad' heart, which had originally been adapted as a film in 1920, starring Mary Pickford. He began reimagining it as a Disney film, and secretly developed a draft treatment, struggling to get it right and sometimes wondering if it wasn't absolutely awful, before eventually plucking up the courage to show his boss. To his surprise and delight, Walt not only liked it, he found the draft very touching, and David was immediately given the go-ahead to develop and finish a screenplay – with Walt's personal creative involvement, of course.

It was not going to be an easy film to make, though. From the very beginning, David and Walt knew that, like any film with a juvenile performance at its core, the casting would need to be just right. Not only that, Pollyanna herself had the extra challenge of being infuriatingly perfect. If her performance wasn't spot-on – if it was played wrong, too sentimental or too cutesy – this pig-tailed sweetie with a heart of gold, who always sees the best in people and never fails to find something to be glad about, risked, as David put it, 'making everyone who saw and heard her puke in their seats'.

Of course, Hollywood has no shortage of children for sale, all chaperoned by their showbiz moms, and, as I understand it, Disney trawled through and tested hundreds of young girls for the role, but none seemed to do it for Walt. 'They don't hit me in the heart,' he kept saying to David.

My name came up unexpectedly, through Walt's senior producer, Bill Anderson, who was then in the middle of developing one of Disney's new flagship projects – *Swiss Family Robinson*, a big live-action shipwrecked-on-a-desert-island adventure epic, following in the wake of their recent box-office smash *20,000 Leagues Under the Sea*. At a meeting for *Swiss Family*, a disappointed Walt confided to Bill that the search for Pollyanna had been so fruitless he was considering cancelling the picture altogether. Bill wished he could help. He knew Walt was a perfectionist who thought that if something wasn't done right it wasn't worth doing at all, but Bill had his hands full with *Swiss Family*. That night, Bill and his wife Ginny flew to London to meet with the film's British director, Ken Annakin, who was set to present him with all the development materials he had for *Swiss Family*. They set up an office, presumably for convenience's sake, in Bill's capacious hotel suite, and before long the place was so filled with scripts and storyboards and overflowing ashtrays that Ginny was driven outside, where she spent a day in London with Pauline Annakin. In the evening the two women went to see a film – *Tiger Bay*.

Later on, when their wives returned, raving about *Tiger Bay*, Bill's ears pricked up. 'A girl, you say? How old is she?' Apparently, neither Ginny nor Pauline could agree on my age – I've been told it was somewhere between eight and fourteen – but the next evening, Ginny went to watch *Tiger Bay* for a second time, this time with Bill in tow. After an hour Bill said he had seen enough and left. Not because he was bored, but because he was so excited to phone Walt, nine hours behind in California. Ironically, when he called, Walt was just about to go into a casting meeting with David Swift, who claimed to have found a promising young actress for the part and was begging for the 'green light'. I don't know what Bill said, but Walt trusted and valued Bill enough to agree he would hold off on any decisions until he had seen *Tiger Bay* personally.

Of course, these were the days before VHS or DVD, when

the word 'streaming' was only used to describe a bad cold – so Bill had to get hold of a 35mm print of *Tiger Bay* to courier to Walt in California. Straightaway, Bill got on the phone to the film's distributors, the Rank Organisation – who back then had a monopoly over the British cinema chains – but Rank refused to help. This could easily have been the end of my fledgling career (thanks guys) but, luckily for me, Bill didn't give up. He managed to persuade Rank to *sell him* a 35mm print, which would not have been easy, or cheap, and then Bill himself flew back to California to hand-deliver the reels to Walt personally.

Bizarrely, forty-eight hours later, when a bleary-eyed and jet-lagged Bill finally arrived back at the Studios clutching a set of film cans, the first person he bumped into was *Pollyanna's* associate producer – who was understandably livid. What the hell was Bill doing sticking his nose into their project? Didn't he have his own *Swiss* fish to fry? Things had been all set to go with this other girl when Walt had told them to wait – now the production was stalled and every day was costing money. Then he said something which really unsettled Bill: David Swift had already seen *Tiger Bay* while in England and didn't think the Mills girl was right! Bill gulped and smiled weakly, and, I suspect, began praying that his boss would react differently.

A few hours later Bill's office phone rang; it was Walt. 'She's terrific! Perfect! Let's sign her up.' Walt was excited, Bill was delighted – also hugely relieved. 'Anything else you want me to do?' he asked. But Walt was more than satisfied, he'd finally found his Pollyanna. Bill took a return flight to London that night.

So Walt flew to the Dorchester fresh from that screening, eager to do a deal. None of us – not my parents, not Laurie Evans – no one knew this backstory: there was a clock ticking on his *Pollyanna* and the longer it took to sign me, the more it was costing his production. If Laurie Evans *had* known this, he would have enjoyed considerable leverage in the deal-making. But Team Walt played their cards very close.

In the poker-game of any negotiation, the strongest play is often to walk away, so I'm sure Disney must have wondered if Laurie Evans wasn't a master bluffer. But the simple truth was my parents honestly could not decide and the Law had simply given them an excuse to say no. Nevertheless, a few days later Disney came back with a new deal and, to quote *The Godfather*, it was 'an offer they couldn't refuse'.

For me it was all very discombobulating. One moment everything was off and I was steeling myself to return to a wintry boarding school, the massive disappointment still not yet sunk in, and the next, we were back in business. The fog had somehow lifted, the seemingly insurmountable obstruction of English Law had been nimbly skipped over (a deferred payment till I was fourteen, when the juvenile law no longer applied) and the deal was back on. Miraculously too, it seemed to me, my parents' moral conflicts and quandaries were all now mysteriously resolved. I was signing with Disney. Hooray!

What had changed to bring everyone to this happy agreement? At the time I was told Laurie Evans and Disney had simply cut a better deal, but that was not the whole story. I would find out the truth eventually, but not till many, many years later, in 2016, when I was leafing through my file at the Walt Disney Archives.

Around the time of these tense negotiations, Walt got a bad case of laryngitis and ended up in hospital, where despite having almost no voice and a rattling cough he continued to stay across his projects, making calls from his sick-bed and talking to people like Bill Anderson, who at this point was still in London working on *Swiss Family Robinson*. When Bill asked how things were progressing with *Pollyanna*, Walt managed to rasp and wheeze about how negotiations had stalled and how deeply frustrated he was. Walt hated being stuck in bed, but even worse than that, he hated not being able to carry out a plan when he'd decided on something.

Now, Bill Anderson was a very smart man, nothing escaped

him; he was one of those resourceful characters who can always spot an opportunity in a crisis, and on this occasion he realised how he could help his boss. 'Walt, I've just been chatting with the casting agent for *Swiss Family Robinson*, and, y'know, funnily enough, we were just going to suggest Hayley's father John Mills be put on the shortlist of potentials to play the dad . . .'

Bill didn't need to say any more. Walt immediately saw the beauty of the opportunity. He told Bill to write a memo (now preserved in Disney's archives) copying in the team, and, within a few hours of the memo being circulated, a Disney master-stroke was delivered to counter Laurie Evans's supposed master bluff:

'If Hayley Mills signs with Disney,' Bill wrote, 'her father John Mills is guaranteed the lead role in *Swiss Family Robinson*.'

It was an offer my father couldn't refuse. A starring role in a big Hollywood movie. For a family trade-off. The deal was closed and everybody won. But nobody told me that's how it happened. Maybe they didn't feel it was important to tell me. Maybe they were secretly embarrassed, or guilty even. I just don't know. It's all quite silly. This really should have been something to celebrate and laugh about: we all lived in the shadow of Daddy's stellar career – but now, little did I know, he was getting offered work because of me.

That's dramatic irony.

★

In the days leading up to our departure for the United States, Mummy and I went shopping in preparation for the trip. I always loved our little jaunts together, it was usually exhilarating, wherever we were. Fortnum & Mason, Harrods and Debenham & Freebody were some of her favourite haunts. I remember how she'd stride through a store with tremendous energy and determination, galvanising listless shop assistants. As she passed by she'd reach out a hand, and, without pausing, grab the fabric of some article of clothing, hanging on the rails – assessing in an instant its quality and desirability, and then dismissing it. I would struggle to keep up, longing to dawdle, but swept along by her momentum. Mummy had such flair and a natural sophistication about her. 'To the manner born', as they say. But the truth was she hadn't always been able to shop in the best places, she'd known hard times, as had her whole family.

Before she and her sisters were sent to English boarding schools, they had lived in these large, beautiful houses, in Shanghai and Macau, surrounded by so many beautiful things, with land and horses and servants, and an *amah* to care for the children. She'd developed her own innate sense of taste and appreciation for the finer things of life. She knew about antiques, about silver and especially china, and when she became a mother and had a family of her own, the homes she made for us reflected that.

But in the 1930s, with Japanese imperial expansion, the political landscape in China changed dramatically, and the Hayley Bells got caught in the seismic shift. Her father, Francis (who had been acting as Commissioner for British Maritime Customs, while spying for Queen and Country), lost his government post and was forced to return to England in much reduced circumstances. There was no generous pension waiting for an ageing soldier. He struggled to find work, and, before long, they were bankrupt. One desperate winter they burnt their own furniture to keep warm. During one especially humiliating visit from the bailiffs, everything that wasn't nailed down in the house was taken away. Apparently, my grandmother surreptitiously stuffed her fox-fur tippet under a cushion and was sitting on it, trying to look innocent, when one of these bailiffs spotted the little tail of fur sticking out. 'I'll have that, thank you, madam,' he said, and literally snatched it from under her backside.

My mother left the Royal Academy of Dramatic Art early because her family couldn't pay the fees, so she went off in search of theatre work, which led inevitably to regional touring, where she started at the bottom, either as a general dogsbody, or a prompter, or as an understudy – ready to step in if the lead actress was unable to perform. 'I'd sit up in the Dress Circle and watch the show,' she said, 'hoping the lead actress would slip and break her neck.'

While Mummy paid her dues in repertory theatre, Francis was dispatched back to Singapore by MI5 (with his eighteen-year-old daughter, my aunty Wyn, as cover, working alongside him), to gather intelligence on the escalating conflict with Japan. As you can imagine, Francis was incredibly relieved to be working again, and no doubt delighted to be serving his country, but unfortunately the mission ended badly. Having reconnected with his former spy networks, Francis learnt that Japan was planning a surprise attack on Singapore, intending to march their army from the mainland via Malaya. If this indeed proved true then Singapore would be quite helpless, as all their guns and defences were pointed out to sea. Francis reported to his superior officer, the then Governor of Singapore, a man called Shenton Thomas, who dismissed the intelligence as unreliable. A major disagreement erupted between the two men and my grandfather was soon fired and sent back to London, a broken man. (Many months later, when the Japanese army *did* eventually attack from the mainland – just as Francis had warned – resulting in the greatest British surrender ever with the capture of 80,000 men, the former Governor ended up in the truly horrifying Changi POW camp, which must have been some consolation to my grandfather.)

By the time they got back to England, the Hayley Bells were on the breadline. Francis managed to find some part-time work writing articles and stories for *Blackwood's Magazine*, but was plagued with self-doubt and insecurity – 'I'm just not that good, Muggins!' he'd mutter resignedly to my mother in his darker moods. And though his passion for writing would always trump his lack of confidence, *Blackwood's* pay was terrible and he couldn't support the family. Francis was a sterling character, resolute and proud, and it was tough, having been an eminent figure in the East, to fall from such a height, but I suspect it was even harder for Mummy, to see her hero struggle like that. I believe that a good part of what drove Mummy to succeed as a writer was a profound desire to honour his memory. He really was her original inspiration.

So one of the consequences of these trials and tribulations was that we were all taught not to waste money, even in Fortnum & Mason. Shopping with Mummy was never extravagant, we bought good stuff, quality stuff that was going to last. For my Californian trip she bought me a blue lambswool jumper and a tartan skirt ('you can never have too much tartan'), plus two pairs of shorts and a summer dress. I loved having Mummy to myself, she was a force of nature; little did I realise just how much time we were going to spend together. The next few years would test our mother–daughter relationship to its absolute limits.

With the shopping done the two of us ended up in the back of a taxi giggling like guilty children stuffing bars of Cadbury's milk chocolate into our mouths, while we made our way to Laurie Evans's office. It was explained to me that the terms of my Disney contract were settled – now all I had to do was sign it.

MCA's London offices were in Mayfair in a large imposing Victorian building with high moulded ceilings, polished panelled doors with burnished knobs and heavy silk curtains, already drawn in the twilight. Laurie seemed to be in his perfect setting. Getting up from his enormous, and astonishingly bare, mahogany desk, he held out his hands and took both of mine. I could smell his expensive cologne; his shirt was made of the finest cotton I had ever seen. 'Hail, hello darling,' he said. 'Mary, darling. Johnnie is already here, shall we have some tea?'

Tea was duly served on a large tray; I searched in vain for signs of chocolate biscuits. Daddy soon appeared from a neighbouring office and Laurie presented me with an enormous stack of paper: it was my contract – or contracts! Quite literally hundreds of white pages, and yellow pages, with small yellow tabs sticking out all over the place. And there were multiple copies to be signed, it seemed for just about everyone I'd ever met in my whole life. Under the glow of a Chinese lamp with a yellow silk shade, I signed, and signed, and signed, increasingly aware that my signature looked like a silly childish scrawl for something so important. I decided I needed to practise.

The headlines of the deal were explained to me in very simple language. The Disney team had been tough, but Laurie Evans had worked his own magic too. The contract was now 'non-exclusive', which meant I could make films for other producers, so long as those films didn't jar in any way with the Disney image. Ultimately, the studio would always have the deciding vote in any disagreements, and could, if necessary, veto the whole thing. As you might expect, this would very soon become a problem.

With regards to fees, I was to be paid roughly £10,000 for the first film (about £200,000 per movie in today's value) and £10,000 more every subsequent year. This very lucrative deal was watertight and non-negotiable, meaning, I would have no share of further profits. At the time, most studios didn't pay 'residuals' to actors, or directors or writers for television or anything else; and of course, this was before the days of mega merchandising and Home Entertainment, and the small print at the bottom of the contract stated clearly and unequivocally that I shouldn't expect any royalties arising from 'whatever developments and new technologies there might be in the future'.

So that pretty much covered everything from the invention of streaming to multiplexes on Mars.

There was also a clause stating that Disney would make every effort to shoot my films during summer holidays, so that I could return to boarding school afterwards (much to my disappointment) and so life would carry on normally – more or less. This turned out to be wishful thinking on everyone's part. Lastly, and perhaps most importantly, it was agreed that a guardian would be employed by the Studios to accompany me at all times. This was a big deal for my mother, since it freed her from the onerous role of 'stage mother', a job she loathed and was fundamentally unsuited for.

I signed the last contract, Laurie poured Irish whiskey from a crystal decanter, my mother had a sherry, and my father opened a box of Du Maurier cigarettes. The atmosphere relaxed; the deed was done, the die cast.

Before we left, Laurie's wife, Mary, came in. She was slim and tall, with calm smiling blue eyes and soft brown hair, and a laugh as sweet as a dove. She'd been a secretary at MCA and Laurie was smitten by her at first sight – you could see why, there was something about her presence that made you feel that everything was going to be all right, just by her entering the room. Mary gave me a present, a very expensive-looking red leather journal from Asprey's. It had gold-edged pages and gold letters embossed with 'My Trip Abroad'. It was beautiful. I took it with me to California and so began my lifelong habit of keeping a journal . . .

A few days later, our BOAC flight to Los Angeles waited immobile on the tarmac at Heathrow in the hazy July heat. I peered out of the window; airport staff were towing the steps away as the jets began to roar.

I had two new suitcases with my initials on them, a white leather make-up case that Lee Thompson and his wife Gogi had given me, and a blue BOAC bag – ready to 'Fly the skies!'

I stared at my new travel journal and hastily scribbled a first entry.

July 15th 1959: 'Hated leaving Bunchy. Cried all the way over the tarmac.'

I paused for inspiration and glanced up. I could see the backs of my parents' heads, close together, talking constantly as they always did; my mother's hand coming up every now and again to touch her hair, the rattle of her gold bracelets, the smell of her perfume – Schiaparelli – a wisp of smoke from Daddy's cigarette. Beside me Jonathan was busy filling out his Junior BOAC Pilot's book, desperately hoping to be taken up to visit the captain in the cockpit. You could still do that in those days . . .

I felt a soft rumble beneath me. The aircraft's wheels began to move. We started our slow taxi towards the runway. I put my journal away and looked out of the window. Before long we were airborne, the green fields of England slipping away below and disappearing under the clouds. I was leaving it all behind: Bunch left on her own, doing her play; Soxie, Suky, the farm, my friends; I was going away for so long . . . The film would take four months. The whole of summer. I reached into my bag and opened my new script:

'Pollyanna'
Screenplay by David Swift
Walt Disney Productions

I felt a little surge of excitement as I leafed through the crisp pages, imagining the scenes on the big screen. Out of the corner of my eye, I noticed my father had opened his script too – 'Swiss Family Robinson'. It felt good, knowing we all had a job with Disney. Daddy was always happiest when he was working. And if he was happy, then Mummy was happy. If they were happy, I was happy. That was my logic anyway.

Our plane was a Comet Jet, but still, reaching California took longer in those days. We had to stop in Montreal, then again in New York (and spend the night); a third stop in St Louis, before eventually arriving in Los Angeles. Two days later, stepping onto the tarmac at LAX, crumpled and dehydrated, we were greeted by an effusive PR man from Disney who corralled us into a small space filled with sweaty photographers, all yelling and jostling for position.

'This way Hayley! Smile! Say cheese!'

'John! Over here! All together now! Look at Hayley!'

'Hey! Little boy, you! Look at your sister!'

'Yeah! All look at Hayley! EVERYBODY LOOK AT HAYLEY!!'

There had been press at Heathrow, some journalists, a few photographers. This was normal for Daddy, he usually got snapped in public, but it was all very English and polite. This lot, on the other hand, waiting for us at LAX, were ravenous. We stood before them like a family of bewildered rabbits staring into the flashing lights. I could see Mummy grinning through clenched teeth. We finally made it outside and were thrown into the back of an enormous black limousine that whisked us away under the shimmering California sun. As we slumped into our cool leather seats, I heard Mummy whisper –

'This is the beginning of Hell.'

CHAPTER THREE

Cabbages and Kings

David Swift was furious when he found out that I had been cast. As usual, I had no idea what was going on, neither did my parents, until David told me many years later when we worked together on the bonus content for the *Pollyanna* DVD release. Had I known what I was walking into I might not have been so relaxed.

But in this instance, ignorance was bliss – and from the moment I stepped onto that carpeted sidewalk, Hollywood seemed to put its arms around me and I hugged it back. The contrast between grey London and boom-town Hollywood in 1959 was like the difference between East and West Berlin before the Wall came down. Hollywood seemed a sort of demi-paradise; the bluest sky, palm trees waving gently in the sun, vibrant colour everywhere, blue and white agapanthus, the scent of tuberoses, the abundant jasmine scrambling over those great Beverly Hills mansions – everything looked so smooth and effortless and beautiful. Mummy already knew Hollywood well – and had mixed feelings about it, to say the least – but by the time the limousine finally dropped us off, and I gazed up at the Beverly Hills Hotel, like a great big pink wedding cake smothered in purple bougainvillea, I was hooked.

Everything dazzled me. The gigantic cars gleaming in the sun all looked new – or maybe they were just clean? Everything was so clean, even the people! And everyone looked rich, even the porters who leapt forward to open the car doors. Maybe it was because they were all so tanned? They would smile showing rows of gleaming straight white teeth, not a snaggletooth in sight! I was fascinated by everyone's teeth. I didn't know the lengths they had gone to in order to reach this perfection. Back home, I went to bed wearing a flimsy removable brace, which invariably removed itself during the night. I'm surprised it did anything . . . how I escaped buck teeth I shall never know.

The Walt Disney Studios had put us up, in great luxury, in one of the Beverly Hills Hotel's famous pink bungalows. Jonathan was beside himself, tearing about like a man possessed, his face purple with excitement. 'There's a television in *every* room!' The studio had sent us lavish gifts, fresh flowers and baskets of goodies filled with fruits and nuts and welcome messages, my first experience of incredible American generosity. My favourite of all these gifts was a clown, made entirely of red and white striped candy, which reminded me of the red and white Harlequin on the door of Walt's suite at the Dorchester.

At first, I assumed it was from Walt. However, it was from David Swift, my new director.

I was thrilled and couldn't wait to meet him.

Not only was I blissfully unaware of the conflict between Walt and David, but, being British, I didn't fully appreciate how much of an American icon the character of Pollyanna was. I might have been a little intimidated had I known just what a remarkable impact Eleanor Hodgman Porter's novel had on the public's imagination. Walt Disney's *Pollyanna* was going to be a big movie.

It was Mary Pickford – 'America's Sweetheart' – who first brought Pollyanna to the screen in 1920, even though she was twenty-seven when she played the part! With her great wealth of thick blonde hair and enchantingly diminutive stature, she was utterly convincing as the twelve-year-old child. She was so moving, with her soulful eyes and funny ways and her incredible

physicality, throwing herself around with almost terrifying aban-
don, as children do. The movie was a huge success and came to be
the role that most defined her.

Thank goodness, I didn't feel like I was stepping into Mary
Pickford's shoes. Playing Pollyanna, as I did at thirteen, I connected very much with her way of looking at life. It rang true
with something that was already there inside me. Children are
naturally inclined to be positive and trusting and to expect the
best in people. This kind of innocent positivity, the power of
gratitude in your life, the power of a smile, of living in the moment, the power of Now – these have become modern mantras
for happiness, but they were all there in Pollyanna's philosophy
in 1912. Even today, over one hundred years since the novel's first
publication, *Webster's Dictionary* includes the word 'Pollyanna' as:
'a girl of irrepressible optimism who finds good in everything'.
Conversely, many people think of a Pollyanna as a 'type' – sickly
sweet and unrealistic about life, a general pain in the neck. But I
never saw her as a goodie goodie. She was a tough, gutsy little girl
(as was Pickford herself), an orphan whose optimism made her
a survivor. She lived in the moment, as children do, and saw her
glass half-full, rather than half-empty.

So Walt and David Swift felt the time was right for a remake;
they had high hopes for *Pollyanna* and Disney made sure that
no expense was spared. A feature film in pre-production is like a
great steam train leaving a station, gradually increasing in speed.
There are so many departments and hundreds of people involved,
bringing various skills and talents, all of them working to come
together at the same moment on the day shooting begins. Pre-
liminary production on a big movie can last for many months.
Pollyanna was due to start filming in just two weeks, so by the
time I arrived in Hollywood the train was already blowing its
whistle and racing along the tracks. My next two weeks were
packed with rehearsals, meetings and fittings and I was swept up
in a whirl of activity.

On the very first morning I was taken to a costume fitting with the legendary designer Walter Plunkett. Of course, I was excited to see all the clothes, but I was also feeling quite nervous. Mummy explained to me who he was, how Mr Plunkett had already won Oscars for *An American in Paris* with Gene Kelly, as well as designing *Gone with the Wind*, all those beautiful dresses for Vivien Leigh. I remember especially loving the green velvet dress that Scarlett O'Hara was supposed to have fashioned out of a pair of old curtains.

Walter's offices were at MGM Studios, where he'd worked on films like *Singin' in the Rain* and *Seven Brides for Seven Brothers*, and it was soon clear to me that Walt Disney had hired him because he was the best. As we were ushered into his work studio, I was introduced to a slim, formally dressed man in black trousers and a black silk shirt, with dark hair carefully slicked back, and a thin moustache. Simple, stylish and elegant. He struck me as quite an impressive figure, but also rather an endearing one.

There is a scene in *Pollyanna* in which she is taken on a shopping trip by her aunt. She tries on one gorgeous outfit after another, shop assistants rushing around her at Aunt Polly's beck and call; Pollyanna finds herself at the centre of a whirlwind of attention, and she becomes quite giddy with it all. As life imitates art, an oddly similar sort of thing began to happen to me during the preparation for the film. It was hard not to get swept away by the whole experience. All my clothes were being designed and made especially for me by Walter – and he was a perfectionist. Every dress was an authentic, lavish recreation of the period, down to the smallest button and piece of braid. There were twelve dresses to try on; I stood for hours while they pinned me up and tucked me in, raised the hem, lifted the shoulder, added more lace, tweaked and plucked; a nod from Walter, a tut, or a shake of the head.

It was all a little overwhelming. The dresses were beautiful, especially the white frock made of broderie anglaise, my favourite.

It had a pale blue satin bow on the front and an even bigger bow on my bottom, with white tights and a pair of very squeaky, brand new white button boots. I stared at my reflection for a long time in the fitting-room mirror while a seamstress, with a mouthful of pins, crawled around on her knees – but the girl in the mirror just looked like me. It made me rather worried. Maybe it was the hair. It was my hair, not Pollyanna's.

After a couple of hours, somebody approached me with a huge menu and asked what I wanted for lunch; pinned into my stiff new dress, I could hardly move, let alone read the menu. I ordered a sandwich, which turned out to be so huge it had to be held together with toothpicks. I couldn't get it into my mouth. Everything fell out the other side. Even sandwiches were something astonishing in America.

I wondered what Daddy and Jonathan were doing – swimming in that sparkling pool, probably.

One fitting led to another. I was taken to Max Factor to get my 'fall' hairpiece done. Everyone was so kind and friendly, I just didn't know what to say, or how to say, that I really didn't like it. Actually, I hated it. Not only did it not feel right – it didn't feel *real*. It was all too big and heavy, with these thick braids hanging down over my shirt. I looked more like Heidi having a bad hair day than Pollyanna. I hoped that when I got the costume on, with the braids, it would all look and feel better, but there was still this creeping sense of anxiety. So I did what any other child would do, I ignored it.

Before long, Mummy and I were taken to Disney Studios in Burbank. The first time I was driven through those studio gates was to meet *Pollyanna*'s writer and director, David Swift.

David didn't give away any of his serious misgivings about my casting, for now. He was charming and friendly, with the bluest eyes, and the baldest head, and he had a very good sense of humour, which would be a godsend later on. David showed us around the Animation Department, where he had started as a young man in 1938. He knew everyone there; he introduced me to the legendary animator Ub Iwerks who'd been with Walt from the early days and helped design Mickey Mouse. He also took me to meet all the girls in the Ink & Paint Department, where I learnt about the thousands of hours they'd spend painstakingly colouring the drawings. It seemed a happy place to work. I could tell everyone loved what they did.

One evening during that first week I was taken out for dinner with a tremendously attractive and charismatic man wearing an outsize pair of horn-rimmed spectacles called Lew Wasserman. Lew was the head of MCA, the largest and most successful agency in Hollywood, and Laurie Evans's ultimate boss. Yet another A-lister in my diary. Lew was not just an agent, he was something of a visionary who created the 'star system'. His empire became so powerful that Attorney General Bobby Kennedy deemed it a dangerous monopoly and ordered MCA to be broken up. Lew's CV was unprecedented. Not only did he represent all the big names, he also started the Universal Studio Tour; he helped his client Alfred Hitchcock create his TV show *Alfred Hitchcock Presents*; he would launch Steven Spielberg's *Jaws*, overseeing the film's promotional campaign, which really started the phenomenon of the summer blockbuster. So Lew was very big fish. He was also my father's agent.

And now he was mine.

I sat and listened to the grown-up conversation and tried to see over a goldfish bowl filled with crushed ice and six absolutely enormous prawns that tasted like wet cricket pads. I wasn't entirely sure who Lew was.

The next time we went to The Walt Disney Studios, I was taken to see Walt himself. He was so warm and welcoming, it was like meeting an old friend. He showed Mummy and me into the office next to his, where he had all these cork boards on the walls, from floor to ceiling, each one covered with little drawings, like the most enormous comic book. 'These are the storyboards,' he enthused. 'Every shot for every scene of the film is pre-planned and illustrated: wide shots, tracking shots, close-ups ... We've already made the whole film here, in this office.' Walt kept a close eye on every aspect of the process, from the script to the shoot; he would work on all the set-ups with the director, he was involved in all the special effects, the editing, and even worked with the composer.

Unquestionably, Walt was a genius, and like all great artists he wanted control, but it left little room for inspiration on the film set. Indeed, I was to experience first-hand the frustration it produced for his more creative directors when their creativity didn't match Walt's expectations. Especially when the film happened to be shooting on location, in another country with a different time zone. No changes could be made without Walt's sign-off, even if we were shooting on the other side of the world. Sometimes the wait for the morning sun to rise in California would cost the production enormous amounts of money.

So Walt showed me all these storyboards, one of which I remember was a close-up of Pollyanna. She had a very surprised look on her face, wide open eyes and a little pursed-up mouth. I rather hoped that they wouldn't want me to copy that look.

In those days, everyone would go to the Commissary for lunch. On that first visit I remember everyone sitting on the grass in the sun eating their sandwiches. Walt greeted them all with a little nod and a smile. He seemed to know everybody; sometimes he'd call out to someone, ask after their families. I could see that he was genuinely loved and respected. It was a family of sorts. The Walt Disney Studios wasn't that big, not compared to Universal or Warner Bros. There was a good-sized backlot with some amazing sets built on it: a Main Street in a Western town, with a saloon and duck walks along the road; a big city street of the 1800s, somewhere in middle America – but it all felt quite contained. When they wanted to film in the open country they'd often use Walt's ranch in Placerita Canyon, which was beautiful, with horses and white wooden post-and-rail fencing. The studio itself was all spotlessly clean and well kept, the streets had wide grass verges and flowers, with names like Dopey Drive and Mickey Avenue; the buildings were only two storeys high, except for the Animation Building where Walt's office was. It was all very friendly and personal.

And of course, Walt was the undisputed Boss. It was his studio, and he loved it. He certainly wasn't a remote figure hidden away in his penthouse office, seldom seen or rarely descending to the studio floor. He was down there often, right in the thick of it. He loved wandering on to the sets when they were shooting; sometimes at the end of a take, you'd look up and Walt would be standing there just behind the lights. He adored movies and the whole process of making them. Sometimes he'd come with his wife Lilly; a sweet person, small and pretty and motherly, with a charming easy way of laughing. Lilly wore this amazing bracelet made up of little golden replicas of all the Academy Awards that Walt had won at that time. It weighed a ton. She'd always say, 'You can hear me coming a mile away.'

That first lunch, Walt took me to meet my screen 'Aunt Polly', the actress Jane Wyman. She was so beautiful, a real Hollywood star. The atmosphere was relaxed but I could sense what a formidable personality she was. I remember her telling me that she had always known what she wanted, that she had just gone out into the world, completely on her own, and simply made it happen. She'd come to Hollywood when she was just sixteen, had lied to everyone about her age, saying she was years older than she was in order to get work. When she was sixteen she married her first husband. It was incredible to think she had done all this when still only three years older than me! Two husbands later she married Ronald Reagan, who, after they divorced, became the 40th President of the United States. So, as you can imagine, I was more than a little in awe of Aunt Polly, but I also thought she was a darling. What I did not know about her back then was her very strong faith. Years later, after she had stopped working in movies, she became a Lay Tertiary in the Roman Catholic Church. When she died she was buried in a nun's habit.

After a couple of days in LA, I was scheduled to begin rehearsals. My mother was my chaperone as usual and we travelled together to meet Karl Malden, who was playing the role of 'Reverend Ford', a fire and brimstone preacher, sadly under the influence of Aunt Polly and her loveless take on Christianity. When I met Karl, he was so tall I had to bend my head back to look up at him. He was an impressive figure with an enormous head, a huge shock of hair and bright piercing eyes. I thought he was sweet and rather frightening. I remember him stooping down to my level and peering at me with those fierce eyes.

'You've got a nose just like mine,' he said.

I tried not to look at his, which was quite difficult.

'When the two of us are together in front of the camera,' he said, 'it will be a scene about two noses!' Then he threw his great head back and roared with laughter. I had a good laugh too; but it worried me for quite some time that my nose would grow up to look like his.

I knew that Karl was a great actor. He was part of Lee Strasberg's original theatrical troupe the Group Theater in New York. Elia Kazan was a close friend, and together they had made *A Streetcar Named Desire* and *On the Waterfront* with the young Marlon Brando. Karl had won Oscars and he was hugely loved and respected. That afternoon, Mummy and I went with Karl and David to an empty office to rehearse the first scene we were scheduled to shoot for the movie. I suspect Mummy was just a little bit nervous to see her young, inexperienced daughter thrown in at the deep end with a heavyweight thespian like Karl Malden. She gave me a brave smile as I walked into the rehearsal room while she was left to sit outside in the office.

In the scene we rehearsed, Reverend Ford is practising his

sermon alone on a hill one afternoon. Pollyanna appears with a message for him from Aunt Polly – notes on Bible texts that she wants him to consider for his sermon that coming Sunday. In this scene Reverend Ford and Pollyanna discuss God and what God might want for us. Pollyanna tells him about her late father, who was also a minister, and all about the 'happy texts' in the Bible. She shows him an inscription on her locket, which her father gave her: 'If you look for the bad in mankind, expecting to find it, you surely will' (Abraham Lincoln).

I always rather liked that, and have never forgotten it. For a short time they would sell these lockets in Disneyland with the famous presidential quote. It wasn't until many years later that David Swift confessed to me that it wasn't actually a quote of Abraham Lincoln's at all. He had written it himself! So as soon as he saw the lockets on sale at Disneyland, with the misattributed quote, he immediately had them pulled.

The rehearsals seemed to go well, but I was starting to worry about Mummy, who had been sitting outside the office the whole afternoon. It wasn't right that she was stuck out there and I knew she must be bored.

The shoot was drawing nearer and every day was packed. There were trips to the city to get a medical check-up, then somewhere else to get a work permit, then back to the studios to meet my tutor Jean Seaman, whose unenviable job it was to try to maintain some consistency in the education of her peripatetic pupils. Jean seemed very nice and showed me the 'little red schoolhouse' on the lot, a long trailer fitted out like a classroom. The red school-house was used by all the children working at Disney at any one time, which included all the *Mickey Mouse Club* kids from the TV series, stars like Annette Funicello and Kevin Corcoran, also known as 'Moochie', who was playing the little orphan boy Jimmy Bean in *Pollyanna*. The thought of having to go to school and study while in this movie playground seemed absurd and I wasn't looking forward to it.

During the second week they screen-tested all my outfits. I enjoyed that. Trying everything on, twirling around, no acting required, then taking it all off again. But the hair was still a big problem for me. The hairdresser kept telling me it would all be fine, and not to worry – but I *was* worrying. I hated it.

Life during those hectic two weeks became such a dizzy whirl-wind of fittings and rehearsals and incredible people to meet, that I slightly forgot I had to make a movie at the end of it. I just wasn't in touch with reality any more, especially when, during the second week, Walt turned up at our door in his car and personally drove us, in air-conditioned luxury, for a weekend at Disneyland. Of course, he had made the offer to take Jonathan and me to Disneyland during that first meeting at the Dorchester, but we didn't think he meant it literally. And yet that is exactly what he did. He took me by the hand and led me and my family through the gates on a personally guided tour of his magical kingdom.

It was a blistering hot day when we arrived, so Walt started by taking us to his private apartment which was located in the town square, at the entrance of Main Street, U.S.A., above the little Fire House. It was like walking into a Western bordello – red flock wallpaper, little red table lamps with bobbles on the shades and rocking chairs. He served us all ice-cold drinks and took great pleasure in being our host. He said he loved staying there in the park. Disneyland truly was his baby. Back at the Studios I remember he kept a huge map of Disneyland pinned on his office wall, which he used to spend hours studying; not just planning amazing new rides or attractions, but also the smaller details – like making sure that there was always somewhere for people to sit down in the shade, to find a cold drink, and that they didn't have too far to walk to find the loo. I thought it was really sweet of Walt Disney to think about things like that.

So we sat on the Fire House balcony with our iced drinks and looked down at the thronging crowds, all pouring in through the gates, oblivious to the fact that Mr Disney himself was up there, watching them.

Once we had polished off our cold drinks, we descended onto Main Street, giddy with excitement. For any child, a trip to Disneyland is as close to heaven on earth as it gets, but to be taken around by Walt himself was unreal. Jonathan and I were practically delirious – we had now gone into Hollywood Hyperspace. Walt not only took us all over the park, he went on all the attractions with us too. He seemed to enjoy every one, even the *Mad Tea Party*, with spinning cups and saucers, which kids love but makes most grownups feel sick. But not Walt. He had been on all his rides, hundreds of times, and still loved them. We could tell he was immensely proud of Disneyland, and rightly so. He told us that when he had first come up with the idea of building a theme park in Anaheim most people thought he was nuts; not even his own company would back the venture, and he had been forced to raise the financing elsewhere.

Although Walt was very famous and recognisable, especially since the launch of his television shows, we didn't see him get mobbed in the park. People seemed respectful and, while they smiled and were thrilled to spot him, they mostly gave him space. One of the great advantages of being escorted by the man himself was that you were spared from having to wait in those endless queues. Walt would walk us straight round to the back, in through a private door, and then up to the front of the line. On one occasion we did this for the *Matterhorn Bobsled* rollercoaster, which had an especially long and winding line. Our shameless queue jump was spotted by a young conscientious worker, wearing the red Disneyland uniform and sporting a nose very liberally covered in white sunblock. He rushed over to us, waving his arms, clearly very agitated.

'Hey! Stop! You can't come in here!' he said. 'Who do you think you are, Walt Disney?!'

There was a tiny pause, before Walt turned around and showed his face.

'Well, yes,' he said in a very quiet voice, 'as a matter of fact, I am.'

The young man went pale under his tan, clapped his hand over his face – smearing the white ointment all over it – tripped and fell backwards into a flower bed.

That whole weekend was a child's fantasy. I was so swept away by the heady mixture of all the thrilling sights and sounds, the rides, the shows, the food – and I was so completely enamoured of Walt Disney himself – that I had quite forgotten about the film I was about to make.

One night, towards the end of those two weeks, Walt invited my whole family up to his house to have supper with him and Lilly. It was awfully exciting.

At one point during the meal, Lilly turned to me.

'Well, Hayley,' she said, 'are you looking forward to the film?'

I looked up at her with my most engaging smile. 'What film?'

There was a moment's silence, then everyone laughed. But I was left with a strange queasiness in the pit of my stomach that wouldn't go away. Oh yes . . . *that* film.

After dinner we were shown to Walt's private cinema to watch a movie. The idea of having a cinema in your own home was simply mind-blowing to Johnny and me, who had never seen anything like it in our lives. We were still impressed by televisions. Walt and Lilly's cinema was so luxurious. As your seat reclined your feet shot up, and magically your right hand was plunged into a bowl of M&Ms. Walt watched very little of the film – he spent most of it at the back in his cocktail bar making enormous ice-cream sodas for the kids.

That night I went back to the hotel and stared in the mirror at my reflection. After a moment's rumination, I picked up my mother's nail scissors, grabbed the fringe of my hair, and cut off my widow's peak.

I remember the satisfaction at hearing the scissors chomping through my hair like pinking shears. It left a little tuft sticking up where my widow's peak used to be. I was due to fly to the first location the following morning where *Pollyanna* would start filming in just two days.

And I had just vandalised my head.

It was an idiotic thing to do and I was told so in no uncertain terms by my appalled mother. It took me years to understand why I did it. Self-sabotage. On the surface children appear to mis-behave and act irrationally, but there's an instinctive logic to it. Mine was that, if I turned out to be absolutely awful, a failure, I could perhaps blame it on something other than myself, like a ridiculous tuft of hair protruding from my forehead. I don't remember *feeling* nervous, but I know I definitely was because I wrote it down in my journal. Maybe nervousness is like pain, you don't remember it.

The next morning, Jonathan, Mummy and Daddy and I all flew up to Santa Rosa to start shooting. Santa Rosa back then was a beautiful and romantic part of California. It had been a wine-grow-ing area for well over a hundred years, with old stone or clapboard houses, and trees draped with lichen that gave the place a sort of ghostly, abandoned feeling. The families that lived in these old houses had apparently been there for generations and the whole town seemed like it belonged to another era.

I don't think I slept particularly well the night before the shoot. The same sickly knot of nerves and excitement that gripped me in Walt's cinema was still there, squirming in the pit of my stomach, and I was worried what the hair and make-up team would say about my hack job.

It was early in the morning when I arrived at our location but the sun was already baking hot. The production base was set up on a hillside, some way outside of the town, amid rolling fields of tall dry golden grass and poison oak everywhere. There was the usual collection of vehicles, trailers and arc lights, with black cables snaking all over the ground, and what looked like hordes of people wandering about, apparently randomly, but actually everyone knowing exactly what they were supposed to be doing, even if it was just drinking a cup of coffee. It was all familiar to me. I'd been on sets many times before, but nothing quite on this scale. It was like a great circus had encamped on the hillside – the only thing missing was a Big Top.

I got out of the car, the queasiness in my stomach almost making me dizzy, and I was taken to my trailer, which turned out to be the size of a small ship. I was thrilled, I had my own private house! Two double bedrooms, a proper bathroom, a huge living room with bouncy sofas, and a real kitchen. There was nothing for Mummy to worry about here though – the catering truck was just around the corner, and what an astonishing sight that was: laden with mouthwatering treats, enormous platters of delicious fruits, huge slices of watermelon, the biggest, reddest apples – like the evil witch gave to Snow White – fabulous giant cookies, not to mention great samovars of tea and coffee and a strange thing called 'Half and Half', which, if you threw it onto the ground, stained the grass like white paint. But most impressive of all were the boxes upon boxes of fresh pastries, cinnamon rolls and donuts covered in icing sugar.

For a short moment I was able to forget about the film and just enjoy American catering.

But all worldly pleasure is fleeting, and I was eventually sent for by the Wardrobe Department, who were waiting in my trailer. They helped me get ready and put on the costume for my first scene with Karl. It was the plaid – my least favourite and least comfortable of the dresses: green and yellow with a high neck and long sleeves – with worsted wool tights and white button boots that you did up with a hook.

Decked out in my new clothes and increasingly nervous, I was taken to see 'Hairdressing & Make Up' who were understandably thrown by my 'new look'. After some mutterings and internal discussion it was decided to shave off the offending tuft and create a whole new fringe by bringing down another line of hair to cover up the shaved bit. Then the 'fall' – with the heavy braids threatening to pull the whole thing off my head – was attached and pinned on, rather too tightly, with the wispy strands of new hair struggling to look convincing as a fringe. My face was then, rather too liberally, covered in Max Factor pancake, as if to make up for it all. I left Hair & Make Up feeling like a boiled egg in a wig. All of a sudden, I found it difficult to walk normally.

The morning sun was by now very hot as the third assistant director marched me up the hill to where the camera and the crew were waiting. David was up there under the bright lights, wearing a Spanish straw hat; he seemed jovial and made no mention of my hair. He introduced me to the crew: the director of photography, the first assistant – there seemed to be an enormous number of people, I couldn't quite take it all in. Further down the hill, I could see the shining silver trailers and the giant catering truck. I thought of all those donuts.

I ambled over to where Karl was muttering his lines and said hello to him. And then, with David watching us, we again went over the scene that we had rehearsed at the studio. There is always a lot of hanging around and waiting on a film set. Often, the bigger the set, the slower things move. It was sweltering before the cameras started rolling and it just got hotter and hotter as the day wore on. My parents stayed out of sight, behind the camera; they didn't want to put me off.

And so we began. Reverend Ford is practising his sermon in a field and Pollyanna is supposed to appear carrying a note from Aunt Polly. All I had to do in the first shot was walk up, observe what was going on, then sit down on the trunk of an old tree and listen to the Reverend, before he eventually noticed that he'd got an audience. That was easy. Then the scene began – and the problems started. Time dragged on, the heat seemed to slow everything down, things kept going wrong, I wasn't sure what,

David seemed flustered, and there was a lot of waiting about before doing the scene again, and again . . . and again. The wig was hot and scratched my neck, my dress was stiff, the long dry grasses got stuck in my tights, and everything itched.

I don't really know why we didn't get a shot in the can that morning. I have a clear memory of the crew, all standing around in the heat, the enormous, blinding arc lights, of glancing over Karl's shoulder down the hill, the sight of the catering truck with all those fresh donuts – and of David, being very patient, but looking increasingly anxious with every take, and Karl being very kind, as his skin got redder and redder.

The pressure was on but I was so unsettled and distracted by everything. I just couldn't concentrate.

David Swift must have been a very worried man. He hadn't wanted me for the role in the first place and now here he was, sweating like a pig on a hillside in Northern California, finally making the film he had worked on for so many years, and his star player was not delivering. Making feature films is an extremely expensive endeavour – every minute costs money. Time is the enemy. The sun is always going down. Especially in those days when movies were shot on film; they used to say the whirring of a camera turning over was the sound of money going through the gate. So when things weren't working, everyone felt the strain. The actors certainly; the director perhaps most of all – the buck stops with them.

Eventually, we broke for lunch, still with nothing worth printing in the can. The unit all moved off down the hill with audible sighs of relief. That was when my father finally appeared. He'd been out of sight, stood among the crew, but he'd seen everything. He took me to one side, to sit in the shade of a big tree.

'What's the matter, Bags?' he asked calmly.

I could see the concern in his eyes. I swallowed drily.

'I don't know,' I said. 'What d'you mean? Nothing's the matter.'

'Well . . . umm,' and then he paused. I could see he was

choosing his words carefully. 'Do you know what you're like? Up there? On camera, I mean.'

'No . . . what?'

'You are like . . . a big white cabbage.' I stared at him. And he nodded back. 'That's right. A great big white cabbage.'

And then, all of a sudden, I knew exactly what he meant.

'Boring,' he said. '*Very* boring. Pull your finger out.'

Being boring was a cardinal sin in our family. It was just about the worst thing he could have said.

But I knew he was right.

With the imprint of Daddy's boot firmly on my backside, the afternoon's shoot went much better. The 'cabbage talk' had jolted me out of my stupor – the acting genes kicked in, and I was much better. I was certainly more professional, but more importantly, I enjoyed it. I know it sounds simple but that really is the key. If you don't enjoy giving a performance, you can be sure no one else is going to enjoy watching it. And on that first day, I loved acting with Karl. It was a well-written scene and he was so fascinating to watch. Unfortunately, by the end of the day, his poor head and nose were the colour of burnt sienna.

I couldn't help feeling slightly responsible.

After that initially bumpy start I quickly settled down. Part of the trick to filmmaking is getting into the rhythm of the process. It's a bit like getting your sea legs: you become accustomed to the ritual and routine, the nerves, the tension, the stops, the starts, the early mornings or long night-shoots. But most of all, ideally, you start to function as part of a team, working together to create something bigger than any one individual. Once I had properly settled in to my new 'circus life', I began to feel completely comfortable, just as I had on *Tiger Bay*. I got over the strangeness of my fake hair and the period costume – although the lure of the catering truck never completely left me.

I loved working in front of the camera. From the beginning it felt like home. The camera gives you its total, undivided attention;

it doesn't judge, it's just there, quiet and steady, to observe, absorb and to listen. I sensed instinctively that whatever I did, whatever I thought, the camera would get it. That didn't mean I always got it right, but that was all part of a fascinating process. The great Charles Laughton, in his own inimitable way, once revealed his secret to film acting: 'You simply feel the emotion – and then let it dribble out of your eyes.' And what huge and expressive eyes Charles Laughton had! In the same way, I loved feeling that the camera understood me, that it could see what I was doing and communicate my thoughts. It was my special friend.

And everyone was very sweet and considerate to me. It could have been absolutely disastrous if I had been overly spoilt. Of course, there is always an element of being pampered, especially when you've got the starring role in Hollywood – and it's very easy to get used to people running around doing things for you – but thankfully, I had my sensible, no-nonsense mother, who kept my feet firmly on the ground, so, although I got star treatment, I understood that it was because I was expected to deliver the goods.

Just as I had been incredibly fortunate to have J. Lee Thompson to direct me on *Tiger Bay*, I struck it lucky a second time with David Swift. *Pollyanna* set the bar very high for the future. David was one of the most patient and gentlest people I've ever worked with. I think he genuinely loved actors. He encouraged everyone to come up with ideas, to improvise if they wanted to – something I'd never done before. I once tentatively suggested to him that Nancy Olson and I could sing 'Early One Morning' as a duet when we're walking along the road and to my delight David said, 'Do it!' He was very like Walt in that respect, always encouraging. Walt would come on to the set after watching the 'dailies' and go around telling everyone how good they were and how happy he was. That kind of support and encouragement was incredibly valuable and made you feel inspired and happy and safe. I have never understood directors who belittle and undermine their actors (and I've known a few), thinking that this approach will produce a great performance. Admittedly, I'm sure, sometimes an overly complicated or tiresome actor needs a proverbial ice bucket chucked over them, but on the whole, as in life, I believe that only love leads; it is care and encouragement, not fear, that brings out the best in people. If someone you respect believes in you, it means more than just believing in yourself alone. I heard a story once about a young actor who leapt off the end of a pier into the sea because his director asked him to – quite ignoring the fact that he couldn't swim!

While things were going well in front of the camera, behind the scenes they rather took a turn for the worse. Mummy was finding the long hot days interminable. When my father was filming it was different, she could come and go as she liked, but with me working she was stuck on set all day, sitting about with nothing to do. She wasn't cut out to be a stage mother – and she didn't want to try. She was a writer, she needed space and she couldn't write a single word stuck on set. Doing nothing was stultifying.

Things got worse for her when Daddy left us to start shooting *Swiss Family Robinson* in the West Indies. My mother had been dreading his departure and when he was gone she began to succumb to her Celtic melancholy.

Around this time, the production returned from Santa Rosa and began shooting in Hollywood. We were moved out of the Beverly Hills Hotel and into the iconic Chateau Marmont, perched on a rise above Sunset Boulevard. I remember the front of the hotel sported an enormous cowgirl, the size of a small building, revolving slowly on one cowboy-booted leg, wearing a Stetson and smoking a cigarette. We had been given a cottage in the grounds, so it felt much less like living in a hotel. We had a sitting room and a little kitchen, which I noticed Mummy eyeing somewhat balefully, cooking being her least favourite occupation – she considered it a huge waste of her time.

Opposite our cottage was the legendary Garden of Allah Hotel, then in the last phase of its existence. The Garden of Alla, as it was originally named, was a relic of old Hollywood, where the stars in the 1920s, '30s and '40s went for privacy and stayed in great comfort. It had originally been built by the beautiful Russian silent star Alla Nazimova, who lived there until the 'talkies' arrived – and with them, the end of her career. Finding herself out of a job she took some good advice, turning her house and swimming pool (shaped like the Black Sea) into a luxury hotel – building twenty-four Spanish-style whitewashed cottages, with red terracotta roofs, surrounded by white roses and beautifully manicured grounds. The Garden of Allah – its spelling was normalised by new owners who took over in 1930 – became a Mecca for the stars; before the days of the great Beverly Hills mansions and wealthy neighbourhoods, when the stars only came to Hollywood to work and needed somewhere to stay. Icons like Ernest Hemingway lived and wrote there; F. Scott Fitzgerald also stayed there with his young lover, Sheilah Graham (while his wife Zelda was safely away in a sanatorium); Humphrey Bogart was enjoying a stay there with Lauren Bacall when his wife turned up one night and tried to attack him with a kitchen knife. Lauren Bacall had to escape through a back door.

Greta Garbo had lived there; the Marx Brothers had lived there; Marlene Dietrich loved to swim naked in the pool, and Clara Bow was famous for pushing waiters off the diving board. It was as glamorous as it was notorious for its wild parties and scandals.

By the time we arrived, the Garden of Allah was run down and practically abandoned, all the contents having been sold off the year before. The stars had all gone, their lights faded from the Tinseltown sky. Such is the fate of all Hollywood legend.

When I returned the following year it had completely disappeared, razed to the ground, the pool filled in with cement. In its place was a parking lot and a bank. No clue left that it had ever existed.

Close to where the Garden of Allah stood on Sunset Strip was Schwab's drugstore, which became a Mecca of sorts for me. It's odd that I should have become so enamoured by something as random as a drugstore, but it seemed to exemplify everything I loved about America. Sitting at the long bar, swivelling on the polished chrome and red leather stools, gorging on a mountainous ice-cream sundae – it was heaven. And if you sat in one of the booths you could have your own private jukebox. For just a dime you could play anything you wanted: Elvis Presley, Ricky Nelson, Connie Francis and my new favourite, Doris Day. And then there were the rows upon rows of American comic magazines. I browsed through endless aisles of hundreds of incredible comics like a connoisseur, discovering *Superman* and *The Twilight Zone*, a far cry from my beloved *Dandy* and *Beano*. I had discovered the New World – and its name was Schwab's.

The longer we stayed at Chateau Marmont the deeper Mummy plunged into her gloom. She felt alone without Daddy, she hated cooking and doing the laundry, and she began to drink too much vodka. At night, Johnny would shove our beds together and we'd all stay up late and giggle and talk for hours. Mummy was a nightjar. Jonathan would usually conk out first, then I would have her to myself. She'd stare into the dark and muse upon some disaster that had happened in the world, and the impact it must be having on the people involved; or if there had been a murder, her imagination was graphic, sometimes horrifying, conjuring ghastly images that kept me awake and crept into my dreams. Neither of us slept much. But she'd also tell me wonderful, funny stories about her early life and experiences as an actress, which all started when she met my father and the theatrical company he was touring with in China. 'The Quaints' had all been invited for tea and tennis at Colonel Hayley Bell's family home in Tientsin one Sunday and she had been instantly enamoured by them all, especially my father; she envied their wonderful gaiety and camaraderie, and the sense of this incredibly glamorous life they all led. Fired by a desire to one day become one of them, and smitten by the magic of the theatre, she eventually studied at the Royal Academy of Dramatic Art before getting her first job with Seymour Hicks's theatrical company – the venerable Edwardian actor knight, who rather took a shine to my mother and mentored her in those early days. Touring Britain in the 1930s was far from glamorous. Actors' digs were wretched in comparison to my charmed Hollywood life. Mummy never had any money and would have to share dreadful lodgings (and often beds) with her companion Sonia Somers. Staying in one such lodging, in Manchester, they realised it must be infested with bed bugs when, at breakfast, they both started itching furiously. A fellow lodger and self-proclaimed expert in bed bugs told them how to deal with the situation.

'It's simple. You gotta get a bar of soap,' he said. 'Get a bar of soap, nice an' tacky, then grab a hold of the sheet and rip it back fast – if you see a bug SLAM down the soap. But you gotta be quick!'

So she did as he suggested, and just as he predicted, there on the white sheet was a small black dot. Her bar of soap was swiftly slammed down and came up with a flat black bed bug stuck in the middle of it. Subsequent forays with soap produced further trapped bugs. The girls then descended the stairs brandishing their bars of soap in the air and threatened to report the unsanitary landlady to the police. The old cow tried to get them to pay a week's rent, to no avail, and they left, itching but triumphant.

I would lie there in the darkness for ages, listening in wonder. Here's me, I thought, aged thirteen, already starring in a movie with digs in Beverly Hills. It had been so much harder for her.

As we drifted off into the small hours, she would inevitably recall her childhood growing up in China: sleeping on the roof under the stars in Macau with her brothers and sisters; riding her pony bareback along the Bund; incredible adventures with her father, Francis, boarding Chinese junks for contraband guns and opium. She loved her father more than anyone in the world and when she met Daddy, of course, she transferred all that devotion to him. He became her emotional lifeline. That's why she struggled so much when they were apart; she always felt she didn't cope well without him. Unfortunately, due to my career, these prolonged separations were to become a regular occurrence.

When we returned to the Studios to shoot all the interior sequences, I discovered that Disney had found a guardian for me, freeing my mother from her onerous duties on set. Initially I was appalled. I was turning into a feral movie brat, wandering the sets and sound stages, often borrowing the messenger boy's bicycle and riding all over the studios, chatting to the chippies, playing on the deserted backlot . . . And then this woman called Lee Bragg turned up, who had been told never to let me out of her sight! Fatal. Poor Lee, wherever she was I would run in the opposite direction; I'd climb up and hide in the gantry, beyond the lights and the electricians, as high as I could; or if she followed me into the loo, I'd jump out the window. After my rather bolshie response to her arrival, Lee and I became great friends. Lucky for me, she had a sense of humour and two children of her own. She was a tall, imposing figure with a big laugh, her hair swept up in a french twist, bleached so blonde that it was always snapping off at the roots. Lee chain-smoked unfiltered Pall Mall cigarettes. When I was fifteen Lee taught me how to smoke.

Eventually September came around and we were still in the thick of shooting *Pollyanna*. Time had crept up on me unawares, because, of course, back home I should have been going back to school, so Jonathan and I were sent to the little red schoolhouse on the lot.

By law, I had to do three hours of schoolwork a day. In America the teacher could literally stop the shoot. On one memorable occasion, I remember we were filming the big summer fete sequence with 125 extras in costume; David Swift needed one more 'take', but Jean, the school teacher, refused permission and I was taken smartly off the set and sent back to the little red schoolhouse, even though it meant bringing hundreds of extras back for one extra take the next morning! They say 'never work with children or animals', and poor David must have been fuming. But that was the law – three hours' schoolwork a day. There was no getting out of it.

It was also a nightmare for me; I was not academically minded and concentration was challenging to say the least. One moment you'd be under the lights, in the middle of filming, possibly a very tricky scene, the next you were being shooed off to the schoolhouse to try to remember dates about Mesopotamia.

On my first day Annette Funicello and all the Mouseketeers were there. I hadn't met any of them before, they were all quite a bit older than me. At seventeen, Annette seemed very grown up; we smiled and nodded at each other and I sat down at one of the desks. It was a very different curriculum to the one I had been doing in England. For a start I was told that I had to write in pencil ... *pencil*!? I was outraged, and tried to explain, slightly pompously, that I had graduated to writing in ink some time ago, but it was useless, and I was given *pencils*! I felt humiliated, and rather superior about doing my schoolwork with a fountain pen. Soon after this, I discovered that none of these kids had started Algebra or even Geometry, let alone Latin. More feelings of superiority – not that I was any good at all at the first two, and I hadn't actually started Latin yet, owing to the fact that I had been filming in Cardiff when my class had begun it, but I didn't mention that fact. So with a martyred look on my face I picked up the offending object and got to work on 'Math' as they called it; another subject miles from my heart.

I made a mistake, and raised my hand.

'Yes, Hayley?'

'I was wondering if anyone would lend me a rubber. I haven't got one, and my pencil doesn't have one on the end of it.'

The whole of the Mickey Mouse Club exploded into hysterical laughter while I sat there bewildered.

It was Moochie who told me later what a 'rubber' meant in America. Now *that* was an education.

I soon realised that, while I may have been writing in ink and studying advanced subjects in England, these kids in the little red schoolhouse knew a lot more about life than I did. Kevin, or 'Moochie', had been acting since he was six (he was ten when he played Jimmy Bean in *Pollyanna*). He was round and unusually small for his age, and, with a great chunk of brown hair almost obscuring his eyes, he looked even younger. We used to squeeze under the wooden ladders that led up to the gantry, where all the lights that shone down on to the set below were hung, and gossip. Despite his age, Moochie was very wise and knew about lots of things, apart from the facts of life. He was an experienced performer, much more so than me. He came from a huge family. I think there were eight children in all, most of them in the acting business, and two of his older sisters had already made names for themselves. It sounded like enormous fun, but it was Moochie who first told me the horror stories about other child actors who had worked all their lives and ended up with nothing to show for it. He solemnly recounted the tale of Jackie Coogan – the first of the child stars – discovered by Charlie Chaplin on a vaudeville stage at the age of five, before taking the world by storm in *The Kid*. Jackie's unprecedented success in his many movies spawned huge amounts of merchandising – images, books, toys and games – and by the time he had reached his twelfth birthday he was reported to have earned $4 million, a staggering amount for the 1920s. When, on his twenty-first birthday, Jackie asked his mother if he might have some of the money that he had earned throughout his childhood, she refused to give it to him. His father, who had always managed his earnings with care, had died tragically five months earlier in a car accident, and his mother had quickly married again, to a man called Arthur Bernstein, who was also their 'financial advisor'. Between the two of them Mom and Arthur had managed to run through almost all the kid's entire fortune, splashing out on holidays and fur coats, diamonds and expensive cars. Jackie eventually sued his mother, and, after a lengthy court battle, was paid just $160,000.

As a result of the embezzlement of Jackie's earnings and the publicity surrounding the court case, a new law was created called the California Child Actor's Bill or, more popularly, 'The Coogan Act'. The Act was designed to protect child actors from the depredations of their parents and advisors, and safeguard their money. The new law stipulated that at least 15 per cent of their earnings had to be put into a trust account for the child. Unfortunately the law was so peppered with loopholes that many of the child actors still ended up working for nothing. The problem was, as it still remains today, that a lot of these families were supported by their children's work; the parents argued that the time and money spent on nurturing their child's careers – dance classes, dance shoes, acting lessons, singing lessons, clothing, and driving back and forth to endless auditions, not to mention agents' and managers' fees – justified their keeping the earnings for themselves and the rest of the family. While there may have been a degree of truth to this, there was no proper legal protection for the child, and so this was often taken advantage of.

Shirley Temple suffered the same fate. Fox's biggest star in the 1930s earned over $3 million. By the time she was twenty and her career began to slow down, she decided that she wanted to retire from acting, and discovered she had only forty grand in the bank as a result of her parents' reckless spending and indifference.

Moochie told me all these stories, and many others, that could chill the blood. The thought of being betrayed by one's own parents and then having to take them to court! But it also made me realise how lucky I was. At least, I was confident in the knowledge that my parents didn't need my money. They had their own wealth. I wasn't having to support the family, and, whatever happened, however much I earned, I knew that they would be able to take care of everything for me.

That's what I believed at the time, anyway.

For me, the whole experience of filming *Pollyanna* was wonderful. Although some of the days seemed endlessly long, hot and humid, I still loved every minute. Santa Rosa had been my first glimpse of old America; the house they used for Aunt Polly's was an 1865 mansion – wood painted all white with pillars and porches and wonderful flowers – owned by a Mrs McDonald who, at ninety-five and in a wheelchair, was I think the oldest person I'd ever met. I loved talking to her. The locations were all full of history; 'Stag's Leap', the house of Mr Pendergast, played by Adolphe Menjou, was completely derelict, and Theodore Roosevelt used to stay there.

And I was surrounded by lovely people. It was an extraordinary privilege to work alongside such talent and I was genuinely dazzled by everyone and how amazing they all were; people like Richard Egan who played Aunt Polly's old flame, who was so good looking that I found it hard to look at him during a scene without drying; and Nancy Olson, who played Aunt Polly's maid, so pretty and charismatic, I loved her immediately. We used to giggle about nothing. Her nickname in Hollywood was 'Wholesome Olson', but she was a peaches and cream sort of girl, with a wicked sense of humour. When we made *Pollyanna* she was married to the songwriter Alan J. Lerner. It wasn't till years later I saw her starring opposite William Holden and Gloria Swanson in the classic *Sunset Boulevard*.

'O Brave new world that has such people in it . . .'

On the last day of filming there was a party on the set. Jane Wyman was an avid baseball fan and at the end of the last take an enormous television was wheeled on to the sound stage; chairs were arranged in a large semi-circle around it, and the whole cast and crew sat and watched the Los Angeles Dodgers play the San Francisco Giants. It was terribly exciting – even I had heard of Willie Mays. There was beer, we ate popcorn, and gave each other presents; we hugged a lot and cried a bit. It was a fitting end to my first American movie.

As it turned out, the shoot for *Pollyanna* had lasted four months – a mini lifetime for a thirteen-year-old. It was an incredible summer that I shall remember for ever. Little did I know it would also remember me. For many people, for the rest of my life, I would forever be Pollyanna, all sweetness and pigtails, just like Mary Pickford before me. It was a role that was to prove both a blessing and a curse. On the one hand, the greatest opportunity a young actress ever had, on the other, a childish label, pinned to my back, which I became increasingly frustrated by, even embarrassed by, with each passing year as I struggled to maturity.

But that was still way off in the future. For now, it was sunshine and happiness. Mummy was already brightening at the promise of being with Daddy, and I was excited at the prospect of regaining my freedom and just going back to being a normal kid again. But, of course, this was never going to happen. In a matter of months, I was about to become a household name – a face on a magazine, a name on a poster, one of Disney's biggest exports – and while nothing on earth could prepare me for the incoming twin meteors of Fame and Success, these paled by comparison to the biggest shock of all, just around the corner.

CHAPTER FOUR

Split Screen Effect

'The nerve of that girl, coming here with your face!'
— *The Parent Trap*, 1961

Ironically, just as my career as a child actor was beginning to take off, puberty started kicking in. Adolescence is a minefield of confusing, conflicting moods and deep emotional changes for everyone, and being in the public eye only exacerbated the whole experience. Becoming self-aware is often agony; it was for me. I suddenly began to question everything I'd taken for granted about myself. Things didn't seem to fit any more. My last days of unadulterated childhood were coming to an end, and I was about to leave that carefree world behind for ever.

My last days of childhood paradise were literally just that. After *Pollyanna* wrapped we flew to Tobago where my father was filming Disney's *Swiss Family Robinson*. Tobago: twenty-seven miles long as the crow flies, just three small hotels and empty beaches, lined with palm trees that leant over the sand, as if trying to reach into the surf that sweeps softly up the beach. Back then, Tobago wasn't the luxury destination it is today and it almost felt like we had the island to ourselves. Daddy had found us a little house on a hill that peered out from under the banana trees and down to the sparkling water. It was here that Jonathan and I spent two ecstatic months running wild, bare feet, and flying wet hair, dashing across shell-strewn beaches, throwing ourselves deliriously into the rising waves, full of iridescent fish, or sometimes a school of barracuda, backlit by the setting sun. We'd stare up in awe at the most wonderful birds: great grey pelicans that flew low and slow across the water; man-o'-war or frigate birds with their angular wings and long forked tails, hanging motionless in the sky. At breakfast, bright yellow warblers would land on the table and help themselves to your papaya.

Walt Disney had taken the brave decision to shoot all of *Swiss Family Robinson* on location. But filming on a tropical island is very different from going there on holiday. Before we arrived there had been a tremendous hurricane with torrential rain and hundred-mile-an-hour winds, which almost destroyed the sets. The film's famous treehouse was through a mangrove swamp, where there were also large and highly mobile land crabs with shells as hard as motorbike helmets, not to mention snakes and scorpions. In the film, the shipwrecked family keep a private zoo's-worth of exotic pets: elephants, lions, monkeys, zebras, all of which had been flown in to the island with accompanying train-ers. There was also a fully grown tiger, which was quite unsettling, and a very ornery ostrich who could only be sufficiently motivated to go in the desired direction by having an electric prod stuck up its tail feathers – enough to make anyone move. Once the poor bird took off with such force that he crashed through a very sturdily built wooden shed and went straight out the other side.

Daddy was happiest when working, and Mummy was writ-ing again, relieved of her domestic duties, thanks to the angelic presence of Mrs Batista, who arrived every day in her bright red commando's beret to provide us with fresh fish, perfectly cooked rice and coconut milk. Everything was perfect.

The only cloud in my sky was Bunch. I had been so excited

to see her again, but when she arrived in Tobago to spend a few weeks' holiday, something had changed. She didn't want to talk to me any more, or share in any of the fun. She was always going off by herself to sit on a rock. I'd watch her, deep in thought, gazing at something far out beyond the horizon, something that I couldn't see. One night, as we lay quietly under our mosquito nets, she finally broke her silence and told me what was wrong: she had fallen in love. He was an actor called Jeremy Spenser. I knew who he was: a rising young star, olive-skinned and rather good looking. He had just made a film with Daddy called *It's Great to Be Young*, in which he played a schoolboy heart-throb and mimed playing jazz trumpet very well. Bunch had met him at the studios and fallen head over heels. She'd written to him so many times but never heard back. He seemed to be completely ignoring her. She later found out he was having a relationship with an older woman – much older, almost thirty years, in fact – a very well-regarded actress called Patience Collier, who was no great beauty. This should have been some consolation, for it was abundantly clear that Bunch simply wasn't his type – and wouldn't be for some considerable time. But she was desperately unhappy. I did try to listen and sympathise but I was too young. I just couldn't understand. It all seemed so stupid to me. And it was ruining a perfect holiday. What a terrible waste! It just didn't make any sense. One thing I was sure of: I did not want to fall in love.

After a few weeks, Bunch had to go to New York where *Five Finger Exercise* was opening on Broadway. As I stood waving goodbye from the little island airport, watching the red tail-light of her plane disappear in the evening sky, it seemed like the end of something – something more than just a departure. I wasn't sure what; but one of us had left. She would have her own life now, alone in that big unfamiliar city, and when she came back to London it would all be different, she'd probably have a place of her own to live in . . .

Then suddenly it hit me. She was grown up. She'd left me be-hind. I felt hot tears stab my eyes. I didn't want her to go, I didn't want to imagine life without her. She gave shape to things, she always knew what to do, she always had plans – but she'd flown the nest. Who was going to make plans now?

When I returned to England in late January 1960, I didn't mind the grey skies, the clouds hanging low over everything, the drizzle, the damp smell of earth; it was home and I relished it. Soxie's smiling face, the barking joyous dogs tearing around like maniacs; I'd been away so long my bicycle was covered in weeds. I'd hardly time to catch my breath and take Annabelle out for one last ride in the wintry woods before my trunk was packed and I was sent off again. Back to Elmhurst.

I said goodbye to my parents at Waterloo, a horrible lump in my stomach as they waved me off on the platform. I found myself an empty compartment and sat down in my seat, upholstered in stiff prickly material that felt like horsehair. Everything seemed to be stained brown and smelt acrid, like the ghosts of a million old cigarettes. I peered through the grimy windows as telegraph poles flew by, and the tenements and smoking chimney pots of London gave way to a greener, rain-sodden country, and the occasional depressed-looking white horse standing alone in a field.

I was wearing my grey school overcoat, long grey socks, brown lace-up shoes and Elmhurst's blue woollen crochet beret. It felt strange to be back in uniform again. I was hoping like mad that no one would come in so that I could spend the whole journey back to Camberley alone, thinking my thoughts; of the summer, of my sister, of Tobago . . . My reverie was soon arrested however, by the sight of a cowboy, twenty feet tall, whose face I recognised immediately. I leapt up and pushed my face against the carriage window as a huge great billboard flashed past: '*The Magnificent Seven* – a movie by John Sturges'. It was an incredible sight: Yul Brynner, dressed all in black, leading his war party, seven abreast, with Steve McQueen, Charles Bronson, Robert Vaughn; and there, among them, astride a suitably magnificent Appaloosa, was Horst. I settled back in my seat and stared into space, imagining Horst galloping around in a cowboy hat. I'd heard all about the movie, people said it was amazing. Akira Kurosawa, the great auteur who made the original, *Seven Samurai*, was so impressed with it he presented John Sturges with a samurai sword. Horst was on his way to becoming a Hollywood star . . . The only place I was on my way to was this bloody school. I wondered if I'd ever see Horst again. My thoughts drifted glumly back to my last day shooting *Tiger Bay*, splashing around in that ridiculous great big water tank; bobbing, sobbing, heartbroken. And drunk.

The train began to slow down as we approached Camberley station. Of course, I was excited to see Jane and my friends. I'd been gone for almost seven whole months, and I was also a bit nervous. No one wants to be the odd one out. Even the most eccentric nonconformist desires 'to belong' on some level, but at school this was becoming harder and harder for me. Not only was I making movies, I had missed all of the autumn term and half the winter, so I was terribly behind with my studies. My parents had attempted to remedy the situation by sending Jonathan and me to a local school in Tobago's capital, Scarborough. We were the only kids not from the island, everyone was very nice and friendly and it was great fun, but we didn't learn very much – except how to play football without any shoes. Now I was dreading going back and being bottom of the class.

Arriving back, amid the hubbub of reunions and registrations, we were assigned to our new dormitories. I was put into 'Green' and Jane was in 'Yellow' just across the linoleumed landing. I was disappointed that we weren't going to be in the same dorm, but I was so happy to see everybody.

That night in the dormitory, after lights out, there was a lot of giggling and talk about boys. Some of the girls had been to dances during the holidays, one or two had been kissed. Some of them had started to wear bras, white cotton ones from Marks and Sparks. I was terribly impressed and longed for the day when I could wear one. I started to tell them about making the film and all the incredible things I'd seen and people I'd met in Hollywood; they seemed to be interested at first, but then it all went quiet.

'So, what do you think . . . Prue?'

Silence.

'Gillian?'

Silence.

They were all fast asleep.

And then something totally unexpected happened: Father John asked me if I would do a play with him. It was a surprise, I didn't know the school priest acted, or even wanted to act. He had singled me out for a 'one on one' rehearsal, which felt a bit odd. I don't remember the title of the play, only that it was about the two little Princes in the Tower of London.

Father John was the son of the Headmistress, Helen Mortimer, a much loved and revered woman who, along with Miss Fischer, had started the school in the 1930s. Father John was tall and thin, his face was almost gaunt, thick black hair with strands of silver and large dark eyes. He walked around the school with long strides, his old cassock flapping in the wind. For some of the girls Father John was rather a romantic figure; rumour had it that he only had one lung which made him seem rather tragic and even more a sort of 'Mr Rochester'. Some girls thought they were in love with him. I wasn't one of them. He gave wonderful, rousing sermons, but he always made me feel vaguely uncomfortable. At meals, sitting at the top table with the other staff, he'd pick one girl out and stare at her with a funny little smile on his face, until, blushing and giggling, she'd choke on her food or drop her fork. It amused him. When he was taking 'Scripture' sometimes he'd lean over to look at a girl's work and snap her bra strap. Yes, if I'm honest I really did think he was awful. So when one night Father

John asked me to come to the Big Hall after prep to rehearse, I really didn't want to go.

It was a cold evening so I wore my coat and gloves. When I entered the hall, Father John was already there, sitting on a chair in the middle of the open space beneath a bright light. He had taken off his dog collar and cassock and was wearing black trousers and a white shirt, open at the neck. I could see his chest. It was cold in the hall so I kept my coat buttoned up and my gloves on. We began to rehearse. In the scene I have to beg for mercy for the little Princes; Father John was playing the Cardinal. I gave it my best effort, which he observed intently, and then he said, 'When you plead for the Princes' lives you should fall onto your knees in front of me.'

This I did.

'And now bury your face in my belly,' he added.

I stared up at him. For a moment, I thought about doing it, but I couldn't. I just couldn't. It was too intimate. It was already excruciatingly awkward to see Father John without his cassock – he was a priest, I didn't want to see his chest, I didn't want to think of him as an ordinary man, *and* he was playing a Cardinal! I didn't really know what he was going to do . . . so I just stood up.

'I'm sorry . . . I'm very sorry, but – I can't do that,' I stammered.

There was a silence. It seemed to go on for ever. Finally, Father John said, 'Well, you had better go then.' Somehow I managed to find my way out of the hall and fled back to my dormitory and told Jane what an agonisingly embarrassing experience it had been.

Next Sunday in chapel Father John solemnly announced that 'Hayley Mills has let it be known that she doesn't want to do the role in the play so Sally Mates will be taking her part.'

No one ever mentioned it again.

Term dragged on. I started to get really homesick. Things had changed, I didn't seem to fit in, not in the same way. Jane was now good friends with Liz and Sally Anne. We were still friends, but I started to feel like the outsider. I'd fallen behind in the lessons, my confidence plummeted, and to add insult to injury I had to do extra classes in the evening with another girl who was a bit slow. I didn't feel I should be there.

With all this going on, *Pollyanna* was released in the spring of 1960. Being locked up at school I had no idea how the movie was doing or what sort of response it had received. I wasn't connected with what was happening outside the school gates, let alone Hollywood; but soon enough Hollywood found me. One day a journalist and photographer from *Life* magazine turned up to do a 'shoot' and follow me around school, 'A day in the life of . . .' type of thing. They roped in Jane and some of the other girls and photographed us all sitting around, rather self-consciously, with our greasy hair and grubby Aertex blouses; we looked like we could all do with a good wash. I leapt about as balletically as possible on the grass tennis courts in my black tights and leotard. For the final shot they wanted to photograph me in a dress they'd brought down with them, a sort of white sailor suit vaguely reminiscent of Pollyanna's broderie anglaise dress, mercifully minus the blue bows. I stood in front of some school sheds and posed for the camera.

The team had brought down the US poster for *Pollyanna*. It was a huge illustration of me, just enormous, and it gave me quite a shock. It all seemed so remote; the whole thing was weird and disconcerting. There was one particular look the magazine wanted me to give: eyes wide open and a little pursed-up mouth. I knew straightaway what they meant; it was the same rather 'twee' look from the storyboard in Walt's office. So, in the end Walt did get his way; I did the look and that was the shot *Life* used for the cover!

Pollyanna had a huge theatrical release. The Disney advertising juggernaut made sure the film was everywhere and it played on screens all across America. The film did well at the box office, and it had some great reviews; *Time* and *Newsweek* praised it and said it was Walt's best live-action film ever. But it wasn't instantly the giant hit they had hoped for and it gradually became clear *Pollyanna* was fighting against her saccharine reputation. Even Walt himself acknowledged this. 'The picture would have done better with a different title,' Walt later said. 'Girls and women went, but men tended to stay away because it sounded too sweet and sticky.' Despite this, the film had a hugely positive impact across America. In those days, films played in theatres for much longer; the initial release was just the beginning and a good film could end up playing for months. 'Girls & Women' did indeed go to see the movie in their droves, and they seemed to identify with the film's heroine. Here was a female character who was not only cute and sweet, but also wise, courageous and loving. Positive word of mouth grew steadily, the film itself was acknowledged to be beautifully made, elegantly photographed, authentically and sumptuously designed, the cast of the highest calibre. David's script handled the subject with intelligence and humour, and really did manage to steer clear of mawkishness and sentimentality.

And the proof is in the pudding. Sixty years on, *Pollyanna* has endured to become a Disney classic.

Things started to change for me in America after *Pollyanna*. Fan mail began pouring into the studio in large numbers – some even made it home. Many were addressed in very strange ways, but the great British postal service somehow managed to work out where I was, based on very little information: 'Hayley Mills. Somewhere on a farm. England'.

I replied to every letter that I received, my mother saw to that. Sometimes they were in their hundreds, and an interesting variety of gifts arrived, among which I remember a monkey-skin rug from Africa, a movie camera, and once a diamond ring with an offer of marriage! I was delighted with the ring and wanted to keep it, but my mother explained that I couldn't unless I was prepared to marry the sender, so the offer was politely declined and the ring returned, as were most of the other things. The letters were so sweet but apart from the fan mail, the impact of *Pollyanna* upon my life back home in England felt minimal. Disney movies were successful in the UK but they weren't released with quite as much fanfare as they were in America; and even if there was a buzz, I had no inkling of it, incarcerated as I was in my boarding school. We never left the school grounds except when parents came down occasionally at weekends to take us to Betty Brown's Tea Rooms in Camberley, to have baked beans on toast, a big treat. Letters to anyone apart from family members had to be left open (so they could be read by a member of staff to make sure that we weren't writing to boys). My holidays were spent on the farm in the middle of Sussex. Hollywood was light years away.

One night, during the school holidays, we were back at the farm; I was fast asleep. The telephone had been ringing and ringing and I stumbled out of bed to answer it. Aunty Wyn's voice sounded thick and strained. 'Hayley darling, Granny has died, go and wake Mummy up. I'll hold on.'

Granny was a nurse with the St John Ambulance Brigade; she had gone with them to meet President Charles de Gaulle at some railway station, and then followed him to a garden party at Buckingham Palace. It had been a long day; she was coming out of the gate at Hyde Park Corner, and collapsed; she'd been in a coma at St George's Hospital for two weeks. I climbed into bed with Mummy and tried to give her some comfort.

'My God!' she said and clutched my hand. 'It's April again!'

My mother associated the month of April with death. Many of her family had died in that month: her younger brother Johnman had died of meningitis at Dartmouth naval college when he was only fourteen; her beloved father Francis died in April; and now Granny too. It occurred to me that this deathly month was also when I was born. This led to a gnawing fear that I too might be cursed. Somehow I felt that I had to try to make up for it. I knew it was impossible, but 'the cruellest month', as T.S. Eliot called it, was both my birthday month and the one that reminded Mummy of the ones she'd loved so much and lost. I lay there wondering if April was like a sort of magnet for the dying, as if they sensed 'It's April, this is when we die.'

And I thought about Granny. I didn't really know her that well. We didn't see her that much. My mother loved her, of course, but they weren't very close. She would say things like, 'Oh, God! Granny's coming . . .' with such a dire tone in her voice, especially as she said the word 'Granny', that it made us all rather dread her arrival. I remembered Juliet aged eight, standing stark naked with her hands on her hips on the top of the stairs, her imperious little voice exclaiming: 'We don't want Granny in the bathroom!' – and Granny pausing, one foot on the bottom stair . . . Poor Granny, my heart ached for her, she never stood much of a chance. She was the only grandparent we had left and we hardly saw her.

I didn't really understand my mother's relationship with her. It was strained and a bit distant and, as a result, I didn't have a close relationship with her either. Granny was an Edwardian. She was conventional and religious and had lived most of her life in China, where her parents were Anglican missionaries. Her grandparents had also been missionaries in China, in Fuchow, and what is more, they were all American. In fact, I was astonished to discover that all of my maternal grandmother's family line were from the East Coast of America – from Connecticut, Maryland and Vermont. These ancestors went back eight generations, with all sorts of colourful characters; most notably the wonderfully named Recompense Sherrill, who was reputed to have been a giant of a man with a great shock of dark red hair, who swam to the shores of the New World in the seventeenth century when the ship he was travelling on was wrecked in a storm! Or the Rev. Joseph Green who, at the tender age of twenty-three, was sent to the village of Salem to try and calm the parish after the infamous hysteria of the Salem witch hunts. His sister, Mary Green, married Rev. Nathaniel Huntting, a 1695 graduate of Harvard who became the Minister of East Hampton, Long Island. I was a direct descendant of Nathaniel Huntting and his wife Mary Green. These stories were a revelation to me when I learnt about the family tree many, many years later. Perhaps, I thought to myself, it's not so surprising after all that a little English girl would end up being wrapped in the Stars and Stripes singing 'America the Beautiful' in *Pollyanna*.

Even Granny herself was born a Connecticut Yankee, but, to my recollection, she never spoke about it. Our main impression of her was of someone very much influenced by her years in China. Eventually, after Francis died, to everyone's complete surprise and bafflement she became a British Israelite. This group, who flourished during the turn of the century, believed that the British were descended from the twelve lost tribes of Israel and were therefore inheritors of the promises and blessing made by God in the Old Testament. My mother, I suspect, would have found all this somewhat dubious and this would have definitely been an obstacle between the two of them. To make matters worse, Granny hadn't approved of any of the men that her daughters chose to marry, including my father; none of them was good enough for her 'swans'. She was 'difficult' and very possessive about her family, something that Mummy inherited and which all three of us would eventually have to deal with.

But I remembered a sweet old lady who would occasionally come to stay with us. She was small and quiet, with a cloud of soft greying hair that seemed to float around her head. She wore ropes of pale blue jade around her neck and gold lorgnettes on a chain; if you blew on them they would 'magically' fly open to our squeals of delight.

When I was quite small I was sometimes sent to stay with Granny in her little flat in Jubilee Place, just off the King's Road in Chelsea. It was dark and terribly overcrowded with the remnants of her life in China. The living room was dominated by a huge green brocade sofa with great silken tassels that held up the arms; there were heavy ceramic Chinese lion gods with fierce grinning mouths, supposed to frighten away the evil spirits; and behind a tall screen, covered with Chinese figures made of coloured pieces of jade, was her single bed. After supper, I would sit on her lap in front of a gas fire that hissed through broken teeth while she read stories from the Bible and told me that the world was soon coming to an end, and then Jesus would return.

Later, as I lay in her little bed behind the Chinese screen and listened to the sounds of Granny washing up in the tiny kitchen and to the gas hissing and popping, I was sure the world was soon coming to an end, and certain that the flat was going to catch fire.

There was so much I'd love to have asked her – and now it was too late. For the first time I realised how life and people can just slip away while you're not looking, while you're asleep. And suddenly someone you have known all your life has gone for ever.

A few weeks later, there was another nocturnal disturbance, which similarly shook my comfortable sense of the natural order of things. I was woken suddenly in the middle of the night by the most horrific blood-curdling shrieks and screams coming through my open window. The curtains and their incongruous pink roses were blowing about in the wind. It was pitch black outside, I couldn't see a thing, but I could hear these hideous noises going on, getting louder and more and more ghastly. I screamed. Soxie came running in in her nightie, her hair all over the place and no teeth.

'What's happening?' I sobbed. I was traumatised.

'It's all right, my darlin'.' She went over to close the window and shut out the sound of all that horror. 'It's them pigs,' she said sitting down rather heavily on my bed. 'The sow has given birth earlier than what they expected, and the boar is attacking the babies.'

'What? Why? Why would he do that?'

Soxie patted my knee under the eiderdown. 'They should've separated the boar from the sow before she gave birth; it's much harder to do it now.'

I didn't understand. Something was terribly wrong – why would a father want to kill his own babies? It was incomprehensible to me. I lived on a farm, I knew about death. On the other side of the road we had a herd of Aberdeen Angus beef cattle. I knew that the male calves were taken away from their mothers soon after they were born, and that the cows would bellow pitifully for their lost babies. It was a terrible sound, it made me so sad. I didn't want to think about it, and never went over there. But then I ate beef. Which didn't make sense, really. I just thought, 'This is what we've always done. This is how life is.' I simply didn't question it. But the boar and the piglets shook me. The violence; this was outside of anything I'd known, or understood. The next morning I went down to the pigsty. Most of her babies had died but there was one tiny little shivering piglet lying in the straw; the whole side of his skin had been torn off and hung down like a flap. Brian put a sack around him. 'What's going to happen to that little piglet?' I asked.

'Don't think he's going to make it,' he said. 'He's too badly injured.'

I picked the piglet up and walked slowly back to the house. I found some bandages and gently wrapped them round his little quivering body, found a cardboard box and a couple of my old sweaters and put him near the radiator in my bedroom. He died in the night. I've never forgotten him. Years later I made the decision to become a vegetarian, for so many reasons. But it all started with that little piglet.

★

'I've got to have a steak!' Mummy said and picked up the hotel phone.

'Room Service? I'd like a steak please. One, medium rare; and a baked potato with sour cream, thank you.'

She put down the phone and lit a cigarette, inhaling fiercely. The ice cubes rattled in her glass.

We were back at the Beverly Hills Hotel, exhausted and jet-lagged. Mummy was self-medicating.

'What about me?' I asked. 'Why did you only order one?'

'One's plenty. Enormous great lumps of dead cow hanging over the side of the plate, they're far too big for one person. We'll share it. When the waiter comes, you hide in the cupboard so he doesn't know there are two of us!' The years of rationing had left their mark, we didn't like to waste food – but at the same time, there was a bit of bourgeoise, false *pudeur* and she didn't want the waiter to think she was being stingy. So when he knocked at the door, I scrambled for the cupboard and stamped all over her shoes.

It was strange being back in Hollywood. I missed having Jonathan around. He'd been packed off to a boarding school near the farm. He desperately wanted to stay at home, but there was no other option – Mummy and Daddy were both going to be away and they couldn't leave him at home with Soxie because she was coming to California with us! He was miserably homesick, made even worse knowing I was splashing around in those sparkling blue swimming pools every day. We were going to be away for months, so he wasn't going to get any visits from the family at the weekends or half-term. He felt terribly abandoned and resentful and hated the whole thing – and I don't blame him.

Daddy was planning on joining us later. Mummy really didn't like being there without him. The gilt was off the gingerbread for Horrorwood. She hated hamburgers, and Coca-Cola was her least favourite drink.

'I like Americans,' she said, 'but I hate the bloody freeways, four lanes of cars that seem to be cuff-linked together and one simply *cannot* get off at the exit; then you're swept on for miles to God knows where!'

This had actually happened to us a few days earlier, while we were trying to get to the studios for a fitting. You wouldn't have thought it but my mother had driven emergency ambulances in London during the Blitz. They must have been absolutely desperate for drivers.

'And as for all those white Christmas cake houses, it looks more like Forest Lawn Cemetery. The only difference is that people can walk out of them!'

The drink was making her dour, but I was quite happy to be in California again. Hollywood was still exciting to me and I was looking forward to making my next movie, which at that point was still called 'Lottie & Lisa' – the original title of a German novel that Lilly Disney had come across and taken to Walt as a possible vehicle for me. The story was about identical twins, separated while they were still babies after their parents' divorce. One twin goes to Boston to be brought up by her mother; the other twin goes with her father to Southern California. Growing up, these two girls have no idea that somewhere in the world they have a sister, let alone a twin sister! Neither of them has ever been told.

So they meet for the first time when, by happenstance, they are sent to the same Summer Camp for the holidays. The girls may have the same faces but they are very different. Sharon, from Boston, is a tidy girl, well-mannered and respectful of those in authority; her life is ordered and well-considered, she plays the piano, wears expensive clothes, knows about 'good taste'. She lives in an elegant town house with her mother and her grandparents and she speaks with a refined Boston accent. Susan isn't any of those things. She has been raised on a ranch with her laid-back dad. She's outspoken, somewhat chaotic and free-spirited, having grown up with little supervision and been treated more like a boy than a girl. She adores her father, and Verbena, their housekeeper, the only mother she has ever known. She leaps on to her horse and goes wherever she wants, for as long as she wants. She is learning to play the guitar, although not very well, she chews gum and bites her nails, and has a Californian accent.

Initially the two girls hate each other and become sworn enemies, doing everything they can to make life as miserable as possible for the other one, thereby causing mayhem. As a result, they're put into solitary confinement together for a week, as a punishment. During that time they discover that their similar faces aren't some weird aberration of nature but that they are in fact twins; and for the first time, they see pictures of the mother and the father they have never met. After this life-changing revelation, the two reunited sisters hatch a bold plan – they will switch places. Each will impersonate the other, and at the end of the holidays return to the other sibling's home to meet the parents they didn't know they had.

I loved the story and David Swift had written an especially charming and witty script. I knew it would be a challenge playing two characters, and I had been warned the shoot would involve some new technical tricks to achieve the effect of identical twins, but I was excited rather than daunted. Perhaps it would have been better if I *had* been more wary – I might have prepared better, especially in regards to the two accents. But I did the work as best I could. I didn't know what else to do.

In June 1960, principal photography began on 'Lottie & Lisa', provisionally retitled *We Belong Together*. Walt had made the smart decision to hire the same team that made *Pollyanna* a success: David Swift was back at the helm. Not only was he a brilliant director but he gave the whole experience a continuity. We just seemed to pick up where we had left off. Going back to work felt very familiar – it really was like a *family*. Disney's magic formula was to surround me with established names, and for the next film they assembled an incredible cast – all I had to do was learn my lines and not bump into the furniture. Actors like Charles Ruggles, who played my grandfather, a hugely experienced actor, and a sweet, gentle, truthful presence; Joanna Barnes, who was absolutely perfect as the scheming, bitchy girlfriend, glamorous and very funny; and the inimitable Leo G. Carroll, a wonderfully charismatic character actor and Hitchcock regular. There was also Cathleen Nesbitt, who played my sophisticated Bostonian grandmother, an actress of enormous charm and class. Originally a star of the London stage in the 1920s, '30s and '40s, she had been the love of Rupert Brooke's life. The great poet had written her many beautiful and now famous love sonnets and they were engaged to be married before he died tragically in the First World War.

One of the actors I especially adored was Una Merkel, who played the Californian housekeeper 'Verbena'. Una was a Hollywood stalwart and a lovely person, so self-deprecating, with her gentle Southern wit. She took me under her wing and would often appear out of nowhere, put her arm around me and make me laugh, as if she always seemed to know when I needed cheering up. Una was someone who had known real tragedy in her life; I think that's why she was so compassionate. Brian Keith was cast as the girls' father, a role he played with warmth and sweetness, and just the right sense of bewilderment at having to deal with so many scheming women. He also really brought across the father's honesty and integrity; a man you could rely on. Aside from being hugely experienced, this cast were all very skilled at *comedy*. The film's tone of playful humour was really carried by them; they made it seem so easy.

And then, of course, there was Maureen O'Hara, who was never lovelier than when she played the mother of Sharon and Susan. By 1960 she was already a Hollywood legend but still so beautiful and radiant, proving that middle-aged maturity is so often the prime of a woman's life. The romantic scenes between her and Brian Keith were so tender and funny. Charles Laughton had originally discovered Maureen in Ireland, when she was only nineteen, and brought her to Hollywood to play Esmeralda in *The Hunchback of Notre Dame*. I knew her from all those classics she'd made for John Ford (who they say became quite obsessed with her) in which she starred with John Wayne: films like *Rio Grande*, and perhaps most famously *The Quiet Man*. They made a fabulously attractive on-screen couple, but were never lovers – according to her.

From the moment I met this formidable woman I admired her enormously; she was so down-to-earth, and although I didn't realise it then, she had a big influence upon me. Apart from her astonishing beauty, and colouring – she was tall and magnificent, and when she came on to the set she really did light it up – most of all I was struck by her joyous spirit. I admired the way she took her great beauty so lightly. She didn't spend hours in the make-up chair looking into the mirror. She got it right and then got on with things. She was very Irish and loved to talk. She said she thought having facials and facelifts was a load of old nonsense! Not something you hear very often in Hollywood. She seemed to take everything lightly, but she was very serious about the things that really mattered, like her family and her work.

I remember, early on in the shoot, we had had a big scene together. The two of us had been walking on a treadmill all morning, in front of a back-screen projection of a leafy Boston park, and now we were sitting on a rug pretending to have a picnic.

'Where's your mother today, Hayley?' she suddenly said.

'She's at home,' I told her. 'My guardian's on set today.'

'D'you know, Hayley, that when I first came to Hollywood I was only nineteen and my mother came with me too. She stayed with me here for the whole time until I got married. You're lucky to have a strong mother behind you, she'll keep your feet on the ground – stop you getting into any trouble!' She said it with a laugh but I knew exactly what she meant. 'I was very lucky to work with men like Charles Laughton and John Ford,' she said, 'but I was never overawed. I saw them for what they were, people just like me. I could always spot bullshit. I can see it coming a mile away, and I've never been afraid to say what I thought, which has got me into some hot water in the past, I can tell you!' She smiled playfully. I got the impression she relished straight talking. 'You know, a lot of powerful men in Hollywood wanted me to throw myself on to the casting couch – but I never would. Things got so bad at one point, I dreaded going to work in the mornings. I was so unhappy, I seriously considered leaving here for good and going back to Ireland . . .' I gazed at her fascinated; I could appreciate she was telling me all this for a reason. 'I know it cost me roles and affected my career but I always had too much self-respect to turn myself into a whore for anything. I knew that I was a bloody good actress; I was a tough Irish woman and I always believed I'd survive.' She stared at me for a moment – then suddenly tugged my awful wig down over my eyes. I looked ridiculous. She burst into her wonderful laugh and gave me a hug. When Maureen O'Hara laughed, you just had to laugh too. She was brave and beautiful and tremendously inspiring for a fourteen-year-old girl.

I took my script and wandered down to the hotel pool to see if I could find a quiet spot. I had a big scene coming up the next day with lots of lines to learn. As I was standing irresolutely looking around at the blue and white striped parasols fluttering in the breeze, I became aware that someone had approached me – a young man, standing there with some white towels. 'Hi,' he said, 'do you want a chair or a chaise longue?' I squinted into the bright sunlight and saw a pair of smiling blue eyes. 'Oh! Yes. Yes, a chaise longue please, thank you.' He led me to one of the chaises longues and carefully spread out a couple of white towels. He was tall and his legs were very brown; his hair was dark and he had a crew cut. Why had I never appreciated that look before? Suddenly I thought it was fascinating. He told me his name was Nick, he was working at the hotel to pay for his tennis lessons – he wanted to turn pro and play at Wimbledon. He was friendly and talked to me as an equal, even though I was only fourteen; he didn't seem to care. Nick said he was eighteen. The Beverly Hills Hotel pool took on a sort of magic I hadn't noticed before.

Mummy didn't enjoy living in a hotel, so she found a house for us on Hanover Drive in Beverly Hills. It sat on a little rise above a quiet road, a rockery of sorts led up to a blue front door, to the left was an overgrown tennis court with a dilapidated-looking net, surrounded by towering old palm trees covered with rustling, dead leaves, which we later discovered was home to a large colony of rats. It was a white, airy house, with wide living rooms, a bar, a big kitchen – and a pool with a mermaid painted on the bottom. When anyone dived in the mermaid stirred sinuously under the water.

My mother and I were in a state of great excitement, rushing about getting the house looking wonderful for Daddy who was arriving from London with Soxie. Mummy had filled the place with flowers, bowls of dark blue agapanthus and tuberoses, candles were burning, all the windows were flung open to let in the golden evening light. When Daddy arrived he was thrilled. 'Oh! Baba, isn't this marvellous! What a divine place!' He loved California, he adored the sun and the life, and the people, everything really. But Soxie had never left England before; the furthest from the farm I ever saw her go was East Grinstead. I imagine that getting on an aeroplane for the first time and flying to Hollywood, to find herself in Shangri-La, must have been like going to the moon. Her beaming face was a picture. 'Oh, yes madam, it's all very nice,' she said as she sipped her welcome glass of champagne. Even so, I don't think she ever really understood quite where she was; it must have been so alien. She was constantly bemused, especially by American money, which looked like Monopoly money. She never believed it was real. She paid a delivery boy one day and told us: 'I give the boy them bits of paper.'

Sometimes Nick from the hotel would come over to the house. I'd sit on the diving board and watch him while he cleaned the pool. Then one day he asked me if I'd like to go out with him. This was the first time any boy had asked me out on a date and I was thrilled – but my mother definitely wasn't. In her opinion, I was far too young to be going out with a boy of eighteen. This was a devastating blow and I must have been quite miserable because my mother finally agreed to let me go – but only on the condition that Soxie came along to be my chaperone. As you can imagine, I wasn't entirely happy about that either. Nick took me to Pacific Palisades amusement park in Santa Monica. We wandered around for a bit, then he took me on a terrifying rollercoaster. I was shrieking with delight and fake fear, hoping that he would put his arm round me, but every time the car came into view – there Soxie was at the bottom, smiling away and waving at us. That was my first date. A strange little threesome.

Filming lasted for over three months. We had two weeks on location in Carmel, Northern California, on the famous Pebble Beach golf course, which is like heaven-on-earth for golfers. Daddy, a certified golf-nut, had somehow managed to wangle himself a walk-on part so he could play at Pebble Beach all day for free! You can see him behind us, during the scene between me and Brian Keith in which Sharon tells her father that she's now at that age when she needs a mother to talk to. The father misreads the conversation and awkwardly attempts to relay to her the 'facts of life'. It's a very funny scene and it was fun to play but I was slightly distracted by my real father doing his 'golfing acting' in the background.

To achieve the illusion of the identical twins, Disney's photographic special effects team had done a lot of research and development into split-screen photography, which was still a comparatively new technique. This magic trick, overseen by Ub Iwerks and his brilliant team led by Bob Broughton, was groundbreaking and unlike anything audiences had seen at the time. To achieve it, the camera was covered by a large black box, which enabled it to expose only one side of the film stock at a time. They would always frame the shot with a dividing line in sight – like a bedpost, or door frame – so they could effectively line up each side of the shot; a line you crossed at your peril. The Special Effects Department had developed a technique for processing the film, applying methods normally only used in animation. When Walt saw how seamless the results were, he ordered David to include more of these shots. Every time we would have to shoot twice: first with me playing one part, then I'd change clothes and we'd shoot the other side of the scene with me playing the other character. It all worked surprisingly well, although sometimes, when we were running out of time and in a hurry to get the scene done, which was most days, the wardrobe and hair changes would get rushed, my wig wouldn't get put on firmly enough, and it would slip off the back of my head making my forehead look enormous. There are a few scenes where I look like Boris Karloff's monster.

In addition to the split-screen effect, Disney found me a photographic double to play all my scenes with. Her name was Susan Henning and she was very pretty, slim and blonde with pale blue eyes. I liked her instantly, she was an actress herself, and it was fun to have someone to hang out with and rehearse with. But it must have been galling for her at times, never being able to show her face to the camera. She was a really good sport and never complained about it. If you watch the film, you can easily tell who's who from the back because Susan had much longer legs and a longer neck than me. She also had a very dainty little nose, unlike mine, so the poor girl had to have a rubber replica of my nose stuck on her face all day.

When Susan and I were both dressed identically, same wigs, the lot, we used to go out of the Studios during our lunch break to 'Bob's Big Boy Hamburger Joint' in Burbank, and pretend to be real twins. I'd always dreamt of having a twin. It was tremendous fun, but I suspect not quite so much fun for Susan, trying to eat a hamburger while breathing furiously through that awful rubber nose at the same time.

Susie later became a dancer and dated Elvis Presley. I was terribly jealous – he was my heart-throb. Like most girls in 1960, I was in love with Elvis. I actually saw him once in a car on Sunset Boulevard. We'd pulled up to the lights, next to a big white shark-finned Cadillac. I happened to notice a man in the passenger seat, he turned to flick his cigarette ash out of the window and for a second I saw – *Elvis*! Dressed in black and at his most beautiful. By the time I'd managed to get the bloody window open his car had pulled away.

Truth be told, it wasn't just Elvis I was in love with. I was starting to be in love with lots of people. No longer did I think falling in love was stupid, it was the most wonderful thing. In fact, life was pretty boring without it. However, I did find it quite unsettling the way 'love' switched itself on and off without warning. One day I'd think a boy was wonderful, the next he'd irritate the hell out of me. I started to become very self-conscious about my appearance, something that I'd never really bothered about. I didn't like my nose and thought my face was podgy, and I got the occasional spot. I'd hang a towel over the mirror in my bathroom every morning so I didn't have to look at it, and I started to worry about the size of my bosom.

One Sunday lunch party, I was horribly embarrassed in Stewart Granger's swimming pool. 'Jimmy' Granger was an old friend of my parents. He had been married to my darling godmother Elspeth March, but they had divorced and by this point he was with the actress Jean Simmons. I liked Jimmy but he was a bit conceited and I was always unsure what he might say next. There were quite a few rather glamorous-looking people standing around the pool, drinking something absolutely disgusting called 'Bull Shots', made of ice-cold beef consommé and vodka. I had stuffed my bikini top with tissues to give a better impression, and Jimmy started teasing me, accusing me of peeing in his pool. He said he'd put some chemical in the water that showed up if anyone had peed. Well, I hadn't and I insisted on my innocence with a sporting sort of laugh, when suddenly he pointed at me and yelled at the top of his voice: 'Oh no! What's all that in the water around Hayley?!' then roared with laughter. All the glamorous people turned and stared, and I realised, to my horror, that the tissues had come out of my bikini top and were floating around me like ectoplasm. I grabbed desperately at the disintegrating shreds, mortified.

But the swimming pool humiliation was a mere prelude to my next embarrassment.

The Summer Camp scenes, where the twins meet, was filmed up in the mountains at Big Bear, but the girls' cabin interior was all done on a sound stage in Burbank – and it was here that I got my first period.

We were shooting the scene where the two girls are in the 'Isolation' cabin, an important scene with lots of switching roles and changing wigs. The set was small and hot and very brightly lit, the camera crew, most of whom were men, were right on top of us. I was sure everyone was staring at me, that they knew there was something different, and they could see that there was something odd about my shorts. I waited for a murmur and then the laughter; I began to feel acutely self-conscious, something I'd never felt before in front of the camera. It was agony.

Thankfully, my mother had given me the appropriate equip-ment to deal with the situation. It was very uncomfortable and felt like a plank of wood between my legs. I was appalled.

'I can't do this,' I told her anxiously, 'I'm wearing tiny green shorts, it will show!'

'You'll be fine,' she insisted. 'Just remember to keep your legs together!'

How on earth was I going to do that? The scene involved a lot of jumping on and off the camp beds.

I tried not to be self-conscious but I knew that the camera heightens everything – and I mean *everything* – every pimple is ten times the size on the big screen.

Somehow I did manage to keep my legs together, and found a way to more or less levitate off the bed. The day seemed to last for ever, and when the studio bell finally rang I couldn't wait to escape. It was the first genuinely stressful experience I'd had in front of the camera. Self-consciousness is the kiss of death for an actor; just the memory of it makes me shudder.

We worked all through that summer. I was woken every morning at 6.30 a.m. by the sound of bluejays shrieking in the eucalyptus trees outside my window; then the drive to Burbank and the inevitable wait outside the studio gates until exactly 8 a.m. when my day officially began, everything already shimmering in the heat releasing that particular smell of the studios. It was hard to define, and uniquely American: hot metal, leather and plastic from the cars, warm dry earth, pine and eucalyptus trees, cigarette smoke and always somewhere the faint fragrance of *coffee*. It certainly wasn't the fragrance of dear old Dettol, and mugs of steaming tea and Wills Woodbine cigarettes, like the studios in England. The days were long and because I was in almost every scene, often playing two parts, there wasn't much sitting around. I'd go home at 6 p.m., a quick swim in the pool with the mermaid, supper, study the next day's scenes, then early to bed.

There were other girls in the film, playing the rival gangs at the Summer Camp. It was fun having girlfriends of a similar age to giggle with, but they all seemed so much more grown up than I was, and much more streetwise where boys were concerned. With their colourful clothes, incredibly shiny hair, and even with braces on their teeth, to me they seemed like little women; I didn't quite fit in. So it was much to my delight that Bunch arrived from New York. *Five Finger Exercise* had finally closed after an incredibly successful two-year run, playing both the West End and Broadway. It had been her rite of passage. She had grown from a girl of seventeen into a young woman, developed as an actress in the greatest school of all, coped with loneliness in a strange city and forged wonderful friendships working with John Gielgud, Peter Shaffer and Brian Bedford, who became a beloved and lifelong friend. And so, trailing clouds of glory, she arrived at the house to announce to my parents that she had met a wonderful man, while ice-skating in Central Park, where he worked as a rink attendant during the winter. In the summer he worked as a lifeguard on that enormous beach at Atlantic City. They were in love and engaged to be married.

The shit hit the fan.

I didn't know what was going on. There were heated conversations behind closed doors. For days the house was filled with raised voices, the sound of feet running up the stairs and doors slamming; Bunch sobbing in her room. My parents told her she was irresponsible and impulsive. They were also concerned that he didn't have any money and wasn't anything to do with the business. He'd be a fish out of water, they said.

After some days, the battle reached a stalemate. There was silence in the trenches.

And then the man all the fuss was about suddenly turned up. His name was Russell, he was of Swedish descent, tall, blond, with the bluest eyes and a gentle, soft-spoken way about him. I could just imagine him plunging into those huge waves at Atlantic City to rescue people, just as he had rescued my beautiful sister from her loneliness in New York. He was sweet, worked very hard and obviously loved her, but he didn't have any money. This didn't seem important to me, they'd find a way, they loved each other, but the rows went on and it was shocking how Granny's latent snobbism came roaring to the surface. It seemed the more my parents argued and hurled all their common sense at Bunch, the more she resisted, and the firmer her resolve.

One night it really got out of hand, the whole house was in an uproar. I could hear shrieks and shouts and crashes coming from my parents' room across the landing, it sounded murderous. I opened my bedroom door and peered out very gingerly, and saw my father with his trousers tucked into his socks brandishing a golf club . . . was he about to attack Russell?

No. A big fat rat from the colony in the palm trees had got

indoors and was trapped in their en-suite bathroom. It was standing on the loo.

Eventually Russell went back to New York to find work, and to prove my parents wrong, but Bunch was heartbroken. It's too awful, I thought, to find the person you love and want to spend your life with – and then not have your parents' blessing. It happens to a lot of families, I know. It would soon happen to me.

Once filming was over, I had to stay in Hollywood for some weeks for post-production: rerecording dialogue and syncing it to the newly edited scenes. Of course, there was no internet then. Nobody could work remotely from London, so I stayed in town and in this instance it was particularly arduous, as I had to do both characters, and I was struggling with my voice. They kept sending me to the doctor to have my throat sprayed with antiseptic or steroids or something, just so that I could speak. But it was a huge relief not to have to get up at the crack of dawn and be in front of a camera every day, and it meant I could have some fun. There were parties and gatherings, which I could finally attend. Once, we were invited to Anatole de Grunwald's house for Sunday lunch. Aside from being a well-known film producer and screenwriter, he was also the father of my friend Liz from school, so I really should have gone along, but Bunch wasn't in the mood for a party, what with Russell having just left. She was still very unhappy so I decided to stay and keep her company. When Mummy and Daddy returned they told us, to my undying chagrin, that Elvis had been there! Not to mention Rock Hudson and Shirley MacLaine. Sixty years on, I still haven't got over it.

I did stay in touch with one kid from the movie. His name was Joe. He was a good young actor and funny. He played the Boy Scout in the scene where we dance together at camp, and the girls cut the back of my dress out – a hot-making experience, which I was well prepared for by wearing eight pairs of knickers. Joe was sweet and a bit shy; he'd call me up sometimes and we'd talk on the phone for an hour. One night he came over to the house for supper. We were having a friendly chat in the living room, when Mummy suddenly appeared. Her eyes were unfocused and she was finding it difficult to stand up. Just as Joe leapt up she passed out, but luckily he caught her. Joe was not exactly a strapping lad, but after a bit of huffing and puffing he finally managed to carry her up the stairs and lay her down on her bed.

Then he said goodnight and left.

I had never seen my mother in such a state before. I didn't understand it, so I didn't know what to say or how to help her. She certainly didn't talk about that sort of thing, at least never seriously, and she would never, at any point in her life, admit to being an alcoholic. That whole generation drank like fish, seemingly all day long, at lunch, at dinner, at tennis . . . When I was young I thought: 'Well, that's just what being "grown up" is: you get drunk.' Daddy absolutely adored a drink but he never turned nasty or lost control, he just got funnier and more affectionate.

But Mummy battled with demons that attacked her self-esteem. On top of this were the frustrations and disappointments she felt with her work, writing play after play for my father, who, after doing the first three successful productions, never managed to get another one produced. The play she most believed in, the last one she wrote for him, was called *Row G on the Aisle*, but Daddy wasn't confident about it and even after countless rewrites, he never felt she had got it right. She wrote all the time, she was prolific and talented, but like all artists, she needed validation, and the tough grind of endlessly waiting for a word from a publisher or manager and the inevitable, dreaded 'rejection slip' wore her down. Daddy was there to bolster her up, put his arms around her and tell her that she was the most wonderful thing in his life, but that put tremendous pressure on him. Because nobody can tell you you're worthy of being loved if you don't believe it yourself. She had very little sense of self-worth. What she *did* possess was a deep and dark sense of foreboding. That was her nervous whistle. She was a true gothic in that regard. All of her stories were about loss. And I believe she was haunted by the memory of her beloved father's own struggles. For all his glorious qualities, ultimately, he had ended his life penniless and rejected; a failure, albeit a glorious one. Now she too dreaded being a failure. Deep down I think she always felt she was one.

One of the great experiences of that summer was when Walt took me to meet the Sherman Brothers. Robert and Richard Sherman had written a number for me in the movie, a duet that Sharon and Susan sing for their parents – so, a duet with myself. The brothers had composed songs for Disney in the past, but at this point in their career they hadn't yet written for a movie. This was to be their first assignment.

Walt introduced me to two warm and immensely charming characters, both soberly dressed in black: Richard was sitting at a shabby old grand piano, he seemed the more extroverted and energetic of the two, while Robert, softly spoken and a little shy, stood quietly by his side. I thought they were both sweet and responded to them immediately. Richard played the piano and they sang together, making gruesome faces, and generally being a bit silly – the song was called 'Let's Get Together'. It was playful and rock and roll and I loved it. When the day came to record I was actually quite apprehensive about how it might turn out. I'd never had a strong voice and I certainly didn't consider myself a singer. Luckily, I wasn't just in 'safe hands', I was about to work with two of the greatest Hollywood songwriters of all time. They both made me laugh, the session was raucous and fun and I was very relieved that it wasn't too challenging. The recording process went smoothly. Although it was a pretty steep learning-curve, being taught how to double track and so on, it all went well and sounded good. Even so, it was still a complete and utter surprise when, after the film's release, the song became a hit. 'Let's Get Together' reached number 8 in the US Hit Parade, and it made

An early family photo, swinging along the front in Brighton.

Above The Hayley Bells in 1923: My grandparents, Agnes and Francis, with the children; Johnman on her knee, Elizabeth on his; Dennis at the front; Winifred (left) with my mother Mary (right) at the back.

Left Bunch (left) and me (right) with Stanley and Elsie, our pet mice; named after our solicitor and his wife, who cast a long dark shadow over the family. Bunch's instinct here was to flatten them both – almost prophetic.

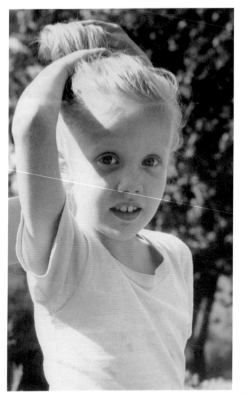

Left At the farm, 1954. Photo by Bryan Forbes. Hair by Nanette Newman.

Above The three of us: Juliet, Jonathan and me in the beautiful garden at The Wick. The house had a powerful hold over my mother.

My parents in 1939, before they were married.

My first day shooting *Tiger Bay*, 1958: J. Lee Thompson (sitting), Daddy (with camera), a cowgirl, an Indian, and Ernie the props man next to me.

Horst on Cardiff Docks, 1958 – I took this picture and secretly treasured it for years.

Premiere of *Tiger Bay* with my parents
and Laurence Olivier. I was completely
overexcited. So was Daddy. We couldn't
quite believe what was happening.

1959: Arriving in America for
Pollyanna. Mummy putting on a
brave face; she loathed Hollywood.

Me, Bunch and Johnny posing with my Berlin Film Festival Silver Bear. Despite winning
accolades and awards, no one in Britain offered me another acting job.

Top The first agonising day filming *Pollyanna* – 'a great big white cabbage!'

Above A tracking shot on *Pollyanna*, with Moochie. When we weren't working he was filling me in on the facts of life.

Right Pollyanna, 1960: Happy in my favourite dress, shooting my first big Hollywood movie.

In Tobago, 1959, trying to look glamorous hanging on to the mast of the *Swiss Family Robinson* shipwreck. The next moment, I fell off.

My favourite picture of Mummy, Walt and Lilly Disney. Lilly appears to be wearing Minnie Mouse's shoes.

With Annabelle, my childhood friend. Riding bareback on the farm.

'You can never have too much tartan.' Happy on a gate at the Farm, 1958, before the bombshell. My parents tried to maintain a sense of normalcy at home, but we were being pulled apart.

The brilliant director David Swift didn't want me for *Pollyanna*. Eventually, we made two classic films together. Here we are on set of *The Parent Trap* with beautiful Maureen O'Hara and her birthday cake!

The Parent Trap with Susan Henning, my photographic double. She had fantastic legs, twice as long as mine!

The same scene – as it magically appeared in the film, thanks to the groundbreaking split screen filming method.

the Top Twenty in the UK – best of all, in Mexico and Hawaii, it went to number 1! Obviously places of exceptionally discerning taste.

The recording went so well, in fact, that once we'd finished filming the movie, I was sent back into the studio to make a whole album. I was slightly bemused by the whole thing as I stood in front of a Neumann microphone, in my little area, cordoned off from the band and orchestra, wearing an enormous pair of head-phones. We recorded a whole LP in one day and I have to say I wasn't terribly impressed with the results. Among the songs was 'Johnny Jingo' – and my least favourite, 'Cobbler Cobbler'. Both became hits.

Extraordinary.

I could tell Richard and Robert were talents, but no one could have foreseen the phenomenon they'd become. In the following ten years, Bob and Dick Sherman went on to write just about every classic Disney song you can think of: all the *Mary Poppins* hits – 'A Spoonful of Sugar', 'Feed the Birds', and 'Chim Chim Cher-ee' – to those showstoppers from *The Jungle Book* like 'The Bare Necessities', and 'I Wan'na Be Like You'. The incredible list just goes on and on, endless, amazing songs that are still sung and adored today. 'The Boys', as Walt called them, turned out to be Disney's very own Rodgers & Hammerstein – and I feel so incredibly proud and fortunate to have worked with them, but more importantly, to have known and loved them both.

As the film approached the end of post-production, Disney needed to agree on the title. I don't think either Walt or David Swift was ever set on *We Belong Together* – it was just a working title, until they came up with something that really fitted. Months later, when we were back in England, Walt wrote to my mother:

We had our first audience reaction this morning on Hayley's lat-est picture – which we have decided to call THE PARENT TRAP.

This seems to be the most provocative title that we have been able to come up with and the boys in the exploitation end feel it will sell tickets. At first, I think it strikes one as an intriguing title and then when you see the picture it "comes to life" so to speak.

The Parent Trap would prove to be an enormous hit for Disney. The lucrative 'family' audience that had somewhat eluded *Pollyanna* now turned up: girls *and* boys, of all ages, flocked to see the movie. And it wasn't just a trick of the marketing men. *The Parent Trap*'s story about divorce, and about two children who take things into their own hands, resonated with audiences. The film came out at a time when divorce was becoming more common, but still not really talked about. At Elmhurst, for instance, there was only one girl among all my friends whose parents were divorced. She told us her father had died; she kept his photograph tucked behind the mirror because she couldn't bear to look at it, it made her too sad. We were all desperately sympathetic and sat on her bed at night to comfort her, and gave her our biscuits. Then, at the end of the summer term, when all the parents came to see the show, a car drew up and someone got out, someone we all recognised – the man in the picture behind the mirror: her father.

I think the film touched a nerve because it focused on the children's experience of divorce. In those days especially, people weren't conscious enough of the damage that divorce can do to the kids. Parents living together in an unhappy, toxic marriage where love and trust have gone is awful, but the destructive effect of divorce upon children, the experience of suddenly losing a parent, or having them replaced by a stranger, can be devastating, and so often it's the child that feels they are somehow to blame.

The Parent Trap was sentimental in many ways, but it was also honest and truthful – and optimistic. This was David Swift's magic touch. He had such heart and intelligence and wit. He walked that tightrope so artfully, never insulting the audience by slipping into mawkishness, always keeping the characters genuine, just as he had on *Pollyanna*. I still receive letters to this day from people telling me how the film helped them through their own difficult and unhappy times. They may not have been able to heal the family rift in their own lives, but nevertheless the film showed children becoming empowered, effecting positive change, instead of being the powerless victims in the mess made by the so-called adults in their world.

When the time came for me to leave Hollywood, I was starting to feel like a yo-yo. Four months is enough time to come to love a place and the people, and to feel at home, but now it was all over. These departures only got harder as I got older.

My parents had arranged for us all to stop off in New York on the way back, to break up the journey. We stayed at the Sherry Netherlands Hotel on Central Park. I was fast becoming enamoured of this spectacular city. For Bunch it was like returning to her second home. She had met Russell there on the skating rink and was so happy to see him again. Not surprisingly, I didn't see much of her after that.

My parents loved the theatre and they took me to see some thrilling Broadway shows; I was there to see the original cast of *The Sound of Music* with Mary Martin playing Maria, and Laurie Peters as Liesl, both of whom won Tony awards for their performances. I remember going to Sardi's afterwards for dinner. Jack Lemmon and Robert Preston were both there. I also saw *The Miracle Worker*, the play about Helen Keller, starring Anne Bancroft and Patty Duke. I thought Patty was marvellous; she was the same age as me, and I was absolutely in awe of her, spellbinding the audience on that huge stage in that enormous theatre on Broadway. We had great seats right in the front. During the scene when Annie Sullivan is teaching Helen Keller to say the word 'water', they fight and water goes all over the stage. Our seats were so close to the stage that the water went all over me. I felt baptised.

My parents also took me to see Laurence Olivier in *Becket*. Unfortunately, none of us liked the play, but afterwards we all got invited to a supper party at the actress Louine McGrath's beautiful apartment overlooking Central Park. The evening has stuck in my memory, not because it was stuffed to the roof full of impressive theatrical personalities like Terence Rattigan, Hume Cronyn and Larry Olivier, but because of her enormous Great Dane, who took up an awful lot of floor space. I remember I was trying to handle some man called Hugh, who had decided to flirt with me and embarrass me as much as he could, when the door to the kitchen was kicked open by the cook, who looked a bit drunk, carrying a large dish.

'Chicken gumbo!' cried our delighted hostess.

At that moment, the door swung back and struck the cook on the bottom – she lurched forward and dropped the entire pot of stew on to the carpet.

There was a confused pause. Then mayhem. The Great Dane leapt forward. Louine leapt at the dog. 'Quick!' she cried, hauling the enormous gasping hound to one side with great effort. 'Take your plates and a spoon . . . and scrape the layer that's not on the carpet, while I hold the dog!' The Great Dane was frantic, straining every sinew, fighting to get at the food. To my lasting astonishment, without batting an eyelid, these distinguished personages all rose from their chairs and with considerable haste began spooning from the pile of steaming gumbo on the carpet.

Apart from Walt, no one had offered me a job after *Tiger Bay*, but things began to change with *Pollyanna*. Thanks to the film's success and the growing buzz around *The Parent Trap*, by the time I returned home there were some amazing offers on the table. Firstly, Lew Wasserman had been approached by the flamboyant and famously unpredictable Otto Preminger who wanted me to play a part in his new film *Exodus*. It was going to be a big movie with a blockbuster budget, all about the founding of the State of

Israel. I was to be cast alongside stars like Paul Newman and Eva Marie Saint, Ralph Richardson, Peter Lawford and Lee J. Cobb, so as you can imagine, I was thrilled to be asked. They offered me the role of Karen, a young girl who falls in love with Sal Mineo (although at that point I hadn't even been kissed).

It was a good part and obviously I was keen to work with Preminger and all these fantastic actors, so I told Laurie Evans and my parents I wanted to do it, but they refused. They thought that I was too young and turned the offer down regardless. But Otto Preminger was not a mogul to take 'No' for an answer, so not only did he offer me more money – he also offered to throw in a Renoir painting! I never did find out which one, but it was academic because they turned him down again, and that was that. Jill Haworth eventually played the part. She was fifteen at the time and very lovely.

I'm a parent now myself, so I can understand it must have been tough for my mother and father to have to make these career decisions on my behalf but, really . . . think about it . . . my very own Renoir!!?

I had actually met Sal Mineo in New York and a year later at a crazy party at his Hollywood home. I really liked him. He was sweet and genuine but also seemed very young and vulnerable. All over the walls of the house were paintings of different parts of his naked body, which I found rather disturbing.

I was also offered a job by William Wyler, who was in pre-production for his next film *The Children's Hour* by Lillian Hellman, starring Shirley MacLaine and Audrey Hepburn, about two women who start a school for girls. Wyler wanted me to play the part of Mary, a disturbed child and a conniving little troublemaker who tells terrible lies about the two women that ultimately destroy them both. It was a good script and Willie Wyler was one of the great American directors. He had an astonishing track record of films which practically defined classic Hollywood; movies like *Ben-Hur*, *Roman Holiday* and *Funny Girl*

– he was a powerhouse who just kept making hits, launching the careers of stars like Audrey Hepburn, winning Oscar after Oscar (he won three Best Pictures and three Best Directors practically all in a row!). So, you can imagine, this was like being summoned by royalty. MacLaine and Hepburn were actresses I loved and admired, so of course I wanted the job. My parents were ambivalent – which I still can't understand to this day – but Walt was adamant. In a letter to my parents he made it quite clear:

> It is not a nice story, and the role Wyler has in mind for Hayley is not nice . . . in fact she is a brat. As I recall she creates quite a scandal. While I do respect Willie Wyler still I think that this particular story is one that should be carefully analysed to determine whether it is the right type to further Hayley's career.

So that was that. Perhaps Walt wasn't wrong, but I was actually rather attracted by the idea of playing a brat. I wanted to do good work. I wanted to act and these were exciting parts to play.

Then came the most interesting offer of all.

A script arrived from Stanley Kubrick – it was called *Lolita*.

Now I could see that it was a good part. This really was an exciting role to play; she was so uninhibited and sassy, and I understood – or rather recognised – certain things about Lolita, without being fully cognisant of the implications. She was teetering on the brink of womanhood, like me; aware for the first time that men and boys are noticing her. She's becoming aware of her looks, of her body, and yet not quite understanding the effect she's having. She's a difficult adolescent, argumentative and bolshie with her poor mother, played by the great Shelley Winters. She wants her own way, she's moody, she wants to be treated like a grownup, but she behaves like a child. I got all that.

The full implications of Humbert's obsession with Lolita were lost on me, but I don't think it would have been to the detriment of my performance. An inexperienced girl of fourteen like Lolita wouldn't have fully understood it either; like me, she grasped it intuitively. There's a big difference between having an 'awareness' of one's sexual power and actually 'understanding' or being in control of the effect it's having. Lolita's feelings towards Humbert are complicated; he's like an indulgent father, he spoils her. Lolita enjoys his attention, she likes showing off to him, while infuriating her mother.

James Mason was going to play Humbert; he was a friend of my parents, so I knew and liked him. Shelley Winters was a formidable talent, and everyone knew and loved Peter Sellers, cast to play Clare Quilty, Humbert's rival for the girl's affections.

For Stanley Kubrick to make such a leap – from *Pollyanna* to *Lolita* – is somewhat mysterious, but on reflection, I suspect it was Lee Thompson's *Tiger Bay* that caught his attention, with its ambiguous emotional relationship between Gillie and Bronik – which Horst Buchholz had played so intelligently, treating Gillie like the child she was, but with the sensitivity of a man relating to a woman.

The crucial difference between Gillie and Lolita, however, is that Gillie loves Bronik and wants to protect him, whereas, for Lolita, the character of Humbert is a curious plaything whom she exploits. The girl doesn't really care about him, or even about her poor mother for that matter.

I had been allowed to read the script for *Lolita*, but my opinion wasn't asked. Unlike *Tiger Bay*, the decision as to whether I could play the role was made by my parents, without any discussion. Naturally, they didn't like the idea of my playing the nymphet and, needless to say, neither did Walt, who made this very clear to them. My reputation was being protected and my image was still in the process of being 'honed' by the studio, to whom I was under contract. To be a 'Disney Star' meant being family friendly, so *Lolita* was politely turned down – and with it went my opportunity to work with one of the masters of twentieth-century cinema.

It was a bitter disappointment.

After the School Nativity, Lolita was the 'role that got away'. That was the one that hurt the most. I've always wondered how things might have gone if I had taken such a radically different path. I know it's fruitless to speculate, but I can't help it. Sue Lyon eventually played Lolita, and very well. She and I were the same age, we both took on roles that were to have a major influence on our careers and on our lives. After the film came out and was such an enormous success, Sue later talked about being forever labelled 'the girl who played Lolita', which she felt affected not only her career but also her private life. She was labelled the nymphet, I was labelled Pollyanna, which could hardly have been more different. Perhaps the Disney legacy was easier to bear, I don't know; but it certainly affected all aspects of my life.

When you're very young, you sense people's expectations and you don't want to disappoint them. You still want to please them, even though a part of you wants independence. Both Sue and I played roles at the very beginning of our careers that left a lasting impression, and both of us experienced how difficult it is to break out of these images once they have coalesced around you, like a fly in amber. It impacted the kind of roles that I was considered for – as well as *not* considered for – and for a long time afterwards, without my realising, it even influenced how I thought about myself.

Once when I was sitting by the pool at the Beverly Wilshire Hotel, a handsome boy came up to me and asked for my autograph; I was delighted. I leapt to my feet and signed my much-practised signature with a flourish and added lots of best wishes and love and handed it back. He stared at the autograph, furrowing his brow. 'Oh . . .' he said, with a look of disappointment. 'I thought you were Sue Lyon.'

I was now fourteen. My time had come. I was about to tip, head first, into the adolescent abyss. So many remarkable things were happening but I didn't feel any ownership, because I wasn't the one making the decisions. I was going through all the inevitable birth pangs of trying to find myself and to mature, while my fame was growing exponentially, like an inflating balloon; it was all beyond my control and beyond the reality that I actually lived in.

At this point something strange happened. As the combined successes of *Pollyanna* and *The Parent Trap* took effect, I began to observe a peculiar phenomenon: there was *two of me.*

There was the me, who I thought I was – looking at the world, trying to make sense of everything. And then there was this identical twin – 'Hayley Mills' – staring back at me: an image projected by my movies, by the Disney publicity juggernaut, by the hundreds of interviews, magazine stories and articles, which combined to create a character that I didn't even recognise. She was having relationships with other film stars and dating teen idols, she was having feuds with other young actresses. All complete fiction and there was nothing I could do about it – suing teen magazines seemed an overreaction, even in those days. And most worryingly of all, the other twin was far prettier, wittier and sexier than I actually was.

Who was this Hayley Mills?

The real one could only be a huge disappointment.

CHAPTER FIVE

Just a Fella

KATHY: 'Jesus? Please talk to me. I believe in you . . . I love you,
I love you.'
THE MAN: 'Go away, kid. Go away.'
KATHY: 'But I've brought you something . . . your snort.'
— *Whistle Down the Wind*, 1961

The farm seemed very empty and very quiet after all the noisy celebrations of Christmas. The cousins had all been staying and Lionel and Eileen Jeffries and their children Elizabeth, Martha and Timothy had come for New Year. We'd jived in the living room, and played 'sardines' all over the house, Daddy had put up the projector and we'd watched *Great Expectations* and gone for long freezing walks, then back home, where Eileen would be waiting for us downstairs in the washroom, pulling off our wet clothes and socks and running us scalding hot baths.

The Christmas tree, denuded of all its finery, was lying outside in a puddle waiting for Brian, the farm manager's son, to pick it up on the tractor. I wandered drearily around, not sure what to do with myself. Bunch had returned to London, where she was playing Wendy in *Peter Pan* with Julia Lockwood.

Johnny had gone back to his boarding school in East Grinstead.

He was a little happier this time. At least we were all in the same country and he could visit at half-term, but I felt sad for him, always being left behind while I went off to make movies. In the meantime, he had discovered a real talent and passion for sport, especially hockey and tennis. When he was thirteen he was good enough to play tennis in the Under-18 group to qualify for Wimbledon; he was also picked as a reserve for England's Under-18 hockey team to play India. All this had raised him considerably in the eyes of the other boys, and distracted him somewhat from his homesickness, which he'd never really got over.

I hadn't gone back to school because it clashed with the start of my next movie. It felt very odd hanging around at home, knowing that Jane and the others were all back there together, laughing and talking about their Christmas holidays, about boys, boys, boys and the plans for the coming term.

I was in limbo. I would ride Annabelle for hours through the dripping woods but it was cold and her hooves kept sliding about in the mud, so it wasn't much fun for either of us. I'd go down to the stables with Hamlet, and a book and my radio. Annabelle always enjoyed company, and she was a good listener. She especially liked the music from the long-running series 'The Archers – an everyday story of countryfolk'.

Then a letter arrived. It was from Nick. The American postage stamp and the sight of his handwriting stirred memories of last summer and my other life. He was coming to England to try out for Junior Wimbledon. I was thrilled and then suddenly dreaded it at the same time. Would it be the same? Would he still like me? Would I still like him? And, oh God, what about my spots?! I prayed they would be gone by the time he arrived. I went to bed with white sulphur on them every night – I looked like I had the pox.

One especially wet and drizzly afternoon I went to the local cinema to see *Fanny*, Horst Buchholz's new film with Leslie Caron. I was terribly excited at the prospect of seeing him, but even so, I wasn't ready for the shock of his giant face projected on that screen in front of me, and hearing his voice again. He looked the same, but more beautiful, like a dream, maybe because the film was in Technicolor, all peachy and golden, and very romantically shot. In *Tiger Bay* he'd looked real. In black & white, the light showed the angles of his face, his dark eyes and hair. In *Fanny* he looked so . . . glamorous.

I was transfixed, sitting alone in that little cinema in Edenbridge, longing to be Leslie Caron and playing that part, standing under a single streetlamp with his arms around me. I wept, and couldn't wait to get home and rush up to my room and write him a letter. I had loved him when I was a child of twelve, but now – now I was practically grown up, I was fifteen! I had to tell him. He had awoken my romantic heart and I poured all my passionate teenage love and devotion on to the pages.

Horst was a married man, and I knew it. I never had any intention of sending the letter to him. That wasn't the point. I just had to write it, and while I was writing it he was in my life, and we were connected.

Tear-stained and emotionally spent, I read and re-read the epic love letter, then folded it up and stowed it safely away with my private journal, at the back of a drawer in my bedside table.

Around this time, Mummy had also received a letter – it was from Walt. He was always good at keeping in touch, and they had become friends, which gave her a direct hotline to the boss. He wrote:

> We had our first public reaction to *The Parent Trap*. The audience loved the picture. It had a very broad appeal and is one of the highest rated pictures ever to come out of the studio. Right now, we are working hard on the script of *In Search of the Castaways*, which will feature Hayley, along with a part for Jonathan if you care to have him pursue a theatrical career. We hope John would

guest star as Captain Grant who is the object of their search. This is definitely the epic type of production, with an audience potential equal to, if not in excess of *20,000 Leagues Under the Sea* and *Swiss Family Robinson*. I feel it is the type of story that is in line for Hayley at this stage of her career.

I was really excited. *In Search of the Castaways* was a story by Jules Verne about two children who set off on a voyage around the world to find their father, a sea captain who has mysteriously disappeared. It was to be an action adventure epic with locations in New Zealand and Patagonia. The marvellous Maurice Chevalier had signed up to do it, and George Sanders and Wilfrid Hyde-White were also being approached. It all sounded wonderful, especially the idea of filming in those exotic places. Most exciting was Walt's idea of Jonathan auditioning to play the role of my brother; we were both thrilled. I think Walt knew that my career was putting some strain on the family. Mummy had probably lamented the fact and told Walt about Jonathan being left behind in England during the filming of *The Parent Trap*; so I wouldn't be surprised if Walt had come up with this idea himself as a possible solution. He was a very family-oriented kind of man, and no doubt assumed, with Jonathan's whole family being in showbusiness, that acting would be like falling off a log, so it was worth an audition to see if he was another natural.

I sometimes wonder how much pressure Jonathan felt, subtly or overtly, to live up to the Mills name. There are challenges in any family, but being the youngest – and the only boy – wasn't a complete cakewalk for Johnny. Bunch and I were as thick as thieves, which often left him out. He was also Mummy's favourite, her darling red-haired boy, which caused a certain amount of resentment from us girls; and although Daddy was a loving father, he was also much harder on Jonathan than he ever was with me and Juliet. I don't know what it is with fathers and their sons – they think they need to toughen them up. Daddy was scared Jonathan would become a mummy's boy. He didn't want him to expect life was going to be easy just because he'd grown up in lovely homes with so much privilege. He wanted him to have the same hunger and ambition *he'd* had as a boy. But that was impossible. Their respective upbringings aside, they were completely different people. Johnny was much more like his grandfather Francis. He looked like him too, with his uncompromising and restless spirit. He was a thoughtful little boy, happy to spend hours on the tractor with Brian, working with the men. For a long time, he thought that he would be a farmer when he grew up.

Bunch and I never argued. Sometimes when I was small, if we were in trouble she'd pinch my bottom to make me own up to something I hadn't done, but that's about it. Johnny and I fought like cats and dogs, yelling at each other and grabbing each other by the hair. Once we rolled all the way down a muddy bank into a stream while a friend from school looked on in horror. There was one occasion, during an argument when we'd been clambering around on the roof of the Dutch barn which was full of hay, and I was so cross I pushed him off the top. I didn't mean to, it just happened – he staggered backwards and disappeared . . . into silence. I looked over with my heart in my mouth and saw him lying there, white-faced and motionless on the concrete. I thought he was dead. I thought: 'I've killed my little brother!'

I rushed down to where he was lying, beside myself, screaming hysterically and begging him to wake up. Thank God, he did. When he came to, he spoke with such extraordinary calm, like an adult. 'It's all right, Bags,' he said, his eyes rolling. 'I'm all right. Don't worry.'

Don't worry?! I'd nearly killed him! I hauled him up and carried him, staggering and sobbing, all the way back to the house to get help. 'Mummy!! Soxie!! Anybody!!' But no one was there. I propped him up on a radiator to keep him warm. I was so afraid of what they would say. More importantly, it had made me realise how much I loved him; that I'd taken him for granted. And that I didn't want him to die.

We never fought like that again.

Walt's suggestion to have Jonathan test for *Castaways* was a godsend in so many ways. It was a chance for us to heal the geographical rift in our family. Jonathan and I would share a more equal footing, we'd be schooled at the Studios together (as we were for *Pollyanna*) and he wouldn't need to be sent back to that miserable boarding school. Maybe he would have a career ahead of him too?

Around this time, my US agent Lew Wasserman stepped back from personally representing clients, to concentrate on his MCA empire, so I was assigned to one of his senior agents, a lovely man called Arthur Park. One day, Arthur arrived from California to pay us a visit. I remember I was sitting at the kitchen table when he handed me a small cardboard box. Inside was my Oscar.

It was an exquisite little thing. I had never seen an Oscar before, big or small. Mine was half as big as a full-size one. I thought it was enchanting. The miniature statuettes were especially created for child actors under the age of eighteen – hugely successful child stars like Shirley Temple, Margaret O'Brien, Mickey Rooney and Judy Garland had been awarded them. And now me.

I must have known I'd won an Oscar, because I wrote in my diary that Daddy had telephoned to tell me shortly after it was announced, but I have no memory of it, which is weird. I can only assume that somehow I repressed it. Daddy had been in the business for years making all these classics, and he'd never won an Oscar. And there was I, on my second movie . . . and especially for *Pollyanna*, as secretly I didn't think I was very good. And now I'd won this great accolade, but it didn't seem real, even though I had this shiny little statuette in my hands.

What I don't understand though, to this day, is why nobody took a photo of me with the statuette. There isn't a single picture of me with it anywhere in existence, which is very odd as Daddy took photos of everything, all the time. If you google my Oscar, the only photo you'll see is Shirley Temple and Annette Funicello holding it together like it's theirs! My Oscar was just sort of absorbed into the general atmosphere and never really mentioned again. I don't even recall where they put it. I know that they were worried that it might all be 'too much'. Meanwhile, I was worried about what Juliet might feel. But, on reflection, she had already decided not to let jealousy get the upper hand, so it's more likely that it was my father who found it too much. This was the family business, after all, and I had just been awarded the most coveted prize – and at the time I was still only fourteen. He was eventually to win an Oscar for his brilliant performance in David Lean's *Ryan's Daughter* of 1970, but when I won mine for only my second film he must have found it a bit galling after his long and distinguished career. I know Daddy was proud of me, but he never spoke of it. In his autobiography he didn't mention it at all. Neither did Mum.

Children are much better at sensing subtle and complex emotions than we give them credit for. My family were dealing with the impact of my extraordinarily rapid rise to fame. It took everyone by surprise. It was like a tsunami that swept up the whole family in different ways, and it changed the dynamics between us. On a practical level, my mother was torn between me and where she really wanted to be, and needed to be, which was with my father. Even before my career happened it had been challenging enough for them, trying to keep all the different plates spinning – but their life together, their work, their great romance, *that* had always been the priority. Now my acting career was becoming alarmingly demanding. Maybe winning an Oscar was just too much of a good thing.

In particular, Mummy was worried about the negative effects that fame and all this attention and adulation might have upon my character. Primarily, she wanted to protect me from a skewed view of my own self-importance, and from turning into a movie brat. It's a double-edged sword – a very difficult path to tread and balance to get right. They would often stress the tremendous importance of humility and gratitude.

'Hail,' my father would say to me, 'you're very lucky. When you were born, God put his hand on your head.' Then he would reach out and touch my forehead with his index finger and say, 'Never forget that. And never forget to be grateful.'

Most children take on their parents' words very deeply, and so I took it to heart. But for all their good intentions, they took it too far. By glossing over things that were real and important, like being awarded an Oscar, they were unwittingly denying milestones in my life. I'm sure if I had been allowed to experience the reality of being given an Oscar, it wouldn't have given me an inflated opinion of myself at all; I think I would have more likely appreciated the responsibility and as a result taken my career more seriously. Instead, the whole thing was played down to such an extent that instead of having a healthy sense of reality, and of myself, the opposite began to take effect. I was left with the overwhelming conviction that somehow my lucky break had been a mistake – and I started to feel guilty about my success.

While the Disney Studios were preparing *Castaways* across the pond, back home things were moving ahead for a project that was especially close to my heart, to all our hearts actually, because it was based on a book called *Whistle Down the Wind*, written by my mother.

It was a beautiful story about three children living on a secluded farm in Sussex, who find a strange, exhausted man asleep in their barn, and are convinced that he's Jesus. That Jesus has come back.

The children decide they have got to hide him, and this time they will protect him from the grownups.

The three children in the book, loosely based on Jonathan, Bunch and me, are all funny and eccentric – actually much funnier and more eccentric than we really were. It's a lovely tale with something to say about children and faith and innocence and the transforming power of love.

Mummy had given her book to the actor Bryan Forbes, who fell in love with it. Bryan then convinced Richard Attenborough that their newly formed production company, Beaver Films, should turn it into a movie. They were both passionate about making their own films, and had collaborated the year before on *The Angry Silence*, the first for their fledgling company. Dickie had co-produced and starred in it, and Bryan wrote the script (for which he won a BAFTA for Best Screenplay).

Dickie and Bryan were great friends with my parents. My father first met Dickie when he was starring in Noël Coward's *In Which We Serve* in 1942. It was Dickie's first film, and my father became something of a friend and mentor to him. Bryan came on the scene when Daddy made *The Colditz Story*, in which Bryan had a small acting part. Bryan loved *Whistle Down the Wind* but he became convinced that they should reset the film in the north of England. Bryan and Dickie were enthusiasts of the British New Wave, which was all about social realism. The previous setting of Mummy's book, in the Home Counties, felt somehow too polite and unreal. Bryan wanted the story to feel more grounded and believable, set somewhere remote, where the kids could lead their lives independently of the grownups, cut off from what was going on in the world outside.

Dickie and Bryan gave the book to Keith Waterhouse and Willis Hall, two powerhouse northern writers. Keith had written the novel *Billy Liar*, which had become a very successful play starring Albert Finney, and later a wonderful film with Tom Courtenay; and Willis Hall had written *The Long and the Short and the Tall* and *A Kind of Loving*, both enormously successful, so they were a vital part of the New Wave. Northern writers were making their presence felt like never before. John Osborne's *Look Back in Anger* in 1956, and Shelagh Delaney's *A Taste of Honey* in 1958, had so transformed British theatre that even established giants like Noël

Coward, Terence Rattigan and Daphne Du Maurier (someone my mother greatly admired) suddenly found themselves out of favour and viewed as almost an irrelevance. This dramatic change in writing for the theatre was one of the main reasons my mother struggled so much after her initial success. Like many writers of her generation, her whole style was suddenly considered to be old-fashioned. Her writing was still as good, but the world had changed.

I expect my mother took on board Bryan and Dickie's suggestions with mixed feelings. On the one hand, she was smart enough to know that adapting a book for film often requires some bold reimagining; but on the other hand, it's likely she took the changes as further proof that she was becoming out of date. In hindsight, Bryan's idea to move the story away from the comparative sophistication of Sussex and relocate it to a remote little stone farmhouse, lying at the foot of the barren, windswept Pendle Hills in Lancashire, was a stroke of genius. It made the story even more poignant and believable.

It was agreed to give Beaver Films the film rights to *Whistle Down the Wind*. This would be an independent, low-budget movie costing £160,000 to make (about £3.5 million in today's money), filmed in black & white. Guy Green had agreed to direct; he was an old friend, originally a cinematographer who had shot David Lean's *Oliver Twist*, and he had just worked with Dickie and Bryan on *The Angry Silence*.

I was brought in to play the lead role, Kathy. After my Oscar I was now 'hot', as they say, so my name made it much easier for them to get financing. I was fifteen years old and it made me happy to think I could help my mum and dad in this way. Although, truth be told, I was still very much considered a child and wasn't involved in any talks or consulted on the big decisions. This was now the established pattern of my career.

Other cast included the wonderful Bernard Lee, who was contracted to play the father, and in looking to cast 'The Man' in the barn, they had approached an exciting new young actor who had just made a big impact on the London stage in Harold Pinter's *The Caretaker* – his name was Alan Bates.

With the project all set to go and financiers in the process of closing a deal, Guy Green suddenly dropped a bombshell, saying he was pulling out. He'd been offered a big movie in America with Richard Burton, and although he was sorry to leave us in the lurch, he said he couldn't turn down such a big offer and such big money. It was his opportunity to break into Hollywood, and he hoped we would understand. Everybody did understand, of course, what else could we do? But it was a blow. We were weeks away from the start of filming and suddenly we had no director, and not much money to attract the calibre that we needed.

One afternoon at the farm, Bryan and Dickie roared up to the house unexpectedly and were immediately closeted in the drawing room with my parents. I knew something important was happening.

What transpired would be the making of the film, and of Bryan and Dickie's future careers. Initially my father had suggested that Dickie should direct it; he was an excellent actor with considerable experience, and Dad believed that he could do a very good job. Dickie said that he didn't want to direct, or at least, he didn't feel ready – he wanted to produce. Dickie then turned it around and suggested that my father should direct it. He was after all massively experienced, he'd produced films like *The History of Mr Polly* when he had his exclusive deal with the Rank Organisation. But Daddy had never directed and he didn't feel comfortable, at the last minute, taking on the enormous responsibility of directing his beloved wife's story, starring his daughter. There was too much at stake.

After all this to-ing and fro-ing, Bryan finally got his chance to speak. He told them that he was actually desperate to direct, and desperate to direct this picture. He'd given an enormous amount of thought to exactly how he would approach the subject and he talked them through the whole film, scene by scene. At the end of his spiel, my father was convinced, Dickie was convinced, my mother not quite so much. She was worried about putting the family project into the hands of someone so totally inexperienced – however much she liked and admired Bryan as a man, as an actor and as an excellent screenwriter. The truth of the matter was that he had never actually even directed traffic.

Meanwhile, I was hanging around outside wondering what the hell was going on in there, when the door was finally opened and they all trooped outside, considerably more animated than when they went in.

'Well, Bags,' my dad said, rubbing his hands together, 'we've finally thrashed it out, and . . .' he paused dramatically, '. . . you have a new director – Bryan! What do you think about that?'

We were all standing around on the grey flagstones in the hall. I looked at their expectant faces.

'That's great!' I said. (Well, what else was I supposed to say?) 'I mean, if you think you can do it, Bryan, then I'm sure that you can.'

'*Do* you think you can do it?' said Dickie looking at Bryan with a wry look on his face.

There was quite a pause.

'Well, we're bloody-well going to find out, aren't we!' said Bryan and everyone roared with slightly nervous laughter.

While Bryan and Dickie were setting up their movie, *The Parent Trap* was released in America and was an instant success. The reviews were excellent, praising David Swift's script and clever dialogue. It was a hit with grownups and had enough fun and gags to have the children screaming with laughter. So much fan mail was now pouring into the Studios for me, they had to employ a special team of people to handle the 7000-plus letters a week; and all the presents too: a mink jacket, a palomino pony, expensive guitars, someone even sent me an otter to keep in the bath! It was a smash. Walt was happy, the studio was happy, but unfortunately there were two people who were not happy: David Swift and Maureen O'Hara.

I believe that Maureen had originally signed up for the film on the understanding that she would get top billing, but her contract was likely to have been negotiated before the release of *Pollyanna*. That film's success, coupled with my Oscar, prompted the studio to change their approach and create a new poster with the star billing 'Hayley Mills & Hayley Mills, starring in . . .' which was fun and eye-catching and capitalised upon my growing fame. But Maureen O'Hara was having none of it. She was understandably upset, as were her agents, but I think there must have been some fine print in the contract that gave the studio the option to change the billing, so . . . that was that. Thankfully, it didn't affect my relationship with Maureen afterwards. She wasn't bitter at me, but she never worked with Disney again.

Another person whose 'stock value' had gone up considerably after *Pollyanna* and *The Parent Trap* was David Swift. He and Walt had always had a slightly strained relationship, as is often the case when a strong director works with a strong producer, but now he wanted more creative control. Both were brilliant in their own ways but they didn't always see eye to eye. In a more equal partnership this would be seen as 'creative tension', which can be very productive, and even bring out the best in an artist, but Walt and David didn't have an equal relationship – how could they? Walt was David's boss and the head of the studio, but after the success of those two films David wanted more power, and perhaps more to the point, he wanted *royalties*. Now, as I've said, Walt was an incredibly sweet and considerate man but when it came to business he could understandably be ruthless. Sadly, it seems that Walt could not or would not accommodate David's demands and the two men fell out so badly that Walt never worked with David again; and coincidentally neither did I. It seemed an unnecessarily bitter ending to their creative alliance, and it was a big loss to me. All of the work I'm most proud of at Disney was authored by David Swift.

★

Back in England, on a cold, grey, early morning in the middle of Lancashire, the crew were all standing around in the mud, huddled in their anoraks, drinking mugs of steaming tea and wondering what this one was going to be like. Many of this crew knew Dickie and Bryan from other films, and many of them had worked with my father too, so there was a feeling of familiarity, of old friends getting together again.

As the car dropped me off at the farm I saw two children – it was my brother and sister in the film. They were waiting uncertainly at the gate. Behind them the Pendle Hills were still shrouded in the heavy mist that never seemed to quite go away. The children looked very small. Diane Holgate, a sweet-faced, rather shy little girl of ten, was playing 'Our Nan', and Alan Barnes, a diminutive figure wearing his own blue school raincoat and cap and Wellington boots, was 'Our Charles'. Alan was only seven at the time. He had a fierce and rather lost expression on his face, terrible teeth and adenoids.

These were my two co-stars.

In keeping with the spirit of the times, Bryan wanted the children to be authentic. He had driven all over Lancashire to find the right child actors for the film. They were vitally important, not just Our Nan and Our Charles, the two main ones – but all of them, especially the 'twelve disciples'.

Eventually he found the perfect cast from local schools. None of them had ever done any acting. Apart from me, the only other professional child actor was Roy Holder, who played Jackie Greenwood, one of the older kids. Diane and Alan were both from the little village of Downham, literally walking distance down the road from the farm.

That first morning, Bryan came over to say hello. He was warm and smiling, and seemed very relaxed and perfectly in charge of everything. I didn't know that the day before, when filming had begun with Norman Bird playing the farm hand, Bryan had been so nervous he'd lost his voice!

Bryan took us up to the old barn where we were shooting. Neither Diane nor Alan had ever been on a film set before, let alone stood in front of a movie camera, and certainly not one the size of the Ariflex which they were both now scrutinising.

On a little rise, just behind the bright lights, some canvas chairs had been lined up with names printed in large letters on the back:

RICHARD ATTENBOROUGH — BRYAN FORBES — ALAN BATES

'Ey up!' said Alan Barnes, aged seven, pointing an outraged little finger at the chair . . . 'They've spelt me name wrong!'

So, the next morning, lined up beside all the others was a very small chair with ALAN BARNES written in black on the back. Courtesy of the props department.

It turned out to be quite appropriate that he should have his own chair, because Alan Barnes was a revelation. And needless to say, he stole the picture.

All the exteriors were shot on location and some of the interiors too: the cafe scene between Kathy and the local vicar, perfectly played by Hamilton Dyce, where she tries to find out what would happen to Jesus if he came back today; the Sunday school; and the arrival of the little boy with spectacles, David Edwards, who was so sweet and funny, he always made me wonder if Dickie Attenborough had looked like that as a child. And of course, the scenes in the barn were shot on location. It was all real – real cold, real hay and real manure, which Alan Bates discovered to his cost.

Bryan had decided it would be better if the children didn't read a script, seeing as they weren't really actors. He wanted fresh, natural performances. The kids would receive the pages to be shot the following day, so they could become familiar with their lines, and then on the set the next morning Bryan would just explain to them what was going on in the scene, and how they were feeling.

Alan and Diane adapted really well to filming but 'Our Charles' always found it difficult to avoid staring at his own reflection in the camera lens, so Bryan never told them when the camera was actually rolling. Rehearsals just merged into a take, and as a result he got some wonderful reactions, especially from 'Our Charles'. Bryan had to tell him repeatedly 'Blow your nose, Charlie!' before every 'take', and Charles/Alan would roll his eyes in frustration. His performance and his indomitable little figure are etched in my memory. He is central to the story: he is the one who initiates their joyful dance to 'We Three Kings'; he saves them all from being discovered by their father and the vet; he is the disillusioned one, and ultimately the one who betrays them – with his line "Ee's not Jesus . . . 'Ee's just a fella' so perfectly delivered, which people still quote at me today. All quite a lot for a child of seven to carry off, but thanks to Bryan's gentle and intelligent direction he really is the heart of the movie.

'Our Charles' did make one film after *Whistle Down the Wind*, a non-speaking part with Vince Edwards in a huge war movie called *The Victors*. It can't have been much fun, because afterwards he decided he'd had quite enough of acting and gave it up for ever.

Alan Bates, who played 'The Man', was a quiet figure on the set. Much like the character, he listened, spoke little and didn't give very much of himself away. I don't know if it was because he was constantly surrounded by children with colds and runny noses, or if he wanted to keep his distance to stay in the character, but it was good for me. He was guarded and mysterious, he let his presence speak for him. I could have gone on looking into his face for hours. He allowed Kathy and all the children to invest him with the qualities they imagined Jesus would have.

By the end of the film, when the police are closing in and the children are pouring down the hills and gathering in silence near the barn where he is hiding, Kathy comes to him and they talk to each other through the wall, and The Man realises that he cannot disillusion her and destroy her love and faith. His heart has opened; for the first time, you begin to see who he really is, and he allows himself to be taken away by the police without any resistance. Maybe it's the first time in his life that he's put someone else before himself. When he goes, he leaves behind him a fragment of hope.

Alan was not only beautiful to look at, it was also a beautiful performance: subtle, generous, and without any ego. Ever since he has remained my idea of what Jesus might have looked like.

In direct contrast to the day's filming, the evening meals back at the Kirby Hotel were some of the most hilarious times that I have ever endured in my life. I say 'endured' because attempting to eat while at the same time laughing hysterically was extremely challenging. Bryan and Dickie both had great funds of the most outrageous and brilliantly told stories. My father was no slouch in that department either, and Mummy threw in her sharp, witty observations. Then add in Bernard Lee to the group, and I was absolutely done for.

Bernie Lee was a darling, warm and kind, a wickedly wonderful individual; a marvellous actor and a great lover of the 'juice'. More often than not he got absolutely loaded and when he did, he would sit down at the piano in the dining room and play so beautifully that it brought tears to your eyes. Then he'd stagger off and spend half an hour trying to get up the stairs to his room singing 'Nellie Dean' loudly at the top of his voice, invariably removing his trousers, presumably to make the climb less arduous.

I remember that I had just bought my first grown-up dress, and wore it down to dinner one night. It was a simple dark blue cotton in a Black Watch design (tartan again) with a white Peter Pan collar, and I had on my first pair of 'court shoes' with a little heel. I remember looking at my reflection in the mirror on the inside of the cupboard door. The dress showed my shape, it made me look like a woman, which gave me a bit of a shock and made me shut the door with a bang – I suddenly felt self-conscious about going downstairs. I felt exposed. I realised that it's one thing to look grown up, but quite another to actually carry it off.

The next day I went to my trailer, on location, and put on Kathy's clothes and became a child again. I was five years older than the other children, and a good head and shoulders taller than most of them too, so the clothes chosen for the film were all too small for me. My coat was above my knees, and the sleeves were above my wrists in an attempt to make me look younger, and shorter.

It was a happy shoot. I developed a painful crush on the clapper boy. He was very attractive and very sweet but I could hardly look at him and found myself sitting around on bales of hay on the set rather a lot, staring into the distance. I was constantly falling in love with people, but I never let them know. I was sure they would laugh, they couldn't possibly take it seriously. It was safer to keep it a secret in my own head, where I could weave my dreams and infuse them with my romantic fantasy. Real life couldn't possibly live up to my passionate inner life, especially as I invariably fell for someone older and unavailable.

Maybe their unavailability was part of the attraction.

Whistle Down the Wind was a joyful experience. It was my second independent British movie and it turned out to be a unique collaboration of like-minded people – the crew were largely handpicked, old friends and new, and family. It doesn't always happen so successfully. Bryan was wonderful, his direction was sure and confident – however nervous he might have felt, he never showed it. He captured the mood and essence of the story perfectly, and his career as a film director spread its wings. It was beautifully photographed by Arthur Ibbetson, and all the performances, especially from the children, were terrific. Everyone on the film was behind

Bryan, and they all liked and admired Dickie, who treated every single member of the unit with consideration and respect. He was always the first to arrive on location at the beginning of the day, and the last to leave at the end. It was no surprise that Dickie went on to become one of Britain's great filmmakers.

After the location shooting, the unit moved to Pinewood to shoot some interior scenes, some pick-up shots and all the post-syncing. My father and Juliet were also working there at the same time; Daddy was filming *Tunes of Glory* with Alec Guinness, while Bunch was making *No, My Darling Daughter* with Michael Craig. It was such fun to be able to visit them on their sets. We practically took over the studios! These days the big studios like Pinewood and Shepperton are block-booked for years on end by mainstream productions from large studios. Sadly, independent British films can barely get in the gate.

Dickie's other invaluable contribution was to bring on board the great composer Malcolm Arnold to write the score. I cannot imagine a more perfect expression of the heart and soul of the film. He connected to it utterly, as he did with the joy and hu-mour of the children. The final brilliant brushstroke was to get Dickie himself to whistle the theme song. Piercingly poignant and unforgettable, and like the film itself the score has become a classic.

There are some remarkable similarities between *Whistle* and *Tiger Bay*. Both were independent, low-budget movies, made in black & white. Both were intrinsically British, part of the New Wave, spearheaded by independent filmmakers like Sir Michael Balcon who broke away and fought against the cultural influence of Hollywood, to make films that showed the country more as it really was, struggling in the aftermath of the war. Most British films never made it across the Atlantic; the tiny percentage that did were considered 'Art House' movies, and there wasn't a big demand for them. British films just didn't attract American au-diences, they couldn't identify with them. Hollywood ruled. The

American Dream was at full throttle. Across the Atlantic it was the land of milk and honey, whereas Great Britain was barely keeping her head above the water.

Whistle Down the Wind was a beautiful film, but it would have struggled to get a distributor like Pathé America behind it without a Disney star being on the poster. I didn't realise at the time – and no one explained it to me either – what an enormously fortunate position I was in, to have a foot in both camps. Few stars in Britain had managed to achieve success on both sides of the ocean. It was incredibly rare and lucky. With a bit more wisdom and foresight I could have used this extraordinary position much more to my advantage. But because nobody, myself included, had really entertained the possible longevity of my career, it was regarded as a sort of novelty. My parents fully expected that once my Disney contract expired I would probably just want to go off and breed horses.

Another uncanny similarity between *Whistle Down the Wind* and *Tiger Bay* was that both films revolve around a secret and serious emotional attachment between a young girl and an older man. I wasn't conscious of it at the time, not at all. In fact it really only occurred to me while writing this book.

Clearly, it was destiny. And it would soon be reflected in my own life.

When Nick, the long-awaited love of my life, arrived from California to try for Junior Wimbledon, the reality of the flesh and blood boy was overwhelming and my journal became superfluous. Shooting for *Whistle* was over and I had a weekend off from school, so he came and stayed at the farm for a couple of days. It was surreal. We played tennis on our ropy old court and went to visit Vivien Leigh in the new house she'd just moved into with Jack Merivale in Sussex. The house was beautiful, decorated with Vivien's unique flair and elegance. I don't think Nick knew who she was. On the Sunday afternoon I had to go back to school and he had to go back to London. I walked him to the local station. There was an awkward pause while we waited for the train. When it finally arrived, he got inside. I was standing by the open door when the guard came up and said in a very loud voice: 'I'm going to close it now. Kiss him through the window.'

I was stricken with embarrassment as Nick's head appeared through the window; his face came closer and closer until all I could see was the blue of his eyes ... then the train was moving and I was waving goodbye. I kept waving until it had gone. I stood there for a moment trying to absorb what had happened.

My first kiss!

A butterfly had brushed my lips.

I was vaguely aware of a sense of disappointment.

While *Whistle* was shooting in Lancashire, on the other side of the planet Disney was busily preparing the shoot for *In Search of the Castaways*. Walt was still very keen on the idea of Jonathan playing the part of my younger brother and a screen test had been arranged. He and I had a scene to do together and Johnny took it very seriously. He asked if he could have a tape recorder and worked for hours on the scene, learning the lines. We were given proper period clothes to wear, and with his little elfin face and huge eyes he looked wonderful on camera, and he was very good. Walt thought so too.

Mummy and Daddy were now facing the prospect of their third and youngest child going into the movies.

★

For three weekends running, a zealous Hayley Mills fan had managed to break into the farm. The intruder had roamed the family home, helping himself to anything he fancied – cameras, silver, jewellery, awards; he ate our apples and left the cores lying around, he drank the sherry. (We assumed it was a male fan because, as well as helping himself to refreshments, he also stole a lot of my underwear.) To our horror, the second time he broke in, Johnny, back from school for the weekend, was asleep upstairs in bed, oblivious to the intruder wandering around the house! The police were called in and searched for clues, but the thief was incredibly bold and, undeterred, returned for a final weekend of foraging, and presumably to finish off the sherry and find a matching bra.

When you've been burgled it can take some time to discover exactly what's been taken, so when the phone rang at the farm one evening and a mysterious caller told my mother that he'd found my Oscar in a ditch, nobody had even realised that it was missing! The caller said it had been wrapped in a piece of our headed note paper, with the address and telephone number on it, and would we like him to return it?

'Yes, please do,' said my mother, quick as a flash. 'That would be so very kind of you, we will expect to see you shortly.' Then she promptly called the local police who rushed over and hid in the bushes. When the mystery caller came walking confidently up the drive they pounced on him and took him off to the station. He had a number of other items stashed about his person, as well as my Oscar. He had my father's Rolex watch on, so there was no doubt that he was the culprit. This was the first time my baby Oscar was stolen; the next time I wouldn't be so lucky.

But that wasn't the last of the story; there was one other personal item belonging to me that was stolen, which I'd been unaware of. The police discreetly returned it to my father, without my knowing.

I was sitting in the bath one night when there was a knock on the door. It was Daddy.

'Hail darling, can I come in?'

Before I could say 'No, I'm in the bath!' he entered – with a very serious expression on his face. He was carrying something.

It was some time since he had seen me in the bath, and the bubbles had all pretty much gone. I was embarrassed although I tried not to show it – he wasn't bothered, so why should I be? I did my best to protect my modesty with a face flannel.

'Hail,' he said, 'the police handed this in to me,' and he held out some handwritten pages. Then I saw to my horror that it was my epic love letter to Horst.

'They found this letter scattered around the field in front of the house and under Mummy's caravan, and they gave it to me. They thought it was sensitive material and better to be kept private.'

I was stunned. The thought of the police reading my letter was excruciating. I didn't know what to say.

'Hail, this is a very dangerous thing to do. Horst is a married man, what have you got to say?'

I stared up at him, but still couldn't think of anything.

And then he started to read bits of the letter out loud to me – 'I dream of you, I dream of your mouth, your lips burning mine . . .' The bathwater was getting cold, I was covered in goose pimples.

He looked at me sternly. 'Something like this could do a great deal of damage to his marriage.'

I hugged my knees into my chest, feeling like a naughty child. 'But I – I never meant – I mean, I wasn't going to send it, it was private, just for me.' I finally managed to get some words out.

'But do you see what could have happened? If someone had got hold of it, like this man, he could have sent it to Horst, or worse still to the *press* – can you imagine what would have happened . . .?'

His voice went on, but I wasn't really listening. I couldn't believe that my father was standing over me, as I sat there naked in the bath, reading out my embarrassingly passionate declaration of love. It was so humiliating. I suppose he thought he was doing the right thing and wanted to make sure that I understood the dangers of this terrible indiscretion, but it felt like a monstrous invasion in more ways than one.

The time had come to make some decisions. The shoot for *In Search of the Castaways* was drawing close. Daddy had been clear from the beginning that he didn't want to play the cameo role of 'Captain Grant', the children's father. I understood, it wasn't a particularly challenging part, and he was about to fly off to French Polynesia to make *Tiara Tahiti* with his old chum James Mason. Mummy explained to us that she planned to go and join him in Tahiti, once I had started filming *Castaways* – and then she revealed that Johnny would be going with her. We were shocked. After months of deliberation they had come to the conclusion that it really would be too much for Mummy if Johnny started acting as well. She wouldn't be able to go to Tahiti, she would have had to stay behind, and anyway, his education was far more important. As you might expect, Johnny was confused and incredibly disappointed. He begged them to reconsider, but they had already turned down Walt's offer.

I suppose my parents felt guilty about messing Jonathan around. Taking him to Tahiti was a sort of consolation prize. But if they didn't want him to act, they should not have allowed him to do a screen test. He'd risen to the occasion, passed the audition and won the part – it really wasn't fair.

I don't think he ever forgave them.

There seemed no logic to it. The whole family was already in the business, making money and having fun. There was one rule for Bunch and me, and another for him. And much like my experience with *Lolita*, this was a life-changing opportunity that was turned down flat, and Johnny had no say in it at all. Maybe it was the right decision, maybe not. But one can't help but be left with that lingering question: 'What if . . .?'

CHAPTER SIX

Laika

'You must remember that you are dealing with a minor and it is up to us as her parents to decide what, in our opinion, is retrogression or advancement.'

– My mother's letter to Walt Disney, 1962

In the summer of 1961 I was kicked out of Elmhurst. The school had had enough of their peripatetic pupil, so, after the exams were over, they politely asked my parents to take me away. They said my comings and goings were disruptive and distracting for the other girls and they had concluded that my place, which was so often unoccupied, would be put to better use by a pupil who was there on a regular basis.

It didn't really come as a huge surprise. I had been struggling for some time to keep up. Often the term would be cut short before I could take any exams, and I'd be back in the little red school trailer at the Studios where the American lessons didn't connect at all with what I was doing in England. I had fallen between these two proverbial stools, adhering to neither one academic system nor the other, while my constant departures made it difficult to reintegrate back into school life when I returned.

That last term at Elmhurst was full of conflicting emotions.

I understood the school's decision on one level, but it also gave me an uncomfortable feeling of being dispensable. In the midst of all this uncertainty, I received a letter from home telling me that our dog Hamlet had died. My darling old friend since I was four, my companion of so many walks and rides had gone. It plunged me into homesickness and memories; the sweet, warm dome of Hamlet's head, his flying ears and wild joyous bark when we finally came home from some faraway place. I always felt he missed us more than the other dogs, like Suky or our moustachioed poodle Charlie Staircase; Hamlet was the one who waited by the front door, who always knew when my father's car had turned off the road, even though the drive was a mile long. For a child, losing a beloved pet is an early lesson in life and death and letting go; but I didn't get the chance to say goodbye. I felt terribly disconnected from home and heartbroken at the news. With Hamlet went another huge part of my childhood.

When my term at Elmhurst finally came to an end, there was the traditional end-of-year service at St Martin-in-the-Fields, at the edge of Trafalgar Square. All of us who were leaving skimmed our blue berets into the Thames in a symbolic gesture of 'goodbye to all that'.

The next question was, what were my parents going to do with me now?

In August 1961, *Whistle Down the Wind* opened to great success and acclaim in the UK.

Audiences flocked to see it, critics called it 'a small miracle of comedy and pathos'. It was one of the top ten films that year – not bad for a small independent British film competing against the big Hollywood fare. It also did well in the States; Bosley Crowther lauded it to the skies in the *New York Times*. Bryan Forbes and Dickie Attenborough were praised and audiences took the film to their hearts. It was a fantastic success for them both; neither Dickie nor Bryan had very much money at that point and *Whistle* would be a huge turning-point in their lives. For my mother too, the praise and recognition of her unique and special story was a tremendous boost to her morale. Personally, I don't remember thinking much about my own performance. While a glance back at some of the old reviews suggests it was well received, I never thought of *Whistle* in terms of my own success. The film itself was the star, not any one performer. Even 'Our Charles' in his little gumboots was part of a greater whole, a magical confluence of the right story and the right talent – at the right time – which is so rare. The success of *Whistle Down the Wind* felt like a massive win for Mummy who had been struggling for so long, but in hindsight I think the biggest winners were Dickie and Bryan, whose careers as filmmakers took a quantum leap.

After the film's premiere Daddy took us for a celebratory dinner at the glamorous Le Caprice restaurant, just behind the Ritz in Piccadilly. Le Caprice was 'the place to be' and it was a huge treat to be taken there as a child. I remember being given Cape gooseberries by sweet Mario Gallati, the maître d' for thirty years, and secretly watching the Anglo-Armenian multimillionaire Nubar Gulbenkian sitting at his usual table, while Mummy whispered to me how he had helped the Resistance during the Second World War, funding and training guides to escort stranded Allied and British airmen over the Pyrenees into neutral Spain. I gasped in awe and glanced over to this intriguing figure who always sat by himself, extremely well-dressed with a waistcoat and a gold chain, a bushy beard and an enormous orchid in his buttonhole.

Bryan and Nanette and Dickie and Sheila didn't make it to Le Caprice. After meeting everyone and his dog at the premiere they walked, skipped and ran the short distance down Piccadilly to the Ritz, where Bryan, in a rash of confidence, had booked a suite. When Bryan, in very high spirits, presented himself at the front desk, he and his guests were in such a rowdy and dishevelled state that initially the concierge didn't believe that he was staying there and flatly refused to give him his key.

While our esteemed producer and director and their respective partners were misbehaving at the Ritz, my father raised a glass of champagne to *Whistle*'s success and announced that he was taking us on holiday, for two weeks in the South of France.

It turned out to be a wonderful but also rather an unusual sort of holiday, sharing a little cottage with Larry Olivier and Joan Plowright who, by that time, was happily pregnant. The cottage was located on a private beach in the grounds of one of the most beautiful hotels in the world: the Cap Estel, which sits on the coast at Èze between Monaco and Cap Ferrat, with the foothills of the Pyrenees on one side and the sparkling blue of the Mediterranean on the other.

Everywhere was the warm intoxicating smell of pine, rosemary, lavender and mimosa. It was an extravagantly romantic place. Larry and Joan were wonderful company. Larry was warm and sweet, tremendously charismatic and often hysterically funny. Joan was great fun too, very down-to-earth, her Lincolnshire accent making her seem very droll. Of course, my parents were glad that Larry had found happiness again, but I think that, for them, Vivien's legacy cast a long shadow. They had been close friends for thirty years and my parents had been there for them throughout Vivien's constant battles with mental illness and the couple's painful separation. This holiday threw the past and the present into sharp relief. Times had changed. It was now a very different group. Not only was Joan a much younger woman, a good twenty-two years younger, a woman in her prime, she was also an actress at the vanguard of the New Wave, which in essence represented everything my mother felt threatened by professionally.

Instead of feeling undermined by this seismic shift in British theatre, like my mother did, Larry was fascinated by the new movement. He recognised it and embraced it (quite literally, in Joan's case), even asking John Osborne – the original 'angry young man' – to write something specifically for him. 'Why don't you write about an angry *middle-aged* man this time?' suggested

Larry, which is what Osborne did. *The Entertainer* became one of Larry's most successful roles. Tony Richardson, who directed it, said that the character of Archie Rice was the 'embodiment of a national mood; he was the future, the decline, the sourness, the ashes of old glory and where Britain was heading'. It was while performing *The Entertainer* that Larry had met Joan and while my parents liked her enormously, I suspect it wasn't easy for my mother to see Vivien replaced by a woman so much younger – and so much embodying the future – while Mummy was being told that her work now belonged to the past. Nevertheless, they all enjoyed each other's company and if my parents had any doubts about Larry and Joan's age difference they kept it to themselves. Unfortunately, when a similar situation was to arise in my own life in the very near future, they would have plenty to say.

Joan was closer to my age than to my parents' and I loved her company. She was funny but also unpredictable. 'It doesn't matter if you've got small breasts,' she said on our first day on the beach, seemingly apropos of nothing, 'so long as you've got a nice bottom.'

'Oh! Yes,' I replied – feeling slightly unsure about my new bikini. 'Well, thank you,' I added – not too sure about my bottom either. I decided I'd have to have a look when I got back to my room.

Those two weeks gave me time to mull over my life and my strange newfound freedom. Elmhurst had kicked me out, I was between movies, I was teetering on the centre of a seesaw – not yet an adult but no longer a child. Even the world around me appeared to be in a sort of limbo; oscillating warily between the nuclear fears of the 1950s and the dawning optimism of the 1960s, initiated by the election of John F. Kennedy, the youngest and most dazzlingly charismatic man ever to have been elected President of the United States. His inaugural speech – 'the torch has been passed to a new generation of Americans' – filled us all with tremendous hope and excitement that this intelligent and progressive young man, with his beautiful family, could truly lead the world to a better, safer place, and that he would know what to do 'before the dark powers of destruction unleashed by science engulf all humanity in planned or accidental self-destruction'.

While JFK was trying to steer his way through the Cold War, I was staring down the uncertainties of my own teenage life, coming at me thick and fast. It was heady and confusing. Perhaps it was the bomb, or just my own burgeoning awareness, but all the wonder and excitement that I had always felt about the world now became funnelled into one overwhelming yearning – for love and romance. Life was unbearably romantic and I wanted to share it all with someone. Sadly, I was always on the move. It's hard to have relationships when you're never in one place for long. The clock was always ticking and I felt an increasing sense of separation nagging at me, which I couldn't shake off. That holiday in France saw the continuation of what was becoming a pattern. I'd fall in love with someone, become romantically obsessed, suffer in sweet agony, keep it all to myself for a while, and then move on. There was one beautiful French boy who captivated me on that trip. His parents owned the hotel. I'd see him by the pool. He'd smile at me, I'd smile back. One evening he invited me to go to an open-air movie in Monaco. It sounded very romantic and I was in a state of great anticipation until he showed up with a whole bunch of friends, including his very beautiful, perfectly tanned French girlfriend. This boy and I sat together, side by side, under a full moon while he held his beautiful girlfriend's hand behind my back. The movie was called *No Love for Johnny*. During a very tense moment in the plot, I managed to spill Coca-Cola all over his lovely white trousers.

Still the clumsy one, but suddenly it didn't seem so funny.

I returned to England full of excitement about *In Search of the Castaways*, which was due to start shooting in August. I'd never made an adventure movie before and I was madly looking forward to riding with the gauchos across the plains of Patagonia, sailing on old steamships and seeing New Zealand. As it turned out, we didn't get any further than Pinewood Studios – all within a few miles of my house. Walt had really taken on board my parents' request that, whenever possible, my films should be filmed in England so as not to disrupt my family and school life. It was a huge disappointment.

Castaways was the biggest film I had ever worked on. It was a big-budget production with lavish sets that took over four sound stages at Pinewood. They used the enormous water tank to build a full-sized replica of a nineteenth-century steamship, perfect down to the smallest detail, with beautiful decks and cabins and rich gleaming panelling, chandeliers and luxurious fittings. On the gigantic backlot, they also built a huge Maori camp and fortress where a riveting troop of cannibalistic warriors would perform their ritual war dance. All the special effects sequences would be shot at Twickenham, including a thrilling glacier ride hurtling through ice canyons on extremely wobbly and precarious boulders! It took set builders two months to erect forty-foot-high mountains for the impressive, if not awe-inspiring, spectacle when huge sections of the snow-covered 'Andes' are completely destroyed by an earthquake.

Walt had kindly asked me who I would like to play the role of John Glenarvan (the son of Lord Glenarvan, in the form of the redoubtable Wilfrid Hyde-White). This was very considerate of him because this was to be my first screen kiss – which, frankly, I was a bit nervous about. I immediately thought of Michael Anderson Jnr, who was one of the child actors in *Tiger Bay*. We'd had fun together on that film, hanging out of the hotel window in Cardiff, dropping stink bombs and itching powder onto the heads of the unsuspecting people walking below. So I thought, if I'm going to be kissed, better it be with someone I knew.

Once shooting began, it all seemed to run smoothly, despite the enormous scale of the production. Maurice Chevalier was a darling, I adored him, he had the most wonderful sense of humour and we got on very well. It's fair to say Maurice was then at the absolute peak of his international fame. He had just made *Gigi* with Leslie Caron and, of course, *Fanny* with Horst. Maurice called me 'Mon petite amour', and I called him 'Mon petit bijou' – 'my little jewel' – and 'Mon petit chou' – which I thought meant either 'my little puff pastry' or 'my little cabbage', I wasn't entirely sure. Whichever it was, he didn't seem to mind. We had a couple of duets together in the film. I've never considered myself much of a singer, but he didn't seem to mind that either. He told me that when he was very young he became the great Mistinguett's dancing partner; he was twenty-three and she was thirty-six. They had a famous romance and were together for years. He said that I reminded him of her. I couldn't see how that was possible; Mistinguett (née Jeanne Florentine Bourgeois) was this beautiful and incredibly glamorous entertainer who had mesmerised and captivated audiences at the Folies Bergère and the Moulin Rouge. He said that her singing was 'slightly off' (perhaps this was where he saw the similarity) but due to her enormous charm and charisma, nobody minded. She had great legs and big teeth, which Maurice thought was madly attractive.

Maurice was 'French' from the top of his head to the tip of his shiny shoes, and while he took great pleasure in playing the part to the hilt, he was totally genuine, as was his charm and natural chic. There was also something strangely unique about the way he spoke English, the way he pronounced certain words and phrases, but I couldn't quite put my finger on what it was. Years later I learnt that when he was a young man, during the First World War, he was wounded and captured by the Germans. Apparently he spent two years in a prison camp where there were a lot of soldiers from the north of England, which is where he learnt to speak very good English, albeit with a slight Lancashire accent!

Again, I was so lucky to work with wonderful actors and learn from some of the very best. One thing that 99 per cent of them had in common was the way that they behaved on set, not only to the director and the other actors, but also to the crew. They were disciplined, courteous and generous. Like Wilfrid Hyde-White, another of nature's gentlemen. Whatever situation developed, however trying, he always responded to it with humour, which immediately defused tensions and put people at ease. I recognised this skill at once, because that was my dad's way too.

Another great actor on the film was George Sanders – the epitome of an upper-class gentleman. His screen persona preceded him slightly. He was mostly known for playing cads and sophisticated villains: from Hitchcock's *Rebecca* to *All About Eve* to perhaps his most famous role, terrifying generations of children, as the honeyed voice of Shere Khan. Initially, I must admit, I found him rather intimidating. However, in reality George was charming and courteous in a very old-fashioned way. He seemed remote and gave one the impression that he found everything vaguely amusing, although I wasn't sure if I'd always want to know what he was thinking. There was something sweet about him but also rather sad, especially when he smiled. George had been married to the much-married beauty Zsa Zsa Gabor. That relationship eventually ended, but in later years he married her sister Magda, so clearly he wasn't lacking in courage!

At the helm of the production was Robert Stevenson, who was gentle and surprisingly self-effacing considering the enormous number of successful films he'd made. He had directed *Old Yeller* for Walt, one of my favourites at the time (to this day I don't think I've ever cried so much in a film), and he would go on to direct many more prestigious features, among them *Mary Poppins*. Yet, in spite of Robert being a sweet and brilliant man, I still missed David Swift. David and I had an understanding. He was an 'actor's director'; he wrote his scripts, he connected with the performers. I didn't feel that that was Bob Stevenson's strongest point and I think it shows in *Castaways*. All the actors seem somewhat detached from the quite extraordinary things that are happening all around them. As an actor, you want to trust your director is keeping an eye on what you're doing, but I suspect that the sheer scale of the production, with its multitude of special effects and huge financial pressures, might have been slightly distracting for Bob.

That said, the film worked out well. It did very well at the box office and it was great fun to make. I had two charming young co-stars in Michael Anderson Jnr and Keith Hamshere, both of whom at some point imagined that they were in love with me. Or so they said. Keith had just enjoyed great success on stage in the West End, playing the lead in Lionel Bart's *Oliver!*, which had changed the world of musicals for ever, and he was now playing my younger brother in the film. This was a sensitive issue, because this was the role that my real brother Jonathan would have had. Thankfully, Johnny wasn't around to have it rubbed in his face. Once shooting began, Mummy and Jonathan flew off to join Daddy filming in Tahiti, which I imagine Walt must have thought a bit odd since he had gone to such a considerable amount of trouble to locate *Castaways* in England – for the sole reason that the family could all stay together! Looking back, I think this could well have been the first fissure in the Mills–Disney relationship. It would soon get worse.

As far as I was concerned, however, my parents' absence meant I was free of their watchful eye and I had a moment of short-lived independence before my guardian, Lee, finally arrived with her Pall Mall cigarettes.

I was beginning to feel my wings stirring. I wanted to experience everything with all the boundless energy of a (nearly) sixteen-year-old girl. I felt an endless supply of joy and love, I wanted to embrace life with all my strength, although I wasn't entirely sure what 'love' meant. I was in love – out of love – in love again; on a swing flying high and kicking my heels at the sky one minute, then crashing down to earth the next. Men flirted with me, whistled at me, sometimes said they loved me. It was all new and exciting and I just went with the flow. One day, during filming at Pinewood Studios, I became fascinated by one of the Maori dancers, in full battledress and war make-up, who was devastatingly handsome. He must have spotted me looking at him, because, during the lunch break, I was waylaid in the corridor when he suddenly jumped out of a doorway, still dressed for battle, grabbed me, pushed me against a wall, kissed me furiously and then walked off. I was left standing there in shock, wondering what I was supposed to do next.

I wasn't traumatised, just stupefied. These days, it's very unlikely a man would ever dare do such a thing for fear of being charged with assault. I was left feeling a bit unsteady for a moment, but otherwise unscathed.

However, my first *screen kiss*, which I had been secretly quite nervous about, was cancelled on the very day Michael and I were supposed to shoot the scene. I found myself feeling both relieved and disappointed at the same time. It would only have been my second kiss ever – well, third if you count the Maori. Strangely, I never did discover why they had decided to cancel this momentous event in cinema history, and I would have to wait another two years for it to happen. Until then, it was always hovering around in the ether as a possibility, which only served to make the forthcoming event even more nerve-racking.

While I was filming *Castaways* my parents finally addressed the ongoing problem of my school education. They had come up with a plan, which I could not have anticipated, that the following year I would be sent to a finishing school in Switzerland. Bizarrely, they had also entertained the idea of sending me to a convent in Belgium run entirely by nuns, where Vivien Leigh had been locked up as a child and recommended it – perhaps as a joke. Faced with these two choices, Switzerland certainly seemed less frightening, but I still wasn't sold on the idea.

'A finishing school? But I haven't even finished my education!' I protested.

'This will finish it. That's why it's called a finishing school!'

replied my mother, glibly. 'You'll love it,' she went on. 'You'll learn to speak perfect French, to cook and sew – and best of all you'll be skiing like a dream by the time you come home.'

Still, I was not convinced.

'It's something I always longed to do,' she added. 'You're very lucky to have this opportunity.'

'Yes, I can see that, but . . . I won't know anyone! I'll be a fish out of water. And I'll be away from home for months! Why can't I stay here and go to a college in London?'

'You probably wouldn't get in,' she replied, rather bleakly. 'Anyway this will be much more fun!'

And that was the end of it. The decision had already been made for me.

I'm sure my mother believed wholeheartedly that Switzerland was what I needed, but in hindsight I can tell you now, it wasn't. What I needed was normality. With Elmhurst gone and filmmaking now completely taking over my life, I was feeling increasingly disconnected from other kids my age. Instead of sending me to a college near home, where I could at least attempt to lead a more normal life, I was being sent to live up a mountain in the Swiss Alps. However romantic it sounded, however much I loved the idea of skiing all day, a whole school full of strange older girls sounded a bit daunting.

And I was just getting a taste for freedom . . .

In October, my darling sister Juliet married Russell Alquist. She walked up the aisle on our father's arm in our little local church in Cowden. The autumn sun poured through the stained-glass windows on to a small pale figure in a dress of gleaming white satin, under a white veil. Russell was waiting at the altar with his best man, Brian Bedford. I was her bridesmaid in a dress made of apricot tulle, with apricot feathers on my head. Jonathan was the usher with an enormous carnation hanging out of his buttonhole.

It was all so very romantic. You'd expect a young girl like me to be endlessly fantasising about my own perfect wedding day, but I never did. Most girls dream of this special day and imagine the beautiful dress they'll wear, walking up the aisle to live happily ever after, but it wasn't something I ever thought about. Perhaps I had a sort of prescience about how my life was going to turn out, or, closer to the truth, about what I really wanted – which was *romance*. Marriage simply didn't strike me as being especially romantic.

For the reception, the barn was hung with drapes like a great tent with blue and white stripes. Gold and red chrysanthemums spilt out of huge vases, champagne flowed and music played as the guests danced and laughed. Finally, their faces bright with happiness, the newlyweds left for their honeymoon in Paris, followed by showers of rice. When they stopped at the crossroads to remove the two chamber pots rattling behind the back of the car, Bunch sat down on the grass verge and burst into floods of tears.

Was it a sense of loss? The sight of all those darling, smiling, tear-stained faces, waving them away . . . A part of her life was over and it was the start of a new chapter; one of responsibility, of being a wife. My parents had resisted her marriage, it had caused difficult days and nights, but now they promised each other that they would never do that to their children again. It was a promise that they could not keep.

Later that evening we were having tea in front of a crackling fire; everything was quiet and rather subdued and I did find myself wondering out loud who I would marry . . .

'I wonder who I'll marry *first*?' said Jonathan, stuffing his face with yet another piece of wedding cake.

He was pretty prescient too.

Gradually we were all scattered in the four directions: Bunch went off on her honeymoon, Johnny was sent back to boarding school and Daddy flew to New York to play T.E. Lawrence (of Arabia) in Terence Rattigan's play *Ross*. So before I began my sentence in Switzerland I went with Mummy to visit him.

This was a personal high point for Daddy. It was his Broadway debut, and he was very excited and terribly nervous. Also, *Ross* was a role that Alec Guinness had played in the West End, to great acclaim, and if there was one actor that my father measured himself against it was Alec. They were old friends and my father admired Alec tremendously, so there was no jealousy there, but it was definitely competition. They had a history going back decades and their careers often veered into each other's orbit. Alec's first supporting role was in David Lean's *Great Expectations*, playing Herbert Pocket, while Dad played the lead role of Pip. They'd had many wonderful, memorable scenes together in that film – like Pip's first night in London, as he struggles to eat politely in Herbert Pocket's chamber, a masterclass of comic acting and timing. But by 1961 Alec's star had risen on both sides of the Atlantic and the two quintessentially British actors were sometimes considered for the same parts. Four years earlier, in 1957 when David Lean was setting up *The Bridge on the River Kwai*, he approached Alec to play the role of Colonel Nicholson. His legendary performance as the honourable but tragically deluded British officer arguably defined the rest of his career, but in the beginning Alec wasn't so sure. Initially he said yes to the role, but as the filming date loomed closer Alec lost confidence and turned it down, plunging the production into crisis. Lean sent my father the script with a frantic telegram begging him to play the role, which of course my father pounced upon immediately.

Then Alec changed his mind again. Naturally and quite rightly, David restored the part to him, but it was a big disappointment for my dad. He knew *River Kwai* was going to be something special. The film eventually won eight Oscars, including Best Picture, Best Director . . . and Best Actor to Alec Guinness.

So when my father agreed to play *Ross* in New York, I think there was a deeper meaning for him. Perhaps he wanted to prove to himself that he could match Alec's performance with something just as good, though different, which he did. *Ross* was rapturously received by the wonderful New York audiences and enjoyed a successful run at the Eugene O'Neill Theater before the play transferred to the Hudson Theater.

With Daddy busy on stage, I had big plans of my own to go out and explore and enjoy the Big Apple, but then something happened that put quite a damper on my activities.

A death threat had come to the attention of the FBI, by way of an anonymous letter, which claimed to know all about my visit to New York and that it was their 'mission to kill me', that I was 'a son of a bitch' and they were going to make sure that I never reached my sixteenth birthday.

Two very nice and quite ordinary-looking FBI agents in suits turned up one day at the door of our suite at the Algonquin Hotel. Initially I was petrified. It was an extraordinary and horrible thought that there was someone out there who hated me so much that they wanted to kill me.

I didn't know what to say – so I laughed.

'We're taking this extremely seriously,' they said. 'We have someone keeping an eye on you right now.'

I felt a sudden urge to glance over my shoulder, expecting to see either a special agent or a crazed killer. From then on, until I left the city, I was driven everywhere in a huge car with blacked-out windows; I had to wear dark glasses at all times and a big hat. Wherever I went, I was followed by the FBI, which was quite exciting, if not a little disconcerting.

Thankfully, my would-be assassin never showed up. In spite of these strange goings-on, I was sad to say goodbye to New York and increasingly dubious about heading off for the finishing school. Although, to be honest, the idea of being hidden in the Alps, far away from crazy fans, didn't sound so bad now after all.

★

L'Institut Alpin Videmanette was located in the little village of Rougemont, 1007 metres above sea level in the French-speaking Swiss Alps. I was expected to speak French, to learn to cook, sew and ski – academic subjects definitely were secondary. Many years later it would be the perfect answer for Princess Diana after she failed all her O-levels, but at least she'd taken them. The same could not be said of me.

I arrived in January 1962, a couple of weeks after the term had begun, which was especially unfortunate, as everyone else had arrived the previous September. So again, I had catching up to do. My mother and Bunch dropped me off, after a long journey by boat and train – and left me to settle in. We said a tearful goodbye. They were heading off to visit Bunchy's godfather Noël Coward, then living in rarefied splendour near Montreux to avoid the merciless British tax man. Mummy told me she expected Disney to send a considerably better script for my next movie, with a much more interesting role than the 'nice' girl I was given to play in *Castaways*. 'If all they want is a pretty face, they should get someone else.'

I found my dormitory and opened my cases, but couldn't face hanging around with all those strange girls and my bits lying around on a strange bed, so I took a walk through the little village that was to be home for the next six months. It was evening, the snow was falling, a streetlamp hanging across the road between two chalets was covered in ice. Everything was silent, just the crunch of snow under my boots. I looked up into the stars; flakes settled on my upturned face, then melted quickly away. Somewhere, up there in the darkness, Laika was circling the Earth in her tiny space capsule. The canine cosmonaut was a husky-mix stray from the streets of Moscow, the first dog to be launched out of the Earth's atmosphere. How terrified she must have been, I thought, how terrible the pain in her ears as the g-forces assailed her, abandoned in the void with nothing to eat or drink. She was dead now, her little body floating on for ever in deep space. I sniffed gloomily. A boy trudged past with his hands deep in his pockets, his red woollen hat pulled down over his ears, the tassel clogged with snow like Hamlet's ears in the winter. Sorrow and homesickness swept over me. The boy disappeared into the darkness like the snowflakes on my face.

It took time to settle in. The girls were mostly very nice; a handful of Americans and Canadians, a couple of Dutch but mostly English. I shared my room with two girls, Lizi and Pip, who were sweet but much older, having left school at the proper time. Initially all the girls kept their distance, they had all made friends the previous term and they were way ahead of me in the French department. Speaking nothing but French from morning till night meant that for the first two or three months I didn't have very much to say for myself. It made things rather lonely and also exhausting. Being desperate to communicate, I was prone to dire lapses into English. Madame wasn't pleased. She'd give me lectures about my hair – not wearing it up – and about my French. I had to learn French poems and write out exercises. 'You came here to learn French!' Madame insisted. 'You will never learn unless you start now!' Then she fell back on the old chestnut: 'Don't think just because you're famous that you don't have to work hard, etc., etc.' That was the final straw. Maddening tears streamed down my cheeks.

It was Miss Dodson all over again. Why did so many people assume that fame inevitably made one conceited or lazy? Or think that I somehow felt myself to be superior, when the exact opposite was the truth. More than anything I just wanted to be accepted for who I was. I don't think many of the girls cared a fig about my acting career, at least not after the initial curiosity. They just wanted to get on with their own lives.

I tried to stay busy and keep out of trouble. All the cooking lessons were in French, so I wasn't given anything too demanding to do and spent a lot of time peeling carrots. Sewing was a whole new world and I embarked upon it with immense enthusiasm, making myself a blue gingham skirt with a broderie anglaise frill along the bottom. I was thrilled. It was enchanting. It fell apart the first time I washed it.

But I learnt to ski, which was a source of tremendous pride

and joy. The experience was the closest thing to flying that I could imagine, like being a swallow, a sensation you could never achieve on your two lumpen feet. It was a glorious, solitary experience, a release for my spirit as much as anything else. And constantly falling on your face, or your arse, is a great leveller. What can you do but laugh? So much for dignity! Of course, the irresistible appeal of the ski instructors kept me going. Their beauty and poise as they swept ahead in a graceful curve, snow flying up like a fan, one ski-tip barely touching the ground, as you floundered around behind – a helping hand reaching down to haul you back up to your feet again, the cloudless blue sky behind them. Gods of the snowy slopes! There were compensations.

Letters became a lifeline. My mother and my sister were good letter writers and so was my brother stuck in his boarding school in Sussex. I also started to get letters from boys. I received two from someone who called himself Frank Sinatra Jnr, who wrote admiringly and promised to take me on a date the next time I was in Hollywood. I had no idea who he was or how he had found out where I was, and I assumed it was a hoax. However, it later turned out to be true . . .

As I struggled with an ever-increasing sense of isolation, not only did I become rather shy and introverted, I also became a complete hypochondriac. I developed a terrible ache in my back, I couldn't sit or stand in one position for very long, or read in bed, and I soon became secretly convinced that the real reason my parents had sent me to Switzerland was for 'the cure' – because they believed I had lung cancer or TB.

I blame Mummy. She was constantly saying she was at death's door. She would often complain of a worrying pain in her back that she'd try to ease by hitting herself with a glass tube of Alka Seltzer.

'Now I have it too!' I thought. 'I've been sent here because they think I'm dying.'

While I was in the Alps grappling with my fears and trying to become a lady, my mother, alone at home, with no one to keep her company but the bottle, had taken it upon herself to intervene in my career. Disney had just sent her the script for my next movie – then called *The Amazing Careys* – and she absolutely hated it. I suspect she was feeling somewhat emboldened by the success of *Whistle Down the Wind* and she was no longer prepared to be simply handed her daughter's projects *fait accompli*, without creative consultation. One evening, Mummy lit up a cigarette, polished off the sherry, and sat down at her trusty old typewriter to give Bill Anderson, Disney's head of production, a piece of her mind.

Alone in that house, inspired by Tio Pepe, and without Daddy's restraining hand, she let rip:

The whole script amounts to precisely nothing. Throughout the whole thing there isn't one scene [for Hayley] worth playing. It's a sort of grown-up *Pollyanna* without the charm or the story of the little girl. In fact, [Hayley's role] emerges from it a rather unattractive character, who merely does all the talking to further one of the most boring tales ever told.

That was just the opening. Leaving diplomacy to the United Nations, she went on:

One wonders if, even in America where this Hicksville type of tale is of interest, the ordinary teenager won't find it incredibly tame. Here is a girl who has won awards for ACTING [Mummy's emphasis], she is a natural actress who can go from strength to strength given the right parts and consideration from the studio ... We do not feel the present script in any way advances her talents and ... if this is the sort of thing she is going to have to do for Walt, she will have to spend the rest of the year working on other things, in order to keep her name on the marquee so that [Hayley] is not lost in oblivion.

Basically, she was telling Disney their script stank. Whatever you want to say about my mother, there's no denying she had balls. What annoyed her most, I can see, was the lack of consultation:

> I have begged Walt a hundred times to discuss his ideas for her with me but he never answers until the last minute when he sends me the script and says he's committed . . . You must remember that you are dealing with a minor and it is up to us as her parents to decide what, in our opinion, is retrogression or advancement.

In her opinion, they should have been sourcing stories like *Whistle* and *Tiger Bay*, which had been both critical and financial hits, winning international awards. As if this were not enough, she then petitioned them to think responsibly about the cultural impact of their films on young audiences:

> When I think, Bill, of all the thousands of stories to which you must have access, which could be a furtherance of talent, and entertainment, of inspiration and imagination, of intelligence, wisdom, feeling and emotion to the children and teenagers that follow Hayley Mills . . . this story entitled '*The Amazing* (?) *Careys*' is rather pathetic and it's no use saying 'it's a lot of fun' 'cos when the critics get at it who takes the can back but H. Mills!!

When my mother was fired up about something, she let caution fly to the winds. As a result, my wonderful relationship with Walt Disney was starting to resemble the Bay of Pigs invasion.

Mummy added that I should not be expected to sing in the movie, to be compared with girls my age who actually could sing, who were trained to sing and made a living from singing. In her opinion it wasn't fair for me to be 'stuck up there to be pilloried and criticised'.

Clearly Mummy didn't think much of my singing either.

Of course, my mother hadn't written directly to Walt, but in sending it to Bill Anderson she knew full well it would end up on Walt's desk. Walt did not take kindly to being criticised. He was used to having his own way and I've no doubt that being harangued by the talent's mother, however much he liked her, would have been a novel experience for him. Walt responded with a terse telegram to Bill Anderson, who was in London at that time.

Basically, Walt took great exception to my mother's letter and to the implication that she was trying to tell him what kind of pictures he should make and how to run his business! He didn't believe she actually knew what was best for me, but that he did.

Walt was so incensed by the whole thing that he felt obliged to remind Bill of my commitment and legal obligations, and that, in his opinion, my mother's attitude was teetering dangerously towards being in violation of my contract.

It was suddenly clear how very different their opinions were. My mother had held up *Whistle Down the Wind* as an example of the kind of film and role that I should be making. Walt's opinion was that *Whistle* was entirely unsuitable for me, that I had been used by my family and their friends to cash in on my popularity and that, anyway, the little boy 'Our Charles' had stolen the picture! (Which I have to agree with.) He maintained his belief that I was too young for heavy dramas or material in any way related to sex. In Walt's mind *Summer Magic* was exactly the right film for me at this stage of my life; the singing was not about showing my vocal ability, more about showing my personality.

Walt and my mother had always had a very good relationship and this letter had left him frustrated and bewildered, and apparently quite angry. But his response also shows how much he cared and the integrity with which he made his decisions.

This was a clash between two families: my professional family at The Walt Disney Studios and my own parents at home.

Card Walker, one of Walt's top executive producers, sent Walt a memo at this time.

I agree 100% with your answer regarding Hayley Mills. I seem to recall that you mentioned after screening *Parent Trap* before the picture was released, they [the parents] were very disappointed, not only in the picture but in David Swift and almost everyone else. I don't believe they can intelligently evaluate a property. What you said about *Whistle Down the Wind* is absolutely true.

I had no idea my mother had even written her letter until I visited the Walt Disney Archives in 2016. History, I think, proves her right (the film in question, despite making Disney money, turned out to be somewhat forgettable) but the fierce, confrontational tone of her letter put everyone at the studio on the defensive and the only dialogue it led to was with the Disney Legals, who were quickly brought in to remind everyone of my contractual agreement. Nevertheless, I was proud to see her stand up to these powerful men, challenging them – arguing passionately, not just as a mother but also as an artist. The fact she failed to change their minds is beside the point. She tried her best and she did it because she loved me.

By the spring term the snow had started to disappear, so instead of skiing we hiked up into the mountains, walking all day, high above the valleys, through fields of long grass and wild narcissi, gentian blue, daisies, columbine and buttercups. My French was by now passable and although I never felt that I managed to completely integrate with the other girls, I could at least talk to people and get out of my hermit-crab shell. With all that fresh air and exercise, the food was my undoing: fragrant newly baked white breads, cheese fondues, fresh cakes and creamy Swiss chocolate . . . I blew up like a balloon and turned sixteen.

While piling on the pounds, I was still dogged by the fear that I was dying. One day a portable X-ray unit arrived in Rougemont and the whole school had to go and have their chest and lungs photographed. I waited in an agony of suspense for the results to arrive. Eventually, one morning, postcard-sized photos of our chests arrived in the mail. I looked at mine; I looked at everyone else's. I couldn't see any difference. Shortly after that I realised that the ache in my back had gone away. It disappeared like Mummy's asthma.

The final weeks seemed to speed by and then suddenly it was over and we were all on the train taking us back to London, officially 'finished' and determined to celebrate our freedom and newly acquired sophistication and maturity – which meant of course getting as drunk as we possibly could in the time between Rougemont and Waterloo station. Four of us shared a 'couchette' that converted into four bunks for the overnight journey, which took us down through glorious mountains covered with wild flowers, to the great gleaming lake of Lucerne and on to Paris and finally crossing the English Channel. The scenery was magnificent but largely ignored. Numerous bottles of cheap white wine were rapidly consumed, then with the bit firmly between our teeth we searched around, determined to find something else to celebrate with. To shrieks of delight, a bottle of kirsch was produced from the bottom of someone's knapsack, a present for her father that he would never get, which would be our undoing. Lizi spent the rest of the journey sobbing in a corner, one girl passed out, and I fell off the top bunk, tearing the zip out of my dress. Staggering out of the carriage to the loo, I made my way past a platoon of equally drunk Swiss soldiers and shut the door with a bang and a sigh of relief and caught sight of myself in the mirror.

'Ohhh . . . shit!'

When we finally arrived and I clambered unsteadily down on to the platform at Waterloo, dishevelled and hungover, my parents walked straight past me, not recognising this balloon of a girl with a face like a big brown bun and half her dress hanging off.

Money well spent at one of the most expensive finishing schools in the world!

CHAPTER SEVEN

Piling on the Pounds

As soon as I returned home from the Alps, I went on a diet. I had one month to prepare for my role in *The Amazing Careys*, now renamed *Summer Magic*, and a lot of weight to lose. All the bread and cakes and Swiss chocolate had gone straight to my face and – to be honest – to my backside, which at least was easier to hide.

My parents didn't seem to be too concerned by my blooming appearance – 'It's puppy fat, darling' – but I was desperate, and so began the long battle with my weight; going on one punishing diet after another, then inevitably succumbing to the unbearable temptation of the local bakery.

Upon entering the bun shop, I would pretend that we were hosting a children's party.

'Oh yes, Susie *loves* donuts – and so does Richard – so two please, yes . . . and Shirley adores chocolate eclairs – thank you . . . of course Pippa loves cream buns more than anything . . .' and on and on.

Back in the privacy of my room I would devour the lot . . . and hate myself.

After Switzerland things were markedly different. The pages of my journal are full of angst and woe. I was growing up and it terrified me. I wasn't that happy-go-lucky child any more. I was morose and struggling with paralysing shyness. The combined effects of fame and adolescence, compounded by the seclusion of Switzerland, had pushed me further into my shell. And now I couldn't get out. I was stuck.

It was a struggle to remember what it was like to feel normal – or natural. I was so confused. I didn't understand it; everything I did felt phoney, I was painfully self-conscious the whole time. I hated my voice, my fat face, my spots. I became quite paranoid. I was scared of growing up and fending for myself. I wasn't sure I was capable. I felt like a total failure as a person: no one liked me, not even my parents. I was like a small aeroplane in a tailspin, my confidence had collapsed, and along with it my sense of self.

I simply didn't know who I was any more. I assumed there was something deeply wrong with me, that I was going through all this on my own, and not that it is a universal experience that virtually everyone struggles with at various times in their life. I wish I had known more back then. It would have saved me literally years of abject misery.

In my early twenties, someone recommended I read *The Art of Loving* by the great psychologist and philosopher Erich Fromm. I appreciated it at the time, although I have to admit much of it went over my head. It's one of those books that is so deep and insightful I find myself going back to it, every decade or so, to discover yet more deeper layers of meaning. I think perhaps the more you've lived, the more you can appreciate it. In his book, Fromm observes that most individuals share a deep-rooted fear of loneliness – of 'separateness' – a sense of being 'alone in the universe', or 'separate from nature'. It's a nagging fear which Fromm asserts is at the root of all our problems. These ideas resonated with me, because adolescence is a time when we naturally become conscious not only of our independence but also of our feelings of separateness; that separate existence from our parents, from other people, from the world itself. As children, we are born with an innate sense of belonging; we feel that connection with Mother and with Nature. We marvel and delight in the world around us, we experience everything as an extension of our very 'self'. It is a state of grace. And then, at some point in our growth, there's a break. A rupture. We are no longer umbilically bound to Nature, we do not feel 'at one' with the world or with ourselves, for that matter. Instead, we become self-conscious, locked out of the Garden of Eden, overwhelmed by a horrifying awareness that we are quite alone. Some people never find their way back. The lonely space inside seems to grow and spread, until that's all there is . . . And sometimes the crisis pushes us on, to go deeper within ourselves, trying to reconnect with that original state of grace, to find our way home – back to each other, back to Nature, and back to God.

At sixteen, however, I was nowhere near finding my way home. Dragging my shyness around with me like Marley's ghost dragging his chains, I began filming *Summer Magic*. To combat my crippling insecurity I'd try to be twice as extrovert and extravagant, which would work for a while but it was difficult to keep it up for long periods, especially when other girls my age were around. I'd start to withdraw into myself like a telescope.

It didn't affect my acting too much, which was a relief. In fact, I discovered that to be able to disappear and become someone else entirely was actually quite therapeutic. It was the chatty times sitting around on the set between takes I found difficult. I'd quickly run out of things to say and then lapse into painful silence. Then there was the question of my physical appearance. I was terribly worried that Walt would be disappointed with me. It's well known that the camera puts pounds on to your face anyway, so I really didn't stand a chance. Staying on the diet was agony. Breakfasts of stewed prunes and black coffee, and then, when all my instincts were screaming to get at the fries and cheesecake in the studio canteen, my lunch consisted of half a melon and a scoop of cottage cheese.

Some of the cast I already knew, like Dorothy McGuire who

was playing my mother. She had been in Tobago with Daddy on *Swiss Family Robinson*, which now seemed like a lifetime ago. It was great to be able to get to know her a little better. She was sweet, gentle and calm – nothing seemed to ruffle her enviable composure. She had this strange, metaphysical little smile. I tried to emulate her serenity, but without much success, and I probably just managed to look like the village idiot.

Burl Ives was a force to be reckoned with. A heavyweight thespian in every sense, in 1962 he was at the zenith of his career. Two years earlier he'd won the Oscar for *The Big Country* with Gregory Peck, not to mention his performance as 'Big Daddy' in *Cat on a Hot Tin Roof* – and he was still Big Daddy to me. Burl was an enormous bear of a man, charming and completely unflappable. He'd sit all day on set in his canvas chair, with a cold-box full of root beers by his side, which he'd consume throughout the day.

My little redhead brother was played by Eddie Hodges, another child actor who'd grown up in the business, starting to perform at the age of three. By the time I met him, he'd already clocked up years of experience in film and TV. He'd even had a *Billboard* hit with 'I'm Gonna Knock On Your Door'. Eddie was incredibly talented. He could sing, play the piano, the banjo, the guitar. He was a born entertainer and still only fifteen.

I did manage to make friends with Deborah Walley, who was lovely and so beautiful. The following year she and her husband John Ashley spent a very white Christmas with us at the farm. We all got snowed in so badly they couldn't leave – the only way out was on the toboggan. Deborah was pregnant at the time, but I remember her hurtling down a very steep hill at ninety miles an hour without even batting an eye!

But what I remember most about *Summer Magic* was being dogged by crippling shyness, which felt like it had me in a vice. It was unpredictable, like a hideous creature from the deep. Camouflaged, it would wait for me and then strike without warning, wrap its tentacles around me and drag me down into the darkness. Then, inexplicably, I'd be released and suddenly find myself back among the living, thrashing around and gasping for air. The bewildering thing about it all was that there didn't seem to be any real reason for its appearance or disappearance. It was just random misery. I took solace in the fact that it didn't last for ever. It gave me a measure of hope; a feeling that maybe all was not entirely lost and that one day I might rejoin the human race.

Before we finished the shoot, adding to my worries and dire imaginings, October was the time of the Cuban Missile Crisis. To think that President Kennedy and President Khrushchev were engaged in a game of nuclear brinkmanship, in which the stakes were so apocalyptic, was simply terrifying. For those weeks in October 1962, before Khrushchev mercifully backed down, most of the planet was on tenterhooks, unsure if the world would still be there when we woke up in the morning. It was as close to another world war as we had come since September 1939.

War or no war, life goes on – and boys and girls will always want to hook up. One night I was invited to a seventeenth birthday party for Kirk Douglas's son, Michael. Most of the evening is a bit of a haze, to be honest. I'd forgotten it even happened until I recently saw a photo of Michael and me dancing the Twist, which was the new dance craze at the time. I remember that at one point Paul Newman arrived wearing a brown-paper bag on his right arm. He'd just been thrown off his motorbike while turning a corner and had put his hand out to save himself from falling, making a terrible mess of himself. We were all allowed to have a look in the bag to see what his hand looked like. It was very odd and not at all pretty.

Also around this time, a big Hollywood producer called Mike Francovich invited my parents and me to accompany him to Las Vegas to see Frank Sinatra's opening night at the Sands Hotel. Mike was a charming, gregarious and extremely generous man who liked to make a splash. So one Friday night, after filming

Summer Magic, I was picked up at the studio and driven to the airport where a party was already getting started on his private plane. Mike's wife, the actress Binnie Barnes, was there, and among our group was also the beautiful red-haired actress Samantha Eggar. We flew into the night and out over the desert. It was a surreal experience having a party in the air! I looked out through my little porthole into the clear starlit heavens and saw what appeared to be a mass of shimmering jewels floating in the middle of black space.

When we arrived at the Sands, Las Vegas, we found our rooms were vast, and on everyone's dressing table was a $100 stack of casino chips, courtesy of our generous host. The hotel was packed with so many people that you could hardly move. All the gaming tables were jammed. Bizarrely, the very first slot machine my mother walked past she put in one of her $1 chips and hit the jackpot!

Our party were sitting at a table at the foot of the stage, so close that I gazed up Ol' Blue Eyes' nose all night.

Frank was everything I imagined: debonair and witty, his voice so beautifully eloquent and captivating, and so *familiar*. I could hardly believe he was real. He sang 'Nancy With the Laughing Face' to his ex-wife Nancy, who was sitting with us at our table. I thought it was madly romantic, though the song was probably written more with his daughter Nancy in mind.

★

Thanks to meeting Frank, I finally met the sender of those letters I received in Switzerland – Frank Sinatra Jnr – who turned out to be exactly who he said he was. Frank Jnr was very sweet and good-natured and when we got back to Hollywood he took me out a couple of times. The first time, my mother came too. Frank Jnr seemed old for his years, although he was only a couple of years older than me. He appeared to be trying to emulate his father, whom he clearly worshipped. He told me he felt it was his responsibility to dedicate his whole life to extending his father's memory and his legacy to the world, by constantly performing his songs. He said, 'Sinatra would live on – in his son.' He took life, and I think himself, very seriously. I suspect that being the son of such a titan was not easy. Frank Jnr was a talented musician in his own right, he played the piano and sang really well, and his voice was pleasant, but it wasn't Frank's – and that was the problem.

The second time we went out he took me to Sammy Davis Jnr's opening night at the famous Cocoanut Grove club at the Ambassador Hotel. It was a huge hotel, redolent of classic Hollywood glamour, opened in 1921. Originally surrounded by fragrant orange groves with thirty separate little cottages, not unlike the Garden of Allah, for years it had been one of the epicentres of old Hollywood; stars like Pola Negri lived there, and Zelda and F. Scott Fitzgerald used to stay for long periods of time. Once, before they left, they set fire to all the furniture in their suite with the bill for the room left on the top! Marion Davies once famously rode her horse through the lobby to amuse her lover William Randolph Hearst.

By the time I went there in the 1960s Cocoanut Grove was a favourite haunt of the Rat Pack, who all appeared regularly. Inside, it was like being in a Moorish palace. Everything glittered, Arabian chandeliers threw kaleidoscopic light on to the walls of real palm trees that surrounded the room. Stuffed monkeys with electrified amber eyes hung from the branches. The ceiling was painted as blue as the night, with hundreds of little stars that twinkled down on the diners as all the beautiful people danced to the band.

Sammy Davis Jnr was at that time married to May Britt, a tall, beautiful Swedish blonde, and they clearly adored one another. That night, after he had electrified the Grove with his performance, we were invited back to Sammy's. There was a very noisy party going on, as apparently there was every night, which would last till dawn. At some point, Sammy suddenly disappeared. His wife became rather alarmed and insisted we all start looking for him. Sammy was eventually found, fast asleep under the grand piano.

Nowadays performers seem to be so much more abstemious, keeping in mind tomorrow's 4 a.m. wake-up call to go to work, but back then people seemed to party like there *was* no tomorrow!

Some years later, the Ambassador Hotel became infamous for very different reasons. On 5 June 1968 Robert Kennedy gave his victory speech to a packed audience of ecstatic followers after winning the Californian Democratic Primary. For the second time, I watched another Kennedy on television; he was a ray of hope for so many people who felt confident the young senator would go on to win the Presidency, end the Vietnam war and help heal their divided and traumatised nation after the shooting of Martin Luther King Jnr. But history had other plans for America. As Bobby Kennedy was guided out of the hotel through the crowded kitchens, he too was tragically assassinated. After that devastating event nothing was ever the same again. The heart seemed to have left the place. The times were changing and the area went into decline. The Cocoanut Grove, with all its ghosts, eventually disappeared, as did the Ambassador itself, gradually falling into disrepair and decay before finally being demolished.

★

For some months, Disney and the Rank Organisation had been cooking up the idea of a joint Mills family tour of the Far East. My father was scheduled to promote *Tiara Tahiti*, his new (and not very good) film with James Mason, and Disney wanted to send me off to promote *In Search of the Castaways*. Both studios saw an opportunity to generate double the publicity heat – with a father-and-daughter act working the press junkets – while allowing them to split the considerable promotional costs. So, after I finished *Summer Magic*, my parents and I embarked upon a tour that would take us to Hawaii, Japan, Hong Kong, Singapore, Malaysia and India.

We travelled in great comfort and style, stopping off to visit so many great cities of the Far East, packing in press conferences, TV and radio promotion and photoshoots; in the evening we were wined and dined and entertained every night for three weeks.

Everywhere we went, there were hordes of people and cameras and flowers: orchids and more orchids. Honolulu was our first destination. We were met by a terrific press reception, and were then taken to a luau – a Hawaiian banquet – where what seemed like hundreds of members of an American package tour, largely female, were watching a floor show and being intermittently forced to shout '*Aloha!*'.

From Hawaii we flew to Japan. As we touched down at Tokyo's Haneda airport, there were hundreds of excited people standing by the terminal, waiting expectedly for someone. I turned to Mummy. 'Hey, looks like there's someone important on our plane . . .' It turned out the crowds were for us!

This was my first experience of fan power – *en masse*. I'd never seen anything like it. A throng of smiling faces, waving flags and posters with my face on them, anxiously calling my name, which they couldn't quite pronounce. It was really sweet. If you closed your eyes it sounded like 'Hairy Mews!' As my journal recorded, it was as surreal as it was thrilling:

Past flashing cameras, we were whirled through customs and into a private room filled with yet more eyes and clicking cameras, geisha girls and bunches of flowers and silence – no questions, just click, click, click. Outside the room there seemed to be millions of tiny little birds, more shuttering cameras and shuffling feet and grasping hands that pushed and snatched and stamped on our shoes and tore at our clothes. It was an incredible welcome, but a little alarming. All the while, these totally silent press photographers were running backwards at great speed, flashing and snapping at us. At one point there was such a chaotic crush of fans trying to get at us for autographs, the security guards had to push us rather violently into an elevator and I lost one of my shoes. It was never found. Collapsed into the car – off to the

Imperial Hotel still with a trail of cameras after us – the suite was so jammed full of flowers, there was no room to put anything. Sank into bed at 4 a.m. Honolulu time.

After a whirlwind of interviews and appearances in Tokyo, we travelled to Yokohama, Kamakura and the beautiful city of Kyoto, where despite the crazy schedule, my father managed to find the time for his first Japanese massage, which he was very excited about. This massage was to be performed by a beautiful little geisha, so my mother and I were ordered to go shopping and told not to return for at least two hours.

When we eventually returned to the suite we found Daddy, greasy and shattered, his hair all over the place.

'How was the geisha?' I asked.

'That was no geisha . . .' he whimpered. 'That was a Sumo wrestler!'

And then on to Hong Kong. Mummy hadn't been back there since she was nineteen, and understandably she found the whole experience quite overwhelming. The first sight of it was instantly familiar, as though she'd left it yesterday. So many remembered faces, and many long since lost, stared at her from such happy places as the Star Ferry and the Hong Kong Club – where, as a child, she'd watched her father in uniform on Armistice Day – and Government House, memories of the crowds waiting to sign the visitors book, evening dresses and decorations, waiting to go to the ball with soldiers and sailors and old friends.

The Repulse Bay Hotel was the same: hot sun and blinds; poinsettias on the lawns standing like guards around the children and *amahs* that still played there, just as she once had.

So many old friends appeared everywhere we went – at the Red Cross Ball, one day at the Hong Kong races, at dinner with the Ambassador, or the opening night of *Tiara Tahiti*, Mummy spent hours regaling us with stories about the old days.

One day we boarded the Tai Lon ferry for Macau, her

childhood home. Mummy was almost sick with excitement and anticipation. It was a beautiful pearly afternoon as we steamed slowly through the islands – Castle Peak, the old Leper's Island, and Nine Islands in the late-afternoon sun. We sailed through the narrow straits crammed with junks and much shouting and yelling in Chinese, while Daddy took photographs with furious speed.

We arrived in the Bay of Macau at sunset and were met by the British Consul and a group of people with flowers and cameras. What a way to return for that small, serious-faced girl with the long red hair who so often trod these very gangways. We stayed one evening at the Reyip Hotel on Praya Grande. It was nice and clean with mosquito nets, always a nostalgic thing for her; and then in the twilight, which disappears so quickly in Macau, we tiptoed with excitement over those same old cobbles to find the house she had grown up in. It was a pilgrimage of sorts and she could hardly keep the tears from rolling down her face. All the old landmarks were there, just as she remembered them forty years ago – the Fort, the Bella Vista Hotel, and behind it, set back on a quiet road behind a high wall, the old house stood among her mother's hundreds of flowers. To her disappointment, however, a Communist building had taken its place behind the wall, and nothing of her old house remained except the servants' quarters. Even the steps to the road had disappeared, although we could see the traces of where they had been. Mummy had to content herself with just being there in that familiar place again as the memories came rushing in. She remembered being led to that spot on her ninth birthday, to find her father waiting for her with a pony. She closed her eyes, brushing the wall gently with her fingers, and imagined hearing voices and the laughter of small children playing on the other side. In her mind, the door in the wall stood open, and she climbed the steep stone steps again, up to the wide sunlit terrace, and it was all as she remembered. Her mother's flowers in their blue porcelain pots, pots everywhere, daisy pots, big round glazed Chinese tubs, every kind of chrysanthemum, the white roses climbing over the old house, the wooden shutters all open to catch the breeze, and the sound of her parents' voices came to her, carried on the wind.

The days we spent in Hong Kong were like a flashback to the last vestiges of the Empire, the lost world of Mummy's childhood. It was all very glamorous and intoxicating but, while we rubbed shoulders with the social elite, Daddy never felt like 'one of them'. My father had rather old-fashioned views on actors and their status in society – which I think I inherited. Even after my father had been awarded a knighthood, he never considered himself 'respectable'. His generation revered the acting *profession* rather than actors themselves. Actors were craftsmen – and it should be a humble profession. Put in perspective, when my father began acting it was only forty years since the great Sir Henry Irving had been knighted. Irving was a huge star on both sides of the Atlantic, the first British actor ever to be awarded such an honour – but that was only in 1895. So, as far as Daddy's generation were concerned, even if you were dining with the Queen Mother at Clarence House, an actor's role was to entertain, tell a few jokes, play the piano and go home. That's a little how it felt in Hong Kong. We were pampered and applauded, but really actors are only ever the visiting curiosities, the 'jesters' – and we were expected to sing for our supper.

One evening during that stay in Hong Kong I was informed that an escort would be taking me to the Red Cross Ball at one of the grand hotels. It was, for all intents and purposes, a blind date. I was thrown into a panic. 'Oh God!' I thought. 'Who is he? What will I talk to him about? What if he's disappointed? He will be disappointed, he's *bound* to be – Oh God!'

I considered making some excuse and hiding in my hotel room, but eventually my curiosity and sense of obligation got the better of me and I just about managed to get dressed and ready in time for the moment the concierge rang to say a gentleman was

waiting in the lobby. Dreading the whole thing, my heart pounding, I went downstairs where I was confronted by a tall, slim
figure who unfolded himself out of a deep armchair, and as he
walked towards me time slowed, strains of the Warsaw Concerto
began playing in my mind, his pale hair drifted over blue eyes . . .
he smiled . . . and my shyness slipped away. Suddenly, it was all *so
easy*. I felt like a woman reprieved!

For the next few glorious days I was free and enjoyed my first
romance. It was all very innocent. We went to dinner, we danced
and laughed, he took me water skiing from his family's beautiful
yacht moored in the harbour, and he was charming and atten-
tive. The whole experience was incredibly romantic. It was like a
dream and the huge yellow moon shining down over the Repulse
Bay Hotel wasn't wasted.

I could have lost my heart but I sensed from the beginning
that this was a 'time out of time', a sort of fantasy, and I was
much more cautious about losing my heart in real life – which
this was definitely not. All the same, I didn't want to leave. That
was the problem. I was always leaving somewhere.

Our final destination was India. After an insanely chaotic press
junket in Delhi we were invited to Jaipur in Rajasthan – 'The Pink
City' – to stay with the Maharaja. Jaipur was the most breathtaking
place I had ever seen. India is an experience that everyone should
have, at least once in their lives. We were lucky enough to stay in
the royal palace as guests of Maharaja Jai Singh and his exquisite
wife Aisha, the Maharani, both of whom were friends of my parents
from polo tournaments back in England. We were given rooms at
Rambagh Palace, one of the royal family's official residences, which
had been converted into a luxury hotel. On the first morning, I
was awoken by the sounds of a terrible riot going on outside; the
noise was deafening, all the wooden shutters in the palace were
being violently banged and slammed, accompanied by murderous
screams and shrieks. Fearing for my life, I gingerly opened my door

and peered nervously through the tiny gap, expecting to see furious hordes brandishing clubs, with the Maharaja's royal head stuck on a pole ... Instead, I saw armies of furious monkeys leaping about trying to dismantle the hotel! Apparently this was all quite normal goings-on before breakfast.

Queen Beatrice of The Netherlands was also staying as a guest of the Maharaja – and we were swept up into all the grand state occasions. I couldn't get over the beauty of everything. We went to glittering cocktail parties, all the women draped in exquisite saris. There was dinner in the palace for thirty people, with a servant in white gloves standing behind every chair. We rode on gorgeously caparisoned elephants around a twelfth-century palace. The whole experience was unreal and magical. I was back in time, hundreds of years, somewhere between the decline of the Rajput Empire and E.M. Forster. I began to feel like Miss Quested in *A Passage to India*. One night we gathered on the terrace at the Maharaja's hunting lodge, which was built by the side of a lake that reflected the moonlight. Our glasses brimming with champagne, we stared down into a little clearing where, under a single light, a small sacrificial buffalo was tethered to a stake – left as bait for a wild tiger. As the royal musicians played and conversation continued, we waited for a tiger to come and tear his captive prey to pieces. The whole scene was so incongruous; all these gorgeously dressed, bejewelled people standing there under the moon, waiting for something so bloodthirsty to happen. Mercifully for the buffalo – and for me – the tiger was too smart to be caught that night. Returning to my quarters, I exhaled a huge sigh of relief. I wouldn't have lasted long in the Raj.

It wasn't until this tour of the Far East, at the age of sixteen, that I really appreciated the international reach and scale of my celebrity. Up until then it had always felt very contained – at school, at home, at work. I'd never had any opportunity to experience the shockwaves of my film career but on that tour I got to see it all up close: the fame, the success, the craziness and screaming fans. I told myself I didn't take it seriously, that it hadn't changed me . . . but I was kidding myself. In reality, I was becoming increasingly confused about who the real 'self' was.

After exchanging a few letters with the boy in Hong Kong, the correspondence withered and died. The moment had passed. Just as I intuited at the time, it was a holiday romance and he belonged to another time and a very different reality, which I would never be a part of. From Hong Kong to Jaipur, I saw the remains of a society that, for better or for worse, still clung to old ideas of Empire. Theirs was a world that tended to look to the past for its identity, whereas I was very much in the present, looking hesitantly into an unknown future – full of surprises, marvels and unspeakable horrors.

CHAPTER EIGHT

The Witch's Stick

Oh God! If you exist, where are you?
                              – Journal entry, 22 November 1963

For some time Daddy had been having a recurring dream about being back at The Wick. He would be standing alone at his bedroom window in the old house, gazing westwards from the top of Richmond Hill, looking down across Petersham Meadows and the Thames beyond it; the sky was a clear blue and he could see as far as Windsor Castle. The Wick had been our family home for almost ten years and so many of my early memories were rooted there. It was an exceptionally beautiful small Georgian mansion, built in 1775 by the young Scottish architect Robert Mylne, who had risen to some prominence in society after winning a competition to design the original Blackfriars Bridge. He was later commissioned by the esteemed Lady St Aubyn to build her a little mansion on Richmond Hill where she could enjoy one of the finest views in the country. Lady St Aubyn named her house The Wick but it was not 'Georgian' in the traditional English sense. Mylne was more influenced by French neoclassical design and all of the rooms overlooking the garden were elliptical with French windows, festooned with twisting vines of wisteria that traced their way throughout the delicate wrought-iron balconies. The garden itself was on three levels, with a gazebo at the bottom, behind which was a stable yard, two garages, the gardener's cottage and a large vegetable garden.

It was an unforgettable house – and my mother had never been able to quite let it go. From the very beginning she had always felt a deep connection to The Wick. There was something there, a presence that she felt attuned to. Not in a dark or haunted way, although there was supposed to be a ghost – the Lady St Aubyn herself was supposed to walk up and down the wide staircase. Mummy never saw it but others said they did; some claimed to have heard a rustling like dry leaves or that of a woman in evening dress passing by. The cleaner once swore blind that a lady in a long grey cloak walked past as she was polishing the banisters. She thought it was someone on their way to see my mother and didn't bother to look up. The Wick had been Mummy's nest and her ivory tower. There she felt safe and in touch with the spirits – the 'tailors', as she called them: muses that gave her ideas for stories and inspired her to write. Much as she loved the farm, it was never really where she wanted to be. It was a creaky old farmhouse full of children and muddy dogs. It would never be elegant, although she tried to make it so. On one occasion she attempted to create a rose garden by stealing part of an adjacent field. I remember the men digging the main rose bed. It was raining and terribly dreary and the bed was still just a muddy hole. I caught Mummy at the drawing-room window, staring out at the sight of it, when she suddenly burst into tears. 'It's just a bloody grave,' she sobbed. We all laughed and made light of it, but I saw an anxious look in my father's eyes as he hugged her. Not only did he want her to be happy – he felt the happiness of the whole family depended on it. Mummy could be incredibly cynical and her caustic wit could cut anyone to ribbons, but she was a romantic at heart and tended to live in her thoughts, some place imagined or somewhere in the past. Just as she idealised her childhood in Macau, she romanticised the old days at The

Wick as a time of near perfect happiness. Life made sense and the future looked rosy. Her children were still young and she was a woman in her prime – a happy and successful writer at the height of her powers.

For a short while, in the early days, my parents had managed to keep both The Wick and the farm, but the cost of maintaining two houses almost destroyed them in the late 1950s when Daddy's career went through a very worrying dry spell. Before he managed to bounce back with *The Colditz Story* – which was a huge hit and essentially restarted his career – our family accountant, Stanley Passmore, told them, in no uncertain terms, that they must choose between selling a house or going bust. I believe my mother agreed to sell The Wick for Daddy's sake. She thought he would be happier at the farm and that the children would be nourished by the freedom of the countryside.

Above the mantelpiece in the drawing room of The Wick lay a peculiar-looking antique walking stick made of one single piece of twisted crystal – it was called 'The Witch's Stick'. This strange curiosity had been left there by the previous owners – and by the owners before them. No one was sure how old it was, some even said it had been there since the days of Lady St Aubyn. The legend was that the Witch's Stick was supposed to remain there on the mantelpiece in The Wick and be passed on to every new owner. But when Mummy left The Wick she did something very naughty. She took the Witch's Stick with her and kept it at the farm. Whether it was her gothic imagination or a supernatural power emanating from the crystal wand, my mother was never able entirely to let go of that house and she dwelled on it with a sense of gloomy regret. She may have moved to the countryside but her heart remained at The Wick.

In those days, before motorways arrived and changed everything, it wasn't so quick and easy to drive down to the farm; the roads were narrow and winding, the drive was long. Mummy found the whole thing tedious and complained constantly throughout the entire journey, especially in winter; she hated the countryside in winter. Adding to her increasing ennui, the truth was that running the farm had also become an enormous and a very expensive responsibility. There's an old saying in the country: 'Unless you're prepared to be a stick-and-dog farmer, keeping an eye on things, you'll never make any money.' This turned out to be so true. Soon all Daddy's money was going into running the 400-acre farm. He couldn't be a hands-on farmer and a full-time actor as well.

It was a dilemma that he mostly kept to himself.

By the time we returned from our glamorous Far Eastern tour it was November. The English countryside seemed so stark and still, just a few of summer's old leaves still clinging on, but the farm wasn't the same. There were empty spaces: Bunchy had left, she was living in London, happily married; Johnny was still locked away at boarding school, and my pony Annabelle had died. The vet had put her down – 'Laminitis,' he said. 'Too much rich grass.'

It seemed like every time I went away, one of my darling companions would die. I went and visited her empty stable. Her old halter hanging on a hook seemed to be waiting for me to take it down and go in search of her. I sat on a gate and stared out across the fields. I imagined I saw her swinging slowly towards me through the wet grass, a beloved phantom, shaking her head to rid herself of those damn flies. My heart ached; I had let her down. If I had been at home, maybe she wouldn't have died? I felt so guilty.

She was buried beside Hamlet under the poplar tree.

I wandered miserably back to the house. It was starting to rain. Mummy and Bond the gardener tramped across the muddy lawn in their Wellington boots, talking loudly about the herbaceous border, their voices breaking into my reverie. So many thoughts, crowding my mind. Annabelle here for months with no one riding her while I was away. Thoughts of Jaipur. Of swallows in an evening sky. Of Hong Kong – and of that boy. It all seemed like a dream now.

Looking back on my journal, I can observe that, like my mother before me, I had aligned myself utterly with the cause of the incurable romantic; each page a testimony to angst, passion and joy:

Sometimes I wake up in the morning and just feel so happy and glad that I exist. To feel the fresh air on my face, to savour all the different morning smells, just to BE; feeling such gratitude . . .

If one loses one's enthusiasm for life, that must be the end. One must be madly in love with everything, or you'll pass over something without realising its value . . . we must savour every moment, because you can never recapture it, never go back. The river can't change its course, it has to carry on to the sea . . .

One of the worst things about getting older must be remorse . . . try to be conscious of every mercurial moment so it won't be so easy to let it all slip through your hands into a thousand tiny fragments of shining silver life.

I'm really happy when I'm not in despair!

I was reading a lot during that time, especially poetry and historical novels. Anya Seton's book *Katherine* about the relationship between Katherine Swynford and John of Gaunt stirred me. I went to the movies and became deeply impressed by Jules Dassin's *Phaedra* starring Melina Mercouri and Anthony Perkins. It wasn't just the story of a great passion that affected me, it was the acting too; I wanted to be Melina Mercouri; she was so powerful and beautiful – and so truthful. She became my icon.

Eventually, Johnny came marching home, dragging his trunk from school, and we all regrouped for Christmas. None of us had any idea that it would be the last holiday we would celebrate at the farm.

★

One of Daddy's great friends was the filmmaker Ronald Neame, with whom he had worked on so many British pictures, often alongside David Lean, including the naval classic *In Which We Serve* (1942), *Great Expectations* (1946), and also *Tunes of Glory* (1960) with Alec Guinness, which my father was especially proud of. Around the time I was filming *Summer Magic*, Ronnie Neame and the Hollywood producer Ross Hunter approached my father to star alongside Deborah Kerr and Dame Edith Evans in a film adaptation of Enid Bagnold's stage play *The Chalk Garden*, which had been a great success on Broadway and the West End. They also enquired whether I might be available to play the role of Laurel, the young lead; an edgy, dysfunctional teenager, hell bent on destroying the lives of people around her – in many ways a thoroughly unlikeable character. However, in the hands of a great writer like Enid Bagnold she was interesting and complex and an exciting challenge for any young actress. Nevertheless, I wondered what Walt would have to say.

The Chalk Garden is set in Sussex, close to the Downs near the white cliffs at Beachy Head, where the grand Mrs St Maugham (played by Dame Edith) lives in a large house by the sea with a big garden where nothing grows, as the soil is chalky and mal-nourished – symbolic of the relationships in the house.

The old lady is looking for a tutor for her granddaughter, Laurel. The job is given to a Miss Madrigal, played by Deborah Kerr, who is the only candidate not to be frightened away by the young child's challenging and disrespectful attitude.

Laurel has been abandoned by her mother and lost all trust in the adult world, becoming emotionally and physically destructive. She immediately regards Miss Madrigal as a threat and sets out to expose her and dig up any skeletons she can about this myste-rious, enigmatic woman.

Walt had already vetoed *Exodus*, *The Children's Hour* and *Lolita* on the grounds that they were inappropriate for various reasons, mostly concerning sex. However, Laurel in *The Chalk Garden*, despite being unpleasant, is ultimately sympathetic and redeems herself by the end of the film with the help of Miss Madrigal.

Perhaps it was because my father was also starring, or maybe Walt just could not find it in his heart to say 'no' for a fourth time. Whatever the reason, I was allowed to play Laurel and take on the most dramatic and demanding role of my career to date.

Once I got the role, I became determined to live up to it. I wanted to prove to myself – and to other people – that I could do it. I desperately wanted to become a better actress, to stretch myself, and by now I was much more aware of my responsibility as a lead actor, of people's expectations, of the faith that the producers had put in me, and not least of all the enormous amounts of money involved. I no longer felt like the performing child who relied on the experienced actors and actresses to carry the film. I realised that I also carried my share.

But I was excited rather than overwhelmed by all this, and also really happy to be working with my father again. I loved going to work with him in the morning, meeting up for lunch, going over our lines. We always had fun and he was such a generous actor, he made it all seem so easy. The same was true of Deborah Kerr, whom I immediately fell in love with. I had enjoyed so many of her films, like *Black Narcissus* and *From Here to Eternity*, and her Mrs Anna in *The King and I* (a role which I was to play many years in the future, much inspired by her). I thought Deborah was wonderful, I couldn't imagine her doing anything that wasn't elegant. She had so much natural grace and composure, but was also great fun to be with. She was a beautiful person.

I celebrated my seventeenth birthday while shooting the film. In the make-up room that morning Dame Edith gave me a beautiful antique green opal ring.

'It was given to me when I was your age, by a boy that I loved very much,' she explained.

I was thrilled. 'Oh thank you, it's beautiful, I shall treasure it always.'

'It's just a little gift.' She smiled gently.

'But it was yours, Dame Edith!' I was so touched by it.

'Oh, come now,' she replied. 'At work I'm *Dame Edith* but at home . . . I'm just an old trout!'

Dame Edith was no old trout, not by any stretch of the imagination. She was a *grande dame* in every sense, and a legendary actress. Unfortunately, I was too young to have seen her when she played all the fabled Shakespearean roles and all the great roles of Shaw, Sheridan, Congreve and Christopher Fry, but I would encourage everyone to see her film portrayal of Lady Bracknell in *The Importance of Being Earnest* and to experience her inimitable delivery of . . .

'*A handbaaag?!*'

Dame Edith's reading of that line has lived on in our collective memory ever since. It remains a challenge to every actress who has subsequently played that part, and probably always will.

Ronnie Neame's shoot for *The Chalk Garden* proceeded happily and efficiently, which is not surprising since Ronnie was a stalwart British filmmaker from the pre-war era, when every second and every penny was made to count. I enjoyed the filming. It was a privilege to work with such fine actors and I came away from the experience feeling that I had made a good account of myself and done my best.

After we returned from filming *The Chalk Garden*, something totally unexpected happened. My parents had been invited to lunch with friends of theirs, Paul and Gaby Bowman – the couple who had bought The Wick from them seven years before. Up to that point they had studiously avoided driving anywhere near the house. Mummy found it all too painful seeing The Wick again, now that it belonged to someone else. But for some reason, they couldn't turn this invitation down. 'Let's just go and lay the ghost,' my father said – and so they did. It was a strange experience for them. My mother described it as 'agony', walking around the house, filled with so many memories. It looked just the same, it was so beautiful, and my father was silently cursing himself for ever having been so stupid as to sell it.

At lunch my father asked the new inhabitants of The Wick, probably through gritted teeth, if they were both happy and enjoying living there. My mother noticed there was a slight pause . . . her first thought was that they must be getting divorced. However, this was not the case. Paul and Gaby announced that, much as they loved the house, they were going to have to sell it and move back into London.

Before the meal had ended my father had bought back The Wick.

When they came home and I heard about it, I couldn't believe it. 'I know, I know, it's totally insane,' Daddy admitted, raising a glass of Famous Grouse. 'We haven't even sold the farm or the flat in London! I've got a huge overdraft and . . . Mummy and I couldn't be happier!' It was typical of him, he was irrepressible and felt that anything which might make Mummy happier was the right thing to do. 'Happy wife, happy life,' as the saying goes – I'm sure he believed that. Even though life at the farm had been wonderful, he felt it had run its course. The kids were starting to fly the nest and Daddy himself wanted to move into another 'phase', only this time they were stepping backwards – in order to go forwards. Something about it didn't feel quite right to me. Daddy was an eternal optimist, but his cup-half-full view of life, which made him such a darling, was also a symptom of his innate reluctance to confront what you might call life's thornier emotional realities. I don't judge him for this. He was the quintessential Englishman, after all, raised by a typically strict and reserved Edwardian father. Daddy was half Peter Pan, half stiff-upper-lip; he wanted everyone to be happy – even if it meant trying to hold back Time.

An example of this was the naming of our dog Hamlet, who was actually the second spaniel they had named after the Prince of Denmark. Their first Hamlet had been run over when we were all on a family holiday in Woolacombe, North Devon, so Daddy went and bought another cocker spaniel – and then another. Each new puppy would be named Hamlet, as if they all became the spirit of one dog. By the end, there'd been five Hamlets in all.

Sometimes, if you're lucky, you make a friend for life when you're very young. The previous year I had been invited to lunch with some of my parents' friends. I was told their son Andrew had seen *Tiger Bay* and wanted to meet me. I went along, somewhat dubiously, to their house in Chelsea. I was always worried that people had very different expectations of me – that the reality walking through their door would be a terrible disappointment. But as it turned out, the relaxed and charming lunch party would prove to be an exception and this chance meeting would become one of the most significant and enduring friendships of my life; one that would survive through all its vicissitudes.

It began as an innocent correspondence when I was in Switzerland. Andrew, like my brother, was imprisoned in a boarding school and he sent me funny letters with eccentric little drawings of his life at Harrow. Not only was it exciting to get letters from a boy, but he cheered me up and made me laugh.

Andrew's mother was the impossibly glamorous actress and *chanteuse* Judy Campbell – a stage siren celebrated for being, among other things, the first to sing and popularise the wartime classic 'A Nightingale Sang in Berkeley Square'. Andrew's father, Lt Commander David Birkin, was in the Royal Navy and had been decorated after the war for running espionage operations across the English Channel, smuggling secret agents back and forth with the French Resistance, right under the Nazis' noses, which sounded incredibly dangerous and heroic. I was fascinated by the Birkin family. They were all totally unique. I had never encountered anyone quite like them and I was instantly smitten. They were bright, intelligent, unusually attractive, interesting people. They never stopped talking – about everything: the theatre, the arts, writers, politics, history, gossip – always talking, always laughing. Judy Campbell was a tremendously animated person, warm and welcoming, interested in everything and everybody, and she embraced people and life unreservedly. She was very striking, with a great mass of dark hair and a marvellously husky voice. Her husband David was quieter and more watchful. I can see him now, standing by the long window, a tall, thin figure holding a glass of white wine in his hand with his kind, sweet smile. He was also a very good painter. Then there was the middle Birkin, Andrew's sister Jane: already, at fifteen, she was effortlessly beautiful and irresistible. She gave the impression of perpetual motion, her long brown hair flying around her like the sails of a windmill, with her wide smile and that big lucky gap in her front teeth, just like her mum. She was enchanting and wonderfully eccentric, and would eventually, and not very surprisingly, become a huge star and a national icon in France. Linda, the youngest, with that same wide Birkin smile, coltish arms and legs, was an artist. She was gentle and quieter, and she was also the possessor of a huge and startling sense of humour.

But it was Andrew who fascinated me most of all. A year older than me, he was tall and dark like his mother, with shining blue eyes. His mind was never at rest, his curiosity about life was endless. Trying to keep up with his mind was like trying to track a swallow. His conversation dipped and soared, ideas weaving in and out, with observations and great discoveries about life. He told me about his hopes and ambitions; he wanted to write and make movies and had all sorts of grand and remarkable ideas. Being in his company was a breathtaking experience – and an education.

The Birkins were my 'Bloomsbury Group'. They were all so artistic and they didn't give a damn what the neighbours thought – the neighbours probably adored them all anyway. They wore what they liked, not because it was in or out of fashion. Clothes were flung on chairs and stayed there for days, beds were unmade – and if a few cornflakes from breakfast were still on the table at tea, nobody was bothered. They were bohemian. Compared to them, I felt very middle class. My life at home was tidy and ordered; breakfast, lunch and dinner at the same time every day; coffee served at 11 a.m. in my father's study; and 4 p.m. tea served in a silver tea pot – China tea with lemon for Mummy. All those things were lovely and comforting, but it wasn't the stimulating, controlled chaos of that wonderful old house in Chelsea. The Birkins opened their arms to me so generously and took me into their unusual and marvellous world.

The Sussex farm was put on the market and sold quickly, so after *The Chalk Garden* we began the physically and emotionally exhausting process of packing our lives into boxes for the return to The Wick. The family's uprooting was felt more keenly by Jonathan than by any of us. He didn't harbour any sentimental memories of the old days at The Wick. He'd been so young when we left, and besides, he loved the country and his outdoor life. He saw the farm as his future. But it was not to be.

Eventually, the day arrived. As Mummy's Romany caravan trundled unsteadily down the drive I turned and looked back for one last time at the old place with its wonky black and white beamed walls, the ancient tiled roof hunched down like heavy eyebrows over the mullioned windows that caught the late-afternoon sun. Last 'goodbyes' and we were leaving; leaving all the people on the farm, the animals, our beautiful Guernsey cows, the ducks on the pond, the fields and the bluebell woods, morning mists full of the smell of woodsmoke and autumn leaves. Leaving behind so many memories: reading my comic in the chestnut tree; Johnny on the tractor with Harold as they ploughed the long meadow; Daddy hay-making in the summer with terrible hay fever and laughing as the tears poured down his face; Mummy, standing on a hill with her easel, painting the farm and teaching me how to paint clouds; Juliet's wedding; and Annabelle and Hamlet under the poplar tree.

So many memories, and so many things that you can't take with you.

And then, as if by magic, we were back on Richmond Hill. It was the strangest sensation returning to The Wick. I felt like an interloper, inhabiting neither the past nor the present, like a ghost looking at ghosts. Then there were other moments when I'd suddenly be able to catch a perfect sense of how life used to be when we were last there – especially when I was alone in a room as the day was drawing to a close, before all the lights were turned on, and I could feel the still, waiting quality of the house; a cigarette crushed in an ashtray, a bowl of fragile December roses on the piano, cushions scattered on the red velvet sofa. Was it real or was I, like Daddy, dreaming it all?

So much was exactly the same – the quality of the air, the clear sparkling morning light, the sound of the front doorbell, Hamlet's bark, his claws skittering across the hall. The furniture had all gone back to exactly the same place, Daddy's piano returned to its old marks on the carpet in the drawing room. It was as if the house had been waiting for us to come back.

But of course it wasn't the same . . . because we had changed. You can never go back, that much is certain. And slowly, day by day, this would become more and more apparent.

I often thought about the farm, in a distant sort of a way, as if I were reading about it in a book and knew the place being described. But I settled back into life at The Wick very easily. Bunch's old room was now mine, and my old room next door was turned into a bathroom. I remembered when I was little, how I used to hang sideways out of that window when I was supposed to be having an afternoon rest, and brush my hair wearing all Mummy's jewellery, her ropes of pearls and Granny's jade, imagining that if anyone glanced up they would see The Lady of Shalott.

Life soon resumed its natural rhythms. Once again the house was full of people arriving for dinner parties, the sound of laughter, the clink of glasses and the smell of cigarette smoke drifting out of the drawing room, and the sound of Daddy playing the piano.

One of the first things I did was buy a bicycle for £18 and instantly felt guilty spending so much money on myself. I cycled across Richmond Park to the stables and went riding with Mummy; she'd taught me to ride bareback in that same park when I was five. Her approach to riding was that if you can stay on a very fat little Welsh pony without a saddle, you can stay on anything.

I loved being closer to London and began to enjoy some of the advantages, one of them being the chance to see more of the Birkins. Sometimes I'd see Andrew with his sister Jane. They were both very alike. I loved them both and enjoyed their company, but while there was an attraction between myself and Andrew, it was clear to me that he absolutely adored Jane and that she was his original muse. It was hard not to feel slightly jealous, she was so beautiful, free, and completely unique.

Most of the time though, it was just me and Andrew. We used to talk for hours – and boy, could he talk – but he was also a good listener, which is the basis for a good conversation. We went out together occasionally, but sometimes my fame seemed to amplify the usual awkwardness. My journal for 30 August 1963 reads:

Spent last night scoffing Sole Veronique at the 500 Club with Andrew and two other men, having seen 'The Birds' which was terrifying . . . every time I see or hear a bird I have to stifle an impulse to throw myself face down on the ground.

After the film was over Andrew introduced me to a friend of his Kits Du Maurier [son of Daphne who wrote Rebecca and The Birds] and we all went in Kits' Jag to the 500 Club. I felt a bit swamped at first, being the sole upholder of my sex, and had to retire hurriedly to the loo to powder my nose and put aside my doubts. When I returned Andrew was behaving so oddly. We were supposed to be sitting side by side, yet he was practically at the next table he was so far away. At first it embarrassed me, then it annoyed me, eventually I decided that, for some unknown reason HE was the embarrassed one. I concluded it was one of three things:

1. I had BO

2. He had BO

3. Neither of us had BO. He just didn't want to sit next to me.

After dinner Kits drove us back in his luxurious car with his gram-ophone thing going, and the champagne in my head going round and round and round ... He dropped us off at Andrew's – we'd decided that I'd spend the night with him (his mother was in) – so we went into the sitting room and talked for a while and ate all the grapes I'd bought for his mother. He showed me the garden, although it was pitch dark, and generally rummaged around a bit ... then went back into the sitting room and talked some more. I realised that he was ter-ribly shy of me, and of being near me at first, as if I was some fright-ening insect. I was worried because I thought my dress had something to do with it, being rather low cut ... Anyway, I forgave him for his behaviour at dinner and at last we stopped wandering around the room and he told me about his work, and we discussed our hopes and fears for coming years and – all the time he talked – I watched him; his face is never still, never dead, there's always something moving and running in his brain, his eyes are like quicksilver and one feels he never misses a thing. Sometimes I think he's extremely good look-ing, tall and straight and so young and eager and enthusiastic about life. He looks at everything through the hazy eyes of inexperience, free from disillusionment. His imagination is like Hans Christian Andersen, like a million-hued rainbow, even the grey rains of life are obscured ... I felt a bit sick after two filthy fags he produced, so we went for a walk and got a bit lost and he hugged me in the graveyard because I got frightened when he pretended to be Boris Karloff ... then we listened to more records and it was 5.30! We couldn't go to bed, pointless, I'd wake up looking like a bullfrog so we had cornflakes, and I talked some more until his taxi came for work and off he went leaving me collecting the milk bottles on the doorstep at 7 a.m. in the morning.

Our relationship was as intensely loving as it was innocent, and Andrew became the linchpin of my life. I wanted his interest and approval. He was so clever; he wrote very well himself and he inspired me to read more than just historical novels. I was desperate to learn and to make up for the yawning gaps in my education. I didn't talk to my parents about it; this was my private quest. But I didn't really know where to start.

In September I went back to work for Disney. The Studio was by now having to rethink how I was marketed and presented to audiences. I was no longer the sweet Hollywood pup but a spotty and slightly overweight young woman with breasts. So they devised a lush romantic thriller called *The Moon-Spinners*, to be shot on the island of Crete, which Walt Disney and Bill Anderson felt was the right kind of story for me at this point.

I was first sent to Athens for a few days of publicity with my co-star Peter McEnery, who had already distinguished himself in films and in the theatre, and who, I was slightly taken aback to discover, was charming and very good looking. For the first time I was working on my own without a guardian and in one of the most beautiful and romantic of settings. On the first night Peter and I ran panting up a hill to see the Acropolis, bathed in the light of a full moon. It was like a great immortal, towering over the rabble of history. There was a warm wind blowing, the smell of wild jasmine and the sound of crickets, but it felt like we should whisper . . . I sat down next to Peter . . . but the monster from the deep emerged, an attack of paranoia that rendered me virtually silent. My mind was whirling but I was paralysed.

For the next three days Peter and I were driven around being photographed, among the classical ruins, against towering columns, ancient history piled up all around us – bleached stones and carvings thousands of years old at our feet – and I was incapacitated with shyness. We posed and smiled at each other but remained strangers. It was agony. At one point Peter was sitting in a chair, staring out into the blue Aegean, when I plucked up the courage to ask him what he was thinking about . . .

'I'm riling against fate,' he said sombrely, not looking up.

What was *that* supposed to mean? I could only guess he meant me. I was dumb with shyness. He was obviously regretting ever accepting the part and wishing he was back home in England rehearsing for a play. Here was an experienced theatre actor of twenty-six; I was seventeen and suddenly felt twelve.

With the publicity trip over we relocated to the Minos Beach Hotel on the island of Crete, a single-storey building that looked down a little hill to the sea. Scattered all the way down to the beach were small whitewashed cottages connected by a red-tiled path – this is where most of the actors were staying: Joan Greenwood and her husband André Morell, Eli Wallach and his wife Anne Jackson, Irene Papas, Peter McEnery, Michael Davies (the young boy in the film) and myself. I already knew Joan Greenwood, she had been in a play with my father called *The Uninvited Guest* written by my mother. She was one of the sweetest, cosiest people you could ever wish to meet and also one of the smallest – a tiny little person with the most divine sexy voice and an enormous appetite. She told me that she always kept a snack by her bedside in case she woke up hungry in the middle of the night. It must have been like sleeping beside a little mouse. Joan and André were both wonderful actors with enormous experience. Joan was famous for starring in so many of the classic Ealing Studios comedies like *Whisky Galore!*, *Kind Hearts and Coronets* and *The Man in the White Suit*; she also played Gwendoline Fairfax in *The Importance of Being Earnest* opposite Dame Edith's outrageous Lady Bracknell.

Eli Wallach was, of course, a great stage and screen actor; I knew him from *The Misfits* and *The Magnificent Seven*. He was also one of the founding members of the Actors Studio in New York with Lee Strasberg who was known as 'the father of Method acting'. I had heard about the Actors Studio and how Strasberg had developed the 'Method' system with Konstantin Stanislavski in Moscow, and subsequently with Stella Adler and Sanford Meisner in New York. These were towering figures.

As Tennessee Williams said of Strasberg actors: 'They act from the inside out.' I was intrigued by the whole thing. I had encountered it before in New York when Daddy was doing *Ross*. Two of the boys in the show were Method actors and I had noticed one of them smelling the stage curtains in the wings every night before he went on, with hot tears in his eyes. One night I hesitantly asked him what he was doing. He told me, 'The smell of the curtains reminds me of my dead brother's clothes.'

I suppose it is a bit strange, but pretending to be other people for a living is a very strange job. I did understand the principle of it, the need to tap into an existing memory, an emotional recall, a feeling that he could use in the scene – how he got there wasn't important. I would notice Eli doing strange things too – for instance, if he had to run into shot out of breath, he would literally run around the set a few times to make himself genuinely out of breath instead of just pretending to be. It seemed sensible enough to me, although we all had to stand and wait while Eli pounded around doing his laps!

Eli told me that much of 'the Method' was just fundamental common sense. So many actors through the centuries already used these tricks, and Stanislavski and Strasberg simply illuminated a process. They identified the tools: motivation, emotional recall. They formulated the grammar, if you will, so that actors could be more conscious of their 'process' when building a character. I found it fascinating. However, there were many great actors who had no time for 'the Method', Larry Olivier among them, who considered it indulgent, while Noël Coward said, 'If you must have motivation, think about your pay cheque on Friday.'

Eli was a dear man, warm and relaxed. He laughed a lot and didn't take himself too seriously, but he and his wife Anne were passionate about their work and true devotees of the Actors Studio. Truth be told, I was rather in awe of them. I loved to listen to them talking in the evenings after work in the hotel restaurant, telling their stories, discussing the theatre and laughing uproariously. It was inspiring. I began to realise there was a huge world outside of my own experience of the profession, and subsequently I began seriously to resent not being given the opportunity to work with William Wyler on *The Children's Hour*. Eli talked of how brilliant he was with actors, especially it seemed with women – so many of his female stars ended up giving the performance of their lives and winning Oscars, which they would all attribute to Willie Wyler's inspirational direction. Bette Davis, who worked with him on *Jezebel* and won the Oscar for Best Actress, said Wyler had been the single greatest influence of her career. Hearing all this was a bitter pill to swallow. I was discovering for myself that the director is the most important person on a film set; TV is a medium for writers, theatre belongs to the actor, but films (good ones, anyway) rest on a director's total vision. The visual language of film and the performances of the actors all depend upon this. A good director is worth their weight in gold. In the world of filmmaking, they are God-like.

I asked Eli about Marilyn Monroe and what she was like, as he had made *The Misfits* with her, and he told me she was sweet and lovely but terribly insecure. Marilyn Monroe!? It seemed extraordinary that someone so beautiful and talented could suffer from paralysing insecurity, but on one level I could understand it. The image of a star is never the real person. Eli apparently took Marilyn under his wing, even when she would be hours late on the set, and sometimes not appear at all. He felt it was important that she always knew he was her friend.

Peter McEnery was also quite a formidable actor, who would soon be celebrated for his performance as the stud lodger in

Entertaining Mr Sloane. Even though he was still young, Peter had done lots of films and Shakespeare and he approached our scenes together in the same way that he would rehearse a play – which turned out to be a challenge for me. One evening, he suggested we rehearse the scene we were going to shoot the following day and asked if he could come over to my cottage after supper.

That threw me into a bit of a tizz . . . What did he expect me to do? My approach had always been to read my lines over and over again until they were second nature; I would listen to what I was saying, imagine that I was in that situation – make believe that I *was* 'Nikki Ferris' or whoever – and try to understand and intuit as much as I could. Beyond that, what else did one do? For me, it only became real once I was in front of the camera, on the set, 'blocking' the scene (learning where I was going to stand, whether I was going to get up, or sit down, or pick up a book). The thought of trying to do that in my room at night alone with Peter was worrisome to say the least. And the fact that I had by now developed quite a sizeable crush on him didn't help.

Later that evening Peter arrived at my door. 'Hello,' he said.

'Hello,' I said. An awful pause. 'So what shall we do?' I asked rather inanely.

We were reading a scene where my character 'Nikki' finds Peter's character 'Mark' wounded in a crypt. They don't have much time, because she knows that 'Stratos', Eli Wallach's murderous character, is looking for them.

'Let's just read through the scene first – then we can get it up on its feet,' Peter suggested.

'Sure, OK.' I nodded coolly – but inside I was panicking. 'Get it on its feet!?' Oh dear.

Peter moved the furniture around a bit, pushed the bed up against the wall to make some space, then he got down on the floor and started acting like he was wounded. I'm supposed to find him bleeding and barely conscious, I try to rouse him and bind his wound with my headscarf, so there was lots of business with knapsacks and cotton wool – all quite tricky to do while crawling around on the floor of my room with no props. I was struggling. Peter wanted to 'investigate the text', but all I could do was repeat my lines and pretend to wrap up his arm with a bath towel.

Being there alone with him and making such a pig's ear of the whole thing was absolutely excruciating. I imagined he was thinking, 'What the hell's she doing? This isn't how we rehearse in the theatre!' And it was at that moment I realised that I *had* to go on the stage, if only for my own confidence. I needed to learn the craft of acting. Simply relying on my instincts had been enough when I was a child, but now I had to understand it on a whole new level. I wanted to know how to 'investigate' and intellectualise the process.

There was another small bone of contention when it came to shooting *The Moon-Spinners*: all these very experienced actors from the theatre were accustomed to being able to contribute creatively to the process, but they found the very strict Disney culture of shooting a 'storyboard', which had been created and agreed weeks previously back at the Studios in Burbank, to be a bit of a straitjacket – especially Peter, who often came to the set with his own ideas, which he was never allowed to try because 'it wasn't on the storyboard'.

One day we were shooting miles out of town on a barren hillside, and Peter felt very strongly about some change he wanted to make in the scene. What it was I can't remember, but Jimmy Neilson, the director, flat-out refused, saying that it was impossible without Walt's approval. Peter thought this was ridiculous and dug his heels in, and so did Jimmy – impasse! The only way to resolve it was to wait until everyone woke up in California, ten hours behind, so Jimmy could speak to Walt personally and get his 'OK'.

It was crazy, we spent the whole morning sitting around on

rocks in the blazing sun, trying to find some shade under little wizened olive trees, waiting for Walt to call. Peter was furious and Jimmy was terribly upset – I think he probably felt somewhat emasculated by the whole situation, poor man. Finally, we got the 'OK' from Walt in Burbank and didn't start shooting until well after lunch. A very expensive morning.

I was still battling with the bulge which, added to my spots and the Disney ethos, made life in front of the camera a bit of a minefield. One night we were shooting in the little restaurant of the Moon-Spinners Inn with Joan and Peter, and in the scene my character is sitting at a table trying to impress Peter, leaning forward over-eagerly, talking rubbish – when suddenly a voice shouts 'Cut!'

The wardrobe girl comes forward and beckons me off camera.

'We have to do something about your cleavage,' she hisses.

'My cleavage? What cleavage?' I was astonished.

'Er – we can see too much,' she says politely. And so, with great difficulty she threads wire all along the top of my sun dress and clamps it to my body.

We start the scene again, then . . .

'Cut!!'

This time there are murmurings behind the camera – then another voice calls out: 'Make-up!'

Harry Frampton appears with his brushes to paint over my spots, then he applies a little sponge and adds some brown pancake in an attempt to slim down my cheeks. I check the mirror. I look like I have a beard.

This went on all through the shoot. Hard as I tried, I couldn't lose weight. In fact I kept putting weight on. My appearance wasn't helped by the pink pedal pushers I was wearing for most of the film, even though the long-suffering Wardrobe Department sewed little lead weights along the bottom of my tunic to try and keep it down. But it was an adventure movie, and we were always being chased, running up a hill away from the camera or hanging upside down from windmills, exposing my behind – there was nowhere to hide!

The final indignity was when they had to make a cut in my espadrilles, because my feet were too fat to get them on.

In spite of all that, I was enjoying my freedom. I missed Mum, and wrote endless letters to Andrew, but I loved having my own little cottage and wandering down to the beach for a swim at the end of the day. I learnt to waterski and would snorkel in the little bay, searching for bits of Ancient Greek pottery. I adored Crete, the barren hills dotted about with little whitewashed churches; the old widows in their black garb; little donkeys tottering along with a mountain of sticks or hay on their backs twice their size; the heat and the dry pine-scented dust, and the incredible turquoise blue Aegean.

But there were hard lessons to be learnt also. One decadent night I spent with the actress Irene Papas became something of a rite of passage. Irene was the embodiment of a Classical Greek beauty. 'Tragic yet serene', she was another accomplished actress, well versed in Ibsen, Shakespeare and Greek tragedy, and she had worked a lot with the great auteur filmmaker Michael Cacoyannis – she had played the title roles in *Electra* and *Antigone*, Helen in *The Trojan Women* and Clytemnestra in *Iphigenia*, and of course she was unforgettable as the widow in *Zorba the Greek* with Anthony Quinn, Alan Bates and Lila Kedrova.

One night Irene asked me if I'd like to join her on a trip up to a little village in the hills, where they were having a fete. I was thrilled and accepted instantly. There were three other men, friends of hers, including the driver of an ancient car. One of them turned up carrying a shotgun, another was a flamboyant-looking man with a strong, rather sensual face and a thick mane of dark hair – a Greek film director whose name was Nicos. We headed off into the hills, up a steep, rough, rock-strewn track. It was pitch black, and you couldn't see anything except the headlamp beams lighting the way ahead, and as we bumped and bounced along the road Irene's friend kept firing his gun out of the window hoping to shoot a hare. He never hit anything, which is hardly surprising.

When we finally arrived at the village they were roasting mutton on a spit over a huge fire in the middle of the little square. People were clustering around, all seemed to be wearing black, and somewhere musicians were playing bouzoukis. It was like something out of an arthouse movie, with much singing and dancing. The Greek film director kept giving me food and drink – strong, rough red wine and mutton stuffed with rosemary and garlic. It seemed the most delicious thing I'd ever tasted. I don't know how long we were there – it all became a blur. Sparks leaping up into the night, faces in the glow of the fire, voices singing, and more wine. On the way back down the mountain, full of the wine and the warmth the Greek film director kissed me expertly in the back of the car and I kissed him – all the way down the mountain and back to the hotel.

The next morning I was stricken.

I could hardly look at my own face in the mirror. What had I been thinking?! I didn't even know this man. I wasn't thinking, that was the point, my mind had capitulated to my senses: the wine, the music, the fire, it had all been too potent to resist.

It all sounds incredibly old-fashioned now, but the sexual revolution of the 1960s had yet to storm my Bastille – and anyway, I was still a virgin. I was so shocked at myself that later when I was swimming and saw him again, standing on the pier and watching me with an inscrutable look on his face, I was so embarrassed that I dived down under the water and stayed there for so long I nearly drowned.

For all my romantic dreams of love and passion, when it came to the real thing I didn't know how to handle it. I was just a frightened little rabbit.

Soon after that my mother arrived on location, quite possibly in the nick of time, because the truth is that although the Greek film director was really very nice and very attractive, at thirty-seven years old he was old enough to be my father.

The *Moon-Spinners* shoot was long, almost six months, and after we finished in Crete the unit relocated to Pinewood Studios in England. It was there that I met Pola Negri.

A genuine legend of the silver screen, she was retired from showbusiness and had been living in San Antonio, Texas, for over twenty years. Somehow, Walt Disney had managed to convince her to come out of retirement to play the character role of Madame Habib.

Pola Negri! What a coup. Pola was one of the biggest silent movie stars of the twenties and thirties and one of the few who survived the transition to talkies. A screen siren, beautiful and mysterious, she had an extraordinary allure that made both men and women love her. Her singing voice was unique, something like Edith Piaf and Marlene Dietrich rolled into one, and when she danced she expressed her emotions so eloquently and with an extraordinary sense of freedom and abandonment; but she was also a very good actress. She had lived for a while with Charlie Chaplin, and also Rudolph Valentino. She claimed Valentino had been 'the love of my life'. At one time Pola was the biggest star in Hollywood with the world at her feet. In 1928 the studios paid her $10,000 a week ($7.5 million per year in today's terms), which was a fortune for old Hollywood. Her house in Beverly Hills was modelled to look like the White House. She still influences fashion to this day – before Pola Negri nobody painted their toe nails bright red, or wore fur boots or turbans!

As you can imagine, Pola's reputation preceded her. I was half expecting her to be rather remote and grand, especially after hearing her demands to the production team before she started filming, which were:

1   That all the jewellery she wore must be real.

2   The mink stole (referred to in the script) must be real sable.

3   Instead of her character owning a parrot, she wanted to have a cheetah – her signature mascot.

The cheetah arrived on set before she did, like a sort of herald. Then Pola arrived in a limousine, wrapped up in a black cape, wearing a large brimmed black fedora pulled down firmly over her eyes and an enormous pair of dark glasses. She strode in, speaking to no one, and ordered the make-up room door to be shut, which it was, with a bang and then locked, with no one allowed to enter. I don't know what went on in there, but when she finally emerged with a jet-black wig and full make-up, a gold brocade dress and wearing all her jewels, she looked *fabulous*. The studio had to employ a security guard to follow her around wherever she went, owing to the fact she was wearing a small fortune in jewels – and the sable stole, flung carelessly over one shoulder, was very often dragging in the dust behind her.

As for being grand and remote – well, she was dignified but she was also very sweet and funny, dry and ironic, which I wasn't expecting. She did things in the scene we had together that made me laugh. It was a pretty silly scene, but she took it seriously and was completely truthful and committed.

I admired that. It was fascinating to watch her work. You could see so many of her old ways of performing in the spotlight. She loved being in front of the camera, and the camera loved her.

For my first entrance into the scene – on Madame Habib's private yacht – I had to run past the cheetah, which was sitting on a big silken cushion. I obviously moved too quickly and took it by surprise because the animal suddenly snarled and lashed out at me, its sharp claws ripping into my dress. I shrieked and leapt away, crashing into a large light and scorching myself. I had two scars to show for my scene with the legendary Pola Negri: sergeant's stripes on my arm, and her cheetah's claw-marks on my arse.

*

A few days before the film wrapped, and still struggling with this hopeless crush on Peter McEnery, the final scene that I was longing for – and dreading – was fast approaching. The kiss. My first 'screen kiss' was to take place in a hearse. I don't know whose idea that was!

On the day we were to shoot the scene, the Publicity Department, in their infinite wisdom, had invited as many ladies and gentlemen of the press as they could cram on to the set to photograph this landmark event. As they all crowded around behind the camera, loading their weapons and choosing their angles, I was becoming a basket case. I started to sweat, for my secret passion for Peter had become an obsession, and when the moment came for him to lean forward and plant a kiss upon my lips . . . well, the Niagara Falls in my ears and the diesel engine in my heart were so loud that I couldn't hear him speak his lines . . . and I forgot to close my eyes. I looked like I was waiting for a bus, or wondering what to have for lunch.

★

There is always a huge emptiness when a long shoot finally wraps. You've spent every day together for six months, then you get 'demobbed' and sent home. Everyone goes back to their own lives, or on to new projects. Sometimes you meet up with them again, sometimes you never do. During filming they become your whole world, especially if you have spent a long time away on location. Filming can be an intense experience, stoking the passions, the nerves, relationships forged under the heat of the arc lights; you share your lives, the fun, the boredom, the laughs, the fights, everything, and then suddenly they're gone.

I returned to England to realise I'd started losing touch with my friends. This had started after I left Elmhurst and had been made worse by the fact that I hadn't made friends in Switzerland. I'd managed to write to Andrew from Crete, but I wasn't very good at writing to people, and when I came back I was astonished and disappointed to learn that Jane Alexander, my old friend from school, had got married at seventeen and was now living in Mexico. I didn't see her or hear that irresistible laugh again for many years.

There was no one living at The Wick either. Mummy had left to be in New York with Daddy, so I went and stayed with Juliet and Russell in their little flat on Duke Street in Mayfair.

On Friday 22 November they invited a few friends over for drinks; the television was on . . .

Out of the blue, the world was changed utterly when President John F. Kennedy was shot while driving in his motorcade through the streets of Dallas. We were all in shock. The whole world was. How could such a ghastly thing happen? I was only seventeen, and I had never experienced anything like it in my life. Everything I thought I knew seemed to be lost. I think a lot of people realised, at that moment, just how much hope and faith we had invested in President Kennedy: to heal America's age-old divisions of race and wealth, to steer the world out of the Cold War and save us all from nuclear annihilation. Now he was dead. If I look at my journal on that day, I'm floundering, trying to understand the enormity of the loss.

Kennedy was the hope of the world! We could believe in him, he was so young, he stood for the best in America, he understood the great potential for the goodness and the generosity of America, he stood for Democracy, and the future of the free world. We've lost Camelot.

Oh God! If you exist, where are you?

What are you doing to allow such a thing to happen, you can't sit back so righteously and say 'I gave man free will' – That's as good as telling us that we're on our own. It's despicable!

I want to cry and tear my hair, but tears are useless, everything and everyone is useless. He's DEAD!! DEAD! I wish there was an answer. But I know that there isn't one.

Who else does Khrushchev respect? Who else would have handled the Cuba Crisis so brilliantly? Who else is as good as him, thinks like him?

I have a horrible feeling that we'll be hard pushed to find another man like John Kennedy. They don't appear very often, we may have missed our chance.

A few weeks later we were all back at The Wick for Christmas. I'm sure that many families around the world, after the terrible shock of 22 November, felt the need to huddle together during that holiday, to support and comfort and love one another. I remember Christmas morning being a riot as we came trooping down, festooned with all our gifts! Daddy presided over breakfast with an Astrakhan Cossack's hat on his head and an alpaca jacket over his pyjamas; Bunchy was wearing a polo neck sweater over her nightie and a huge pair of earrings; Johnny buttered toast while wearing great leather gloves. I wore my fur boots from Mummy under my nightie and Russell turned pea-green after valiantly puffing away on his new pipe.

It was a gorgeous happy day with only the family. In the afternoon, we went up to the Star & Garter Home for Disabled Soldiers, Sailors and Airmen, which was a tradition that we had always observed when we lived at The Wick as kids. As before, it was a sobering and inspiring experience. The home, which was just two doors up from us on top of Richmond Hill, had been built after the First World War. The inside was spacious and elegant, with enormous windows that led out to a huge terrace that ran the whole length of the building. It was a fitting home for the men who had sacrificed so much for their country. We walked through the wards and chatted with the men. Some were lying in bed, some were in wheelchairs, and some were sitting wrapped up against the chill out on the terrace. It made me feel ashamed of my selfishness and pettiness and lack of forgiveness. These people understood the value of life more than we did and yet they smiled at us, with sadness in their hearts, to make us feel at ease.

On Christmas night we were back in that beautiful old house, sitting around the polished table and the flickering candles in the dining room. There was a moment of quiet and Daddy suddenly got up from his chair and raised his glass.

'To my darling Baba, back where you belong. Welcome home!'

'Welcome home, Mummy darling,' we all chorused and then hugged her and filled our glasses and laughed and hugged again.

For a moment it seemed she was happy, really happy, back in the old house she had dreamt about for so long. The years seemed to just slip away, as once more the house was bright with lights and filled with the sound of voices and laughter. A fire was burning in every grate, in the hall the Christmas tree glistened, and on the mantelpiece in the living room, the Witch's Stick gleamed, back where it belonged.

CHAPTER NINE

The Beautiful & The Damned

'You know that old saying about not losing a daughter but gaining a son ... well, this is sort of like losing a daughter and I didn't
gain any son ...'

— Walt's letter to me, 22 December 1965

By 1964 my contract with Disney was almost at an end, and it
seemed like the whole world was changing. These were exciting
times. Andrew had managed to be hired as assistant to Richard
Lester working on the Beatles' debut movie *A Hard Day's Night*,
which was huge. The Beatles were everywhere, their music was
in the very air you breathed. With their arrival came the rising
tide of youth culture, sweeping away the old order in its wake,
changing values and perceptions about everything from music, to
sex, to fashion, to self-identity, to God! Everyone and everything
in Britain seemed irretrievably transformed. Everyone, it seemed,
except me. I was seventeen and should have been in the vanguard
of the revolution, but I felt strangely outside of it all – an observer
rather than a participant, even when my life criss-crossed with the
Fab Four, which happened a lot over the next few years. I was a
full-time working actress, and although there were perks, it came
with a responsibility, which increasingly felt like an impediment

to enjoying the joys and freedoms of teenage life – including dating.

My journal entry for 31 January 1964 is typically awkward:

Watched a rough cut of 'Moon-Spinners' *in a small stuffy screening room in the West End, it was a pretty nerve-racking experience, I stuffed my face with chocolates and chain-smoked all the way through it. After the purgatory was over I didn't think the film made much of an impression, and felt my performance was disappointing, and wanted to sob, but instead did the opposite which invariably proves to be fatal, laugh too loudly, over-gesticulate / under-articulate until everyone was exhausted!*

On 8 February, I left for Los Angeles with my parents, to do some promotion in America. We were put up in the Beverly Hills Hotel, bungalow number 19. It was very glamorous. There were flowers waiting for us with hampers of fruit and bottles of Jack Daniel's, which Daddy was very happy about.

The next day, still woozy with jet lag, my father and I began rehearsals for the *Danny Kaye Show*, which was a very popular TV show at the time. We had some dance routines and a couple of numbers to perform. I can't remember much about it. I think my journal speaks volumes about my rather blasé attitude to fame and celebrity back then, as it says very little about the event.

Feb 19th
Daddy and I wanted to rehearse some more but Danny didn't, so end of story.'

Recorded the show, seemed to go alright, hard to judge, wish I'd had more time – hope it doesn't show!

Dinner later with Danny at his house, he is a fantastic cook and has a fantastically enormous ego! He was rather rude to his wife – didn't like that much.

20th
Lunch at Disney Studios with Walt and Bill Anderson, and lovely
Arlene Ludwig from publicity.
  p.m.: Party for us at Alan Brown's house, very sweet producer of
my next movie 'The Truth about Spring' with Daddy; met James
MacArthur son of Helen Hayes, he seemed really nice, he's my 'love
interest' in the film, poor man!

22nd
Grauman's Chinese Theatre on Hollywood Blvd. I put my hands and
feet into cement! And wrote 'Dad's birthday' in the space, because it
was – he was delighted and made me feel we'd done it together.
  He should have done one, I wish he had.

Somewhat telling, that. Rather than being thrilled to have my
hand and footprints on Hollywood Boulevard, alongside Mary
Pickford and Shirley Temple, I was feeling guilty that Daddy
hadn't been asked to do his.

On the 23rd we flew to New York, to the Algonquin Hotel for
more press and promotion – a typical day.

24th: Press all day in the hotel suite 11 a.m.–5 p.m. then photographs.
25th: Press all day 9.30–4.30
26th: Ditto Press all day and photographs in the suite.
  p.m.: Supper at 21 Club interview with Gossip columnist Sheilah
Graham – F. Scott Fitzgerald's mistress.

Meeting Sheilah Graham was a life-changing event. Until I met
her, I had always been dogged by my lack of education. It hurt
my confidence, made me doubt myself and created so much inner
anxiety. But if there was one person who really understood this
and set me on the road to my own personal education, it was
Sheilah Graham. She was small and blonde, in her fifties, with
tremendous energy, an engaging smile and a fascinating story to

tell. For once, the interviewer told me more about her own life than I spoke about mine and, compared to her, my life experiences seemed incredibly tame.

Sheilah was English, born into the slums of London's East End, and poverty forced her mother to put her into an orphanage while still a small child. Her mother remained a stranger to her all her life, leaving Sheilah alone in the world, but this was a woman who was both intelligent and determined, not only to survive but to *rise up*. She managed to get herself to New York and the land of dreams and possibilities. She was not well educated, but she was smart and a fast learner and moved steadily up the ladder, eventually landing a job in Hollywood writing about the lives of movie stars and the business. Along with Hedda Hopper and Louella Parsons, she became one of the three most powerful (and often feared) gossip columnists in Hollywood. It was a genuine rags to riches story.

Despite her success, she said she had always felt terribly insecure and inhibited by her lack of education. She knew that it was a huge obstacle to her ambitions, not only her dreams of getting ahead in society but, more importantly, to becoming a really good writer.

Everything changed when she met F. Scott Fitzgerald and they fell in love. In her 'Memoir' she wrote: 'Here is the person for whom one has been searching so desperately, who will give one comfort and love and anguish – and the education for which one has longed.'

At that time Fitzgerald was still married to Zelda Sayre, although she was in a mental institution suffering from schizophrenia. Scott often lived in one of the bungalows at the Garden of Allah, where they kept their relationship discreet. It all sounds wonderfully romantic, but one has to remember that Scott endured years in the wilderness, and though it's still difficult to believe, much of his work – even *The Great Gatsby* – was not fully appreciated until after his death.

As well as being her lover and mentor, Scott took on Sheilah's education enthusiastically. He called it her 'College of One' and, over the next two years, set her an almost impossible number of books to read, starting with Proust's *Remembrance of Things Past*. 'But not more than ten pages a day,' he instructed, as he felt it would be difficult to finish if she took on too much.

'College of One' was a brilliant concept, a syllabus spanning the Humanities – I found out later that Scott had simply divided H.G. Wells's *Outline of History* into forty sections, each interrupted by an appropriate novel or a play:

Serious music
Greek and Roman History
Medieval History
History of France
Morton's A People's History of England
The English novel
The French novel
The American novel
Russian writers
Etc ...

The course covered almost all the great poets – but no Maths, no Biology, no Latin or French. In a broad sense it was what was taught in a Liberal Arts College.

At that supper, at the 21 Club in New York, Sheilah gave me a list of a few books to start my reading, jotting them down on a page of her notebook.

Vanity Fair — *Thackeray*
Man and Superman — *Shaw*
The Red and the Black — *Stendhal*
Bleak House — *Dickens*
Androcles and the Lion — *Shaw*

The History of Henry Edmond — *Thackeray*
A Doll's House — *Ibsen*

I was thrilled. It was as if I had been given the key to my own self-improvement – my own empowerment by F. Scott Fitzgerald himself! Convinced that I could educate and transform myself, I tore into the list like a fiend. However, by the time I reached Shaw's *Androcles and the Lion* I was seriously starting to flag. I hated to admit it but, to my shame and great disappointment, I was struggling to get through it – and Stendhal was such hard going I hadn't been able to finish it at all. I think I might have fared better if I'd had F. Scott Fitzgerald to talk it through with every evening. I was so busy filming. My reading was interrupted, my application suffered from a lack of concentration – I needed a hands-on teacher. Nevertheless, it broke the ice for me and meeting that remarkable woman when I was seventeen opened up the world of books to me in a whole new and exciting way, setting me on my own path. I soon experienced the excitement of discovering great writers like Ernest Hemingway, Joseph Conrad, E.M. Forster and George Eliot, Daphne Du Maurier, Charlotte Brontë. Books have been a passion and a solace ever since.

You would be forgiven for wondering why I didn't discuss this with my mother. She was a writer, after all, and would have been fascinated. But the truth is I wanted it for myself. I was beginning to feel the need to assert my independence. We were very close, we did everything together, and I adored both my parents. The last thing I wanted to do was hurt their feelings, but I needed to have something that was my own.

Back home in Richmond the almost daily disagreements and disputes had begun to cloud the days. Mummy's drinking was now a serious problem, although it was barely acknowledged. After a night of angry rows and recriminations, the next morning everything would go back to normal and we would all carry on as before. But Mummy was in trouble. It would be easy to blame my father for not wanting or not being able to accept the truth staring him in the face. The fact is, none of us could. To apply the word 'alcoholic' to your wife or mother was almost unthinkable, it was a taboo subject. We told ourselves 'she just needs to know when to stop' – but I knew from my own experience that this wasn't always so easy. Part of the reason I think we allowed it to carry on for so long was that she never let herself go – she always looked wonderful, she dressed beautifully, her hair was brushed and shining, and she left a trail of perfume behind her wherever she went. The house always ran smoothly, meals were on time, everything was the same and functioned properly, and there were no outward signs that anything was wrong, except for those Alka Seltzer before breakfast.

Looking back now, I see that I was retreating so much into my own private teenage world, becoming so completely absorbed in my books and my music and my thoughts of boys and the Beatles, I simply didn't *want* to know.

So it's deeply ironic that it was actually thanks to my mother that I dated George Harrison.

The occasion was a big charity night for the Red Cross and I had been invited – with my parents, of course – to go down to the house of actor Richard Todd (of *The Dam Busters* fame) outside London in Henley, where he was hosting a reception party. It was one of those old-fashioned charity events where film stars and celebrities turn up to attend a premiere or a first night and raise money for a good cause. On this occasion my mother decided that her daughter needed an escort – and that my escort should be George Harrison.

To this day, I can't explain why she was behaving like a character from a Jane Austen novel, matchmaking her daughter with the eligible young bachelor. I remember being in the study with her at The Wick, sitting in front of a crackling fire, the curtains drawn against the fading light. 'What about George Harrison?'

I nearly choked on my tea. Mummy rose to her feet and marched towards her desk . . .

'What?! Are you serious? I hardly know him!' I gasped. 'You can't just call George Harrison up out of the blue and say, "Hey, George, do you wanna take my daughter out?!"' I was absolutely horrified.

Now you may be thinking that the lady doth protest too much – and you'd be quite right – because, beneath my panic and embarrassment, I was of course hoping desperately that this would happen.

She picked up the phone . . . I leapt over the sofa to stop her.

'Don't! Mum – *stop*! Suppose he doesn't want to – but feels he has to because it's rude to refuse?!'

Now, I had met the Beatles the previous year, albeit very briefly, at the Royal Variety Performance, where they put on a famous show that made them superstars in Britain. But the reason George in particular was on my mother's mind was because we had met him a few days before at another charity event. Mummy had liked him very much and asked if he'd like to come and visit us at The Wick, to which he had replied, 'Yes, I'd love to.' 'Well,' I thought to myself privately, 'he couldn't very well have said no!' My embarrassment went from 'slight' to 'acute' when she asked him for his telephone number – and he had given it to her!

Now I couldn't quite believe what I was seeing. She seemed to be dialling in slow motion. I watched helplessly, paralysed, unable to do anything but stare and wheeze. I could see she was clearly speaking to someone; then, before I could gauge what was happening, the receiver was put down again, almost too quickly for my liking, and my mother looked up at me with a wry smile. The die was cast – George Harrison was going to come round on Friday evening to pick me up and drive me to Henley.

I was in shock. In fact, the whole house was.

As you can imagine, the anticipation leading up to that night was just unbearable: Christmases, birthdays, weddings, they don't even come close. I was a seventeen-year-old girl, it was 1964, and

I was going on a date with George Harrison. I described the evening in great detail in my journal.

It was one of those nights that you thought would never come, and after it's gone you can't stop thinking about it. George was late picking me up. The maddening thing about it all was that, waiting for him to arrive I was as calm as a cucumber, and curiously, the later he got the calmer I got, which was just as well because Soxie was driving me crazy, flying back and forth in front of the window of my room like Scarlett O'Hara with her candelabra, looking out for George's arrival. She'd suddenly spot a passing car and shriek in a voice I'd never heard before – it got higher and higher until I almost wanted to hit her. And it wasn't just Soxie. The whole house was in an uproar, from Kathleen [the cook] tearing around the kitchen in a state of nervous excitement to Barnes [her husband] upstairs who must have opened the front door at least eight times calling for a non-existent cat. When at last George did arrive, Barnes overdid the whole butler thing to such an extent George must have thought that he'd arrived at a madhouse. As soon as I walked down the stairs and saw him standing there in the hall with his black corduroy coat and his hands thrust deep into the pockets and all that shining hair, my carefully cultivated calm vanished, my knees started to tremble and I threw my eyes up to heaven for some fatuous reason that was lost on both of us, and which I regretted the moment I'd done it!

George and I tore off together in his black E-Type Jaguar. The rain was pouring down and, when my heart had finally settled more or less into its proper place, I began to enjoy myself. I looked at him out of the corner of my eye. He didn't seem to mind that I had been foisted on him by my very determined mother. He reminded me of a little foal peering out from under a bear skin rug; his smile is rather wicked but in the most innocent sort of way; when he laughs it's as if there's a tiny leprechaun sitting on his shoulder who pulls one side of his mouth up and whispers wicked things into his ear. It was wonderful, just the two of us sitting there in the red leather warmth, droning down the wet, black roads, staring past the three windscreen wipers fighting with a wall of rain. I wished we could just get lost and never have to go to the event, or meet the press, or make conversation with a lot of strangers, but keep on driving into the night. When we finally arrived at Richard Todd's house, where the reception was taking place, I got nervous all over again. Inside, it was packed with large men, and women with sloping shoulders. As soon as they saw George they all rushed at us and plied us with plates of food which neither of us wanted to eat. George had a habit of getting to within an inch of your face when he spoke, and I immediately started worrying if I had spinach plastered across my teeth – or something even worse. There was nobody there we knew except for Mum and Dad and Richard Todd. At one point George thought he saw TV personality Gilbert Harding's back view – but I said it couldn't have been because unfortunately Gilbert Harding was dead. After a while we were driven in convoy to the cinema, where the charity screening was taking place – George and I climbed into the back of a black limousine, while in the front seat a neurotic-looking Marine sat chewing his white gloves. There was a huge crowd of fans waiting at the cinema. When he saw them poor George went slightly green and cowed-looking.

'Just follow me!' shouted the Marine as he leapt gallantly out of the car and instantly disappeared and was never seen again. In all the chaos, someone managed to open the door and George sprang into a snakepit of shrieking, scratching, maniacal girls. One of them nearly took my eye out with a jabbing Biro pen . . .

This was unlike anything I had ever seen, before or since. My experiences in Japan paled by comparison. Beatlemania was still in its infancy, and George hadn't become completely exhausted by it all yet, but it's easy to see now how this mass hysteria would soon wear them all down.

It was practically murderous. George couldn't go anywhere. These girls would have stopped at nothing to grab a tuft of Beatle hair. It was a miracle he still had so much of it. Somehow we managed to fight our way through the melee into the cinema, clinging to our clothes for fear they would be torn off our backs. We miraculously found our way to our seats. But there was no oasis of calm, for as soon as we sat down it seemed the entire Red Cross descended on us. We were surrounded, people leaning on our heads, their sharp elbows and grumbling stomachs in our faces. I remember George was marvellous the whole time, the way he handled it all, signing autographs and smiling at everybody, however pushy. One woman actually knelt in my lap to get at him!

The film we were due to see was *Charade* with Cary Grant and Audrey Hepburn, and we were looking forward to it. As it turned out we didn't get a chance to watch much of it, because throughout the entire film people were crawling on their hands and knees up the aisle with autograph books in their teeth to reach him.

We decided to try and get out before the film was over, so there was another mad scramble to escape the crowd. But it didn't work, and there was more screaming, fighting and stabbing pens. George jumped into the car and some fool slammed the door shut, leaving me stuck outside! I saw George's face looking back at me helplessly as the car sped off, girls still chasing and banging on the windows. Eventually, I got a lift back to Richard Todd's house, where I found George sitting in a big winged chair in front of the fire, a bit like the Queen Mother. Within minutes the whole room was drawn to him. Looking back, I don't think it was simply because he was a Beatle either, George had a certain something, which not very many people have, especially young people: a mixture of great poise and composure, a sweetness and an ordinariness. He was unaffected, completely his own man, and people loved him for it. But there was also a certain reserve about him too, an aura that kept people just that arm's length away. We stayed for quite a while. It was the early hours before we headed off and were once again closeted in that luxuriously upholstered Jaguar. The drive home was much more relaxed. We had survived the evening and I think it had created a subtle bond. I now understood what it was like for him to be in the eye of that storm. I even managed a few jokes. I remember at one point, in a burst of daring merriment, saying, in my worst Lancashire accent, 'Hey, y'up! It's a great life, George!' We both looked at each other and burst out laughing, although it wasn't that funny. On the way back we passed a sign for Excel Bowling. He said, 'Hey! Let's go bowling, Hayley!' And we both bellowed with laughter again, because it was impossible for him to do anything normal – and not least because it was now 3.30 in the morning.

For a long time afterwards I remembered the conversations we had, and I would inwardly and outwardly cringe at all the asinine remarks I felt I had made from sheer nerves, while working out all the beautiful, perfectly intelligent exchanges that never happened.

When we finally got back to The Wick, Daddy was still awake – waiting for his daughter to be returned. He answered the door and suggested we have scrambled eggs, so we all trooped down to the kitchen and Dad cooked. I'd never seen my father cook scrambled eggs before in my entire life. It was most surreal. Then George suddenly leapt to his feet, saying he was sorry to rush off. Ringo was packing up their home, they were moving house together at 4.30 that morning – with a police escort.

I remember thinking that night what a price they had to pay for their success. On one occasion, many years later, I bumped into George at the Chelsea Flower Show with his lovely wife Olivia. We had a good laugh about our mad night together, and he confessed that one of the thrills of his life was having scrambled eggs cooked for him by John Mills at four o'clock in the morning!

★

Just two weeks before my eighteenth birthday, I received my first really awful reviews – for *The Chalk Garden*.

I had always tended to avoid reading reviews after my first

awkward experience with the notices for *Tiger Bay*. There was something deeply unsettling about the whole thing, reading about oneself – good or bad. When they are good it's weird – possibly unhealthy if you believe it too much. And when they are bad it's worse. Nobody likes to be criticised, but getting criticised in public is a whole other level of discomfort. The reviews of *The Chalk Garden* were the first time I had been singled out for criticism, and it felt like a serious blow, as I noted in my journal on 1 April 1964:

The Chalk Garden has laid an egg and the critics have smashed the shell to pieces, and me too like Humpty Dumpty . . .

I was destroyed for a few days, my confidence plummeted. There was one line especially that I couldn't forget. It stayed with me, taunting me, spinning around in my head.

. . . Hayley Mills is given too much rope for her limited dramatic talent.

Interestingly, while researching for this book I went back and re-read some of the notices for *The Chalk Garden* and was surprised to find that actually they weren't *all* bad. Why is it that actors only remember the bad notices and never the good ones? Perhaps it's just a human trait. We're all much more likely to remember some harsh criticism than we are a kind compliment. Maybe it's because it speaks to our inner demons, our self-doubt. I've spoken to the finest actors, who all share a strange, secret fear of being exposed as a fraud. I recall Peter Firth, the original star of *Equus*, recipient of countless awards, confessing he was terrified of being 'found out'. Or maybe it's because actors have a struggle being objective about their art. They can't step back like a painter, observe the canvas and make adjustments – they *are* the painting.

After reading the bad *Chalk Garden* reviews, I spent the next few days in a state of deep depression before eventually picking myself up and pulling myself together. I steeled myself with fighting spirit, leaning into my Scottish ancestors, who didn't take shit from anyone – and told myself that I now had something to fight for, as I vowed in my journal:

The idiots! I'll show them, I must show them, I will . . . I must believe that I can show them. Oh, God! Help me show them!

Of course, insecurity is not something unique to actors. Standing strong and weathering criticism, separating and discriminating between what is fair and what is plain vicious, is a test that everyone has to go through at some point, not only people in the theatre. For me it was a big test, as I had always been deeply critical of myself anyway, and now that other people were wading in too, and in public, it began to scare the hell out of me – because there was a dark, negative voice inside of me that agreed with them. In fact, truth be told, I was a much harsher critic of myself than they ever could be.

Joan Collins and her husband, the singer-songwriter Anthony Newley, were famous for giving wonderful parties, and there was one I remember especially well at the Pickwick Club in London. At that time the Pickwick Club was a Mecca for people in the business: celebrities, actors, writers, musicians, everybody went there to hang out, and on that night the Beatles were there too. All musicians loved and respected Anthony Newley. He was a great performer and his songs, co-written with Leslie Bricusse, had influenced so many (perhaps none more so than David Bowie!), and of course Joan Collins has always been famously smart and incredibly glamorous, so it's not surprising their parties were a big hit. Paul McCartney was at the party that night, accompanied by his beautiful girlfriend Jane Asher. I remember having a lovely chat with Ringo. At one point I thought 'This is all going very well', until we came to say goodbye – and

I realised that I'd left one of my false nails in the palm of his hand.

My parents were good friends of Tony and Joan and they reciprocated by throwing a party at The Wick for seventy people. The house was jammed. It was a good cast list: apart from Tony and Joan the guests included Leslie Bricusse and his gorgeous wife Evie – Leslie had just written the score for the Bond film *Goldfinger* with John Barry, which everyone knew was going to be massive; Trevor Howard; Larry Olivier and Joan Plowright; David and Judy Birkin; husband-and-wife actors Michael Denison and Dulcie Gray; producer Glen Byam Shaw; playwrights Terence Rattigan and Beverley Nichols; Dickie and Sheila Attenborough; Bryan and Nanette Forbes; Lionel and Eileen Jeffries. I remember Paul McCartney and Jane Asher arriving late. Jane was dishevelled and very upset; they had just run the gauntlet, having practically been torn apart by fans in London. Her coat was in tatters and she was fighting back the tears. I took her upstairs to my mother's room to help her calm down. Apparently it had been a really frightening experience. Somehow she'd got in the way of some screaming, hysterical kids trying to accost Paul, and they had attacked her, pulled her hair and ripped her beautiful rainbow-coloured woollen coat to shreds. It was completely insane. I could sympathise with her after seeing what happened to George in sedate Henley, and my own experiences during our trip to Tokyo and the Far East – but I had never actually feared for my life. All this certainly helped to put my own success into perspective, but it didn't make it any simpler.

Before I started shooting *The Truth about Spring* I had to have four wisdom teeth removed, which meant spending a week in the Fitzroy Nursing Home in London. It seemed rather extreme for just a few teeth, but when I woke up from the anaesthetic I was extremely glad to have been incarcerated – my face looked like a huge overripe pear.

As it turned out, a few days in a nursing home did me some good and I had time to contemplate my life. In that quiet little room overlooking Fitzroy Square, with the muted sound of cars skimming along the wet road, and the wind in the peeling sycamore trees, I realised that it really was time to leave home, and yet I knew the chances of that happening were pretty remote. I was just eighteen; I felt life waiting, like a huge map laid out before me without any roads or tracks on it, like my face without any lines. I knew life would soon supply all that, but there was so much out there, so many dreams to follow and adventures to be had. I didn't want to hurt my parents, I adored them, but they were a towering influence and I was struggling to stand on my own feet.

The bed was spikey thanks to bits of old toast, which I'd struggled with at breakfast, but I felt I could go on lying there for hours doing nothing, just staring at the string that held up the window.

I wondered secretly, if I were bedridden for years, would I write? I'd always imagined that I would one day. At Elmhurst that's all I wanted to do. I wrote short stories and privately was rather proud of them, and some pretty awful poetry.

I thought about Mummy sneaking off to swallow some of that poison that she loves, and Daddy at lunch, pretending that he hadn't noticed. I thought how I hate myself when she tells me how much is done for me, and how much has been sacrificed on my behalf – *sacrificed*, what an awful word, like being burnt at the stake – and how little I give in return, how I take everything for granted.

I kicked off the sheet and got out of bed, stared through the window at the rain and the sight of the awful new Post Office Tower with its bulbous, onion-like nose. On the radio Cliff Michelmore's *Two Way Family Favourites* was beginning to depress me. I opened my powder compact and looked at my big face in the mirror. Now that I'd cut my hair I really did look like a suet pudding.

I was going home the next day. I was looking forward to it and dreading it too. It seemed I was always quarrelling with Mummy, and it was awful. I loved her so much but she needled and aggravated me and I would often go off to bed hating myself for being such a moral coward. I'd give anything for peace. 'Perhaps I'm just like Daddy,' I thought. Arguments exhausted and frustrated me. It felt like my parents would tell me a thousand times a day how young and irresponsible I was, and yet they would never let me make my own decisions. Like any normal teenager trying to find her feet, I just wanted to be allowed to grow up, simply and quietly, without having everything I said or did criticised. On the one hand I knew how lucky I was to be successful and to be loved – but I was made to feel so aware of my privilege that I was now consumed with guilt. My parents' control over my life had become suffocating.

Something would have to give.

In my next movie, *The Truth about Spring*, I was going to be working with my father again. Privately I wondered if it was such a good idea – like we were a comedy duo. It would be awful if people got bored with us. The film was a romantic comedy, and the whole thing was going to be shot in Spain on the Costa Brava. We were playing a father and a daughter (the 'Spring' of the title) who live on a ramshackle old boat and manage to make a ramshackle sort of a living, not always strictly above board – and they have some pretty shady friends as a result. I can't remember whose idea it was for us to work together, or where the script came from. I think it was another one of the decisions I wasn't really a part of. Anyway, whatever misgivings I had about the film I kept them to myself, which was, in effect, cowardice. I should have spoken up, but I didn't want to rock the boat – if you'll pardon the pun.

Instead of flying to the Costa Brava, Mummy and Daddy decided it would be more fun to drive to Spain, make a road trip of it and stop off in the South of France for a week at my favourite hotel in the whole world, the Cap Estel in Èze. The plan was to have a little holiday before we started filming, and Johnny could be with us for the first few weeks until he would have to go back to boarding school.

It was three years since I'd been in Èze with Larry and Joan. It was practically the same room I'd occupied the previous time I was there. For a glorious week there was nothing for me to do but swim, sunbathe and enjoy having my own space, where I could read my books, learn my lines and doze ecstatically on the cool white bed, listening to the constant, rhythmic lull of the sea. During our stay, my parents had heard about a small villa that was for sale across the bay, and they decided to go and view it. The day before we went I had looked at it through binoculars from the sun-baked terrace of the hotel. The villa was called 'La Solitude'; it was painted white and set back into the steep side of the rock above the water. It appeared to have two floors, each with a long, wide terrace, and balconies. There was a graceful pine tree growing below it that threw its shadow on to the lower part of the house. I closed my eyes and prayed that they would fall in love with it and buy it. I could think of nothing more perfect than to own a holiday house in that beautiful place on the edge of the Mediterranean.

The following day we drove around the coast on the Moyenne Corniche, to Cap d'Ail. We turned off the main road and followed a very narrow, steeply winding track down to the water, and there, through a little iron gate, down some rather wonky steps and past a few neglected-looking shrubs, stood the villa. The owner was waiting at the front door to show us around. He told us his wife had recently died and he wanted to sell the place as soon as possible, fully furnished, down to the smallest teaspoon. It was a dainty little house, but it seemed bigger because of the large windows that opened out on to the sea. We walked up and down the little marble stairs, stood about on the terrace and looked down to the villa's landing stage, where you could tie up a boat. Across the water was the Cap Estel hotel, and just around to the right was the tiny Cap d'Ail beach. As my parents discussed the pros and cons of it my fingers were crossed so hard behind my back it hurt, but then to my dismay I heard my father saying, 'No, it's just too extravagant, Baba . . . too much of a responsibility . . . we would have to spend months here to justify the expense and, lovely as the idea is – no, no . . . I don't think so.'

I had been holding my breath in anticipation for so long that I heard my voice burst out of me as I said: 'Well, if you're not going to buy it, then I will.'

There was silence as everyone turned and stared at me.

I had just had my eighteenth birthday. The most expensive thing I had ever bought was my bicycle.

In 1964, I bought Villa La Solitude in the South of France – for £24,500.

I was thrilled and felt immensely proud being able to buy my own property.

★

When we finally arrived on the Costa Brava for the film shoot, we were put up at the Hostal de la Gavina in S'Agaró, which again was right on the coast and very beautiful. We had a week before filming began, mostly spent in preparation: wardrobe fittings and rehearsing lines. So now it was Jonathan's turn to be splashing happily around in the pool, swimming off the beach and turning golden brown in the sun.

For all my doubts, I could see 'Spring' was a good part for me: she was fun, outspoken and independent, living all her life on this little fishing boat, brought up by her father as if she were a boy; perfectly happy and comfortable with her situation until an attractive young man (in the shape of James MacArthur) appears on a yacht and, in spite of herself, turns all her ideas about life upside down. My parents' dear old friend Lionel Jeffries was playing the villain, alongside the wonderful Irish actor Niall McGuinness; and while this was perfect casting, I knew it was going to be a challenge. When my father and Lionel got together, things quickly got out of hand. They were like two schoolboys – and Niall was mad as a hatter too.

The whole film was shot on location, 90 per cent of it on a very small, very rocky little tub of a boat. The camera had to be lashed on to the end of a plank to get the shots, and the camera operator was constantly being dipped in and out of the water like a biscuit into a cup of tea. Despite all this, everyone was having fun and there was constant laughter from Daddy, Lionel and Niall, but secretly I was getting a bit distraught, worrying about this picture, as evident from my journal:

If I'm not good in this one, it could be the end. This part seems so right for me . . . If I mess this one up I'm not sure I've got the courage to mess up anything else!

There is such a thing as having *too* much fun when you're making a picture. The hilarious times we had on the set didn't go down well with the film director. If, instead of preparing for the next scene, the actors are chatting away and falling about, laughing like drains, it's going to show. And in our case, it did. There are many directors who don't like too much laughter on set. Some are even quite superstitious about it, especially when filming comedies – it's like, if there's too much laughter on set, there'll be none left for the audience.

As my father later remarked, 'If the picture had turned out to be half as good as the food, the wine, the time and the laughs we had on that location, it would have been a sensation – unfortunately, it wasn't!'

I tried to remain professional; after my bruising reviews for *The Chalk Garden* it felt like my entire career depended on it. 'You must not get carried away,' I told myself. 'You must be totally single-minded and focused on the job... And you must not fall in love with anyone.'

Easier said than done. There was a boy; he was Spanish, his

name was Ramón and he worked at the hotel. He was a year older than me, sweet and very good looking. He would turn up at my little rented house with gifts, roses in one hand, a fresh fish in the other. And yet, as romantic as this must sound, I didn't believe him when he told me he loved me. I thought, 'It's my fame. He doesn't see me, he sees "her".'

At eighteen, it seems as if every fibre of one's being is so finely tuned to being in love – to feel its yearning, to experience it. I wrote that summer:

Unless you are in love, life lacks a little lustre. Love is the shimmer in a new day, the lightness in your step and the song in your heart.

I would fall in love so easily, become so carried away by the currents of my emotions, I started to think the only way I could control all this energy was to become a nun! I began seriously thinking about taking my vows. It was the 'all or nothing' that attracted me. 'I could definitely do that,' I thought. I imagined sublimating everything into a great love of Jesus, swathed in a nun's flowing black robes, leading an austere life of prayer and service to the community. Yes, *that* would be a romantic life – but when I discovered that the flowing black habit had disappeared and had been replaced by short skirts, thick, grey woollen stockings and heavy brogues, and that the white veil had morphed into a very ordinary blue scarf, I'm ashamed to admit the idea suddenly lost a lot of its appeal . . .

Andrew and I wrote to each other constantly. He had started to write beautiful letters to me – poetic, romantic – and it was only to him that I dared to bare my soul, sharing my thoughts and experiences during those long days filming on the water, in the baking heat. But this worried me too: Andrew was my best friend – my only friend, really – and I loved him, but I was becoming increasingly afraid that if we fell *in love* and it all went wrong, I would lose him. This was what I told myself, anyway. What I *truly* feared, deep down, was the chance that if he got to know me too well, ultimately he would be disappointed. I couldn't bear that. It was all so confusing. I longed for love but I was afraid of it: the commitment, my unreliability and of revealing my true self – whatever that was. I knew I couldn't possibly live up to people's expectations; and a deeper relationship that inevitably involved sex made me nervous. I wasn't ready for the great unknown.

★

Back in the early 1960s, we had a charity show in Britain called *Night of 100 Stars*, which was something of a national institution. It was held at the London Palladium in the royal presence of Her Majesty the Queen. In 1964 I was asked to appear on the bill as one girl in a chorus line with Susan Hampshire, Anna Massey, Miriam Karlin and Barbara Windsor – all of us in fishnet tights and sequins, and a huge bouquet of ostrich feathers on our backsides. It was enormous fun. I loved rehearsing with the other girls, and it was a completely new experience to be dressed in such a sexy, provocative way. I learnt the potency of a chorus girl's dress when I encountered the great operatic tenor Placido Domingo at the top of the backstage stairs and nearly lost a handful of my tail feathers!

It was a star-studded night that included Zsa Zsa Gabor and Gloria Swanson, Laurence Olivier, Placido Domingo and Cilla Black. I was able to watch from the wings when the Beatles played their set. This was actually the second Beatles gig I had seen, since the year before at the Royal Variety Performance. On that night I had watched from the wings when John stepped up to the microphone and famously quipped, 'For the people in the cheaper seats – clap your hands. The rest of you just rattle your jewellery!' It brought the house down. John was so clever, I loved his voice and admired him from afar. He had a magnetic quality, I felt if my eyes caught his I'd never be able to tear them away, but there was this sense of danger about him. He was completely unpredictable, and you never knew what he was going to say next. As he demonstrated on this very night when the headlining artist took the stage.

You see, the performance that everyone was really talking about that night was not actually the Beatles; it was Judy Garland, who was going to sing after emerging from hospital only that very day.

I was standing in the wings, still wearing my ostrich feathers when she appeared. The Beatles had finished their set and we were all waiting together, whispering and giggling, jammed up against those musty velvet curtains, when the lights went down and suddenly, out of nowhere, Judy Garland breezed past us, into the spotlight, to a tumultuous roar of applause. It was not a well-kept secret that she had been in hospital after another attempt to end her life. She had explained it away in the press as 'just a few cuts to my hands, trying to open a tin box', which of course no one believed for a moment. She seemed a tiny figure, alone on that enormous stage, trapped in a great beam of light, facing the yawning darkness of the auditorium, which was packed to the rafters with over two thousand people, all waiting with a mixture of admiration and naked curiosity. She was dressed in a scarlet, full-length, figure-hugging sequinned dress with long sleeves. The applause died down to a deafening silence – there was a pause, just as she took a breath to speak – when John's clear voice rang out from beside me in the wings:

'Show us your wrists, Judy!'

I'm sure John hadn't really intended to be cruel, his humour was sardonic. His own life's experiences had left deep fissures of anger in him and I'm sure he recognised another's pain. His often caustic humour had become the way he dealt with his own demons.

Judy Garland's story frightened the hell out of me.

Three years earlier, in 1961, our dear friend Roddy McDowall had taken me to see Judy at the Greek Theater in Los Angeles. I'd been so excited to see her, but the reality of Judy Garland in 1961 was deeply unsettling. Clearly, beneath the veneer of this consummate professional was a very frail and damaged person; she had trouble remembering the lyrics and had barely been able to get through 'Somewhere Over the Rainbow'. Some of the audience weren't very forgiving and there were dreadful catcalls, which chilled the blood, but she refused to dignify it, or wasn't aware of it, I'm not sure which. We went round to her dressing room after the show. You could hardly get through the door, there were so many people crammed into the small space, and in the middle of this hazy melee was Judy in a dazzling white dress, trying to talk to everyone at once, and laughing at the crush as she waved us in. She seemed wired; so small and thin – too thin – and even with high heels she was still only the same height as me at fifteen. I looked at her with awe. I did know something of the horrendous childhood she had endured in Hollywood, and the abuse, some of it at the hands of her mother, and of the permanent damage it had inflicted upon her for the rest of her life. But unlike me, she hadn't been able to leave Hollywood and go back to living some semblance of 'normality'. Her reality was the *unreality* of Hollywood and its many questionable values. She was trapped. Like me, as a child of thirteen she had signed a long-term contract and had worked non-stop, but she had been left at the mercy of the system and her mother hadn't shielded her from the worst kinds of abuse. The studio dictated every aspect of her existence: what she looked like, what she wore, how she did her hair. They worked her long hours, feeding her drugs like Benzedrine, which resulted in a lifelong addiction. They bound up her bosom to make her look younger. They forced her to wear caps on her teeth and a cap on her nose until she was twenty-one when a make-up artist refused to do it any more, and told her it wasn't necessary because she was, and always had been, a pretty girl!

She was someone with very little self-esteem. Here was a woman adored by millions – talented, beautiful, funny – and yet she saw no reason to value herself, because despite her success, everyone treated her like dirt in her personal life. Her mother threw her to the studio wolves, where she had lousy father figures (Louis B. Mayer used to call her his 'ugly duckling', or his 'little hunchback'). She had no say about what her next picture would be. She was studio 'property'. She belonged to them body and soul, she was their 'product', their little goose with the golden voice.

If I had had to deal with half the things that Judy did, if Walt Disney, who I loved and looked up to, had said things like that to me when I was struggling with my weight, it would have been devastating – but I was lucky. Walt would never have dreamt of being so cruel and, unlike Judy, I had my parents behind me who were familiar with the pitfalls inherent with the job. My father was a popular figure, held in great esteem within the business. It wouldn't have been so easy to take advantage of me. I was protected.

Seeing Judy made me count my blessings, but nevertheless, I could see some worrying parallels. I could relate to those same feelings of powerlessness, of being a studio 'asset', and the intangible pressure and expectation a child feels. Judy's was a cautionary tale and I started to worry that unless I broke out of the limitations of my own life, I could end up in a similar place.

In 1965 my contract with Disney was going to finish. My final picture, *That Darn Cat!*, would mark the end of five years and six films with the studio, a huge chapter in my life; but as it turned out, Disney weren't ready to let me go and they began discussions with my agent Arthur Park about renewing my contract.

I felt pulled in two directions. On the one hand I was aching for my independence, to spread my wings and fly the nest, and, for better or worse, to make my own career decisions and possibly make films that didn't necessarily fit my Disney image. But I was also hesitant to 'leave home' – which is what Disney had become. To all intents and purposes, they were my surrogate family. They had raised me, cared for me, mentored me, and Walt was a towering father figure. So while I felt frustration at being 'Disney property', there was also a sense of security, of being protected. They were 'my people', they had shielded me from the worst of the Hollywood jungle – and not least they provided me with a steady flow of work. Naturally, I was apprehensive of letting go and I struggled privately wondering 'what to do?'

Everyone has to leave home at some point. It's a healthy impulse. If you don't 'come of age' and strike out on your own, it's like missing a fundamental evolutionary step in your development. It should have been a simple no-brainer for me, a natural parting of the ways; but it wasn't that simple at all. The thought of leaving the safe, protective sphere of my 'family' was actually very frightening. Instinctively, I felt the urge to leave, but in my gut I didn't feel quite ready. I lacked confidence – I was completely torn. It was a bit of an existential moment. Leaving home and braving the horrors of the jungle without the support of my 'family' was daunting to say the least, but the thought of remaining where I was, where I had been since the age of twelve – and unable to make my own choices? That frightened me even more.

That Darn Cat! began shooting in October. My parents and I moved into a large, comfortable house on Cordell Drive, high on a hill above Sunset Strip. The house had originally been built for Ronald Reagan and Jane Wyman, but it was now owned by the choreographer Gower Champion, who was away in New York directing his smash hit *Hello, Dolly!* with Carol Channing.

The view from the house down the valley would have been spectacular but for the smog. Most days everything below us was hidden under a noxious brown and sulphurous miasma. Only the tallest buildings were visible, rising out of the fumes like stark fingers reaching desperately up to the sky.

My father was busy making a film, which Bryan Forbes had come to Hollywood to direct, called *King Rat*, about British and American POWs in Burma during World War Two, starring Tom Courtenay, James Fox, Denholm Elliott and George Segal. *King Rat* is etched into my memory because the studio had built, twenty miles outside Hollywood, a replica of the infamous Changi prison camp, and it looked extraordinarily realistic. Unfortunately they hadn't factored in the intense dehydrating heat of the Californian sun, and within a couple of weeks the lush green hills around the camp had burnt to brown sienna. It was much too late and too expensive to relocate, so they hired an enormous tanker full of paint and sprayed everything within sight jungle green!

I was relieved and thrilled to discover *That Darn Cat!* was a very funny script, perhaps the best since *The Parent Trap*, and Disney had assembled another marvellous cast: Dean Jones (soon to become a Disney favourite in the Herbie *The Love Bug* franchise), Dorothy Provine, Tom Lowell, the fantastic Frank Gorshin (forever known as 'The Riddler' in *Batman*) and the inimitable Elsa Lanchester, one of the all-time great character actresses, whom I had been mesmerised by in *The Bride of Frankenstein*. But all these very fine actors were really just supporting players to the movie's *true* stars, five incredibly talented cats, all masquerading as the one 'DC' – Darn Cat! I never managed to bond with any of my fellow feline cast members. There were too many of them, and sometimes the methods employed by their trainers to get the desired 'performances' were upsetting, to say the least. Once they waved a live pigeon in front of the cat to get it to hiss and lash out. Unfortunately, the cat was quicker than the pigeon handler and Dean Jones and I were spattered with the pigeon's blood.

One of the great pleasures of making *Darn Cat!* was working with Roddy McDowall, who played my screen sister Dorothy Provine's pathologically suspicious boyfriend. Roddy was one of the sweetest and most generous people you could hope to meet; he had started acting as a child and became a big star in films like *How Green Was My Valley* directed by John Ford. Nobody knew more about the business than Roddy did. He knew everybody and everybody knew and loved him – and he gave great parties. It was at just such a party in Malibu that I met Francesca Hilton, the daughter of Zsa Zsa Gabor and the hotel mogul Conrad Hilton. For all the dazzling Hollywood stories of beauty, fame and wealth, there were the ones who didn't quite fit in, who didn't live up to 'expectations'. While the favoured ones lounged in the sun around aquamarine pools, these misfits stood in the shadows, unnoticed, unsung. Such a one was Francesca.

It was a Sunday lunch full of glamorous people like Natalie Wood and Robert Wagner, James Fox and Tuesday Weld. I became aware of a girl, about my age, standing uncertainly on the edge of the crowd. I noticed her because, like her, I too was hovering about on the fringe of things. She stood out particularly because it was a very hot day and everyone was either in bathing suits or a variety of Emilio Pucci and Ferragamo patterned silks and cottons, big hats and sunglasses, but this girl was wearing a pink woollen coat buttoned right up to her neck.

I caught her eye and smiled and she walked rather tentatively towards me.

'Hi, I'm Francesca. My mum is Zsa Zsa Gabor.' She gestured at an overdone-up woman sitting under an umbrella, holding a very grumpy little dog in her arms.

Francesca was a year younger than me. She had a heart-shaped face with a very pronounced widow's peak, clear skin and thick dark-blonde hair. She didn't resemble her mother at all. In fact she looked ordinary, and in contrast to her preening mother she seemed very sweet. She was friendly and a little shy.

'Aren't you a bit hot in that coat?' I said, smiling.

'I don't want to take it off because . . . of my weight,' she said, and we both grinned. I understood and my heart went out to her – she must have been sweltering. She told me who her father was but she never saw him. Basically he had disowned her. Her mother had lots of boyfriends, who all tried to bribe Francesca by buying her expensive presents, so that she might encourage her mother to marry them. But Zsa Zsa never stayed married to any of them for very long.

Francesca invited me back to her house in Bel Air. It was enormous, like a palace with marble floors, all very expensively furnished, but it didn't feel like a home. It was too big, too grand, too empty. There was something hollow about it. She told me she loved horses and loved to ride, but I got the impression that she spent a lot of time on her own there, in that huge house.

Zsa Zsa later alleged she had been raped by Conrad, resulting in Francesca, so I cannot imagine the effect that must have had on their relationship, or how it made Francesca feel about herself. She was already very fragile. When Francesca was older, struggling in her personal life and unsure what to do with herself, her father's generosity would only extend to getting her a job as a receptionist at one of his five-star hotels. When he died, worth billions, he left her only $100,000, which she contested in court, and lost. Francesca ended her life homeless, sleeping in her car, and died aged sixty-seven. Zsa Zsa Gabor lived to be nearly a hundred.

Francesca was another Hollywood casualty, the only child of a mother who married nine times, accumulating husbands and great wealth, who showered her daughter with presents but never really gave her any of her time.

★

While I had been filming *That Darn Cat!* and grappling with professional dilemmas and an assortment of Siamese cats, Andrew was backpacking across America, hobo-style, travelling from New York to California, following in the footsteps of so many dreamers and pioneers across that vast country, hitching rides, sometimes jumping on to freight trains. He finally made it to Mecca/Hollywood, where he managed to supplement his meagre savings with a bit of entrepreneurial brilliance. One of Andrew's skills, which I haven't yet mentioned, was his uncanny knack for *forging* signatures. I'm not sure who taught him, whether it was one of his father's spy colleagues or if he just taught himself, but it's an art that came in handy on this occasion because, thanks to his stint working on *A Hard Day's Night*, during which Andrew had been in a privileged position to snap the Beatles at his leisure, he had all these original prints of John, Paul, George and Ringo. Needing to make some money in Hollywood, he made a killing flogging 'signed' Beatle photographs outside the studio gates.

Having Andrew around to talk to was a big help in all my deliberations. Talking to Andrew, meeting Francesca, seeing Judy Garland, all these together made me realise I had to leave Disney, however good the offer was to extend the contract. Not only was it a tough decision professionally, it was going to be tough personally too. I was going to have to say goodbye to all my family at the studio – and ultimately to Walt himself, whom I loved and owed so much – to take 'the road less travelled'.

By the time *That Darn Cat!* wrapped, everyone at Disney knew I was leaving. Arthur Park didn't burn the bridge entirely, though. There was still talk of me possibly working for Disney again, if the right project came along. Now those six long years at the studio where I'd grown up were drawing to a close, it didn't seem real. I couldn't imagine that I'd never see Walt again, that I'd never look up from a scene and see him standing there, smiling, just behind the lights.

We were slowly getting the house on Cordell Drive packed up. Daddy had finished *King Rat* and the suitcases had all been dragged out again. Another four months gone; by now I think I'd become hardwired to want to move on again after four months.

The Wardrobe Department had given me some of the clothes from *Darn Cat!* – they were now lying across the bed – all lovely, but, strangely, after a short time I couldn't wear them. I'd left that life behind.

I lay down on the bed and looked around the room. It all looked so bare, empty and abandoned. I caught sight of my gold bracelet. I picked it up and held it in my hands.

When I first arrived at Disney, Walt had given me this beautiful gold bracelet. On the completion of every film, he would present me with a heavy gold disc with the film's title engraved on one side and a little image or symbol relating to the film on the other. The image for *Pollyanna* was her profile, with a tiny diamond at her throat. For *Moon-Spinners* it was a windmill with a pearl for the moon. He also gave me a little golden replica of my Oscar. But the final disc I received was larger and heavier than the others. On the back he'd had engraved the titles of all six films I made for him, and on the front was a door, like a dressing-room door with a star on it, and the star was a diamond; the door opened and inside it just said: HAYLEY.

It was so thoughtful and generous and touching – and so *Walt*. It still makes me want to cry just thinking about it. By the time Walt sent me that last medallion, I had already been back in England for some time. *That Darn Cat!* had been released and was well received, so logically I should have been upbeat, as should have Walt, but instead both of us seemed to be feeling a strange sort of loss.

Dear Hayley,

Realising that this is the last medallion to add to your bracelet kinda brought tears to my eyes. You know that old saying about not losing a daughter but gaining a son . . . well, this is sort of like losing a daughter and I didn't gain any son to make it worthwhile.

I'm sure you have heard how well 'That Darn Cat!' is being received . . . even in England, it is doing great. And it is breaking box office records for this time of year at the Radio City Music Hall. We have our story scouts looking for the perfect vehicle for the mature Hayley, so maybe you'll be with us again yet.

In the meantime, this comes with all my love and best wishes to you and yours for a Merry Christmas, for the New Year and for many years to come.

Walt

By the time I finished *That Darn Cat!* the bracelet was already becoming very heavy. I had the last disc made into a key ring, and thank God I did, because years later Walt's bracelet was stolen from my hotel room while I was making a film in Europe. The story of my teenage life, woven in gold.

I never saw it again.

CHAPTER TEN

Bats With Baby Faces

'And bats with baby faces in the violet light
Whistled, and beat their wings . . .'

— T.S. Eliot, *The Waste Land*

For twelve months my mother had been working on a new story called 'Bats With Baby Faces', which both my parents felt would make a wonderful film – with a good part for me. And I thought so too. The role of Brydie was tragic and quite complex: a naïve sixteen-year-old girl who has suffered a severe childhood trauma after the boy she was playing with was killed in a shooting accident. All the people in the village blame Brydie for this tragedy and ostracise her from the community. Her mother, devastated with guilt, turns to drink and becomes incapable of caring for her daughter, which leaves Brydie to cope and grow up on her own. The only people she can relate to are the local children who frequent the church graveyard, all of whom are much younger than herself. That is, until she meets the gypsy, Roibin . . .

Daddy took the story to John Davies at the Rank Organisation who liked it and agreed to produce. He also gave his blessing for my father to helm the project, taking the director's chair for the first time. On the face of it, it all looked pretty good, albeit pretty incestuous; a story by Mary Hayley Bell, directed by her husband, starring her daughter. There was even a role for Hamlet! Were we asking for trouble?!

Whatever reservations I may have had, I brushed them under the carpet. I loved the story and the idea of being directed by my father. I knew he would handle the story beautifully, and as the experienced and intelligent actor that he was, he felt ready for the challenge of stepping behind the camera.

Unfortunately, at home the atmosphere was becoming impossibly strained, with nightly rows fuelled by alcohol. A terrible feeling of chaos seemed to descend on the house and sit there, straddling it like some evil entity, distorting everything.

I would tell myself, it's just the drink that makes my beautiful, intelligent mother appear idiotic and pour out those ridiculous, hurtful, sometimes even cruel remarks. I didn't stop and consider *why* she was drinking in the first place. These horrible scenes seriously shook my confidence in both my parents. I soon began to doubt the film as well – was this going to be a disaster? Could I even be objective? I became more and more worried about Daddy. I knew how desperately he wanted to make a success of this, especially for Mummy, and I could see it starting to weigh heavily upon him.

We had all the conditions for a perfect storm and I feared Daddy would bear the brunt of it. It's hard enough to direct a movie, even in ideal circumstances, without the addition of family complications. Directing a movie is like waging a war – it is literally 'dreams versus reality'. The director must struggle to realise an incorporeal vision in their head while facing a myriad of oppositions. There's no such thing as a smooth ride. The studios are always interfering, budgets are always being cut, something is always going wrong and, with so many moving parts, it's the director that everyone turns to for every decision. It takes a hundred times as much energy as acting. Of course, my father knew all this – but only in theory. He was a conscientious and hard-working actor but this would be another level of responsibility. Once the ship was launched there would be no respite, no relaxing with a glass of wine at the end of the day. As soon as the actors were wrapped, it would be off to view the 'dailies' from the previous day with his dinner on his lap, then back to the production offices to plan the next day's shoot, with all the inevitable hitches and stitches, casting issues, production issues, budget issues . . . It's endless. It takes enormous determination and willpower to hold the vision before your eyes and never lose sight of it.

So I worried whether my father would have the energy, since he was already fighting an emotionally exhausting battle on the home front. I felt helpless. Nothing I said made any difference, Mummy never stopped talking and Daddy became her punch bag. I wished just for once he would lose his temper – I'm sure this is what she really wanted. She was a wild and tempestuous woman who seemed to be scratching at the walls of her own self-made prison. She was desperate for a fight, a good old-fashioned barney. It would have been stimulating, satisfying, dangerous, but that's what she longed for – a knock-down, stand-up row!

But my father never obliged her. He was too gentle, too nice.

One night we had dinner together, just the three of us as usual. Jonathan was at his boarding school and Bunch was in New York doing *Alfie* with Terence Stamp. The meal was over and we were down to the cheese and nuts. Mummy had been haranguing us throughout the meal.

'Actors!' she snapped. 'The only people we ever see are bloody actors! Oh *God*!' She groaned and drained her glass. 'All they ever talk about is the business, we never see anyone interesting with something to say. Writers, thinkers – we never talk about ideas or books . . . just actors, actors . . . boring, bloody actors!!'

Suddenly I'd had enough and shouted at her. 'Why do you do it, Mummy? Why do you drink so much?'

'Excuse me?' she said witheringly.

'Why do you drink so much?' I pursued her.

She stared at me, long and hard.

'Because I like it,' she said defiantly. 'I'm Irish . . . the Celtic people are all psychic.'

'What has *that* got to do with anything, Mummy?'

She scoffed, waving me away like I was too unintelligent to grasp the subtler truths of Celts and booze. 'I'm like Uncle Bones,' she proclaimed, pouring herself another.

All I knew about Uncle Bones was that he was Irish and riotously, unapologetically alcoholic.

'Yes, Uncle Bones died of drink! How is that a good thing? And why do you never stop complaining? You have so much to be grateful for, not least of all a man who adores you!'

'Ha!' was her only retort.

'When you're drunk you just become stupid and ugly!' I knew I was getting out of hand . . .

She was shocked; that was unlike me. She fixed me with a look.

'You'd better be careful, you're becoming nasty, you're losing all your charm! You've no idea how much we've sacrificed for you, you selfish girl, how much is done for you, and how little you appreciate it, taking it all for granted!'

As usual Daddy said nothing; less said soonest mended . . .

'I just can't sit here night after night,' I said suddenly. 'I think it's time I left home and got a little flat in London. Johnny could share with me, we've talked about it—'

'Ha!' she snorted dismissively. 'You wouldn't last a minute, you'd be hopeless and miserably lonely.'

'I'm nearly twenty! I need to stand on my own two feet and not have everything done for me!'

There was a long, very awkward silence. I was beginning to regret my outburst.

'Well . . . at least, I could just try it out for a bit . . . maybe Chelsea. Not far. I'd come home a lot.'

Daddy looked at me across the table with a hurt look in his

eyes. Finally he said softly, 'Oh, Hail, we would never have bought back The Wick if it was just for the two of us.'

'Oh, Daddy . . .'

But I didn't know what to say. I loved them both so much, I didn't want to hurt them, but I didn't want to have to deal with their pain and their problems. It was self-preservation. Or maybe I was just selfish.

Mummy's drinking became our family secret. It was all kept behind closed doors, locked away in the attic like mad Mrs Rochester. Thankfully, society these days is much healthier and more honest, people can admit they have a problem, get counselling and go to AA. Wild horses couldn't have dragged my mother there! She'd make flimsy excuses: she didn't 'want to risk being recognised'. It was shameful, and deep down she did feel shame. She didn't want people to know, least of all the press, which is understandable – although by today's standards the press then were discreet. The truth is she was chained to the bottle and she didn't want to stop. She had a remarkably strong constitution and very rarely got a hangover. But mentally it was slowly wearing her down and as the years passed she turned to it more and more.

She began to find herself increasingly alone. Soon everyone had either left home or was working, Daddy was often in the theatre night after night, and when she found that she couldn't write any more her despair was profound. Nevertheless, a 'respectable' pretence was kept up, the facade maintained, while all the while my father's heart was breaking and my mother was in danger of falling apart. This was partly the English way, of repressed emotions, but they also believed that being in the 'public eye' meant one had a responsibility to set an example. I was taught that too, but we had our problems like any family, and we simply were not dealing with them. Locking the drinks cabinet for a few days wasn't going to change anything.

Writing was the only way she knew how to heal herself, or at least process the complex emotions she was grappling with. As with *Whistle*, the story for *Bats With Baby Faces* centred around a group of children and a strong young female protagonist. My mother wrote about the lives of children repeatedly. It was an undisguised attempt to recapture her own childhood, those paradise years in China when the world made sense to her. I know she mourned the loss of her adored father, and her brother who had died so young – just as she mourned the loss of her own youthful self. When she met Daddy, he took the place of her father in many respects, his enthusiasm for life filled so many of those empty spaces. But in the deepest recesses of her soul, because she never dealt with them, they were always there.

My mother once told me about a dream she'd had. What she remembered of it had disturbed her greatly, although she had no clue as to its meaning. In the dream she was dragging a large, heavy suitcase 'full of her things'. It weighed so much her arms hurt. Passers-by remarked, 'Why are you carrying that old thing? What's in there?' But she wasn't entirely sure. So she stopped, unlocked the case and looked inside – only to discover it was full of water.

Keith Waterhouse and Willis Hall were approached to write the screenplay for *Bats*, which by now had been retitled *Sky West and Crooked*. They had both done such a wonderful job with *Whistle*, steering the children's story clear of sentimentality by grounding it with realism and humour. However, both writers were now in great demand and unable to take on more projects. Rank were eager to get a script as soon as possible, so my father turned to John Prebble, an excellent writer, who had just had a huge hit with his screenplay for *Zulu*, which had made Michael Caine into a star. So Prebble got typing and delivered a good first draft, which was promising but not entirely right. My father kept it to himself. He didn't let me read the first draft – I think he was genuinely excited by the script but there was a way to go before it was ready to shoot and he knew we were running out of time.

In order to make a big film you need both the financing and the talent (aka, the 'stars' – both literal and celestial) to align at the same moment. This is the chicken-and-egg scenario that plagues the film business. Luckily for my father, he already had my name attached, as well as his own, before he approached Rank. However, my schedule was jam-packed, and we were both booked to make other movies in America directly after the shoot. If the dates for *Sky West* were pushed back I would have to drop out, which might scupper the financing. So my father had two choices: stop everything and get the script right, or strike the iron while it was still hot, and try fixing the script as they went. He decided on the latter and ploughed on with pre-production. Sets were built, locations scouted, cast and crew finalised as they advanced towards the first day's filming. Dickie Attenborough once said that even if a director is struggling, so long as the script is good, they will probably be able to make a decent movie; but without a decent script even a good director will struggle since the blueprint is fundamentally flawed. As the saying goes – 'if it ain't on the page, it ain't on the stage'.

But Daddy couldn't turn back, he was so emotionally invested in the film. He was also hoping that it would lift Mummy's spirits. He told her not to worry, that there was as much to look forward to as there was to be anxious about. So he kept on, while behind the scenes constantly revising the script, giving himself this added handicap, which was not ideal for his first venture into directing.

I could feel the pressure he was under, but I had my own job to focus on. I desperately needed a few days alone to prepare for the role, so I took myself off for a long weekend to Brighton. I saw myself having bracing, solitary walks along the seafront and on to the piers, the gulls circling above me, breathing in the lonely sea and the sky . . . Also, I had a new 'miracle diet' to try out, which I could only do on my own.

Brighton has always had a special place in my heart. This famous seaside town has gone through so many vicissitudes:

from its beginnings as a small medieval fishing village to be-coming the Hanoverian royal retreat with its great Pavilion and beautiful John Nash Regency terraces, to its latter glory days as a popular Victorian seaside Mecca. To this day it still has an aura of decaying romance about it. Behind every fish'n'chip shop or bowling alley you'll find those elegant old Georgian houses, standing like ghosts, their arches and pillars crumbling in the salt breeze. It's that haunted grandeur that was captured so brilliantly in the Boulting Brothers' noir classic *Brighton Rock*, which made Dickie Attenborough a huge star in Britain, playing baby-faced psychopath Pinkie.

I arrived at the Metropole Hotel, a majestic Victorian relic on the seafront, checking in under the name 'Heather Miles', to match the initials on my suitcase. Unfortunately, I kept forgetting that my name was now Miles and more often than not failed to respond when spoken to.

I was given a spacious sea-view suite with large Georgian win-dows. As I looked out across the beach I could hear the sound of revving motorbikes. I peered down towards the promenade and could see a few Mods and Rockers zooming by on their respective wheels of choice: Lambrettas for Mods, motorbikes for Rockers. The British papers were always going on about teenage delinquency in the 1960s, and Mods and Rockers were the fa-vourite bogeymen for a while. It seemed a lot of fuss over nothing to me, just kids letting off steam. Of the two fashions, I felt more inclined towards the Mods – the miniskirts, the Italian shoes, Motown, Pop Art, bands like the Who. They took amphetamine pills, which allowed them to stay up all night, and I became rather intrigued by these 'blue pills' because, apparently, they also made you very thin. But annoyingly, I hadn't as yet come by any. As far as the Rockers went, I liked their music – Elvis Presley, Eddie Cochran – but I couldn't quite see myself hanging on to the back of a Norton motorcycle with my arms wrapped around a Greaser.

I stepped back from the window, took the script out of my bag and reread my character description: 'Brydie sits on a church wall, watching the children play. She is sixteen, curious, waif-like.' I stopped reading and looked in the mirror – oh shit. By no stretch of the imagination did I look 'waif-like'. Not at all. Obviously, the priority was to focus absolutely, completely on the script, and my character, but, oh shit!! I also needed to lose as much weight as possible! I was quite plump, which I could see made me look too old; Brydie was supposedly about sixteen; naïve, innocent, emotionally arrested – and *waif-like*.

The new 'miracle diet' was vital and so, as soon as I was settled in, I embarked upon it enthusiastically. It sounded simple enough, even enjoyable too – it included lots of things that I loved like eggs and white wine, and . . . well, actually, that was pretty much it.

Breakfast: Two hard-boiled eggs and a glass of white wine.

Lunch: Two hard-boiled eggs and another glass of white wine.

Supper: Two more hard-boiled eggs, a glass of white wine, or two . . . or . . . finish the bottle!

I was plastered for three days, slept like a log and became as constipated as a crow. In those three days in Brighton I lost five pounds. On the way home I stopped to fill up the car and bought two Mars bars.

I became exasperated by myself and my inability not to eat! The only way that I could see to deal with the problem was to throw up after every meal, which I proceeded to do with alarming regularity. With this regimen came all the feelings of failure, self-loathing and depression that inevitably follow. I had no idea that other people did this, or that it actually had a name – 'bulimia'. I didn't discover this for years.

I once met the champion jockey Lester Piggott while staying at a health farm and he told me that, in order to keep his weight down, he sometimes ate grass to make himself sick. I liked the idea of keeping my weight down, not so much the eating grass, so at first I had to stick my fingers down my throat. After a while, with practice, I got so good at it I didn't need to any more. I'd just lean over and throw up, simple.

Whoever we are, whatever our backgrounds, whatever crisis we face, whether it's struggles with money or teenage hormonal Armageddon, I believe that, at its core, the reason anyone becomes trapped in habitual self-harm is the same for everyone: low self-esteem. Not being able to accept who you are; not feeling happy in your own skin. Back then, when people talked about 'self-love' I didn't really understand it. To me it sounded indulgent, narcissistic even, but I mistakenly associated the word 'love' with 'romance', which is misleading. It's not about being 'in love' with yourself. To be 'loving' to oneself, to take care of oneself, to be kind, in the same way that a parent cares for their child – this love is a source of spiritual strength. Without being able to love oneself, it is so hard, perhaps impossible, to be a source of strength for others. And let's face it, life is hard enough as it is without needing our own self-sabotage.

To this common human problem, I added my own special layer of fear. It was more than just a desire to be thin (especially on camera), to look better, even beautiful, or the pressure to live up to a certain ideal. Subconsciously, there was also the fear that I was growing up – something I felt no one wanted me to do – and that if I stayed small and thin and looked like a child, maybe people would be more prepared to accept me. They didn't want the new Hayley; they wanted the charming and appealing child, not the chubby, introverted adolescent. Who was this new 'me', anyway? I had no idea. She was a complete unknown and that was scary. The child, I knew – and of course, she had been very successful.

So I took the situation into my own hands, literally, throwing up regularly and keeping my weight below normal. Before long I stopped having my periods, the glands in my throat became infected and my skin erupted – I had to take antibiotics for years to try and get rid of the acne that developed under my chin.

The years of secret eating and bulimia took their toll psychologically as well. When I look back at pictures of my younger self, she's not nearly as gross as she thought she was; in the fullness of time, all that weight she had despaired over simply melted away naturally and everything settled into the shape she was born to be. And there's the irony: one spends the rest of one's life trying to recreate that youthful bloom with ridiculously expensive creams and facials and surgery. Then, one day, you realise you're actually getting old, your hair dries up, there are lines on your face that don't go away after a good night's sleep. It all seems to happen so suddenly. Where was the time between youth and middle age when you were supposed to just enjoy the experience of being grown up?

With all my secret issues bubbling away and family drama hanging thick in the air, we began shooting *Sky West* in the little village of Badminton, on the Duke of Beaufort's estate in Gloucestershire. The hotel lodgings were a short drive away in Bristol. My father had personally hand-picked every member of the crew, many of whom had worked with him in the past. He'd also made sure that they all received a copy of the script, so everyone felt personally connected to what was going on in front of the camera. As a result, there was a wonderful atmosphere on the set. I was especially happy because my father had brought Andrew on board as third assistant director. It would be fun having him around – as it turned out, too much fun.

In spite of all my worries for *Sky West*, I was excited to play Brydie. Earlier that summer, in the South of France, my mother had come across a painting, by a street artist, of a slightly strange-looking girl, with a thin face and pale untidy hair tied back with a bit of black string. It was Brydie. I based my idea of her on that painting. And thanks to my strict bulimic regime, I'd lost the weight, bleached my hair even blonder, and now Brydie looked back at me from my dressing-room mirror.

My father had assembled an excellent cast: the young Ian McShane was perfect to play the gypsy 'Roibin' who falls in love with Brydie, and Annette Crosbie was very moving as the desperate drunken mother. We also had dear Geoffrey Bayldon playing the bewildered vicar, and Hamilton Dyce as the local gravedigger – he'd previously played the wonderfully fastidious vicar in *Whistle Down the Wind*.

My father was the soul of calm and courtesy on the set, and with the actors he was the soul of tact. Knowing how it felt to be in front of the camera, he understood how to play on an actor's strengths, or gently moving them away from a direction they may have been taking if that wasn't what he wanted. However tense things got, he never shouted or lost his temper and his sense of humour was inexhaustible.

Nobody would have guessed that at night he was tearing his hair out back at the hotel.

Daddy was a very focused, organised person, without ever being pedantic. He had a tidy mind, which was second nature to him. Even when speaking on the telephone he would automatically be rearranging things harmoniously on his desk. All the notes in his script were meticulous, like the entries in his pocket diaries, which were written in tiny writing. Everything he did was considered, everything he owned was appreciated, and every moment of his life he attempted to live consciously, joyfully and with thanks.

However, my work ethic, which I acquired from my father, and which I usually adhered to religiously, was now falling to pieces due to having Andrew on the set. Although we were both nineteen, we still had a lot of growing up to do and we often behaved like kids. Andrew hadn't lost his macabre fascination with graveyards and so sometimes, after work, the two of us would take his small portable record player and risk getting piles sitting on ice-cold gravestones as we listened to Wagner. He was always poking around in derelict

Top With Alan Bates in *Whistle Down the Wind*, 1963. It was so easy to imagine he was Jesus.

Above We Three Kings: With Our Nan and Our Charles (Diane Holgate and Alan Barnes) on *Whistle Down the Wind*. Alan's wondering where the tea trolley is. I'm wondering if I'll ever kiss the clapper boy.

Right *In Search of the Castaways* was an epic adventure movie. I was looking forward to riding with the gauchos across Patagonia, but only got as far as Twickenham.

An old darling, 'mon petit chou' –
singing with Maurice Chevalier,
1962. The quintessential Frenchman,
he spoke English with a slight
Lancashire accent.

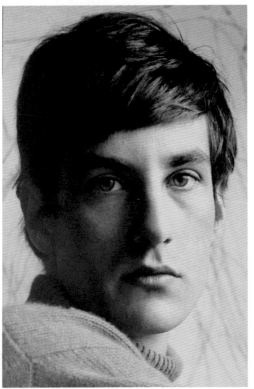

Andrew Birkin in 1962. His hysterical
letters to my Swiss finishing school
helped me to stay sane. The Birkin
family were my Bloomsbury
Group; eccentric, glamorous
and all quite brilliant.

Summer Magic, 1963. Walt would often wander onto the set and hang out with the cast and crew. He knew everyone's names.

Sixteen and still with a big bow in my hair! Here I am waiting with Dorothy McGuire at the end of a long day on *Summer Magic*. My star was at its zenith but my confidence was crumbling.

With Peter Brown and Burl Ives on *Summer Magic*. Our very own 'Big Daddy', Burl was a formidable actor, fueled almost exclusively by root beer.

Flanked by two sweet geniuses, (left–right) Richard and Robert Sherman, 1962. From *The Jungle Book* to *Mary Poppins*, the Sherman Brothers wrote so many classic songs for Disney.

London, 1964: At the Pickwick Club with George, Jane Asher and Paul. I'm not thrilled at all.

Filming *The Moon-Spinners* with Pola Negri and her alter ego, 1963. She insisted on the cheetah, and that the sable wrap and all jewels she wore be real.

Disneyland, 1962, with Walt, Mum and Dad at the Swiss Family Treehouse. Dad was thrilled. You know you're part of history when you become an attraction at Disneyland!

With 'D.C.' on *That Darn Cat!*, 1965. He weighed a ton and dug his claws in at the slightest provocation. He needed to go on a diet. So did I.

Left Tom Lowell, Dean Jones, Dorothy Provine, Roddy McDowall and me enjoy a visit from Walt during production of *That Darn Cat!*. It was to be my last film with the studio. Walt died two years later.

Below right 'The terrible twins': With the Boulting Brothers, Roy and John, filming *The Family Way*, 1967. It was to be a life changing experience.

Below The debacle of my twenty-first birthday party – with a few of my closest friends from Fleet Street. (Daddy, second from left, posing as a press photographer.)

The calm the before the storm: Roy and I on the *Queen Elizabeth* sailing to New York to promote *The Family Way*. It was the first time we formally 'came out' as a couple.

With Crispian, 1974: The view from Cobstone Mill. You could see five counties!

Crisp and Ace – my two little boys in their Brittany jumpers, 1978.

old tombs hoping to find human remains. One night he was successful and found a pile of bones and a skull, which he took back to his hotel room, laying them out neatly on his little bed, with the skull on the pillow. The next morning, the maid gave everyone a heart attack with her blood-curdling screams.

I was hanging out with Andrew and Ian McShane a lot after work. It was fun and Ian was great company but he was also a bit of a Lothario. He boasted to Andrew that before we wrapped he was going to try 'to get me into bed'. Obviously, Andrew shared this information and I scoffed at the idea, but I was secretly flattered. I was no angel in white either. Ian was very attractive and I often found him hard to resist, but I had never slept with anyone and it certainly wasn't going to be with him.

I tried to remain professional but my rules about self-discipline were getting stretched to breaking point. Drinking red wine and brandy in the evenings, which I didn't even enjoy that much, began to take its toll. For a time, I just about got away with it, but inevitably the consequences appeared on my face, and the smallest suggestion of cheekbones soon disappeared. While my father grappled with the enormous responsibilities of the shoot and trying to keep the show on the road, I was in danger of sabotaging the whole project, up at all hours, knowing that I had to work the next morning. Thinking about it now, it was a rebellion of sorts, the inevitable teenage stuff. It was just unfortunate that my father's first opportunity at directing had to suffer my ill-timed attempts at growing up.

One day during the shoot, I saw the strain on my father's face and I felt awful. I realised I had to take the job more seriously, for him and for myself. I couldn't take it all for granted; I needed to have self-respect, stop cavorting around with randy actors – and I didn't want to get a reputation.

★

Fortunately, I managed to complete *Sky West* without giving my poor father a nervous breakdown and also without becoming another notch on dear Ian's bedpost. As soon as I wrapped, I was flown back to Los Angeles, this time completely on my own, to start filming *The Trouble with Angels* at MGM Studios – playing a wayward novice nun! The movie had an unusually female-heavy cast, starring the dynamic and charismatic Rosalind Russell, who I was rather in awe of. Rosalind was very beautiful and very intelligent, and dressed up in the black robes of Mother Superior one couldn't help but feel daunted.

I dyed my hair red, inspired by my mother who, you will not be surprised to hear, had been an out-and-out rebel at her boarding schools in England. Her exploits were family legend so I wanted to channel her spirit. *Angels* was being made by William Frye, who had also produced *The Chalk Garden*, and his production had given me a trailer the size of a city block. It was very good for my morale and I adored it. It was huge and freezing and always empty, like living in a big gold-tinted glass box. This was my first Hollywood movie without Disney, and without my parents, so it was all incredibly exciting, but it also felt very strange being at a foreign studio, walking on to the set and not knowing anybody.

Bill Frye had hired the amazing Ida Lupino to direct. Ida was one of the very few female directors in Hollywood at that time. She was an exceptional person and an excellent director. Born into a family that had a centuries-long history with the theatre in England, she had been an actress herself since the age of three, and wrote, produced and directed for her own production company – a real trailblazer for women. She was strong but knew how to tread a careful course. On the set she was very decisive but never lost her feminine touch or her sense of humour. She called everyone 'Darling' and 'Sweetie' and wanted everyone to call her 'Mother'. On the back of her chair was written 'Mother of us all . . .'

Bill Frye, who adored working with Ida, had a very sophisticated eye for costume and production design. At his suggestion, Ida only ever dressed in black and white – just like the nuns

– and, to complement this image, Bill's office was also decorated in black and white – and I mean literally everything was black and white, even the candies in the ashtray – so Ida could merge into her monochromatic surroundings like a stylised Cecil Beaton sketch! Initially, I admit, it was an adjustment to be directed by a woman. To have Ida in a position that had always been male made the atmosphere and balance on the set feel quite different and it was an unfamiliar experience for most of the men, being told what to do by a woman. But Ida's experience outstripped most people's; everyone respected her and she was a darling. I admired her enormously.

As well as Ida and Rosalind, the cast was predominantly women: a sweet and very good actress called June Harding played my best friend, and there was also Binnie Barnes and the lovely Mary Wickes, both playing nuns. I'd first met Mary on *The Parent Trap*. She was a very funny person and seeing her in a wimple made her even funnier.

The most remarkable bit of casting, however, was that of the famous burlesque dancer Gypsy Rose Lee, who, in the story, comes to the convent one day to teach the girls how to be graceful young ladies.

I couldn't quite believe it. She was someone I never thought I would meet in a thousand years. It was almost as extraordinary as meeting Mata Hari! I had to pinch myself. Rosalind Russell already knew Gypsy well, having played her mother so brilliantly in the film based on her memoirs, co-starring with Natalie Wood. But for the rest of us, being in the presence of the Queen of Burlesque took a bit of getting used to. In *Angels*, Gypsy plays a slightly tongue-in-cheek version of herself, hired to instruct the girls in grace and movement. She was quite fabulous, and I could appreciate that her approach to stripping was just a natural extension of her own character: unique, charming, intelligent and very funny. There was an air of amused detachment, as if she wasn't really taking it that seriously. She seemed to be above it all, yet she never looked down on anyone. And she never gave too much away. I marvelled at the confidence she must have had in her own sexuality and I wondered if she'd always had that, or if that was something she employed to develop her act – as humour so often covers our deeper feelings and insecurities.

Every film is an education of sorts and on *Trouble with Angels* I took away a huge amount of inspiration from this company of strong, talented women leading the caravanserai. All of them had, in their different ways, flourished within a traditionally male-dominated 'system' and built extremely successful careers for themselves, each with their own unique personal style.

While I was shooting, Juliet came to LA on business and we rented a lovely old house together belonging to the actress Gladys Cooper. When she was young, Gladys had been a great Edwardian beauty, celebrated both as a thespian and as one of the most beautiful women on the London stage. I remember her coming to visit us; a small, slim, elegant woman, browned by the sun, with amazingly clear, smiling blue eyes and shining white hair. She must have been nearly eighty and still very beautiful. Her house, on Napoli Drive, in Pacific Palisades, overlooking the golf course, was built of white clapboard, with a long, wide veranda and deep, comfortable rattan chairs. No one walks in LA, or uses the subway like in New York, so I hired a gorgeous little Ford Mustang runabout and we settled happily into Gladys's digs. It was lovely to spend time with my sister and we drew closer together again. She was now a mother and I loved being aunty to her beautiful little blond boy Sean, then aged three. Like any actress in Los Angeles, she was busy meeting agents and casting directors, and was very excited because she was on the shortlist for the lead part in an upcoming movie adaptation of *Doctor Dolittle*, starring alongside Rex Harrison.

It is only very rarely that the showbusiness of Tinseltown gets overshadowed, but in August the only show anyone was talking about was the upcoming Beatles gigs at the Hollywood Bowl.

The band were a phenomenon when I met George, but by the summer of '65 they had conquered the world and America was now the screaming epicentre of Beatlemania. Bunch and I shamelessly exploited our Hollywood contacts to secure two prized tickets. So, one hot afternoon, delirious with excitement, we fired up the Mustang and drove to the Hollywood Bowl. It's hard to describe the concert. It was unlike anything I'd ever witnessed before or have seen since: a mind-blowing, ear-splitting experience, packed to capacity with twenty thousand screaming girls. When the boys walked out on to that stage, the sudden surge of noise perforated your eardrums like a million starlings swooping down over you in waves. At one point a private helicopter appeared, hovering very low, right over our heads, with people clinging precariously from a swaying rope-ladder holding binoculars and cameras, trying to get a better look. With all the shrieking, fainting girls and the thundering chopper blades, you couldn't hear a single note from the band.

After the concert somebody up in the Hills gave a party at their house. I never did find out whose house it was, but they were very brave whoever they were – the whole of Hollywood seemed to be trying to get inside. It took us an hour to park the car, then another hour to get into the house. Inside there was a mash of guests and we found ourselves carried along, as if by a current, towards a brightly lit room, eventually finding ourselves next to the four Beatles who were jammed up against a wall, facing a barrage of flashing cameras and a crush of gawping people. It was all very surreal. I couldn't tell whether the boys were the welcoming committee or if they were just stuck there, unable to move. I ended up next to John. He seemed taller than I remembered, and was wearing a grey suit with a small silk Union Jack hanging out of the top pocket. 'Hello, Hayley,' he drawled in his unmistakable voice. As I looked up from the Union Jack I found myself staring into a pair of mirrored dark glasses where two tiny versions of myself stared back at me – and we both laughed.

It was literally a madhouse. Hollywood parties can often be larger than life, but this one took the biscuit. It was impossible to have a conversation with anyone as we were all stone-deaf by that time thanks to the screaming girls. We hung out for a while with Peter Noone from Herman's Hermits, who was especially sweet, but the place was so heaving and it was so dark you could neither see nor hear who you were talking to. To make matters worse, the music was brain-meltingly loud. If you tried to escape to the garden for some respite you found the helicopter from the concert, with its intrepid hangers-on still clinging to the rope-ladder like limpets, now hovering over the house! This added to the general cacophony. Over by the pool someone had found a hose and was soaking everyone in sight: actors, musicians, film stars, models, directors – they were all fair game. It seemed like the whole world was using Beatlemania as an excuse to go completely mad. Just brushing shoulders with the boys in their rarefied orbit of interstellar fame was heady stuff. God knows what it must have been like for them living through that madness every day.

After I finished *The Trouble with Angels* I stayed on for a while in Los Angeles to do the *Andy Williams Show* with co-guest Richard Chamberlain who, back then, was a household name as 'Dr Kildare' in his extremely successful TV series of the same name. Dick was a fine actor and a huge heart-throb – I'd had a crush on him for years, so I was thrilled to work with him – and Andy Williams was lovely and very genuine. To be honest, it was refreshing to be in the company of two gorgeous men after all those nuns!

I had a couple of song-and-dance numbers with Andy and Dick, requiring a week of rehearsing; but it all went swimmingly. I managed to sing in tune with Andy, and avoided stepping on Dick's toes. Everyone was happy and confident, so on the Friday afternoon, we took a break before taping the show that evening. It was a warm California afternoon, so I decided to take the Mustang out for a spin. It all happened so quickly: the glare of the setting sun in my eyes, the lights turning red, and the other car hurtling off the freeway straight into me ... We both smashed through a fence on to somebody's front lawn; the other car's horn was stuck and wailing away, and the woman driver kept fainting – and then fainting again. The police appeared from out of nowhere. And then, somehow, I was being escorted, somewhat haphazardly, back to the studios with trickles of blood and a lump the size of a chicken's egg on my forehead.

I must have been in shock because all I could say was 'Where is Dr Kildare?'

I found him in a bar across the street from NBC having a sandwich, but to my great disappointment, when he saw me he was horrified. Instead of tending to my wounds as I'd hoped, he panicked and handed me over to the barman who gave me a napkin full of ice and sent me back to the studio.

Although I was still struggling with my social awkwardness, I was markedly better at doing parties. I was bouncing back, having hit an all-time low at a Milton Goldman party a year or so before, and I couldn't let that happen again. Goldman and his partner Arnold Weisberger were two charming, high-powered showbusiness lawyers, and it was a tradition that they came to London from New York every summer and gave a number of famously glamorous parties at the Savoy Hotel, to which everyone who was anyone in the business was invited.

I'd been stuck in the corner of a room, struggling for some time to think of anything to say and, finally, to avoid the look on people's faces, had given up and retreated into the ladies' loo. I had been sitting in there for a good hour, making airplanes out of the loo paper and flying them out of the little window, when I heard two women come in. They were talking to each other and I heard my name mentioned ...

'She doesn't have any star quality though, does she?' said the woman.

If I was already deflating like a balloon, after hearing this I was well and truly popped!

How on earth was I going to go back into the party after that?

Listeners never hear good of themselves . . .

Thankfully, I'd picked myself up a bit since then, and spending time on my own in Los Angeles had given me a little more confidence. I went to a party with Roddy McDowall on his thirty-seventh birthday. The boys told dirty stories all night, while I drank water with lime and ice to pretend I was drinking, because I had to drive. I remember sitting there, holding my hands tightly in my lap and smiling weakly while the actor Kevin McCarthy told me how unhappy he was. I didn't know what to say. At half past eleven I left – I couldn't stand it any longer.

Determined not to give up, I gave my first dinner party at the Luau – the Hawaiian restaurant at the Beverly Wilshire Hotel. I invited Margaret Leighton and Michael Wilding, Richard Chamberlain, Bunch and Russell; I drank too many rum punches, danced and flirted with Dick Chamberlain and made a complete fool of myself falling into some geraniums.

Then something truly awkward happened; much more awkward than any of these social situations – quite horrible in fact. The role Juliet was up for in *Doctor Dolittle* was not offered to her, as everyone had expected; instead they offered it to me. It was acutely embarrassing. I should have been thrilled, instead, I felt like crap. When I told my sister, she smiled lovingly and was wonderful about it, which only made it worse. How could I possibly do it now? I wouldn't be able to enjoy it for one moment.

Of course, it was inevitable that this sort of thing was going to happen, more and more, as the gap between us closed. We were going to be considered for the same parts. 'And then what?' I thought grimly. 'We'll become competitors? We'll start avoiding each other?' I couldn't bear it. I'd rather marry a pig!

I did have a meeting with the film's esteemed musical creator Leslie Bricusse at his house in Beverly Hills and I liked him very much, he was charming and very friendly. He played me the music and talked about the film. I could see that it was going to be something quite exceptional, especially with 'Sexy Rexy' in the starring role, but I bottled out and told him I wasn't confident enough about the singing. But that wasn't entirely true. My heart just wasn't in it. The whole thing with Juliet had left a bad taste – I was scared it might damage our relationship. I told myself it wasn't worth it, so I turned it down. Looking back, it was obviously a blunder. I should have taken my career more seriously and done what would turn out to be a classic (the role was eventually played by the beautiful redhead from my trip to Las Vegas, Samantha Eggar). Ultimately, I made a wrong decision for the wrong reasons: guilt and embarrassment. Juliet would have supported my decision as she understood the business better than I did. You can't turn down good parts in good films, they may never come round again. I just wasn't savvy enough to appreciate that and instead of seizing the opportunity I sank back into those secret feelings of guilt about my 'undeserved' success.

I still wrote regularly to Andrew in England. Sometimes they were normal letters, other times it was just a stream of consciousness . . .

It's Saturday, I'm alone and a little cold, it's so silent even the birds are singing in a whisper.

The house is quite empty, I don't know what time it is, I should be doing so many things; making my crumpled bed, putting things away in my room, learning my lines, writing to Mummy and Daddy.

My tummy feels odd, kind of jumpy, maybe I'm going to be ill. Very ill, a long drawn out sickness, weeks will pass as shadowy anxious figures hover about my bed!

Big, wicked black clouds lie over the golf course, the sun is out, the afternoon is saffron and black. There's a palm tree in the distance on a bluff, standing thin and alone, with a ruff of topaz leaves surrounding a small green tuft like the top of a carrot, it's the only tree hit by the sun against a black sky.

I'm so glad that I've seen it. I want to cry.

It wasn't until December that I finally escaped from LA and made my way back home. On the way, I planned to stop off in New York. My summer in LA had given me a taste for freedom and I fancied a week of adventure in the Big Apple, taking in some shows and doing a spot of Christmas shopping.

I booked myself into the Algonquin on 44th Street. The famous old hotel was quite run-down but it was cosy and familiar which was good as this was my first time all alone in New York. I was nineteen years old, with money in my pocket, completely independent and free to roam in the most exciting city in the world.

And it was winter, the most thrilling time of year to be there! It was dazzlingly cold and bright, all those glittering buildings soaring into sharp blue skies and the piercing wind . . . I loved it all: the sound of my footsteps snapping on the sparkling sidewalks, the sight of the manholes in the streets belching out steam . . . There was joy and excitement in every breath I took. It was like living on champagne.

I fell in love with the energy and the excitement of it all, the sense of unimaginable possibilities; many moons later I would fall in love with a New Yorker and live there for a few magical years. I walked for hours and hours, into Central Park and up and down Fifth Avenue and Madison Avenue, gazing into all the incredible shops. At one point I found my way to the Diamond Exchange on 47th Street. I'd never seen anything like it, a whole block of nothing but jewellers. It was like Aladdin's cave: everywhere you looked there were dazzling diamonds and jewels and, I was told, great bargains to be found! I had saved up all my daily allowance from *Angels* and now I managed to blow the whole lot on presents for my family. I went mad. I bought a beautiful ring for my mother, like a rose with a ruby in it, and a gold bracelet with sapphires. I found a gorgeous opal and diamond ring for my sister, and a wristwatch for my brother. It was just the most fantastically enjoyable shopping experience I'd ever had, or would ever have, buying so many fabulously expensive things for the people I loved. It was addictive and I continued with this madness when I got back to England.

Just as well then that the majority of my earnings were safely locked away in a trust until my twenty-first birthday – or I probably would have spent the lot.

Defying the jet lag, I went to see as many Broadway shows as I could squeeze in. I adored the wonderfully eccentric Carol Channing in *Hello, Dolly!*; I wept noisily in *West Side Story*; I also managed, with great difficulty, to get a seat for Peter Shaffer's extraordinary new play *Royal Hunt of the Sun*, although unfortunately, in the middle of David Carradine's brilliant performance as the Inca King 'Atahualpa', jet lag overwhelmed me and I fell fast asleep, striking my forehead hard against the back of the seat in front. I woke myself up and had to stagger quickly out of the theatre before I fell asleep again.

Since I was alone in New York, Juliet, partly as a safety precaution, and partly because she enjoyed playing 'matchmaker', had given me the telephone number of an old friend, from the days when she had first come to New York with *Five Finger Exercise*. He had been a 'rookie' cop then; his name was Joe.

So I called him up and we arranged to meet in the Blue Bar at the Algonquin.

By the time I arrived, all wide-eyed and breathless, Joe was already there. He had graduated from the force and was now a plainclothes detective with the NYPD. He was tall, blond and very charismatic. He exuded confidence, but frankly I was rather disappointed – I'd hoped he was going to be wearing his uniform.

After we'd said hello he smiled and leant closer – 'I want to show you something.' He took hold of my hand and before I realised, guided it into his trouser pocket where my fingers closed around a thick wad of rolled-up dollar bills. He winked and told me that he had just been on a sting operation and the drug dealers had 'paid him off' – he'd agreed to take a bribe!

I was astonished, and rather shocked that he was so open about this kind of thing, but Joe said he liked giving people second chances, especially since it was Christmas. So he took me out to dinner – I can't remember where, I just remember him driving very fast, backwards, down a one-way street. He had his detective's badge, so he could park anywhere at any time. He behaved as if he owned the city.

I'd never met anyone like Joe before; he really did belong to another world. He told me all about working in the Homicide Division in Harlem. It sounded like his life was unpredictable and fraught with danger, and he always carried a gun. I told him British police didn't carry guns, all they had were big wooden truncheons – Joe was impressed. Going out with him was surreal, it bore no relation to anything I'd ever experienced, it was like leading someone else's life. Maybe that's what I should have done, taken off for a year, just disappeared, travelled around, discovered new places, found out about myself. I'd dropped my shackles somewhere between Hollywood and La Guardia airport and I reimagined myself in some black & white romantic affair, like Audrey Hepburn and Gregory Peck in *Roman Holiday*. We'd fall in love, then I'd fly away, back to my real life, the tears streaming down my face, and never see him again.

I decided I wanted to sleep with Joe. I just needed to jump through that final hoop and move on with my life. On my last day in the city I went to Bloomingdale's and found a sort of Grecian, off-the-shoulder, long white silk nightdress. Back at the hotel I lowered the lights and lit some candles and later, when Joe came to my room, I asked him to stay.

Almost immediately I regretted it. I suddenly realised that the nightdress had been a mistake – it wasn't me, it felt ridiculous and I wished I hadn't put it on. Everything was so calculated, so stage-managed. I didn't know what to do, so I pressed on, but as I attempted to strike what I hoped was a seductive 'Gypsy' pose by the bathroom door, I found myself thinking, 'What *am* I doing?'

Then the truth rushed in. 'I'm not in love with this man, this isn't right . . . I don't want to do this!'

Everything fell apart after that. It was like one of those ghastly moments on stage – which happened to me once – when suddenly you're not the character, you're just yourself, wearing someone else's clothes.

To make things worse, I started to laugh and I couldn't stop. It's a maddening quirk – I think it's nerves or something. Not everyone appreciates it. Sometimes, in the middle of a row when things are really intense, when I'm just about to throw a saucepan, I'll start to laugh. Which is what happened, standing there in that ridiculous Greek nightie. I wasn't laughing at him, it was everything about the situation. It all seemed so terribly funny. Luckily, he had a sense of humour. Needless to say, he didn't stay the night.

Gypsy Rose Lee I was not.

On my way to The Wick for Christmas, I drove through Berkeley Square where I spotted a shining white Lotus Elan sports car in the showroom window – so I went mad and decided to buy it for Daddy.

Christmas morning was a riot. I had the joy of giving my family all their presents, and leading my father to the front door to give him his Lotus. It was parked outside the house, wearing a big red bow.

He was thrilled but almost speechless. 'Oh, Hail!' He was so taken aback, but then he laughed delightedly. 'But what a compliment! This car is for a much younger man!' My father's love of cars was legendary. We even had a joke that he would much rather go to bed with a copy of *What Car* than a copy of *Playboy*. The Lotus Elan was a really elegant little car and at that time it was busy winning world championships. It was the closest thing you could get to an affordable Grand Prix car for the road. Unfortunately, the first time he took me out for a drive we realised there was a little problem: you could see the grass verge tearing past through a gap in the door. The car was very high-powered, going from 0–60 in six seconds; it was made of fibreglass and not very solid – frankly, it felt like sitting in a matchbox on top of a bomb. The Elan was also available in kit form, for home assembly, which probably explains the gaps in the bodywork. After a decent interval he quietly exchanged it for something a little more appropriate and weather-proof.

My return to England also meant reconnecting with Andrew. I couldn't wait to see him again – after the debacle in New York, I realised he was the one. This is really when I fell in love with him. All the time I'd been in America I'd gone out with far more men than ever before, flirted with more, kissed more, but I knew that not one of them held a candle to Andrew. Not one of them possessed an atom of his gaiety or companionship. Was I overthinking it? Andrew was the obvious choice for me, but I was scared that if we broke up it might ruin our friendship and I would be desolate. He was my best friend, I trusted him. I played endlessly with the thought that he wouldn't love me for ever, that nothing lasts for ever. One day he would be gone, his little room in the roof of his parents' house would be empty, his clothes gone from the cupboards; it all depressed me so unutterably.

I kept looking for you last night, I felt dismembered without the knowledge that you were there; I stared at my stupid face in the mirror in the loo, my eyebrow pencil poised at the ready in my hand, and wondered why do I bother, you wouldn't see it anyway.

Even as I was falling in love with him, I was imagining the end. What the hell was wrong with me? I had no balance, no equilibrium. I was constantly ricocheting between being on top of the world, 'Queen of Manhattan', one minute, then down in the depths the next.

Andrew meanwhile was going from strength to strength. He now had a great job as Stanley Kubrick's personal assistant on *2001: A Space Odyssey*. He had managed to get Jonathan a job on the film too, as a runner, after he left school. This would prove to be a profound influence on Johnny's life.

One day I drove down to Shepperton Studios to visit Andrew and meet Stanley. The great man was up on a platform with the camera team, about ten feet off the floor, and I had to climb half-way up a ladder to say hello. He bent down to shake hands; he was very sweet and I thought perhaps a bit shy. It was fascinating to watch him work. He was very taciturn, all his attention clearly focused on the scene he was shooting. He reminded me of one of those saturnine chess grandmasters, staring intensely at the pieces, planning the next gambit. After our brief introduction I stayed well back and didn't attempt to make further conversation. I certainly didn't feel like reminding him that we had nearly worked together on *Lolita* – something I was regretting more and more now seeing him in his element.

A few weeks later, Andrew was sent off on an assignment – along with Jonathan and a cameraman – to shoot some aerial footage from a helicopter for the climactic sequence of *2001*, which became known as 'Jupiter and Beyond the Infinite'. It sounded like an adventure, so I decided to go with them. They were sent way up into the north of Scotland, to the Outer Hebrides, and the plan was to film all along the coast. That part of Scotland is magnificently beautiful: jagged, rugged and totally deserted – it was also the dead of winter and below freezing. We arrived in the late evening at the only little hotel in a very remote village on the Isle of Lewis. It was a Sunday, so everything was closed on this strict Presbyterian island; the hotel we were staying in was only barely open. There was no heating, the television had a black cloth over it and the cock had been locked safely away from the chickens. We presumed the hotel chef was in church, but the host did the best he could for us: he found a bit of ham and some lettuce, and a bottle of ice-cold red wine – strictly for pagans like ourselves. When I asked if it might be warmed up a little, it came back in a bucket of boiling water. When the cork was removed steam shot out!

We all knew Stanley's film was going to be special, but I don't think any of us gathered there in that little igloo of a hotel on the furthest reaches of north-west Scotland had the slightest idea that we were participating in cinema history. When I see that climactic sequence of *2001*, the mind-expanding journey through space and time, I can't help but think of Jonathan and Andrew huddled together in that freezing cold helicopter, soaring over the rugged coastline – and that scalding-hot bottle of red wine.

★

Sky West and Crooked was scheduled for release in February 1966, so as soon as I got back from Scotland, I was booked for a week of non-stop press junkets. As my journal attests, I was not in the mood:

> *Hectic rushing days before 'Sky West' opens, averaging four hours of sleep a night. Been drinking far too much and consequently don't feel that good – and look God awful! Felt drained, interview after interview, beginning to hate my own company and the sound of my own voice; now I know what Mummy means about boring bloody actors! As I rabbit boringly on about myself!*

My parents were understandably nervous before the film came out. Talk about a family production, we were all facing the firing squad together! Thankfully, the reviews were kind enough – critics being among the first hurdles one has to clear – but the film didn't break any box office records. I think my father was simply relieved it was over and that it hadn't been a total disaster. The film had successfully retained the spirit of Mummy's story and he had survived the ordeal without slitting his own throat. The reviews said the directing was accomplished, and my parents kindly didn't blame me in any way for the poor box office. But I knew that the film itself must have suffered due to my extra-curricular activities, which made me ashamed. Of course, Rank were disappointed the film didn't make much money, but 'that's showbusiness' – and by the time *Sky West and Crooked* came out, my father was back acting again, filming in the city of Bath, with his old chum Bryan Forbes in a movie called *The Wrong Box*, shooting most of his scenes with his great friend Sir Ralph Richardson. My father enjoyed the experience of directing, but he *loved* being in front of the camera much more than he did running the whole damn circus.

Just as Daddy had moved on, so was I looking forward to the future. My twentieth birthday was coming up, something I couldn't quite believe. At one time I didn't think I'd make it to sixteen!

I spent a lot of time alone in my room, contemplating life, surrounded by my books and my things, pictures and objects that I loved. I was happy being alone. I saw myself, rather romantically, like a wild seabird, just the tips of my wings a little grey where they had dipped into a muddy puddle or two. Being alone was my familiar state; I could see myself years from now, travelling the world, still alone, going where the wind blew me, answering to no one. 'What is happiness?' I wondered. 'Is it different for everyone?'

My grandfather Francis always said he believed it was good health.

I suspect that my great-grandfather, Revd John McGowan, the missionary, would have said faith.

I would have said love. Love of life, love of every living creature.

For me the answer was all three.

I had all the yearning, the romantic aspirations – but not the wisdom or experience to back it up, to ground it. It's all very well wanting to throw your arms around the world, but if you can't love and care for yourself, what real help can you be – to anyone? I told myself, if I could only hang on to my strength of spirit, keep my feelings of insecurity and inferiority under control, or better still batter them into oblivion, I might stand a chance. That was my goal for my twenty-first year: to be confident and happy. And more loving.

And to stay on a bloody diet.

A week after my twentieth, I was scheduled to fly to San Francisco to narrate a television special about the San Francisco Ballet. I have no clue on earth why they asked me, or why I said yes, but that was the plan.

It was on this fateful trip that I realised something was profoundly wrong with me.

For the entire week leading up to the journey, I had irrational and vivid premonitions of doom. I should have confided in someone but I didn't even tell Andrew. I was too afraid that, if I spoke about it, it would only solidify the intangible, elusive terror that seemed to filter out the light from me. On one hand, the world looked infinitely beautiful, my parents infinitely beloved, my whole life a silvery cobweb of a dream; but it was all too good, my life, my luck. And it was soon going to end.

I ploughed through the days, grinding my teeth at the thought of the impending flight halfway across the world – surely this would be the occasion of my imminent and untimely death? I kept this knowledge secret and solemnly resigned myself to fate. Nothing could change what was to happen, so I pressed on nobly and tried to make the best of what was left of my short, tragic life . . .

That last morning at The Wick was indescribable. I breakfasted in bed with Daddy; Mummy was away, in Chester, at the Crown Court, following the Moors Murders trial. She was grimly obsessed by the murders and wanted to write a book about them. Ultimately she gave up on the project when she discovered that another writer, Emlyn Williams (who wrote *The Corn Is Green*), had the same idea. So, with Mummy away, scribbling notes in the spectators gallery in Chester, it was just me and Daddy at home. Only I knew that this was likely to be our last breakfast together and I wondered how he would remember me, how they'd all remember me.

I wore my red coat, and before the car came to pick me up, I put Rachmaninov on the record player.

When I arrived at the airport my plane had already left! 'Of course,' I thought, 'this whole trip is jinxed, I'm not supposed to go.' But I was told to wait by the desk and they changed my ticket for another flight – only twenty minutes till take-off. Then suddenly, I was up in the TWA lounge. I couldn't sit still. There was only one other man in there, oblivious of me, sitting behind an enormous newspaper. He didn't even look up as I paced the room, twitched the curtains and stuffed my face with nuts. 'I'm already dead to him,' I thought. Then they called the flight and I found myself walking to the gate, trying to be gay; minutes later I'm strapped tightly into my seat, like the electric chair. I kept my coat on. My brain seemed to be plunging about in my head, hideous pictures forcing themselves in. I looked for the emergency exit sign. 'Not too far,' I thought. 'I'll be needing that.' I decided to brace for impact, just in case, so I reached up with shaking fingers and yanked out two pillows from the rack; the seat beside me was empty, nobody there, I was alone – so alone; I stared avidly at the stewardess demonstrating the life-jacket drill, then forgot it all. I couldn't remember anything, anything at all.

In my mind, I could see myself struggling alone, screaming helplessly as the aircraft plummeted towards the cold sea. I heard a 'clunk!' and snapped out of it – the doors were shut and we were moving. The horror was building inside me. I tried to concentrate on the buildings moving past – I thought, 'I'll never see them again!' My mouth was dry. I tried to read a magazine but the words jumped and blurred before my eyes. I was becoming hysterical inside, the fear was so bad I wanted to scream; there was a voice in my head, screaming, shrieking, the same two words again and again – '*Get out! Get out!*' I was suffocating, drowning, gasping for air . . . so I did the only thing I could think of: I groaned, doubled up, pushed the button for the stewardess, and fell onto the floor.

I gave the greatest performance of my life as a girl with suspected appendicitis. The plane stopped on the runway and turned back. The doctors and nurses at the airport were all fooled. I was sent home and spent the next two days lying in a darkened room. My doctor was mystified – 'possible food poisoning', he said. I didn't tell a soul what really happened, not for quite some time. But during those days at home in bed, I realised I needed help. I had no idea where to start looking, but something had to change.

The joke was that eventually I had to retrace my steps; the San Francisco Ballet were still very keen and I felt so bad about letting them down that I had to go back. Three days later, pale and much more subdued, I climbed on another plane. This time we made it off the runway and the flight was fine and completely uneventful . . . that is, until we were over San Francisco. Minutes before we were due to land, the captain's voice came over the loudspeaker to tell us they were having 'technical troubles' with the instruments – and he couldn't tell if the undercarriage was down. They were going to circle around the control tower and added that perhaps, just as a precaution, we should all take our little pillows and assume 'brace positions' for landing – but that there was 'nothing to fear'.

'Nothing to *fear*? Oh God. This is it,' I thought. 'It's all happening exactly as I imagined it! You can't cheat fate!'

I looked out of my window and saw flashing lights and fire

engines gathering near the runway.

I swallowed drily, my heart thrashed – I couldn't believe it was happening.

Then I became aware that someone had sat down in the empty seat beside me. It was a reserve co-pilot from the flight deck. I must have looked terrified, because he smiled and took my hand.

The jet landed drunkenly, jerking us around, but we remained intact, and I walked away as calm as could be – until I got into my room at the Fairmont Hotel in San Francisco and started to shake.

The American Evangelist Dr Billy Graham had been in London for a month and his 'Crusade' was drawing enormous crowds to Earls Court. There was a lot about him in the newspapers and on the radio. I didn't know very much about evangelicals at that time but I understood he was part of a movement that had abandoned the extreme narrowness of Christian fundamentalism. I was fascinated by his story and I wanted to go and hear him speak.

It was a very relaxed affair. His words were simple, he talked about real things, real issues in people's lives; in fact, he seemed to be talking about one's own life – everything he said related to the human condition, so it all connected personally. He had a powerful voice and a tremendously strong presence and he was totally sincere. You couldn't take your eyes off him.

Among other things, he talked about the importance of 'Now'. I'd known this all my life – why is it that one has to be constantly reminded? I remembered a story my mother told me, of being on a beach with her father. He had written 'NOW' in the sand with a stick – only to watch the sea come in and sweep the word away.

It all sounded so obvious, so simple: 'Do the important things now, don't wait, don't put them off; reach out to those you love; don't wait to tell people you care about them, help them now, do it now, read the books you need to read, give the money you need to give . . . now!' (I don't think he meant give it to him.)

But the most important thing he spoke about was our relationship with God. 'Man's hunger for God is just as deep as his hunger for food and his thirst for water . . .' he declared. And when he talked about tolerance and love, his words challenged every individual sitting in that arena. I think he sincerely wanted to change the world for the better, one person at a time.

Listening to him preach, surrounded by all those thousands of people in that vast hall, I found myself going back to that tiny little chapel at Elmhurst, to Father John's stirring sermons. And as a child, reading my mother's dilapidated old bible – and beginning to sense something of the existence of a spiritual life. As children we had always said our prayers at night, kneeling by the side of the bed. Later, as I grew up, I prayed less and less; other things filled my life and I felt I had outgrown it. But after that evening listening to Billy Graham, I made a personal reconnection and I started to pray again. Even though I'm lazy, and often let far too much time go by in neglect of any kind of spiritual practice, I know that it is always there, like a beacon, shining in the dark. Prayer has helped to carry me over some of the most challenging and stormy times of my life, and that evening at Earls Court was the beginning of my spiritual search.

'If the spirit of God is speaking in your heart,' Dr Graham said, 'then just stand in your place, and make your way down the aisle, come down to the centre and stand here in front of the platform.' He paused, then he said, 'Now, you come!' There was dead silence, nobody moved. It seemed to go on for ever, then somewhere in the stadium was the sound of someone getting up out of their seat, then another person got up, and another, and suddenly hundreds of people were pouring down the aisles to stand in front of the stage. They were young and old, I saw priests and nuns. It was very moving and I found myself walking with them. I wanted to be swept up, to be part of this energy.

When it was over I was taken backstage to meet Billy Graham

and I found myself enveloped in a huge bear hug; he was warm and extremely charismatic. A few days later someone from the Crusade called me up and invited me to go to church with them, but I shied away from it. I didn't want to join a church, or feel under any obligation to a group. It had been an inspiring experience and I recognised the need to search for God in my life – but for now, it was personal and private.

★

One day, out of the blue, a job offer came for my father that would not only provide him with one of those gift roles that every actor is always looking for, it would also have a profound effect upon our lives.

The offer was from the Boulting Brothers, John and Roy, also known in the business as 'the terrible twins'. These identical brothers were a fiercely independent producer-director team whose career had already spanned thirty prolific years, during which time they had been responsible for some of the finest and most successful films to come out of British studios. For most of their careers, one produced while the other directed, but the result was always a 'Boulting Brothers film'. They were famously versatile. Starting their careers during the war with groundbreaking documentaries like *Desert Victory*, which won an Oscar in 1943, they then moved into noir thrillers with *Brighton Rock*, and later into their hugely successful satirical comedies like *I'm All Right Jack*, *Lucky Jim* and *Private's Progress*. They had also been responsible for launching the movie careers of stars like Richard Attenborough and Peter Sellers, so my father, who had never worked with the brothers, naturally jumped at the chance when they offered him the lead part of Ezra Fitton in the film adaptation of Bill Naughton's new play *All In Good Time*.

The film, which would eventually be retitled *The Family Way*, promised to be something very special and quintessentially British. Bill Naughton was much admired and respected after his massive hit with *Alfie*. The Boultings had written an excellent screen adaptation of the play; and even Paul McCartney was on board to compose the music. Everything about it sounded remarkable.

I don't know who was offered their part first, and it doesn't really matter, but Laurie Evans called to tell me that I was also being offered a role in the film, and that a script was on its way. In the meantime, Laurie went ahead and had a meeting with the twins at their offices, just off Wardour Street, Soho. They sat across from him at a desk, side by side. Laurie said, 'It was like being interviewed by two headmasters.'

A deal was agreed in principle and a date was arranged for me to meet the brothers for lunch the following week, at the Mirabelle Restaurant in Mayfair. I was quite nervous. I had heard the stories about Roy and John, they were disconcertingly alike, and I was concerned about how I was going to tell them apart. Laurie Evans reassured me, saying that it was simple: 'John wears glasses. Roy doesn't.' In the taxi on my way to the rendezvous to meet the two 'headmasters', I found myself nervously repeating it like a mantra: 'John wears glasses, Roy doesn't . . .'

When I arrived at the restaurant and was directed to the table, I saw two identical men sitting together reading the menu. When they looked up, they were both wearing glasses!

The Boulting Brothers were, without question, two of the most striking-looking men I'd ever encountered. They were in their mid-fifties, each still with a very good head of hair that flopped over their bright blue eyes. They had unique voices, strangely clipped and plummy, but were obviously quite brilliant and they seemed to find everything amusing; it was a very animated and exhilarating lunch. I could see they enjoyed being twins. Often, as I soon discovered, in business meetings they would play Good Cop/Bad Cop, delegating roles accordingly, depending on who was in the mood, and then, to further confuse people, they would often switch again. I had heard that John was the more relaxed and jokey of the two, but they both seemed very warm to me – I think it just depended on which brother you had met first.

They were as connected as identical twins could possibly be, often finishing each other's sentences. Roy said many times he would reach for the phone to call John – and John would call him before he could lift the receiver.

The Boultings offered me the part of Jenny Piper, Ezra's daughter-in-law. This would be the fourth time in six years that I had acted with my father, but I didn't have the same doubts and reservations that worried me on *The Truth about Spring*; this script was much better and the casting felt like a good fit. I'd seen the play at the Mermaid Theatre in London too and enjoyed it enormously. It was about a small community in the north of England in the 1960s; the story focused on two very different working-class families, from opposite ends of the town, who come together for the wedding of a son and a daughter. The innocent newlyweds are conned by a dodgy honeymoon travel agent who steals their savings, forcing them to live for months with the boy's mother and father, in a tiny bedroom with paper-thin walls. Tensions mount, family secrets bubble up, generation gaps widen into chasms, and the young couple become unable to consummate their marriage. It was a charming story and Jenny Piper was a great role.

As it turned out, *The Family Way* would be the last film of my childhood. If there was ever a moment that marked the end of my child career, this was it. This was my chance to grow up. It was a 'coming of age' story, and as the adage goes, 'art imitates life' – it certainly did for me.

It was also a wonderful part for my father. He understood the Ezra Fittons of this world. There were echoes of his unforgettable performance as Willie Mossop in David Lean's classic *Hobson's Choice*, artfully balancing the comedy and the realism, the loud-mouthed, working-class dad, with his touching inner vulnerability.

The Boultings were famous for their ensembles of pitch-perfect British character actors and *The Family Way* was one of their best. Ezra's wife was played by Marjorie Rhodes who had been in the play in London and on Broadway. Hywel Bennett, in his first big

movie, was cast to play Arthur, my husband. Hywel was an exciting, very handsome up-and-coming young Welsh actor who later
married Cathy McGowan, herself a 1960s icon as presenter of the
music show *Ready Steady Go!* The one and only Barry Foster was
cast to play the local cad, with the lovely Liz Fraser playing his
wife. Avril Angers was extraordinary as my bitter, unhappy mum.
Murray Head was to play the feckless brother-in-law, and we had
the much-loved actor Wilfred Pickles to play my Uncle Fred.

We started filming in June 1966. I hadn't made an independent
British film since those mud-drenched farmyard shoots of *Whistle
Down the Wind*, so it was funny to find myself back in Lancashire
again, filming in the freezing rain, on a wet and windy morning
in Bolton town square.

The shoot was fast and efficient. Pretty soon I realised that Roy
was an exceptional director. He was a fine technician, a gifted
screenwriter, and he also loved working with actors; you could see
all the emotions in the scene crossing his face as he stood by the
camera watching the actors work. He appreciated them; he never
said too much, he just gave you the 'key' to unlock the scene.
I trusted him absolutely. In some ways he reminded me of Lee
Thompson: the pleasure he took in it all, the way he would come
around from behind the camera after a take, smiling. And the
way he was with the crew, who were like the Boulting Brothers'
second family, having worked together countless times.

However, all of this didn't make my nude scene any easier. My
first screen kiss for Disney was certainly a rite of passage, but this
was altogether different. Taking my clothes off was an extraordinarily awful and rather hysterical experience from start to finish.
I had agreed to it in principle because the scene wasn't gratuitous
and the story justified it – the tense and awkward moment when
Jenny is caught bathing in a hip bath in the family's kitchen, by
Arthur's younger brother, played by Murray Head.

It often takes a whole day to shoot a three-page scene. I sat
there for hours and hours, like a skinned rabbit, trembling in the

tiniest hip bath. I felt hideously undignified, my legs screwed up in front of me, the puddle of water grey and slimy and getting colder and colder by the minute. And I was supposed to look as if I was adoring every moment of the excruciating experience! The day started off on a rather humiliating note when Trevor, the make-up man, insisted upon applying pan-stick body make-up with a piece of sponge the size of a penny. I did my best, attempting to appear like a woman of the world rather than a pointlessly modest adolescent trying to protect – what? Two undernourished little cold raspberries perched on someone's unsuccessful attempts at crème caramel!

We rehearsed without any water at all. Clanking around in that ridiculous oversized bucket, I began to feel so uncomfortable, so acutely self-conscious, I must have been scarlet with embarrassment. At one point, my eyes drifted up towards the gantry – a burly, tea-drinking electrician was sitting right above my head. I covered myself in a flash, only to realise his face was buried in the newspaper. He'd obviously 'seen it all before, love' and was much more interested in finding 2-Down in the crossword than 2-Across on the star.

It may have been my nightmare in the hip bath that set me off, or perhaps it would have happened anyway, but soon afterwards, about halfway through the shoot, my old demons began rearing their ugly heads again. I could feel the sticky threads of a web, tightening around me, as all my fears inched, inexorably, towards me like black spiders. 'Am I even any good? Everyone's brilliant in this film, apart from *me* . . .' I began to dread going to the studios, pretending everything was all right, trying to have relaxed, normal conversations with Hywel, or Murray, or with Marjorie, or Liz – even talking with Daddy. All the time I was imagining their conversations – 'She's really not very good, is she? Oh dear . . .' – and becoming sick with worry that I was disappointing Roy and John.

It got to such a point that I started to seriously doubt whether they were even bothering to put film in the camera when they shot my close-ups. I remember we were shooting the big recon-ciliation scene between Jenny and Arthur, a pivotal moment in the story – and when Roy turned the camera around to shoot my side of the scene, I honestly believed they were just going through the motions, pretending to film me, because they thought I was so awful they wouldn't be able to use it.

On my way to Shepperton Studios the next morning, I felt so desperate, so hopeless and wretched, so utterly consumed with gloom, that I resolved to end my life.

'At the next corner, I won't turn,' I decided. 'Whatever happens, I'll just put my foot down and accelerate, I'll close my eyes and just keep driving. And that will be that . . .'

At the next corner I drove straight into a large hedge.

It wasn't a very impressive crash. I sat there for a minute or two staring through the windscreen at a lot of tangled greenery. I was numb. Slowly, and with a lot of noisy grinding of the gears, I managed to back out of the little ditch and continued on my way, driving through the studio gates, past the startled-looking guard, oblivious that half the hedge was sticking out of my radiator.

At the end of filming I went back to the now empty Wick.

I was keenly aware that I had lost touch with all my friends. My parents were both in East Africa, in Kenya, where Daddy was making another picture, Bunch was on tour with a play, and Jon-athan, now seventeen, had left school (having vigorously resisted my father's attempts to put him into a Swiss finishing school). He was now thoroughly enjoying working with Andrew on *2001: A Space Odyssey*.

Even Andrew and I seemed to be growing apart. He was still the boy I loved, and I always would, but that was part of the problem, he was still a boy. Although we shared so much and could talk to each other for hours, we were both changing, going in different directions – wherever that was. It was a very sad and difficult time. We went to the villa for a holiday, hoping it might solve all the difficult questions and put things into perspective. We had been together for five years and I knew I would always love him. All that time Andrew had been my constant companion; whatever happened, whatever passing crush, Andrew had always been there. Moving beyond our childhood love was the problem – as I wrote to him in a letter, 'It's like we're running hand in hand, but we haven't yet learnt to walk.' I think we knew each other too well. We had reached the end because we just didn't know how to take the next step. The trip ended with us having a terrible row, which was the end of any hope – or any kind of a holiday for either of us.

So I found myself at a very low ebb, my relationship struggling, while being convinced I was awful in the film. Even my half-hearted attempt at killing myself had been a joke. It all seemed to be piling up. I felt increasingly isolated and couldn't reach out or connect to people.

I've since read a report about scientific tests which have been done on adolescent rats and mice that are deprived of social interaction. Neuroscientist Shannon L. Gourbey wrote: 'Lack of social intervention during adolescence has lasting consequences in adulthood, changing the structure of the brain, altering normal development and decision-making behaviour. This lends a lot of support to the idea that adolescence is a critical period during which social experience is sculpting the brain.'

I don't know what effect it had on my brain, but hanging out with friends is obviously one of the strongest protective factors against mental health disorders, depression and loneliness. We need each other.

While kicking around that big old empty house, I got an invitation to visit my father in Kenya. He was making a movie called *Africa Texas Style* with Hugh O'Brian, who was very famous back then for playing Wyatt Earp in a wildly successful American TV series. Hugh's production office had offered me the chance to fly out there and would pay for my ticket providing I was happy to agree to make a brief cameo appearance at the start of the film. The chance of flying to Africa? For nothing!? I leapt at it.

It was the best thing I could have done.

My parents had a little cottage in the grounds of the Mount Kenya Safari Club. The entire world seemed to be dominated by that majestic snow-covered mountain. Golden crested cranes and pelicans tiptoed like models over the grass, and an eagle would sometimes land for a moment on a post by the swimming pool. It was all so beautiful, but inside I was a mess. I remember spending one entire lunch struggling to stop the tears from streaming down under my dark glasses – as Mummy talked on and on. She didn't notice, she was in the middle of writing her autobiography entitled 'What Shall We Do Tomorrow?'

When the film finished shooting, my parents and I took a tiny twin-engine plane and flew into the centre of Tsavo National Park. For three days we drove in battered old Land Rovers through the African bush, and at night we pitched camp in a dried-up river and gazed, enraptured, into the depth and blackness of the night sky littered with uncountable stars. One night, as I drifted off to sleep I heard the hoarse cough of a lion coming from the opposite bank. In the morning the fire had died and the footprints of a curious little hyena could be found at the very end of our beds. The vastness of this beautiful, endless country, the savannah stretching into infinity, the soaring sky and the sweeping clouds of Africa, the ancient silence, the warm winds, the smell of dust and rust-coloured elephants, gazelle, giraffe and lion – it stirred my soul and had a profound effect upon me. When you encounter the great aloneness of Africa there's a sort of recognition, a deep primal connection, and all the pettiness of one's life falls away. Things you thought you needed suddenly seem less important. Africa was an expansive unfolding of my spirit and just by being there I felt cleansed, like Tom the chimney sweep in *The Water Babies* after he'd fallen into the river and all the dirt and grime of his life was washed away. Africa made me think and feel in a new way. I felt closer to God.

While I had been contemplating the Infinite, my father received a nasty reminder of home in the shape of a letter from the Inland Revenue, who had decided that the golden handshake he had received from the Rank Organisation after he was released from the exclusive contract, many years before, was taxable, and at the full rate – 98 per cent!

Daddy had already spent most of this money and he had no idea in hell how he was going to pay the bill. On the advice of our family accountant, the aforementioned Stanley Passmore, my father fought the case. And lost it – ending up with enormous legal costs on top of the crippling tax bill.

He was furious. And in deep financial water.

Daddy always considered himself a lucky man, he often talked about 'The Mills Luck', but now, after the taxman's *coup de grâce*, he may have been starting to doubt. The Wick was an expensive household to run, he was between jobs (having recently lost out on the lead role for *Gilligan's Island*, to his best friend Dickie Attenborough!) and there was only so much golf he could play before he started to panic. Thankfully, or I should say luckily, by late October he received an offer to do a pilot for a television series in Hollywood. The salary was large – large enough to pull him out of his financial hole – but the hitch in the plan was that he would be required to sign to CBS for five years if they chose to pick up the option.

Strange how elation and gloom can coexist so closely. Five years away from home sounded like a penal sentence, but he simply could not afford to turn it down – this opportunity might never come again. But they both dreaded having to be away for so long. Despite the punitive taxation in Britain, my parents had never even considered escaping, like so many other high-earning artists had been forced to do. They were English, and it was to England my father felt he owed his loyalty and where he belonged; it was

England that had given him the life that he loved, the opportunities that he had enjoyed, and he couldn't imagine abandoning ship, despite the lure of the sun and living the life of the lotus-eaters in Tinseltown – which of course Mummy hated anyway. So the decision was made.

There was a strange emptiness in the house that week. Our voices and our footsteps echoed across the hall, as if the house had already been abandoned. And it felt cold now; the only fire was in the study, and it only warmed you one side at a time. Mummy was doing a lot of whistling through her teeth, dealing with suitcases, sorting things out and packing everything up. Daddy was endlessly on the phone or playing the piano, doing his best to hide his anxiety. Jonathan was the least affected by this unexpected alteration of our already disordered existence – he was caught up in his own life and plans.

So he and I decided to move out and we rented a little furnished flat in the heart of Chelsea, just off the King's Road. I was terribly excited: something I'd dreamt about for so long had finally arrived. It was just saddening that it should happen under such difficult circumstances for my parents, but at least it made my move away from home seem more natural – and necessary. Despite my excitement, I had a strangely bleak feeling that our days of all living together as a family were coming to an end. Just as Juliet had gone, Johnny and I were now leaving; I expected we would share a flat together for a while, then eventually he would go off and find a place of his own, and then . . . it didn't look likely that I would ever move back to The Wick again. It would just be 'the two of them' in that big house, as they had been in the beginning.

I decided it was time to get myself in hand, starting with stopping smoking; forty a day was forty too many, and I stopped drinking spirits – how many mistakes and compromising situations could be blamed on too much alcohol! Johnny and I settled in together, two extraordinarily incompetent flatmates. Neither of us knew how to boil an egg, neither of us had ever had to make our own beds, and after passing an item of discarded clothing on the floor for at least a couple of days, it finally dawned on me that if I didn't pick it up, nobody else would. We got along together pretty well considering the size of the place, although I did draw the line at jam on the doorknobs. It was quite a small flat, but I adored it. We had two small bedrooms and one little sitting room with a dilapidated old velvet sofa and two comfortably tatty armchairs that leant soft with age over a fading Persian rug – and a large grainy mirror over the fireplace that reflected Johnny and me as we stumbled about adjusting to our new life. There was a little balcony from which you could look through rustling sycamore trees to the river and the Albert Bridge, which became as fragile and insubstantial as a cobweb of twinkling fairy lights when darkness fell. Standing on the balcony a couple of days later, the startling coincidence of my location suddenly hit me: quite by chance I had rented a flat on the same road where Andrew lived! I was still getting to know the streets of London, and when I had visited his parents' home in the past it was usually in the evening, and I had never really looked at the 1920s block of flats on the opposite corner of the street, which is where I now was – practically facing his house.

Was it fate?

Johnny and I adjusted happily to our new situation. He went to work at the film studios and I went shopping up and down the King's Road, discovering all the wonderful little boutiques that had sprung up: Zandra Rhodes and Bill Gibb, Granny Takes A Trip (although I had yet to understand what that meant) and, just around the corner, Caroline Charles and the Biba store on Kensington High Street. In 1966 the King's Road was the place to be. Vidal Sassoon had his salon there; the area was full of hip, happening little cafes and restaurants, antiques, book shops, and a classic cinema. Jonathan and I went to film premieres together, me wearing my new black dress that looked like a nightie, Johnny fighting all night with his bow tie, which kept escaping from his neck and sticking out at right angles. We were having a ball, away from home – young, free and independent.

Returning one very blustery day from an afternoon foraging along the King's Road, I spotted a familiar figure ahead of me. He was leaping about on the pavement trying to stop a taxi. The wind, blowing his coat-tails out, made him look like a demented bird trying to take flight, except that he had a rather mangled half-smoked cigar clamped between his thumb and forefinger. It was Roy Boulting.

'Hello!' he said, his hair in his eyes. He'd obviously dressed in the dark as none of his garments matched, not even his socks. 'What are you doing here?'

I laughed, I was so delighted to see him. 'I've moved! I live here now, just down that street,' I said, waving my hand across the road towards Chelsea Manor Street. 'What are you doing here?'

'I live here,' he said and waved at the building we were standing in front of – a bank.

'You live in a bank?'

'No!' he laughed. 'I live *above* the bank, you must come and visit me, have some tea!' Then a taxi pulled up and he was jumping inside.

'I'd love to,' I said, as the door slammed and it drove away.

Walking back down Chelsea Manor Street I began turning over the extraordinary thought that, in the whole of London, I should find myself living with Andrew at one end of my street and Roy at the other.

I had just bought myself a new car: a Mini Minor, somewhat inspired by Roy himself. During the shoot for *The Family Way* he had taken me to lunch at a local pub in Shepperton, in his custom-built souped-up Mini. It was the first one I'd seen; the exterior was black and racing green, with small racing wheels and little carriage lamps on either side, with black leather seats and a black carpet. It was exquisite and went almost as fast as the Lotus

Elan, but with Roy at the wheel it was even more frightening, a white-knuckle ride all the way. My new Mini was a gorgeous Mediterranean blue with a white leather interior and racing wheels. It sounded like a Maserati and went like a bomb. I drove over to the Boulting Brothers' office at British Lion in Soho.

'Come down and have a look at my new car!' I said as I burst in on the twins. Roy was sitting in an armchair and John was perched on the end of the desk, both of them smoking like chimneys. I was enjoying my independence, just turning up at their office unannounced, and they seemed delighted to see me. No wonder they were famous for their comedies, they never stopped laughing.

We went out into the street to look at the car. Roy was suitably impressed.

'I say, do you have to go?' he said suddenly. 'Come back up to the office and have a drink!'

I had tea. Roy and John drank whisky; they both had an astonishing capacity for alcohol but however much they drank they never appeared to get drunk – if anything they became more sober and dignified. They were thirty years older than me but it wasn't something I felt overly conscious of. We got along great, but in reality they were the same generation as my parents, who fought in the war and drank all day long.

The Family Way was about to open the following night at the Odeon Leicester Square. Roy said he was heading over to the cinema later, to check the sound and the print, and to screen the movie to make sure everything was good and ready for the premiere. He asked me if I'd like to go with him.

I arranged to meet him at his apartment beforehand. You can tell so much about a person by their home and how they choose to live – and I wanted to know more about Roy. He intrigued me. I knew that he had been married three times, that the last wife was a successful and very beautiful South African model and that they were now divorced, that he had a number of children

– but that was all. Later that evening I arrived at his apartment, above the bank, walked up some rather dark stairs to the first floor, pushed open a heavy wooden door with a solid brass knob, and walked into a room. It had high ceilings and long tall windows – a picture of Miss Havisham in *Great Expectations* flashed into my mind. Roy was in the far corner, sitting in a deep wing chair; behind him oak shelves ran the full length of the wall, filled with books and objects, some photographs of his children in silver frames and the occasional antique lamp with a glass shade that spread a pool of amber light. There was a large desk and numerous paintings hanging on the walls, one by Ted Hughes with black crows being blown chaotically across a stark wasteland by a wild invisible wind. It was huge and dominated the room – there was something disturbing about the picture, but it was the only one that I didn't like. There were a few wide antique chairs and some expensive-looking old rugs lying across the wood floor, but no flowers. The room was comfortable but there was something missing; it felt empty, with a sense of long solitary hours. Roy came towards me smiling and gave me a kiss and a glass of red wine, and we talked. We talked about the film, we talked about his paintings and he told me about his life. We talked for hours, and as I watched the glow from an old lamp accentuate the long austere lines of his face and the deep pools of his eyes, he reminded me of the American poet Ralph Waldo Emerson. He told me that he had been married three times, had six sons, and a stepdaughter who was very beautiful like her mother and wanted to be an actress . . . and this explained it, the sense of emptiness in the house: it was the presence of a woman that was missing.

Later Roy and I went over to the Odeon Leicester Square, now completely empty after the customers had left, and we sat side by side and watched *The Family Way* with the whole cinema to ourselves. I hadn't seen anything of it up to that point. Not even the dailies. I was astonished. The film was so wonderful and so deeply moving, all the performances were superb – my father, of course, reduced me to pieces – and Paul McCartney's soulful score, brilliantly arranged by George Martin, cleverly used the evocative sounds of brass bands, typical of the industrial north. I didn't even mind my own performance; the whole film worked together so perfectly that I appeared to have escaped by the skin of my teeth. My own coming-of-age struggles during the filming seemed to have been absorbed into those of my character, Jenny – coming to terms with her own immaturity, her own rite of passage.

When the screening was over and the final credits began rolling I was so moved that I leant over to Roy impulsively and whispered 'Thank you' and kissed him on his cheek. Roy had made a beautiful film.

My heart was lighter as we walked back to Chelsea, across a deserted Trafalgar Square, down The Mall.

On a pedestrian crossing, in front of Buckingham Palace, Roy kissed me.

The Family Way opened the following evening to the sort of publicity that only exists in dreams. Critics praised the film and they praised Daddy to the sky – if only he had been there, it would have really cheered him up. Roy, who had put his heart into the film, was overjoyed to have his work recognised and appreciated.

Roy and I celebrated far into the night. We finally slept together and the following morning he took me for breakfast and champagne cocktails at the elegant Connaught Hotel in Mayfair. I don't know what anybody else thought seeing us having breakfast together at such an early hour and I really didn't care. I adored him, I didn't care that he was so much older than me. I was ready for a mature relationship with an older man.

I may have been ready for this – but unfortunately, everyone else was not.

CHAPTER ELEVEN

The Girl Who Wouldn't Grow Up

'Second to the right, and straight on till morning . . .'
— J.M. Barrie, *Peter Pan*

The same week that *The Family Way* opened I received a call from the BBC asking if I would go to Broadcasting House for an interview that day. The production assistant I spoke to had assumed that I already knew what it was about, but no one had told me.

'Walt Disney has died.'

I dropped everything and ran for a taxi. I must have been in shock as I remember feeling strangely disconnected to the news: he had lung cancer, he was sixty-five years old. It was so unexpected: I had absolutely no idea he'd been ill, it had been kept secret. I simply wasn't able to process the information. Walt Disney was larger than life, he couldn't just die! It didn't seem possible to me that he wasn't there any more; he was still up there in his office, meticulously scanning those storyboards or working on designs for the latest Disneyland attraction. I can't remember what I said to the BBC, it was more of an out-of-body experience than an interview. Walt had been my boss, my mentor, my friend throughout half of my childhood and I had genuinely loved him. His studio had been like a second family and, just as Walt had been a father figure, a part of me would always remain 'Disney's daughter'.

With Walt's passing, I felt like my childhood had finally disappeared over the horizon for good. One life was ended, a new one was opening up. Although I grieved his loss, I felt strangely elated; I was looking forward. It felt true to Walt, who was an optimist to the end.

So 1967 dawned with great expectations: I had my independence, I had, by now, bought my own flat in Chelsea (two floors above the one I rented with Jonathan), and I was about to come of age – my twenty-first birthday would finally allow me access to all the money I'd earned and saved during the Disney years and I could now take charge of my finances. *The Family Way* had been well received and much to my surprise I had escaped censure; and, of course, Roy was in my life now. I was consumed by him and gave myself to him without reserve. I trusted him, I believed he loved me. I would not have to flounder around any more – I had Roy to support me and he would know what to do.

I felt my life was answered, it was complete, my quest for something – that frail, indefinable something that so often eluded and perplexed me – was over. Everything in life that I valued and loved was within his being.

I just hadn't told my parents yet.

The occasion presented itself in March. I was due to leave for Singapore to make a film called *Pretty Polly*. My parents had been in America for months shooting the television series, but now they were heading home during a break in the filming. Their flight was arriving on the day I left, so I decided to surprise them, very early, at the airport. I've never been known as an early riser, so my parents were quite taken aback to see me smiling and waving at them in Arrivals.

'Hello, my darlings!' I said, hugging them both. 'I've missed you so much!' I was perhaps overly exuberant, because, of course, deep down I was very anxious about how they would take the news. 'Why don't we go and have a coffee?' I suggested. 'I've got something I want to tell you.' We shuffled off to find a cafe. They were both bleary-eyed and jet-lagged but I think they twigged that something was up since the whole situation was most irregular. We found a brasserie in the terminal serving breakfast and sat on high stools at the counter. Once they began tucking into their scrambled eggs, I couldn't wait any longer.

'Look at this!' I said, holding out my left hand so they could see the blue enamel ring surrounded with little diamonds on my finger. They both peered at it for a moment.

'It's lovely, darling,' Daddy said curiously, swallowing down some toast. 'Where did you get it?'

I took a deep breath. 'From Roy. I'm in love with him.'

'Roy?'

'Yes.'

'Roy *Boulting*?'

'Yes.' I nodded, my heart melting with joy.

There was a stunned silence. My father leant forward to have another look at the ring, his stool tilted, his elbow nudged the plate, and the next moment he was flat on the floor covered in egg.

Mummy helped get him restored to an upright position again, which I think gave both of them time to take in my news. So I pressed on.

'Well, what do you think?'

Daddy pushed his hat on to the back of his head. 'Well . . . I'm poleaxed!'

I turned to Mummy. She fixed me with her gimlet eye. 'So. You've finally been in the hay!'

She snorted knowingly and lit herself a cigarette. This was not the conversation I had imagined. Now we were *all* in shock.

'Daddy . . . I can understand it's a surprise . . . but you do *like* Roy, don't you?' I said anxiously.

'Are you really serious about this?' he said. 'I mean . . . are you going to get married?'

Married? I hadn't anticipated this question.

'Well, not right away,' I recovered, 'but one day, I hope so, Daddy, yes . . .' I was improvising furiously by now, but I didn't want them to think our relationship was anything other than real, or that Roy was taking advantage of me – or me of him.

'Bags, darling, I do like Roy, I really do, and I admire him, he's very erudite and intelligent, and . . . and he's . . . a very, *very* good director, but – really, darling, he's as old as me!'

All the while, Mummy remained conspicuously silent. Perhaps she had a headache.

Daddy continued: 'Look, you might not feel a thirty-two-year age difference is important to you now, but . . .' He cleared his throat. 'Later on, I mean when you're forty, which is a *marvellous* age for a woman, isn't it . . .' He looked to Mummy for some kind of affirmation, but she just puffed grimly, so Daddy kept on: 'But just think, when you're forty, Roy will be *seventy-two*! And all his friends will be too. Really, Bags. What will that mean for you?'

'Oh, we've talked about that,' I said, trying to laugh it off. 'We have a joke that I'll have to push him along the seafront in a wheelchair!'

I could tell instantly that this picture did not sit well with them. They stared back horrified.

'Come on! Look at Charlie Chaplin,' I said. 'He married Oona when he was thirty-six and she was eighteen! They've had eight children and they're still going strong!'

I tried to keep it light but there was no escaping the fact that this was a huge shock for them. Of course, the awkward truth was that Roy *was* my father's contemporary; John and Roy Boulting were as much of a British institution as he was. To put it in context, it was the Boultings who had given Dickie Attenborough his first big break with *Brighton Rock*. John Boulting and my father were both godparents to Dickie's son, Michael. So I'm sure it felt to all of them as if Roy and I had crossed the generational divide and entered into a sort of incestuous taboo.

'Darlings, I know this must be a bit of a shock and I'm sorry,' I continued. 'I just couldn't wait to tell you, especially since I'm flying off to Singapore any minute.'

'The most important thing,' he replied gently, 'is that you're happy.'

'I am happy.'

'Well . . . good. You look happy.' He smiled warmly.

I turned to my mother hopefully.

'I just hope you know what you're doing,' she said, stubbing her cigarette out in the remains of her scrambled egg.

The meeting over, we hugged and went our separate ways. A part of me could understand how strange it must have seemed to them, but when you're truly, madly, deeply in love you believe no obstacle is insurmountable – and it only made me all the more determined to prove them wrong.

Pretty Polly, which was based on a short story by Noël Coward, was directed by Guy Green (who had originally been recruited to direct *Whistle Down the Wind*). The film also co-starred Trevor Howard and the wonderful Brenda De Banzie (who had worked with my father many years before in *Hobson's Choice*, playing Charles Laughton's daughter, Maggie Hobson, who marries the timid but brilliant little shoemaker Willie Mossop, played by my father). Unfortunately for me, Brenda's character dies quite early on in *Pretty Polly*, so I didn't get to work with her very much. My main acting companion was Shashi Kapoor. Shashi was already a big star in India back then, although not quite yet the Bollywood icon he would become in the 1970s when he teamed up with Amitabh Bachchan in *Deewar* and other classic films. Those films are not so well known to English-speaking audiences, but they are some of the biggest and most famous movies ever made in India, which is still arguably the largest film industry in the world. Shashi was, in all respects, a gorgeous man – *Shashi* translated means 'moonbeam'; he was beautiful to look at and with the greatest natural charm and an irresistible sense of humour. I found him very interesting because he was married to English actress Jennifer Kendal (the sister of Felicity) who was herself quite glorious: with her radiant smile and long silken wheat-coloured hair, and her beautiful clothes, she exuded warmth and goodness.

Both Shashi and Jennifer came from theatrical dynasties. Shashi's father was the great actor Prithviraj Kapoor (who starred as Emperor Akbar in the famous 1960 historical epic *Mughal E Azam* – which is India's equivalent of *Gone with the Wind*) and all the Kapoor family began their acting careers performing in his theatrical troupe. Similarly the Kendal family belonged to a touring theatre group, which performed Shakespeare and the Classics to the outer reaches of the British Empire, travelling in and around India – a story dramatised in the early Merchant Ivory film *Shakespeare Wallah*, which starred Felicity. My father had done this too, travelling the Far East with a rep company in the late 1920s. In fact that was his first proper acting job – before this he'd always been just one of 'the boys', dancing and singing at the back of the stage. I think perhaps it was because of our shared background that I felt a kinship with both Shashi and Jennifer. It was also the first time that I'd seen such a wonderful fusion of the East and the West. Shashi was an absolute darling of a gentleman, while Jennifer could speak fluent Hindi and designed all her clothes herself using exquisite Indian silks and cottons, creating her own unique style of little embroidered jewelled waistcoats and pantaloons, flowing dresses, tunics and smocks. She was effortlessly elegant and I sought to emulate her for years, without much success. Jennifer was the love of Shashi's life and she adored him. I think they had to overcome a lot of deep cultural prejudices, on both sides, in order to be together, but Shashi and Jennifer broke the mould in many respects, and they were so breathtakingly beautiful that I fell in love with them both.

The tropical humidity in Singapore was exhausting and so it was fortunate that we did a lot of cooler night shooting. We were filming along what was then Bugis Street – the Far East's red-light Mecca for transvestites and transsexuals – before the whole area was razed to the ground and sanitised for tourists. Back in 1967 Bugis Street was still pretty wild and all the sailors arriving on ships from across the world made a beeline for it. It was busy and bustling, crammed with stalls and wonderful little street restaurants and thronging with the most beautiful and exotic girls that I'd ever seen. However, on closer inspection one could see that these were no ordinary girls – some of them had a five o'clock shadow and an Adam's apple, some were slim and smooth-cheeked, with immaculate hairdos and long tapering painted nails, many wore sequinned cocktail dresses and traditional Malayan costumes. Altogether they seemed to me like brightly colourful tropical birds that had flocked to Bugis Street from all four corners of the Earth. It was something of a safe haven for trans people, but still, their lives were not without risk, for not every sailor appreciated the fact that the pretty girl he thought he'd picked up wasn't quite what he'd bargained for.

The Bugis Street girls were all sweet to me – one of them made me a traditional dress, another baked me an amazing cake, and still another sang to me in the most exquisite falsetto. They were very gentle and generous and charming and I wondered what would happen to them all. They were the odd ones out, the misfits, 'outcaste children of the East' – funnily enough, that's what Mummy used to refer to herself as, although for rather different reasons.

But throughout all this, my heart and mind were with Roy, back in England. When he came out to see me, the press photographers made it difficult for us to be together. I didn't like having to sneak in and out of the hotel as if we were ashamed of ourselves. I was proud to be with him.

Roy and I never made any official 'announcement' to the press that we were together, there was no hiring of publicists or PR managers to 'control the narrative', we simply started to be seen together and the story was left to run amok – which was probably a mistake. Earlier in the year we had travelled to New York together on the *QE2* to promote *The Family Way* and it wasn't long before the press began writing about us. Inevitably there was gossip and speculation about our motives. I took most of the flak: stories ranged from cod-psychology and 'father fixations' to cynical accusations of gold-digging. To the accusation of father fixation, I replied coolly that I already had a perfectly good father and I didn't need another one, but the insinuation that I had ambitiously selected Roy because of his influence in the film business was quite hurtful – especially when this gossip persisted among people whom I knew personally.

Ironically, being with Roy did nothing to help my career at all, in fact it did the opposite. The press sometimes depicted Roy as a sort of Humbert Humbert from *Lolita*, taking advantage of my youth and inexperience, but we got used to being mocked. On the face of it, Roy seemed less bothered, but it affected him too. What genuinely did distress me was the reaction from some of my fans. Many were shocked, some even felt betrayed. They wrote to me saying that I had let them down and set a bad example. I didn't know what to say, it was awful. I told myself there was nothing I could do except reiterate that I had fallen in love. For me, it was as simple as that.

Roy and I were living together in London, but he kept his house on the King's Road, and I was excited to get back to my new flat on Chelsea Manor Street as I had only managed to furnish it very basically before leaving for Singapore. I couldn't wait to go back and make it my own, but while I was away filming Roy had gone ahead and ordered all the china and cutlery, glassware, cooking pots and utensils. So, when I returned, all of these very expensive gifts were waiting for me in huge boxes from Peter Jones and Asprey's.

I thanked him profusely, it was incredibly generous and thoughtful, but secretly I was a bit disappointed. It was my first home and I had been looking forward to deciding what to buy for myself.

My twenty-first birthday was by now looming and the producers of *Pretty Polly* had been talking to my mother about having a 'promotional' birthday party back in England, to tie in the film's upcoming release with my coming of age. The producers wanted to invite all the press to The Wick, and in return promised to supply all the champagne, a big cake and even throw in a tropical parrot.

I went along with the plan, as was the custom, deferring to the producers and my parents' wishes, but when Roy heard about the event he was appalled.

'That's not a birthday party, it's a freak show! A circus!' he insisted. 'Cancel it, at once!'

'But . . . I can't,' I replied. 'Mummy has already sent out the invitations.'

'Here you are, once again, being exploited and controlled by your parents.' He tutted disapprovingly. 'How many of your own friends will be there?'

I had to admit – not very many.

'Exactly. It's all their friends. Is this what you want for your twenty-first? A crowd of photographers and lots of people you hardly know, and all from your parents' generation?!'

'But . . . it's already been agreed,' I said feebly, beginning to feel stuck between a rock and a hard place. 'The champagne, the cake, the parrot and the press. Mummy will have gone to a lot of—'

'The press! It's all about the press! Your mother is the only one who wants this, not you. This is your birthday,' he insisted. 'You should be allowed to have it to yourself.'

'But you're not listening, Roy!' My voice sounded like a last gasp. 'The invitations have gone out!' He shook his head in exasperation. Surely the die had been cast. I could imagine what Mummy would say . . . They wanted to throw me a party, but now, everything Roy said made it seem like a cynical publicity opportunity.

'Do you even want to have a party?' He looked at me expectantly, because he knew how I dreaded them.

'Well, not really,' I said. 'I really don't mind, I'd be happy if it was just the family . . .'

'Well, there you are. Just stand up for yourself and tell them "no!"'

I'd had some awful rows with my parents before, but this was drawing a deep, very defiant line in the sand. On the one hand, I was attracted by the idea of asserting myself and defying my parents, as I instinctively wanted to break free, but on the other hand, I just wanted to make them happy. It was their daughter's twenty-first and I completely understood why they wanted to celebrate it. This party would have given them a lot of pleasure, especially Mummy.

However, in Roy's view this was a 'rite of passage'. Sooner or later, he said, I must stand up to my parents. Perhaps he was right. Truth be told, I really didn't feel that strongly about it one way or the other. In the end, an absurd compromise was reached: the promotional party for the film would go ahead – champagne, press, parrot etc. – as I'd already given my word, but the big gathering for friends and family was cancelled.

On the day of my twenty-first, I drove over to Richmond alone. Roy wanted to avoid the press, so he planned to meet us later that evening for dinner. There was already a throng of photographers, well-oiled with champagne, waiting for me at The Wick, corralled on the garden terrace with an absolutely enormous birthday cake, big enough to feed forty, along with a rather intimidating macaw parrot, who seemed more relaxed than anybody. I cut the cake and smiled while the cameras flashed, Mummy and Daddy raised a toast, the press enjoyed the free booze and the parrot squawked interminably. In the middle of all this, the front doorbell rang and, to our horror, Trevor Howard turned up for the celebrations

– he had never received news that the party had been cancelled! The dear man was given some champagne, and after profuse apologies, he went on his way – talk about a Brief Encounter. He left me a little gold charm to hang on my bracelet. I was terribly embarrassed and felt awful. I think my parents felt even worse.

Dinner wasn't any better. It was just me, my parents, Jonathan, and Roy; a lot of drink was being consumed and everyone was making an effort but underneath the chatter and the laughter the atmosphere was strained and Mummy was throwing tiny psychic daggers at Roy. By the time the brandy came out, I think Roy was finding me irritating too. I was sitting beside Jonathan with my arm draped languorously around his neck, when Roy suddenly leapt to his feet and marched out of the room. We all looked at each other, bewildered, then my mother went out to find him. I heard their raised voices arguing upstairs in the drawing room, then Roy's footsteps crossing the hall and the sound of the front door – slam! Mummy came back into the dining room, quite furious – 'Well, how bloody rude!'

I didn't know exactly what had been said but I had a pretty good idea, and I was pretty furious myself by this time: with Roy, with my parents, and, if I'm honest, with myself too for that matter. It had been a tense day with lots of champagne, followed by wine at dinner, and so, white-hot with indignation and emboldened by drink, I threw open the door and ran outside. Roy was already halfway along the street, striding back towards town, when I caught up with him opposite the Roebuck pub, on the top of Richmond Hill, city lights twinkling below.

'Where the *hell* do you think you're going?!' I shouted rudely.

'I'm going to catch the train,' he replied coolly, without stopping.

'Hey!' I grabbed his arm. 'You can't just walk out! It's . . . bloody rude! You were eshtremely rude!' I hiccuped. 'To my mother, to the whole family – and you've ruined my birthday dinner!'

I summoned up the most offensive word in the English language and hurled it at him like a witch's curse. To my complete astonishment, he slapped me. I was stunned. Nobody had ever hit me before. I became vaguely aware of two people coming out of the pub on the opposite side of the road. I shrugged his jacket off my shoulder, turned on my heels and marched back to the house with Roy calling after me. I was devastated and sure it was the end of our relationship.

When I returned to the house everyone was just standing around, looking quite unsure what to do. There was a silent acknowledgement that Mummy had finally met her match.

I briefly considered staying at The Wick and not going back to Chelsea but I knew I had to face Roy sooner or later – and it was my flat, so if anyone should go, I thought, it should be him. Eventually, against his better judgement, Jonathan agreed to drive me home. It was a pivotal moment. When I walked into the flat, I could see Roy sitting up in bed reading. We started arguing again and after a while I decided that I'd had enough – I got out my make-up case and began to pack a few things and announced: 'I'm leaving you.' As I strode to the front door, Roy suddenly leapt, stark naked, out of bed and rushed down the hallway. He grabbed me, ripping my dress, and hurled me back towards the bedroom, whereupon my twenty-first birthday deteriorated into a naked wrestling match until my shrieks and screams brought a neighbour knocking on the door. We instantly became silent. Roy threw on a dressing gown, answered the door and very calmly reassured her that we were just playing a rather noisy game and that everything was absolutely all right – but thank God, her intervention stopped us and defused the situation.

He wasn't a violent man, he was as shocked as I was about what had happened. We never had a fight like that again. But once you've been on the receiving end of a man's strength you never feel quite the same in the relationship. 'Rites of passage', indeed.

Looking back, I think we were as bad as each other. Although I didn't realise it for a long time, Roy was just as insecure as I was. He may have had power and responsibility in the film business, but emotionally he wasn't any more 'grown up' than I was. Interestingly, I've heard so many psychotherapists talk about how children of alcoholics often unconsciously gravitate towards partners with addictive personalities who can supply those familiar patterns of intense emotion. I wasn't aware of any of this back then, but after so many years, one does start to look back and connect the dots.

★

I was twenty-one years old and in the morning of my life. Apart from wanting to buy a little house in the country and a horse, I hadn't made any concrete plans for the future. But, as yet, I hadn't had access to my trust money. Now everything was about to change: my twenty-first meant I was finally allowed to take control of my finances and access all the money I had earned throughout my eight years of child labour! I didn't expect this forthcoming independence to change me or the way I looked at life, but I felt the promise of new freedom and endless possibilities. It may seem extraordinary to most people, but, at this point, I honestly had no idea how much money was in there. No one had informed me or supplied me with statements – the trust company was this amorphous entity, watched over by the wise and venerable old trustees.

One morning, just after my birthday, I dressed with particular care so as to look my very best for the momentous meeting at my solicitor's office in Mayfair, where I was to be finally handed the keys to my trust. JD Langton & Passmore had been my parents' firm of solicitors for as long as I could remember, which with hindsight was not necessarily such a good thing.

Stanley Passmore was in his seventies, dignified, a little pompous and rather short. He dressed in the regulation black suit and waistcoat of the City of London, a grey silk tie, with a gold watch and chain stretched across his generous stomach. He always wore a black bowler hat and carried the obligatory umbrella, like an aged Mr Banks from *Mary Poppins*.

'Good morning, my dear, come in, come in,' said Stanley warmly, as I was ushered into a small panelled boardroom where a couple of serious-faced junior solicitors were already sitting at a long table covered with a green baize cloth. I gave Stanley a polite kiss on his cheek. A decanter of water and some glasses rattled as I pulled in my chair and sat down. Eager to get started, I smiled brightly at everyone but their faces were blank. There was a pause. I looked at Stanley expectantly.

'Well, here we are,' I said, for want of something better, hoping to get the ball rolling.

Stanley cleared his throat behind his carefully manicured hand and gently pushed a Manila envelope over the green baize cloth towards me.

'This is for you, my dear. I think it's better if you read it yourself and then we can talk about it.'

I reached for the envelope and saw that it was from the Inland Revenue. There was total silence in the room as I opened the letter. I don't even remember a clock ticking. Time had frozen. I read it once – I looked back at Stanley because I couldn't quite believe I had read it properly.

'I'm not quite sure that I understand this.'

Stanley laughed, rather nervously.

'Well, my dear, basically the Revenue have attacked your trust company. They are going to tax you at the full rate – on all your earnings.'

'The full rate?' I whispered, the blood starting to drain.

'Ninety-one per cent. Of the entire trust,' he explained calmly, as if he were telling me the bus fare to Piccadilly.

I looked down at the letter again. The typed words blurred before my eyes. It might as well have been written in Chinese. 'Oh, I see,' I said – not seeing at all. In an instant everything had changed and become like a bad dream. 'But . . . how can this be, Stanley? I mean, how did it . . .' I faltered, I didn't even know what question to ask. 'What am I supposed to do?'

Stanley gave his little old man's rattling laugh. 'Well, nothing you *can* do, really. You could contest it, but if I were you, I'd leave the country!' And he laughed again.

I stared blankly, my mind reeling. Leave the country? My home? My family?

'Ideally,' Stanley added, 'you should have repudiated the trust before you reached twenty-one . . . but I'm afraid it's too late for that now.'

I staggered home in a daze. I can't remember whether I drove or caught a cab. I may well have sleepwalked down the middle of The Mall into oncoming traffic. I felt like I had been beaten over the head, mugged in an alleyway, jumped by thugs – which isn't far from the truth.

'Oh Hal! This should never have happened!' My father and I were sitting by the fire in the study. He rubbed his brow painfully.

'It's not your fault, my darling,' I said, trying to comfort him. He looked shattered. 'I think it's got something to do with the trust Jack Hawkins set up in his father's name, for his children.'

The actor Jack Hawkins had set up a similar arrangement, some years before, after *The Bridge on the River Kwai*, and been royally skewered by Her Majesty's Inland Revenue. Jack fought it in court but lost and so the taxman merrily made off with 91 per cent of his children's inheritance. The knock-on effect of this case was that it set a 'precedent', and now all the Revenue hounds were on the scent of more celebrity trusts to 'attack' and bleed dry, regardless of their age.

Daddy was looking a bit pale. He quietly got up from his chair and stared out of the window; the streetlamps had come on and it was beginning to rain. 'I don't understand, it was all totally legal,' he said, despondently. 'It's not as if we were trying to pull a fast one! Stanley's team assured us that if we put the money into a trust your pennies would be safe until you were twenty-one. The money was never even touched!'

'Don't worry, darling. It's not over yet,' I said, still doing my best to console him – I could see he felt responsible. 'I shall contest it. Stanley says I have that option – although he also said that the best thing I can do is leave the country!' I laughed and sounded like Stanley.

Later that evening, having dinner at San Lorenzo's in Chelsea, I told Roy. He was furious.

'You should sue the bloody solicitors,' he said, trimming the end of his cigar with his little pocket guillotine. 'They were the ones who set up the trust, they're responsible. *They* must pay, not you.'

It's fair to say that if Stanley Passmore had lost a staggering 91 per cent of John and Roy's earnings over ten years they would have hung him upside-down from the top of Nelson's Column, *by his toes* – figuratively speaking, of course – until he paid them back. But that just wasn't my style. The truth is, I had a history with Stanley: he'd been my parents' solicitor for years, for decades! I had named my first pet white mouse after him for goodness' sake! The idea of suing these old boys that I'd known all my life was unthinkable.

'And after all,' I insisted, 'we haven't broken the law. We took good advice.'

Roy lit a match and held it aloft as the chemicals burned away. 'Good advice?' he replied drily.

'It was totally legal, I mean. And above board.'

Roy puffed his cigar to life and looked unconvinced. I ignored him. Believe it or not, at this point, I still wanted to defend everyone, especially my parents. I knew they had simply done what they thought was best for me. And deep down, I was actually quite upbeat. It sounded like my situation was a very different case to Jack Hawkins. I felt sure justice would prevail. In the meantime all my 'assets' were frozen. I would have to wait another two years to contest the case.

★

In August, Roy and I took off for a holiday at La Solitude. It was an enchanted time. I was completely in love with him and didn't need anything or anyone else. We saw no one, sunbathed and swam off the little jetty, played tennis, went out to the expensive restaurants along the coast: La Réserve in Beaulieu, the Eden Roc Hotel in Antibes. We ate rich food and drank expensive wine; it was all wonderfully indulgent until I had the most ghastly liver attack, couldn't keep my balance and had to stay in bed sipping Vichy water for two days. I realised I had a long way to go to equal Roy's capacity, which far outstripped mine.

We were complete. We both loved to read, Roy liked to paint, we appreciated the same music, we both loved classical and jazz. I would play records by Antonio Carlos Jôbim and the French chanteuse Françoise Hardy. Roy didn't share my passion for Elvis but he did love the Beatles.

There were a few little clouds on our perfect horizon, all of which I tried to ignore. One of them was my insecurity and jealousy – if I wasn't careful I very quickly fell into the trap of feeling like the second Mrs De Winter, in Daphne Du Maurier's *Rebecca*. Roy's past was filled with beautiful women, especially his last wife, a fashion model at Chanel; she was the antithesis of me: tall, elegant, incredibly chic and sophisticated. I came upon a photograph of the family – she and Roy with their three sons Fitzroy, Rupert and Edmond when they were little. I stared at the photo for some time. They were all so beautiful, it was like a dagger in my heart.

It was so silly of me to compare myself or our relationship to the previous marriage, especially when it had been far from ideal, for while the boys' mother had been incredibly beautiful she was also extremely complicated and had walked out on the family more than once, abandoning the twins when they were only seven. It was a pattern for her; she had also abandoned her five-year-old daughter Ingrid, by a previous relationship, leaving the girl with her grandparents in South Africa in order to follow

Roy to England. Ingrid didn't join her mother until she was eight years old. Ingrid was an exquisite little thing; by the time I met her she had become a successful actress and model as the face of Biba, the famous hippy emporium of Barbara Hulanicki. Ingrid's huge blue eyes and almond-shaped face were iconic and literally plastered across London during the late sixties.

At fifty-four years old, Roy was a man with a considerable past. He had six sons from three earlier marriages and another relationship, so, as you can imagine, it took time for me to meet them all. The younger boys were still at boarding school: Fitzroy was seventeen; the identical twins Rupert and Edmond were fifteen. There were also two older sons who had already left home: Jonty, the eldest, a Professor of English at the University of Zagreb, and Larry, a writer and filmmaker, who was only a year older than me; there was also the sixth son, a sweetheart called Rufus, who came to stay with us once when he was nine. Rufus was a serious boy, with a quiet charm and an interest in things beyond his years. When his eyes rested upon his father they would light up, he was so eager to know him. He would watch his father with tremendous attentiveness and I could see how much he admired him and wanted his approval. Roy had left Rufus when he was a year old – the relationship with the mother had been a disaster. Apparently, Roy had told her he was going out 'to buy some milk' and never returned. Roy was very good at producing beautiful children but not very good at being a father. He was an Edwardian patriarch really, and needed an army of nannies to take care of them all, and then whip them off to the nursery when he'd had enough.

They were all attractive, intelligent, extremely witty people, and I enjoyed the few times we spent together, but it was a complicated, sprawling family and I didn't really feel part of it. Ingrid had her own flat in Chelsea. The boys were away at school, their mother had remarried, and I later learnt that the boys often stayed at school for half-term holidays because there was never anyone at home. Roy loved them all, in his own detached way, but he didn't seem to be connected with their lives and activities. His life's passion was his work, making films, and I often had the impression that he had absolutely no idea what his children were up to, or even where they were.

One year, Roy and I invited the three boys, Fitzroy and the twins, Edmond and Rupert, and a friend of theirs to come out to La Solitude for a 'family holiday'. Roy chartered a motor yacht called *Thelma* and the plan was to go sailing around the Mediterranean for two weeks. My journal entries reveal the genuine affection I felt for them, but also a strange awkwardness and underlying tension.

The boys arrived the day before we were to set sail. Suddenly the villa seemed terribly small, every space taken up with the four of them and their luggage. Edmond always has the most extraordinary pallor, there is a luminosity about him, those pale blue eyes and that curtain of blonde hair that obscures them. The twins are beautiful and ethereal, they're like moon children, sort of fragile, whereas Fitzroy is of the earth: earthy, square and agile like a young boxer, he has a joyful boxer's laugh. After breakfast of coffee and croissants we all waited eagerly for the moment when she would appear around the Cap. Small at first and vaguely blue in the distance, hours seemed to pass, we checked and rechecked our cases, opened a bottle and raised our glasses to the trip to come, then fell silent, musing, half eager, half apprehensive. Then suddenly – activity! There she was, 'Thelma' coming into view just around the corner of the bay. Shutters were rolled down, windows and doors locked, as Thelma rocked gently on the water, a rather grey and ageing old lady. Once on board, the boys reminded me of domestic animals as they prowled around the boat, stared out to sea, sizing up the situation until they found their chosen spot to settle. The boat took off and silently we all watched as the familiar land slipped by and disappeared into a violet mist behind us, the engines throbbed and rumbled under our unsteady feet. I stared

across the scrubbed deck, across polished rails, to the dark blue sea and
felt excitement shoot through me, what an adventure we were on,
and the boys were with us, it was going to be wonderful!

We sailed on to Tuscany and spent a pleasant day in Via Reggio
on the Tyrrhenian coastline. Early next morning, we weighed
anchor and sailed on. As the safety of the harbour disappeared
behind us, a deep sense of fear began to grow steadily with the
mounting waves. The fear grew as the sea dashed into *Thelma*,
sending vast waves sprawling over her decks and threatening to
swamp her. We sat on the aft deck, squashed into the long seat
behind the table like terrified birds on a telegraph wire, staring out
at the heaving seas. The launch had lost its mooring and was now
attached only by its sharp end, leaving it crashing from side to side.
As *Thelma* heaved, and her propellers reared up out of the water,
we all shared the same thought: that we might soon die . . . and
we remembered how dry London was and how we longed for it!

Eight excruciating hours later, with darkness fallen, *Thelma*
finally limped into safety in the lee of Corsica, which had definitely not been on our itinerary. The near-death experience had
brought us closer together, for the holiday, at least, and we had
a couple of funny, happy dinners in local restaurants where the
boys became enormously rowdy, with the exception of Edmond
who was stricken with *la grippe*. Roy took me to visit museums
and art galleries but the boys preferred to go off and explore on
their own.

I understood that my presence in their father's life must have
been difficult to deal with. We hardly knew each other; Roy lived
with me in my flat, and they lived in the house at the top of
the road above the bank. Maybe Roy didn't want to overwhelm
me with his large family, but honestly, I would have loved it. The
situation was just a bit strange; we were all of similar ages. I was
barely an adult myself and unsure how to behave. Was I supposed to behave like their *stepmother*? What did that even mean?

Without doubt, the last thing they wanted, or needed, was Roy's new partner interfering in their lives, and I certainly didn't feel that I had the right or the qualification to do so. So I remained very much on the periphery.

By 1968, Roy had a new writing partner, Leo Marks, and they were working on a screenplay together called *Twisted Nerve* – in which there was a part for me. Leo was small, stocky, barrel-chested, his huge hands always holding a cigar. He had a knowing gleam in his eye, which made me slightly uncomfortable, as if he could read my thoughts and see my secrets. He was married to the painter Elena Gaussen, a gentle, retiring person. She reminded me of a little brown bird that had found its way into the room and couldn't get out. They were an odd couple. Leo was a polymath and had a very colourful past. During the war, when he was still only in his early twenties, he had been put in charge of the Codes Office established by the Special Operations Executive in Baker Street, London, supporting resistance agents in occupied Europe. He created so many espionage codes including the unforgettable 'code poem' for the secret agent Violette Szabo, which became famous in the film *Carve Her Name with Pride*, about her life. As well as being a giant brain, Leo was also something of a radical; he had written the screenplay for Michael Powell's film *Peeping Tom*. The maverick director who made *The Red Shoes*, *A Matter of Life and Death* and *Black Narcissus* was held in high regard by everyone in the business, but *Peeping Tom*, with its serial-killer 'voyeur' protagonist and lurid Technicolor, proved too much of a shock for moviegoers in 1960. The film was castigated by the critics and Powell attacked so violently and personally in the press that he left the country, which basically killed his career.

This sort of controversy didn't put Roy off one bit; rather, I think it made Leo more attractive. They had a lot in common – both were raised by strong Jewish mothers and expressed a fiercely independent spirit. The two older men regarded themselves as free-thinking non-conformists and soon became inseparable, spending long hours writing, drinking, billowing cigar smoke, ridiculing poseurs and hypocrites, essentially righting the wrongs of the world, while psychoanalysing everyone and their dog.

Leo's knowledge of psychology and hypnosis brought a very different element into Roy's writing and *Twisted Nerve* took him into the realm of psychological thriller. Hywel Bennett had been contracted to British Lion after *The Family Way,* so he was co-starring again; there was also the marvellous Billie Whitelaw and Frank Finlay; I was brought in to play Susan, the object of Hywel's obsession.

I was dieting constantly, as ever, trying to lose weight for the camera, and preparing extensively for the role. I was eager to do a good job, to impress Roy and help make the film a triumph. But it was to no avail; *Twisted Nerve* turned out to be an unmitigated disaster. Not as bad as *Peeping Tom,* but close. The film garnered some serious criticism as people complained at the contention that there was a link between Down's Syndrome and psychiatric or even criminal behaviour. All this was really Leo's area of interest but Roy was deeply shocked by the accusations. He added a voiceover disclaimer before the titles, but it was too late, the controversy overshadowed the film and Roy plunged into depression.

The experience did me no favours either. I never should have got involved; it wasn't my kind of film, it wasn't even a good role – playing supporting victim to Hywel's prowling maniac. No one wanted to see Pollyanna being stalked by a pervert. The only reason I agreed to the role was because my partner was directing, and Roy, blinded by his love for his projects, was even less objective than me. We weren't helping each other's careers. It was a bit of a mess.

Apart from Timothy West's police superintendent's immortal line 'Watch out, this bloke's a nutter', the only memorable thing to come out of *Twisted Nerve* was Bernard Herrmann's eerie whistling theme, which Quentin Tarantino reused so effectively in *Kill Bill*. Bernard's creepy little tune has now entered pop culture and features on many a mobile ringtone – including my son's. It's a far cry from Dickie Attenborough's poignant little whistling for *Whistle Down the Wind*!

★

I was always grateful to be working, but my next film, *Take a Girl Like You* in 1969, although fun to make, was fraught with problems. On the page it all seemed interesting: a script based on a novel by Kingsley Amis, with Jonathan Miller at the helm making his directorial debut. Working with Jonathan was extraordinary and unlike anything else; he was a brilliant man, multi-talented, creator of *Beyond the Fringe* with Peter Cook, Dudley Moore and Alan Bennett. He was a theatre and opera director, an actor, an author, a physician and a trained neurologist! He would come on to the set in the morning and approach things as if he were at rehearsals in the theatre, often without having any plan of the scene that we were going to shoot. Instead, he would spend literally hours talking with great erudition about whatever interested him at that time – sometimes it would be about the diseases and disorders of the central and peripheral nervous system. At other times it might be his thoughts on the latest autopsy that he had just performed, for which he would provide us all with the most graphic and horrifying photographs to illustrate. Fascinating and educational though it certainly was, it didn't serve to move on the shooting of the film very much. Jonathan was an intellectual in the truest sense; he was also an extremely funny man, his humour classic 'undergrad'. He was so witty and I was eager to learn anything I could from him, especially about comedy and timing. Unfortunately he was also an actor, and he was often unable to stop himself from 'acting out' the moment he wanted, but with such brilliance and to such hysterical effect that it was virtually impossible to emulate it – one could only be a pale imitation at best!

Take a Girl Like You was a modern tale of an inexperienced girl from the north of England and her courtship and seduction by a schoolmaster, played by a young Oliver Reed, and his friend, played by Noel Harrison. It revealed a lot of the prevailing attitudes towards women and sex that still existed from the 1950s, and, I think, viewed today it's very interesting from that perspective. The film had a great cast with Sheila Hancock, who was excellent and very funny as the suspicious and bitter landlady, John Bird as her molesting husband and Labour councillor, Penelope Keith, Aimi MacDonald and Geraldine Sherman, who would become a lifelong friend. And also my sweet and beautiful cousin Pippa Steel, who it was wonderful to be able to work alongside.

Much to my disappointment, I did not warm to Ollie Reed. We had a very different approach to acting. I liked to rehearse, he didn't. I was happy to do another take, he wasn't. I preferred to stay on the script, he preferred to improvise. I could have worked with that but I felt less inclined to indulge him as I really disliked the way he talked about women as if they were a lower species. Maybe I was a bit of a prude, but I found his constant sexual innuendos tiresome – as such he was well cast as the character in the film. Doubtless he was a complicated individual, intelligent and very effective on screen in the right part. His performance on *The Johnny Carson Show* with Shelley Winters is an extraordinary example of his brazen misogyny which resulted in Shelley pouring her whisky and soda on his head, which he thoroughly deserved! I rather regret not doing the same thing myself.

Take a Girl Like You was produced by Hal Chester, who was a shameless trailblazer for 'product placement' in movies. In any given scene there was always something being flogged: French copper cooking pots, bottled beer, a certain brand of cigarettes. Before a take, Hal would quickly step in front of the camera and reposition the props so that the cigarette packet or beer bottle label was clearly visible. At the end of the shoot Hal went home with boxes of cookware, beer, cartons of cigarettes – not to mention all of the half-chopped vegetables that had been used in the kitchen scene!

Sadly, for all its potential, the film failed to find an audience and was a total non-event. One of the big problems with the film was that there was no consistent tone or style, either in the acting or the filmmaking. Miller and Chester had very different ideas about the sort of film that they wanted to make. Hal wanted a sexy commercial comedy, whereas Jonathan leant more towards observational satire; Hal hated this and became very nervous and controlling. It probably didn't help that Jonathan spent half the shoot day talking neurosurgery and autopsies. Ultimately, if the film had been allowed to be one thing or the other it might have been quite interesting but their conflict undermined the creative process and subsequently it failed either as Hal's or Jonathan's film; they were like oil and water. These sorts of counter-productive conflicts happen a lot in movie-making and it's terribly disappointing when it doesn't work out.

After the disappointments of *Twisted Nerve* and *Take a Girl Like You*, I felt like I was 'spinning my wheels' as an actress. I'd been stuck in the same place for too long. Somehow, I had to break out, play different kinds of characters, push myself and see what I was capable of. I longed to work in the theatre, a desire that had been growing in me for years. I knew instinctively that I needed to 'go back to school', go back to the beginning and start again, and that the theatre would teach me important lessons.

I wanted to tackle the masters: Chekhov, Ibsen, even Shakespeare, although I was quite afraid of it. From a purely emotional, expressive, 'acting' point of view, I felt I could do it, but I knew I had to brush up on technique. My voice wasn't very powerful, which I needed to address, especially when you're doing Shakespeare, when one really needs control. I started taking voice lessons, learning about breathing, focusing my voice, connecting with my breath; I realised the power was there if I was able to relax. It was exciting to learn new techniques and I felt I was really making a difference – years of playing ingenues and light comedy roles had left me with a very light breathy voice, which also betrayed my insecurity and was not conducive to playing Juliet.

I went along to see Sir Bernard Miles when he was running the Mermaid Theatre in Blackfriars on the River Thames, hoping that he might put me in one of his plays. Bernard was an old friend of my father's after they first worked together on Noël Coward's wartime naval classic *In Which We Serve* – although he is perhaps best remembered for playing Joe Gargery the blacksmith, Pip's lifelong friend in David Lean's *Great Expectations* – also with my father.

So Bernard and I had lunch together in the theatre cafe, but his prognosis was not good.

'You'll never work on the stage, Hayley,' he chuckled, eyes twinkling as he poured a small bottle of Guinness. 'You make too many faces, you screw your face up too much.'

It was a bit of a shock. As a child, people had commented on my 'mobile face', but I'd always felt that this was one of my 'charms'. Now I realised he was right. I did make faces – terrible faces. It was partly shyness, partly an attempt to make people laugh. But struggling with shyness is the kiss of death for an actress, especially when you go along to meet producers and casting people; they'll find it difficult to see beyond the tortured-looking girl wringing her hands in front of them. I didn't give up on my dreams of being a stage actress after my lunch with Bernard – far from it, I wanted to show him I *could* do it – but for some time I did walk around with a bit of Sellotape stuck between my eyes to stop me frowning.

It wasn't until Christmas 1969 that I finally made my stage debut, in *Peter Pan* at the New Victoria Theatre in London. I adored every minute of it, despite the New Victoria being a great black barn of a place with nearly two and a half thousand people – that's a lot of bums on seats.

Richard Wordsworth was directing and the lovely Bill Travers was going to play the dual roles of Mr Darling and Captain Hook, but sadly Bill had to drop out due to a bad throat infection at the last minute and so Richard took over both directing and acting and ended up playing both parts. His Captain Hook was absolutely lethal in the sword fight!

What a joy it was to play Peter Pan. I knew from the start that I was right for it, which is an immensely empowering feeling. I had a beautiful little wig and a red leather tunic, and when I looked in the mirror I saw Peter! I looked *and* felt like him; flying around the theatre seemed the most natural thing in the world. Oh, if only, when one feels ecstatically happy, one could just take a great deep breath . . . and lift off like Peter did! It was such a wonderful sensation – when you got it right. The flying was of course not the result of exhilaration but of mechanics: the wonderful Kirby Flying apparatus, which had been providing actresses with lift-off since Nina Boucicault first played the 'Boy Who Wouldn't Grow Up' in 1904. I was following in the footsteps of so many wonderful actresses who have played the part, and that story is so deeply embedded in the hearts and psyche of children all over the world. The play has a real magic about it and performing to thousands of children every night was like another kind of flying!

Not that there weren't problematic moments. Kirby Flying is actually quite tricky to get the hang of and can be extremely uncomfortable as the webbing goes right up between your legs. The secret to achieving the effect is that someone stands on a ladder in the darkness of the wings, holding onto the other end of the rope – and when they jump, you take off! As you might expect, it is not without its risks. You have to be very careful to stand in absolutely the right place when lift-off occurs, or you may be launched into the scenery. Once I was standing in the wrong position and instead of flying across the stage and landing gracefully on the Darlings' nursery mantelpiece, I ended up flying backwards, very fast, offstage, disappearing into the darkness – and crashing into a ladder and some buckets. My sister Juliet had played Wendy a few years earlier; one night she misjudged her position and crash-landed on a table, cracking her ribs.

One of my favourite moments in the play was when Peter first arrives in the sleeping children's bedroom. It had always thrilled me as a child, and now I was actually doing it myself! As Peter, you are waiting, crouching down behind the big double-windows of the bedroom. The orchestra strikes up; your cue, a 'green light', flashes backstage – the windows are flung open and you, or rather Peter, is suddenly lifted up, flies in and lands centre stage! It's incredibly exciting. One evening, the left side of the windows didn't open, and, as I flew in, my arm clipped it; I went twirling in like a corkscrew, making a perfect landing, arms outstretched – but facing upstage!

I felt strangely at home on that vast stage. Maybe it was all those children out there, knowing how much they were loving it. When Tinker Bell is dying and all the children start clapping and cheering to bring her back to life, it gave me goose pimples every night. The longer I performed Peter the more I could understand how actresses like Maud Adams could play him for ten years. Jean Forbes-Robertson appeared in so many other classical plays but it was the role of Peter, which she first took on in 1927, that became her most famous – and the role that most got under her skin. Legend has it that she used to receive guests into her drawing room while sitting perched on the mantelpiece.

To play Peter Pan an actor has to be in touch with the child within. It's all a wonderful game of make-believe anyway and Peter Pan is the ultimate return to innocence, for the actor as much as the audience. It's a sort of rebirthing! He falls out of his pram and goes off to Never Land to live with the Lost Boys. It occurred to me that, in a strange way, Peter Pan was my life in reverse: for years I had been running away, *trying* to grow up, surrounded by people who didn't want me to.

★

In April the following year, the Beatles broke up. As with Walt's passing, when I first heard the news I couldn't quite grasp it. John, Paul, George and Ringo belonged together – for ever! Up to that day, however bad or confusing things were in the world, you could always take comfort in the knowledge that the Beatles were out there, singing their songs, weaving their enchantments, expressing how we all felt, secretly, deep down inside – because they understood us.

And now they were gone too. It was so sad.

But then, something happened, something clicked inside me, and I understood how *they* felt. They were trying to grow up too, to live their own lives, to discover themselves, to find their own voices as individuals, to break away from the safety of the group. If you want to find out who you are, on your own terms, to be truly free, you have to be prepared to stand alone. And that's scary.

I wondered if I had the courage to do the same.

CHAPTER TWELVE

Irina's Piano

'A Robin Redbreast in a Cage
Puts all Heaven in a Rage'
                    – William Blake, 'Auguries of Innocence'

I should have left Roy in 1970. Deep down I knew I had to end the relationship, but my head got in the way of what I felt in my heart, and I simply couldn't admit it. In hindsight, it's ironic that it was Roy who used to say 'The sword is quick – the sword is clean', it was an adage he truly believed and lived by. I liked the sound of it – no mess, just the swift flashing of the blade, the *coup de grâce*, and it's over – but of course, the reality was more untidy than that, as I would discover.

Early that year, Roy and I went down to Brighton for the weekend and took a suite at the old Hotel Metropole. It was January and the weather was dismal – thunderously cold with driving English rain; the mood was awful and we both wanted to do different things. One night Roy had fallen into a deep and stertorous slumber, I was restless and couldn't sleep. Sitting by the window, looking past the ranks of haloed streetlamps and out into the pitch black sea, I ate grapes and lined up all the pips like ants along the sill – and found myself sobbing silently as Roy snored in the other room.

Not only did I not have the courage to end it, I didn't feel I had the right. We had been together for three years and I felt a responsibility to him. For, despite his age, and for all his success, his prestige and standing in the world, the truth was, I saw him as quite vulnerable. I had always seen him like that, from the beginning in fact; all alone in that big house, deserted but for the painted crows. That was the person I'd fallen in love with. And still loved. That lonely soul. Maybe this was it, right from the start – I thought I could save him.

But in the meantime, no one was going to save *me*. All my child-acting monies remained 'frozen' by the government, pending our upcoming appeal, and I was desperate to get out there and do some work.

There is a sweet little theatre in Leicester, in the East Midlands, called the Phoenix Arts Centre. It has an apron-shaped stage that juts out into an auditorium, holding less than three hundred seats, and it was here in the spring of 1970 that I played Irina in *Three Sisters*. While *Peter Pan* had been a wonderful experience, the Phoenix was my true initiation into the theatre. I found it far more frightening walking onto that tiny stage than flying across the great open spaces of the New Victoria in London. There was no hiding place at the Phoenix. The audience was so close that they would sometimes put their shopping bags on the stage. One matinee a lady sat with her knees apart, treating us to the sight of her blue bloomers for the entire performance, and when Dr Chebutykin's beard peeled itself off his cheek – and hung down like lichen from an old American oak – everyone could see that, too.

The Phoenix was the perfect place and the perfect teacher to learn about working in the theatre: to learn about stillness, not waving my arms around like a demented scarecrow; not making faces; how to use my voice and how to project it clearly to the back of the stalls without shouting – although, to be honest, the sound didn't need to travel very far. I also discovered the joy of starting every performance at the beginning of the play and going right through to the end, experiencing all the dramatic threads leading to their natural conclusion, with nothing performed out of context or continuity – as so often happens when shooting a movie. Most importantly, it was during this run that I discovered that thrilling, emotional and electric connection with a live audience.

Three Sisters is the perfect play by the perfect writer. Chekhov's characters were a revelation, and for me, Irina was the perfect part. She and I were the same age. When the story opens it's her 'name day' and she is full of hope and optimism for the future. She feels as if everything on God's earth is opening up to her, which makes the disappointments and pitiful compromises that follow all the more tragic. Chekhov seemed to understand perfectly the heart and mind of this young woman; I especially loved her line 'My soul is like a wonderful piano which is locked and the key has been lost.' How brilliant. Playing Irina was like living another life and I felt a soul connection to her in many ways. When eventually Irina agrees to marry Baron Tuzenbach, although she doesn't really love him, she grieves the fact because, while she has always dreamt of love, she has never felt capable of really loving another person. Deep in my heart this struck a worrying chord, for I was well aware how easily I fell in and out of love. I had abandoned my faithful Andrew so cruelly – and I wondered if I was truly capable of loving someone for ever.

Emboldened by my time at the Phoenix, I dived almost immediately into another tour and another classic – playing Hedvig in Ibsen's *The Wild Duck*. And so two of my dreams had come together in one year and privately I hoped that Bernard Miles had noticed.

It was very exciting. We were set to tour the country and then move to the West End. I was grateful for the work but I was also glad for the distraction, since back in London Roy was under enormous pressure to save a floundering production for

British Lion, awkwardly titled *Mr Forbush and the Penguins*.

Mr Forbush was an original screenplay by a promising new writer named Anthony Shaffer (who would go on to write *Sleuth*, Hitchcock's *Frenzy*, and most famously *The Wicker Man*) about a vain, frivolous young biologist, played by John Hurt, whose life is turned upside down when he is sent into the solitary wilderness of Antarctica to carry out observations on a colony of penguins. The film had been shot in two halves: one in London and the other in Antarctica. All the footage of John with the penguins looked amazing, masterfully shot by the Swedish documentary director Arne Sucksdorff (who made *The Great Adventure*, about a little boy and his wild otter, one of the most beautiful, poetic and unforgettable films I have ever seen). However, the Boultings felt that the London half of the film was just awful – so awful and pretentious, in fact, that the entire first half needed to be rewritten and reshot, or the film would be unreleasable. Roy fired both the director and the writer, taking over all script and directing duties himself, leaving his twin brother with the unenviable task of having to ask EMI Films for more money.

Back then, it just so happened that the head of production at EMI Films was my old friend Bryan Forbes – and this is where I came in. The original actress in the story was no longer available so the Boultings asked me to add my name to the project. Roy promised to write me a great part as 'the girl he leaves behind' – and he and John both felt confident that adding my name to the mix would give *Mr Forbush* the extra 'marquee' value required to get EMI to turn out their pockets.

'I'd like to help, of course,' I said. 'But what about *The Wild Duck*? I'll be in the West End by then.' Roy calmly reassured me that the shoot would be only two weeks at most, and he'd make sure all of my scenes were filmed near to the theatre, so I could dash off after work and play Hedvig in the evening.

Despite a very clear voice yelling in my head '*Nooo! Don't do it!!*' I said: 'Great! I'm in!'

And so, leaving the Boultings to salvage *Forbush*, I began work on *The Wild Duck*.

It was my first proper touring experience and I adored every minute. Arriving in a strange town, looking eagerly for the posters announcing our production (and seldom finding any); the camaraderie of travelling with a troupe of actors, just as both my parents had done before me – mercifully, without the bed bugs. Being part of the town for one short week and then moving on; adjusting to the shape and sound of the new theatre, and the dressing rooms, with their dangerously threadbare carpets; the naked lightbulbs around an old mirror, and always the ghosts of past occupants: a mysterious telephone number scribbled on the wall, a smudged message in lipstick on the mirror . . . and the thrill of the Tannoy calling our names to go on stage.

I felt I was really beginning to spread my acting wings. I was in good hands and good company: Glen Byam Shaw was directing, a tremendously experienced craftsman. A friend of Gielgud and Olivier and also Siegfried Sassoon, as a young actor he had performed Chekhov, Ibsen and Strindberg and for many years had run the Shakespeare Theatre in Stratford upon Avon.

I was also blessed to be working alongside the legendary husband-and-wife team of Michael Denison and Dulcie Gray, playing the roles of Hjalmar and Gina, Hedvig's parents. Michael and Dulcie were theatre veterans and travelling with them was an education in the 'old school'. They were often referred to as the English equivalent of Alfred Lunt and Lynn Fontanne, the famous American husband-and-wife acting team, known affectionately to all as 'The Lunts'. Michael and Dulcie had worked together for decades, ever since they first met at drama school in the thirties. Not only did they have a vast amount of touring experience, they did it all in remarkable style, travelling in their ancient old Rolls-Royce with their yellow Labrador 'Titus'; and while the rest of the company were assigned humble

337

digs in pubs or hotels, Michael and Dulcie would invariably be invited to stay with friends in their stately homes or lovely old country houses. Both of them were always beautifully dressed, even at rehearsals. Michael was charming, humorous, courteous and dapper in suits and jackets, often with a silk cravat, while Dulcie, small and pretty, with her sweet face and lilting voice, always looked glamorous. She wore lovely jewellery and always a wig. Quite a few ladies on the English stage wore wigs at that time, something I discovered while still quite young, when, at a dinner party, Vivien Leigh astonished me by pulling her wig down over her eyes for a gag. It gave me quite a shock, as I had no idea that she was even wearing one. Dulcie was from this 'old guard'. Professional and industrious, she was also a very good writer; she would write every day before she went to the theatre, turning out successful crime thrillers that were a useful supplement to their income. But what intrigued me most of all was the fact that she and Michael were so clearly still in love. He adored her and still found her just as enchanting and funny as he had in their youth. Dulcie loved him equally. I didn't know what their secret was. Laughter? Luck? Drink? And who knows what problems they may have been through in the past. Even my parents had their struggles. I remember when my father did the musical *The Good Companions* starring alongside a young and rather gorgeous Judi Dench, whom he adored, Mummy became quite jealous – she made sure she was at the theatre a lot! Whatever Michael and Dulcie's secret, what was abundantly clear was that, like my parents, they had a wonderful gift for friendship, and they swept me up so generously into their theatrical caravan. Wherever we went, all over the country, at the end of every performance their dressing rooms were always filled to overflowing with old friends, shouts of laughter and the pop of champagne corks.

The play itself was a wonderful discovery – and again, I found a personal connection with my character. Hedvig was another doomed romantic, and I discovered her just as I had found my Irina in *Three Sisters*.

The whole experience was a joy, until, that is, one night in Newcastle, when the police arrived at the stage door saying they were going to have to escort me back to my hotel. It appeared my mystery stalker, from whom I'd had FBI protection in New York, had tracked me down again to north-east England; the police had intercepted another letter threatening to bump me off. At least, I *assumed* it was the same stalker. After all – how many people wanted to kill me? It was a worrying thought.

Every night for a whole week, the police took me back to the hotel and a couple of them would sit in the very dreary lounge all night, keeping watch in shifts, taking turns for one constable to be stationed directly outside my room. I was extremely grateful and touched, but concerned at the miserably uncomfortable night they were all having. At around seven o'clock in the morning there would be a gentle knock on my door and I would frantically scrub the sulphur off my spots and drag the rollers out of my hair, as the tired face of a Geordie copper appeared at the door to let me know that he was going off duty.

At the weekend, Roy came up for a couple of days. On Sunday, we hired a car and drove to Bamburgh Castle. We walked along the empty, windswept, sandy beaches and lunched at the medieval Lord Crewe Arms. Sitting in straight-backed wooden pews, we ate good pub food and drank good red wine and talked about history – the Moorish castle, the Virgin Queen, and Shakespeare – and all the while I looked long and hard into that dear face that I still didn't really understand.

After eight weeks touring, *The Wild Duck* finally opened in the West End for the three-month run. It was a milestone for me and I should have been focused entirely on the play and relishing the whole experience, but instead I was tied up with the shoot for *Mr Forbush and the Penguins*. Roy was solely focused on the job, as was his way, while I was exhausted from travelling, so living in my small flat was proving to be stressful. We both needed more space and there just wasn't any in that tiny place. On top of that I was struggling to do both jobs – getting up at the crack of dawn, filming until 6 p.m., then travelling to the theatre to play Hedvig, returning home at midnight, still buzzing with adrenaline and unable to sleep – and then starting it all over again at dawn the next day. The shoot was supposed to be two weeks but ended up being five. Not very surprisingly, I eventually lost my voice and was consigned to bed with acute laryngitis.

After a few days, I returned to the theatre and went into Dulcie's dressing room before the show. I was exhausted and terribly worried that I wouldn't be able to give a good performance. Dulcie was already in costume and make-up, sitting at her dressing table playing Patience, as she always did before she went on. Confiding in her about my anxiety, she opened a drawer and took out some little blue pills. 'Take this, my darling,' she said, her eyes twinkling at me from under her wig. 'This will take all your tiredness away,' and she handed me a pill. I was delighted, a pill that would magically restore my energy? This sounded marvellous! I thanked her profusely and by the time I went on stage I was feeling great and gave a splendidly energised performance. It was miraculous but I knew I couldn't simply keep stealing Dulcie's pills. A few nights later I went back to ask her what these little blue pills were called because I was definitely going to have to get some. The doctor was startled when I asked for a prescription. 'What do you want sedatives for?' he asked.

Sedatives? I couldn't believe it, I thought I was taking uppers or cocaine or something, not a pill to make me calm! But it taught me something – the pill had perked me up simply because it had taken away the tiredness and the stress. It could just as well have been a placebo! It was the power of the mind.

Despite the strain of juggling two jobs, I did enjoy spending time with John Hurt. I found him to be very sweet, very smart, delightfully funny . . . and incorrigible, even then. One Sunday, he and Roy and I went out to dinner in Richmond, near the studios in Twickenham. It was all going very well, we were having a great time, laughing and talking and eating and drinking, with John doing a lot more of the latter than anyone else. Suddenly I became aware that he was sinking down into his seat. First his face landed in his plate, and then, before anyone could do anything, he slid very, very slowly under the table and disappeared from view. I gave a little squeak as I felt something bite my ankle, before feeling the dead weight of John's head settle on my foot, where he promptly fell asleep.

Mr Forbush and the Penguins turned out to be a disaster for British Lion and another career misstep for me. It was a 'nothing' sort-of-role, just 'fluff' as Mummy would have said, which didn't do anything for my name. The promise of John Hurt and penguins at the South Pole failed to attract audiences; and the film's over-inflated budget and the subsequent flop resulted in dear Bryan Forbes being fired from EMI.

Mr Forbush became my third consecutive flop and I was starting to feel jinxed. How could I not?

However, in December 1970 I decided to push any negative thoughts to the back of my mind and steel myself for the tax appeal with Her Majesty's Special Commissioners, which had finally arrived! The headlines were:

i) The trust had been set up by my father.
ii) All the money I'd ever earned had been transferred into the trust – *after income tax had been paid.*
iii) The trust funds were never distributed.

The money had essentially never been touched. Prior to my sixteenth birthday I had been given 'expenses'; after I was sixteen I had been paid a salary of £400 p.a (about £10,000 in today's value), and given my own cheque book and also allotted a Post Office savings account, but couldn't draw out more than £10 at any one time.

When the trust was originally set up, I was only fourteen years old. I had signed the forms without even reading the endless pages of densely typed and largely incomprehensible contract – all written in legalese, so even if I had read them I doubt very much that I would have understood any of it.

I understood even less of what was said in the court case. But the final verdict was clear enough.

My appeal was rejected.

I felt utterly hopeless – I was being ordered to hand over essentially *everything*. Stanley Passmore told me not to despair; it wasn't over yet, he said, and he quickly advised that we should appeal to the High Court of Justice. I agreed to the plan and wrote another very large cheque to JD Langton & Passmore solicitors, while they assured me that the case would be put before a High Court judge very soon.

A date was set for December 1971, by which time my money would have been frozen for almost five years.

I became very dispirited by losing the case and at the same time things were far from harmonious with Roy. Christmas was coming and the thought of the two of us jammed into my little flat in Chelsea was making me worried. I needed a proper break and to get away. I decided to fly over to California and be with my family who were all gathering at Juliet's house for the holiday. Roy was already busy prepping his next movie, *There's a Girl in My Soup*, starring Peter Sellers and Goldie Hawn, and he was locked away in a darkened editing suite anyway. I think he was relieved to be alone.

The writing was on the wall but I couldn't face it. We were such different ages. I had so many more things I wanted to discover about the world. Not only had he already lived a life of rich experiences, more importantly, he had made up his mind and set his opinions about so many things, which wasn't healthy for me: I was still trying to grow and evolve. It didn't help that we hardly ever saw people; the only socialising we did was with Leo – and he was even older than Roy. My Christmas diary entry did not bode well for 1971: confused as ever, lurching between loving Roy and wanting to be free of him.

Alone in the Beverly Hills Hotel, left Roy in England. Had to go, be alone, very important, necessary, so tired after the London slog in the play and shooting the film for five weeks. Got ill, ghastly throat infection. Nothing seemed to be working for me. It's a stupid, negative attitude and I shall shake it off once I've sorted myself out.

Brought down terribly by losing my Tax case, cannot believe that such injustice be upheld by the law and that after ten years hard labour there should only be the villa to show for it, nothing else. Some bits of those years I enjoyed and some bits I hated. I had no friends, and no freedom. This lack of freedom or threat of freedom has always bedevilled me. Now suddenly I found I couldn't stay, couldn't be with Roy, who I love and risk losing because I'm in search of . . . what? My own free self, free expression . . .

Freedom. But what does that mean?

I left him at Christmas time, alone, snow fell Christmas Eve, I wasn't there, but terribly missing him.

I must wait and think and hopefully learn a private lesson of my own, mine, mine alone.

He and I are strangely good together, he's loving, patient, indulgent and full of concern and so true, never a truer heart I know that. Yet, still I feel not quite light at heart because my spirit's not quite free.

I want my heart to be his, but my spirit must, must fly free and full of joy!

Christmas with Juliet was very therapeutic, back with my big sister and all the family; we had lots of long walks and talks and laughter. Juliet had landed a hit TV show for ABC, with the actor

Richard Long, called *Nanny and the Professor* in which she played a psychic nanny wearing a blue Inverness cape and a little deerstalker cap perched on her head! She looked enchanting and was very good in it. I've noticed my sister is often cast as 'supernatural' types. She has a natural magic.

The popularity of *Nanny* required Bunch to relocate to Los Angeles and it changed her life. She loved Southern California and embraced everything about it. She put her little boy Sean into a local school and within no time he'd lost his slightly 'Artful Dodger' accent and began to sound and look like a little American: beach blond, dirt-bike racing, surfing his brains out and winning all sorts of competitions. Juliet never looked back, she has a wonderful life out there and, as a result, half my family's now American.

Juliet has always been 'the star' to my 'wandering bark' that 'looks on tempests and is never shaken'. Through all of her own life's often considerable upheavals, she's always had time for me and mine. Bunch and I have always had a strong connection. I can't count the number of times that she's just miraculously turned up in my life when I've been going through some tumultuous experience. I have always known how lucky I am to have her; an older sister who has been down a similar road to me just a little while before. Some people bring out the best in us – what more can I say? Like all of us, she's had to confront her own demons and, in doing so, she can recognise other people's struggles. She's learnt wisdom and compassion, she's smart and terribly funny – and, despite being one of the very few people in Hollywood who has never had any cosmetic surgery, she is still incredibly beautiful. Again, natural magic.

Spending Christmas with my intimate family felt like coming up for air. Jonathan was also now living in California so we were all together. It was at that time I first heard George Harrison's 'My Sweet Lord'. Perhaps it's too much of a cliché to talk about 'the soundtracks of our life', but some songs not only transport us back to a special moment, or where we were, they also recall that moment of *who* we were. When I first heard George singing 'My Sweet Lord', I remember feeling an immediate response, like recognising a familiar old face or a long-lost friend. Music is natural magic, too. The poignancy and joy in the voices made me want to play it over and over again. The Beatles were always pioneers and George seemed to have emerged from the storms and confusions of the sixties with a deep and profound spiritual message. George was leading the way; but unlike the Pied Piper leading the rats to their watery doom in the river, George was leading us to higher ground. Like so many who followed George on the spiritual path, I came across *Autobiography of a Yogi* by Paramahansa Yogananda, which was really my first introduction to Eastern spirituality and helped me to appreciate the universality of all faith.

In a fortunate coinciding of events, also partly thanks to George, I encountered the Hare Krishna devotees; their beautiful philosophy and the Hare Krishna maha-mantra made a deep impression on me, as did the exquisite paintings of the devotional artists Dhriti Devi Dasi and Rama Das, whom I was lucky enough to meet and who became lifelong friends. Wherever I go in the world, whether travelling or touring, I always carry a small framed picture of Dhriti's beautiful 'Sri Govinda' – Lord Krishna as the divine cowherd.

I returned home to London refreshed and rejuvenated after the California sun, determined to make a new start with Roy. So much was changing. My parents had finally decided to sell The Wick. It was a house that needed 'staff'; the kitchen in the basement was enormous, it had a pantry, a flat for the cook and the housekeeper, a washroom and a billiard room – it was just too big and too expensive to keep up. And now that we had all gone, there were too many empty bedrooms. So once again, the dreaded removal vans were lined up outside the front door and all my parents' belongings disappeared inside and were driven off. For a while they kept a very smart flat in Mayfair, and they also bought a small water mill in Oxfordshire, but unfortunately neither place turned out to be very successful. Mummy hated living in the centre of London, she missed her garden, and every night, with Daddy working in the theatre, she became terribly lonely and too often turned to the drinks cabinet for solace. They soon realised that the mill was far too isolated for friends and family to get down to for the weekend. They couldn't find any staff and were soon shocked when they realised how much time was spent cooking and cleaning! It was a very difficult time for Mummy and it didn't help that she was having difficulty with her writing. She did her best to embrace the necessity of the move but The Wick had such a strong hold on her heart and her imagination that she grieved its passing and with it the life that was now gone. It would be some time before they found the right place for them both to live.

By now Jonathan had flown the nest too. Of all the kids, Johnny was the first of us to seriously explore spiritual life. While I was living my safe, grown-up life with Roy in Chelsea, Johnny was driving to India in a VW bus with Chrissy, his wife-to-be. They drove across Europe, through Afghanistan and on into India via the legendary Khyber Pass, an adventure that would be impossible today. In Nepal, they walked up to the base camp of Mount Everest in sandals! Jonathan returned in the summer with Chrissy and that October had a wonderful 'hippy wedding' at the church nearest The Wick. All the colourful guests were wearing beads and bandanas and the aroma of marijuana was in the air. St Peter's is an ancient little church in Petersham, with high box pews and small leaded windows, nestled at the bottom of Richmond Hill below The Wick. It was high summer and very hot and we were all waiting for Chrissy to arrive. I don't remember why she was late but she chose to run all the way down from The Wick, completely barefoot, down Richmond Hill and across Petersham Meadows in her white wedding dress, her long tawny hair streaming down her back like a veil. She burst breathlessly into the church, where the air was thick with smoke, and Daddy, delirious and unseen in one of the pews, groaned out loud with a temperature of 104.

After their wedding, Jonathan and Chrissy went off on more adventures, to Mexico and beyond. They eventually settled in California; my brother was the first of us to live in America. Johnny can turn his hand to anything, from building a house to deep sea fishing! He's got green fingers, he can grow anything, and he's a brilliant photographer and writer – but true to the Hayley Bell spirit, he is eternally restless. By the autumn of 1971 I was the only one still left in England and I missed my brother and sister terribly.

In May that year Roy and I had been down to the villa. The South of France is so beautiful in early summer, before the heat and the tourists arrive. We fell into our familiar pattern – quiet days and meals together. I worked on my script, learning my lines; Roy read and painted. But happy as I should have been, I felt like Irina's piano, locked up, without a key. I was listless, in a sort of limbo; everything seemed so nebulous there was nothing concrete to hold on to.

One evening, I stood for a long time on the lower terrace gazing into the twilight, past the black limb of the pine tree reaching out into a lilac sky, and across the quiet water beyond. I could see the Cap Estel hotel on the promontory and remembered that summer when I'd first spied the villa through binoculars. It all seemed a lifetime ago. Roy was upstairs, Astrud Gilberto was on the record player, it was peaceful and lovely – so why was I so restless? I realised I needed to make a decision. I couldn't go on like this, it wasn't working . . . It just wasn't working.

I could feel myself being driven by some instinct as I turned and walked quickly inside from the terrace and crossed the room, with its enormous bed and the art deco mirror, and climbed the narrow marble steps up to the little sitting room and found Roy seated at the table painting a still life – an arrangement of fruit and an earthenware jug. I stared at it; something about it depressed me. I took a deep breath.

'Roy?'

He paused and looked up, with a distant smile.

'Roy, I've been thinking . . .' I faltered, suddenly unsure what I wanted to say.

'Yes?' he said, wanting to get back to his painting.

'I've been thinking . . . I feel . . . I feel that . . . that either we should separate or . . .'

The smile faded from his face – and I realised I couldn't do it, I didn't have the courage, I wasn't even sure what I wanted. 'I mean, either we should separate or . . . we should get married!'

Was that what I wanted?

Roy looked at me carefully, a cautious light coming back into his eyes. 'Really?' he said. 'Are you sure?'

No going back now. I'd gone too far, I couldn't take back those words.

'Yes. Yes!' I said, starting to believe it the more I said it. 'And I want to have a baby before I get too old!' That much I knew was true.

'All right!' he said. 'Let's get married!' So we laughed . . . he went back to his painting and I turned and went back down the little marble stairs to the bedroom.

'Maybe that's it!' I told myself. The answer to the conundrum. I just needed to make a definite decision; no more drifting, I needed a destination. Either I wanted to be 'in' and married, or 'out' and free!

I persuaded myself that I couldn't just walk out on him. We'd been together for years, I'd made a commitment and I didn't feel I had the right to just abscond . . . It wasn't as if I didn't love him, I did. He needed me. Not like Andrew who was still young and had his whole life ahead of him. Roy was older and more vulnerable.

I stared fiercely out at the dark blue sea and tried to imagine the future ... We will be married, I will make a success of it, I'll be a good wife, and with any luck I might just become a mother.

And at that, I began to feel the old excitement and optimism stirring in me again. The future had a purpose. Of course, of course this was what I wanted, I just hadn't known it!

The wedding was set for later that summer. Roy suggested we have it in France: a little civil ceremony in the *Mairie* in Cap d'Ail; the local grocer, who we knew, was also the *Greffier* or Registrar, so he would officiate. Roy preferred it to be as quiet and private as possible: no press, no family. He did not want my parents to be there, reasoning that, if they came, it would be impossible to keep the ceremony secret. I sympathised to some degree – after all, I would be Roy's fourth wife, I was thirty-two years younger than him and he didn't want to attract any attention. 'The press would have a field day,' he said. 'Beauty and the Beast.' But it didn't make for a very celebratory wedding day. In fact, it bordered on the farcical.

As usual, I went along with the plan. I told myself that I didn't really mind, I'd never dreamt of having a big white wedding anyway and having a secret marriage seemed rather romantic, like rushing off to Gretna Green. Understandably my parents were quite saddened, although they tried not to show it. But by this time I was lost to them, they knew that. I had hitched my wagon up to Roy's and his word and his opinions were law. I had merely substituted one straitjacket for another and I didn't even know it.

Roy booked a 'honeymoon' suite at the glamorous Hotel du Cap-Eden-Roc in Antibes, so we would have to drive the fifty minutes to Cap d'Ail to be married. The suite was beautiful, absolutely enormous and completely empty, save for a large bouquet of dark red baccara roses from John Boulting.

The morning of my wedding didn't start well. I awoke with my period, a headache and a disturbing weight on my heart; I was sure it was just nerves.

I'd thought long and hard about what to wear for a civil wedding in a little town hall. I had no idea what to buy. Having gone through things I already had in my wardrobe, I finally settled on a long white cotton skirt with a frill along the bottom and a Mexican hand-embroidered blouse with big wide white sleeves, and a raw silk sash in Mediterranean blue and pink.

I looked at myself in the long mirror. I thought it looked rather good, white enough to get married in, but the sash stopped it from being absolutely bridal – after all, who was I kidding, we'd been living together for four years.

Roy walked in and caught sight of me in the mirror, the morning sun streaming into the room behind me.

'You can't wear that!' Roy said, looking aghast. 'It's totally transparent, I can see your underwear!'

He was right. This was before the days when the sight of a pair of knickers was acceptable and I became frantic. Apart from casual stuff and beach clothes this was all I had with me. I had no choice; the best and really the only alternative was a pair of knitted, white cotton trousers. Well, at least they were clean. So I changed and we set off on the Moyenne Corniche to Cap d'Ail. The road hugs the coast between Nice and Menton and is one of the world's most beautiful drives. We were both quiet, thinking our own thoughts.

I gazed down over the wide blue Mediterranean as we drove past the hilltop village of Èze, the windswept pines, like dancers, frozen in mid-gale, silver-green olive trees and endless bougainvillea cascading over walls and across rooftops. I breathed in the ravishing smell of the cypresses and cedars of the Côte d'Azur and the warm air soothed my aching head.

Rounding the final corner, I saw in the sky ahead of us the biggest, blackest cloud hanging ominously over Cap d'Ail. It looked like an omen.

Arriving at *La Mairie*, my French solicitor Gordon Blair and his American wife were waiting for us. They were to be our witnesses – and our only guests. As I stepped out of the car, Gordon's wife shrieked 'Oh, my gahd! She's wearing pants!' and thrust a few flowers into my hand that she had picked from her garden and wrapped in some kitchen foil.

The ceremony was in archaic French and I didn't understand a word. I felt I was walking through the whole thing like a somnambulist, and not understanding the words of the ceremony further increased my feelings of detachment – it was only because Gordon's wife started randomly clapping that I realised the Registrar had just pronounced us 'Man and Wife'.

Roy kissed me; I smiled at him and looked at the unfamiliar little gold band on my finger. I was proud of it, but it felt strange. That's when you need your family and friends around, but there was no one there.

The four of us went to a little restaurant on the port in Beaulieu-sur-Mer for lunch. Everything was so unreal – this wasn't how you were supposed to feel on your wedding day, was it?

Then I remembered that when Bunch got married she'd sat down on the grass beside the road and wept.

★

Not only had I become Roy's wife, I was also, by now, his regular employee. My next movie, *Endless Night*, was once again made for British Lion. I had been so focused on the theatre, where I felt I was learning and evolving the most, that I had entirely neglected to pursue my film career. I didn't instruct my agent to go hunting on my behalf in the intensely competitive jungle that is the film industry. I would go to Hollywood to see my sister, but never capitalise on the trip by having meetings with directors or producers. Perhaps a part of me was happy to step back from films – I had made two a year since the age of twelve and I wasn't driven to further my career. As a result, the only jobs I heard about were through Roy.

Endless Night was an Agatha Christie novel adapted by Sidney Gilliat, who also directed, and his long-term creative partner Frank Launder. (At a late stage Gilliat's younger brother Leslie took over production duties from Launder.) Sidney Gilliat and Frank Launder were two old boys with decades of filmmaking between them. As a partnership in the 1950s they had created the enormously popular 'St Trinian's' films – but *Endless Night* was another world from the dorm fun and jolly hockey sticks of St Trinian's. *Endless Night* was a murder mystery thriller, and basically a vehicle for Hywel Bennett, who was still signed to British Lion, with Britt Ekland, George Sanders, Per Oscarsson and Patience Collier among the supporting cast. The locations were all on the Isle of Wight, where a stunning house was built on a hill looking down to the sea. My role – an American heiress studying opera at the Met – wasn't particularly challenging but I enjoyed it. Sidney skilfully infused the film with an uncanny, haunted atmosphere, much helped by Bernard Herrmann's score, whom the Boultings had successfully lured to England for *Twisted Nerve*; now Bernard surpassed himself with an even more unsettling theme – which was to be sung to William Blake's 'Auguries of Innocence':

Every Night & Every Morn – Some to Misery are Born
Every Morn & Every Night – Some are Born to Sweet Delight
Some are Born to Sweet Delight
Some are Born to Endless Night . . .

This strange little 'Air' was meant to be sung by my character in the film, but Sidney chose to overdub my voice with that of his own daughter who was actually a real opera singer. No actor wants to be dubbed, but on this occasion I said 'fair enough'. Unfortunately, she was also a contralto and her deep and sonorous voice, lovely as it was, coming out of my seven-stone body sounded like I was possessed by a demon.

All the actors were put up in the beautiful and historic

Farringford House Hotel near Freshwater Bay, once the beloved home of Alfred Lord Tennyson. Britt Ekland and I hung out together quite a lot at the bar; she introduced me to her favourite drink – vodka and freshly squeezed grapefruit juice. 'It won't make you fat or your breath smell, darling,' she said. 'No one will even know that you've been drinking!'

I enjoyed spending time with Britt, she was just as beautiful in real life as she appeared on screen. She always dressed with great flair and possessed a wonderful dry, sardonic sense of humour, which her Swedish accent only made funnier. We spent hours together in her trailer, talking about her life, and often about her marriage to Peter Sellers. Peter was an old friend of the Boulting Brothers, who had helped to catapult his film career with the enormously successful *I'm All Right Jack*. Britt's relationship with Peter had been stormy; the much older husband was mordantly jealous and it all ended in divorce after four years. Despite being a genius and a huge star, Peter remained pathologically insecure and convinced that Britt was flirting with everyone behind his back, which made him manic and intensely controlling. Britt was very funny about that too: she told me the final straw had come when he chopped up all her clothes and she'd hit him over the head with a photograph of his beloved mother (who was definitely part of the problem) – and had then stamped on it! The few times that I met Peter I found him enormously entertaining and charming, but after hearing all Britt's tales, I realised that here was yet another wounded creature playing at being a grownup. And a whispered voice at the back of my mind worried about me and Roy.

Wounded creatures abound in the arts and I was very happy to be working with George Sanders again. It had been ten years since we were together on *In Search of the Castaways* and he was just the same, just as sweet, although there was a new kind of vagueness about him. He had some difficulty remembering his lines and for some reason he could never remember Hywel's name and kept calling him Margaret. I was never quite sure if George really couldn't remember or if he did it on purpose just to make us laugh. It wasn't until much later we discovered that the dear man was struggling with the after-effects of a stroke.

George made only one more film after *Endless Night*. The following spring, I was deeply saddened to hear that he had checked himself into a hotel in Barcelona and swallowed five bottles of barbiturates leaving a typically wry note of farewell. It explained that he was bored, he'd lived too long and that he was leaving us with 'all our worries in this sweet cesspool. Good luck, George Sanders.'

Unique and enigmatic to the end.

Endless Night turned out to be rather good and unusual entertainment, although in 1972, the mystery horror, set to the swirling romances of Bernard Herrmann, seemed a bit out of sync with the times. Sadly the film didn't really make much of a splash. But it has aged well. With its nightmarish dimensions and eerie atmosphere it has gone on to become a cult classic and I'm constantly surprised to find people still discovering it. The immensely talented writer and actor Mark Gatiss and his husband Ian Hallard went as far as to say *Endless Night* was perhaps their favourite Agatha Christie adaptation ever.

So there you go. As is so often the case in the arts – and it was even true for the mad old genius of William Blake himself, who died virtually unknown – even if one succeeds in creating a masterpiece, there's no guarantee you'll live long enough to hear the audience applaud.

★

At the end of 1971, after four years that felt like crossing the Nefud Desert on foot, Stanley Passmore finally brought my appeal before the High Court of Justice. The name of the court was reassuring and I felt confident that justice would indeed prevail. After all, I reminded myself, I had acted in good faith on the advice given. I sat in the High Court of Justice and watched the old judge peer over his spectacles and listened while they argued my fate for three days.

I lost.

I was punch drunk. I couldn't speak. Stanley chuckled and assured me that I must not give up, I must take it even higher! To the Court of Appeal! I took out my pen and wrote another enormous cheque to his firm of solicitors – as the wheels of law resumed turning, painfully slowly. I would wait another year.

By now, Roy had reached the end of his tether. He didn't like the way Stanley was handling the case and he was sure there must be another way. He suggested that I go and meet with Lord Goodman, a high-profile lawyer and a friend of his who was, among many other things, chairman of British Lion.

Goodman's reputation preceded him – it was a bit like suggesting that I go and meet with God. Not only was Lord Arnold Goodman a renowned lawyer with a brilliant mind and a phenomenal memory, he was also a leading troubleshooter for successive British Prime Ministers. He knew everybody and moved in the highest circles of the realm, where, it was alleged, he had consistently employed his inestimable personal influence to smooth over/suppress some of the British Establishment's biggest scandals.

'If anyone can find a solution,' said Roy, 'Arnold can.'

The meeting was arranged for nine o'clock in the morning. I made my way to the address I had been given, fully expecting it to be Lord Goodman's offices, but it turned out to be his private home. I was shown into a high-ceilinged room, every inch from floor to ceiling lined with books. Within minutes, the two wide double doors were flung open and the noble Lord made his appearance, still in his dressing gown which was dark red silk with a quilted black collar and cuffs. Despite the beauty and richness of the flowing gown he still gave the erroneous impression of being completely shambolic. To say he was a 'man of girth' does not quite do him justice. Arnold was a man of gargantuan proportions, huge and very tall, his hair wildly uncombed – but on his enormous unshaven face his smile was beatific.

He moved towards me like a great galleon in a storm and dropped anchor into a capacious leather chair. 'My dear,' he said rather breathlessly, 'I've looked at your case and I am afraid that there really is very little that you can do. In the end, by hook or by crook, the Crown will win.' He then proceeded to underline the problems with which, by this time, I had become only too familiar.

In his opinion, the landscape had changed since my trust was set up. As a direct result of the Jack Hawkins case, which had created a 'precedent', the Revenue were now legally justified in attacking my trust. Just as Stanley had said on that first morning, after my twenty-first, if I had repudiated or liquidated the trust before that birthday (or rather, if *he* had climbed off his backside and done it), the Revenue would not have been able to attack. But that was all with hindsight and not much use now.

In Arnold's professional opinion, that left me with two realistic options:

1.   I could sue Stanley Passmore and his firm, or
2.   Sue my father.

I thanked his Lordship, begged him not to get up, and left the room.

Right from day one, Roy had encouraged me to sue Stanley, but I still could not imagine doing such a thing. He was a family friend and, despite the failures so far, he was still confident we could win an appeal.

Of course, suing my father was out of the question.

So I decided to pursue the appeal, to keep on and see it to its natural end (with my assets still frozen). However, this time, rather than become disheartened and depressed, I began to sing!

I accepted the role of Rose Trelawny with the Bristol Old Vic to perform in my first musical – *Trelawny of the 'Wells'* by Arthur Wing Pinero, with music and lyrics by Julian Slade, directed by the company's artistic director, Val May. I had been having singing lessons for six months in preparation for this new and marvellous and terrifying adventure. I desperately wanted to stretch and challenge myself, so when I was offered the chance to play Rose Trelawny at the Theatre Royal, I couldn't turn it down. The ingenue Rose is star of the 'Wells Theatre Company' and the character has quite a few numbers to sing. I worked very hard on my voice with the musical director, Neil Rhoden, whose gentle guidance, experience and wonderful encouragement empowered me and taught me so much. I loved the music and the character of Rose and I was determined to do it well.

The cast was full of so many talented performers, all of whom had fantastic voices, and I was buoyed up by them every night, especially by John Watts who sang like an angel. (I later discovered he actually was one.) We also had the wonderful Shakespearean actor Ian Richardson as the aspiring young playwright Tom Wrench; Timothy West played Arthur's strict grandfather, and Elizabeth Power was cast as Rose's friend Avonia. There is nothing quite like being part of a big company in the theatre, except maybe being in the trenches. I know that sounds ridiculous but the great camaraderie that you find there, especially in a musical, is enormous. People have to go to extremes, pushing themselves through exhaustion, injury, illness and often personal tragedy as on they go every night, 'over the top', their faces drawn and white under their make-up, swallowing their tears; smiling, singing, dancing and entertaining as if their lives depended on it. I had such enormous admiration and respect for them that all I could do was dig into the furthest reaches of my own spirit and abilities.

I was reminded every night of words my mother imparted to me, the same advice that she had been given by her father years earlier: 'Direct your voice to the back of the stalls, imagine that

I am sitting there and I'm deaf!' And the advice of her mentor, the great theatrical actor/manager Sir Seymour Hicks, who came from a time when dissatisfied punters would heckle and sometimes even throw things: 'Keep your eye on the audience, they're the *enemy*. Never let them out of your sight! If they get the upper hand, we're done for!' Not that I considered the audience the enemy, but the idea of losing the attention of eight hundred or so people, coughing out there in the darkness, is every actor's nightmare.

But the music lifts everything to another level: the sound of the orchestra tuning up, the thrill of the overture, until finally the curtain rises and you're off – there's no going back, nobody to shout 'Cut!' If you forget a line, trip over your skirts or the scenery falls down, you just have to improvise.

In *Trelawny of the 'Wells'* the show begins with a farewell party for Rose, who's leaving the Wells Theatre to marry Arthur. In our opening number Rose, wearing an enormous crinoline, sings to the assembled company from a flower-covered bridge, centre stage. It was a beautiful song called 'Ever of Thee' and the first note I had to hit was E flat, which was quite a tall order, as there were no microphones of any kind in the theatre back then. As the rehearsals progressed, they had to move the flower-covered bridge further and further downstage until it almost fell into the orchestra pit, just so I could be heard. Thankfully, I was saved every night by the arrival of John Watts on the bridge, when, mercifully, my solo became a duet. Singing with John was like being lifted up onto the back of a great white swan, his voice as strong and beautiful and effortless as a feather. As I struggled and developed my confidence throughout that show, John became something of a beacon of light and goodness in my life. We'd have deep conversations at the pub about life and love and God. One day John said that he didn't need to be in a church to find God – he said he could just as easily go off and find God in the middle of a field. It made me think of my time in Africa.

I think it was the first time I'd heard anyone else of my age talk like that. John became a lifelong friend and is still a touchstone in my life.

On one level, things were starting to come together for me. I was making my own friends, discovering what I felt was important about life, about friendships, my work, my contribution, and I was asking important questions, like . . . what did it actually mean to make one's life more spiritual? But the first night threw all that personal freedom into stark contrast. The opening of *Trelawny* was a big occasion in Bristol because it was the inaugural performance of the new Theatre Royal. They had incorporated the Palladian front of the Coopers' Hall, which stood beside the venue, and now the theatre's entrance was through those majestic Georgian columns. The Mayor of Bristol and the Aldermen were present, local dignitaries and celebrities, and the show was rapturously received. Afterwards there was a party in the old cellars of the prestigious Harvey's Restaurant – home of Harvey's Bristol Cream sherry. With all the sherry casks and hundreds of candles it was quite Rabelaisian.

Roy had come up from London for the opening but he didn't seem at all comfortable. It's not easy being an outsider to a close-knit theatre company, all sharing that strong common experience and on the collective 'high' of a first night. Nevertheless, he reacted strangely, and while the company partied downstairs Roy preferred to sit upstairs in solitary splendour.

I sat beside him dutifully, listening to all the laughter and merrymaking below, realising that I didn't want to be up there, away from all of them – and for the first time I found myself resenting his behaviour and furious with myself for accepting it.

★

There is a fundamental instinct in all living creatures – regardless of how happy or unhappy one is in a relationship – when one's chattering mind is pushed firmly aside, and Mother Nature takes the wheel, with an all-powerful, often subconscious, inspiration to build a nest and start a family. I'm not sure how aware I was of this impulse, but, after a brief holiday in Barbados in March 1972, Roy and I set about finding a house to live in. We looked at properties both in London and the country, spending weeks tramping in and out of impossible dwellings, through empty rooms with echoing walls and hollow floors, looking at houses, apartments and cottages. Some were awaiting the next family to come and bring them back to life, some were still complacently full of their present occupants, as we tried to superimpose ourselves onto their lives, their things, their furniture, and to imagine our children running across the garden.

In May this need became more urgent and pressing, as I discovered I was going to have a baby.

I was deeply happy, Roy seemed to be delighted, my parents professed to be thrilled – although I sensed some reservations, which did not altogether come as a surprise.

Ever since that famous astrologer had come to The Wick and looked at my chart, I had secretly feared that I would never be able to have children. I have had many remarkable experiences with astrology over the years, so I don't want to throw the baby out with the bathwater, so to speak, due to one false prediction by the *Daily Express* – but whatever fear or cloud of doubts I may have had were now lifted, thanks, I suspect in no small part, to my relaxing and romantic holiday in the Caribbean.

By midsummer, we had found a house in London, on Lower Belgrave Street. A tall, rambling old terraced town house with five floors, it needed complete gutting and starting again to make it work for us. It was an enormous project and Roy took it on with alacrity. I would visit regularly, tiptoeing about the planks of timber and pots of paint and the clutter of the workmen. Sometimes I would go outside and reconnoitre the area. I had no idea that this dignified Georgian street, with its rows of elegant, terraced houses, would soon be the scene of one of the great murder mysteries of our time. Roy and I had bought the house next door to Lord and Lady Lucan and their three children.

I would often see Lady Lucan out walking, always on her own and always wearing the same pink, sleeveless wool dress by Mary Quant. She was very thin, her arms were white and bony; she had mouse-coloured shoulder-length hair, pushed back off her face by a thick blue Alice band. There was something very strange about her. Sometimes I would be in the basement kitchen of the house and she would stop and crouch down, and peer in through the railings, like a child. We were in on the night the respectable calm of Belgravia was ripped apart by Lady Lucan running down the street screaming hysterically 'Murder! Murder!' as she flung herself into the pub, claiming her husband, 'Lucky' Lord Lucan, had attacked the family nanny, Sandra Rivett, in the basement and battered her to death with a metal pole.

The police suspected he had got the wrong woman – and that the intended victim was his wife.

For some time afterwards, our street was a crime scene. The murder launched one of the biggest and longest criminal manhunts in British history. But Lord Lucan had 'disappeared' and was never seen again.

The building work went on endlessly. I was becoming increasingly pregnant, so we rented a more practical apartment in Ennismore Gardens in Knightsbridge, a rather gloomy flat with two huge, eight-foot wooden Nubian warriors flanking the entrance hall! But it had enough room for a baby and it was just a short walk across the road to Hyde Park. The first thing I did was to buy the most beautiful Silver Cross pram and parked it under the watchful eyes of the Nubians.

While I became more and more immersed in the baby bubble, Roy withdrew into his next project. When he worked, that's all there was in the world – and now I felt very alone. Foolishly, I had allowed my friends to slip away, and very few of Roy's friends came to see us. Roy's life was always his work; whether that was the script he was writing or the film he was shooting or editing, it was an all-consuming passion. He would become so wrapped up and focused on his work that he was almost impossible to reach. He disappeared into this creative world and everything else became irrelevant.

Now that I'm older I would be able to accept it much better and just get on with my own life but, back then, I needed to talk, to share my feelings, my day, my joys and woes. But he wasn't there. He retreated even further when I became pregnant. I could understand it in the beginning, I certainly wasn't feeling or looking my most attractive – I felt blown out and my skin went haywire – but Roy reacted quite strangely. The whole process made him uncomfortable and he kept his distance from me for eight long months.

Roy hadn't learnt his lesson from the disaster of *Twisted Nerve* and he was writing with Leo Marks again, this time a comedy called *Soft Beds, Hard Battles*. It was a vehicle for Peter Sellers, a 'sexy-romp' centred around a bordello during World War Two, with Peter playing multiple roles, from French Resistance agents to the Führer himself. I didn't feel Leo was a healthy influence on Roy, he brought out the drinker in him, as well as the pseudo intellectual. Throughout all Leo's screenplays, from *Peeping Tom* to *Twisted Nerve* to *Soft Beds*, women were either objectified or abused, which made me wonder about his relationship with the opposite sex. Roy was not the sort of person to be easily taken advantage of, but Leo was a complicated character with a knack for feeding off another's weaknesses, and I thought he and Roy became oddly co-dependent. Leo certainly didn't inspire Roy to make great films. *Soft Beds* was just awful.

While Roy was locked away with Leo, I kept an eye on what was going on at Lower Belgrave Street, and, becoming bigger every day, I took to rambling around the country on my own. One afternoon, driving through the winding lanes and fields of Buckinghamshire I spotted something extraordinary standing on a hill in front of me; I followed it up a steep narrow lane, where, leaving the car, I scrambled under an old gate and, breathless with excitement, walked to the top of the rise, where before me stood – a windmill.

I recognised it at once as the children's home in *Chitty Chitty Bang Bang* and it was love at first sight. I was utterly captivated; the tower was twelve-sided (dodecahedral), with white painted weatherboarding and wooden sails, and, apart from the great millstone which had gone, it looked to be in working order. The view from the top of the hill was staggering; it was like being an eagle hovering on the wind – you could see for miles and miles, you could see five counties. A sign stuck into the ground said 'Cobstone Mill – For Sale By Auction'. I looked around the property, imagining us sitting outside in the dappled afternoon sun, watching our child laughing and rushing about in the long grass. That night I told Roy about this incredible place that I had found and how wonderful it was – but of course, how utterly impractical. He laughed. As I did. It was one of my romantic pipe-dreams and I put it out of my mind.

But Roy didn't. Without telling me, the following week he quietly slipped off to the auction and bought it for £30,000. It was crazy, completely, marvellously crazy, and I was reminded how thoughtful and considerate Roy could be – not to speak of being extraordinarily generous.

The windmill would be my dream home in the country, the family nest, and I had great plans for making it all habitable, developing and extending the existing shed into a cottage and landscaping the whole area. It was a major enterprise and I was now spending money like there was no tomorrow, with two properties in a state of development, while renting a large flat in Chelsea, and my first baby on the way.

The costs were as breathtaking as the view from Cobstone Mill. I prayed to God my appeal would succeed.

In October 1972, the day of truth arrived. My tax case went up before the Court of Appeal and was presided over by the unique personage that was Lord Denning, Master of the Rolls.

Lord Tom Denning was often known as 'the people's judge' since he had a reputation for not always simply following 'the letter of the law' like some impersonal machine, rather he was known as a man who sought to understand the subtleties of a case and to carefully arrive at a 'justice' that took into account the uniqueness of each individual. Crucially for me, he was known for his willingness to override 'precedent', which was the cornerstone of the Revenue's case.

So, all things considered, I was very hopeful as I settled myself into my seat in the court and waited for his Lordship to arrive. He was not what I had expected. He wasn't wearing the ceremonial robes and long curled wig of the High Court Judge, but a modest gown with wide white-fur cuffs and a short wig like a barrister. The horsehair wig was thick; it stood quite high off his forehead and looked as if it must be extremely itchy. His cheeks were round and his complexion was ruddy, like someone who spent a lot of their life out of doors, which I believe he did, not in musty old chambers in the law courts. He had a sweet, genuine smile and small, twinkling blue eyes. The whole effect suggested a charming cherub in a wig, which, from time to time, he would absentmindedly push around on his head, forgetting to straighten up.

The proceedings dragged on for four days. Most of the legal arguments were incomprehensible and I waited with a pounding heart for Lord Denning's summing up. Interestingly, whenever he spoke I could understand exactly what he was saying, which could not be said for anybody else.

'If the contention of the Crown is right, the greatest beneficiary of Miss Mills' services will be the Revenue themselves!' he declared, pausing with a benign smile. 'For the first year alone they received £18,000 in income tax from the company* – and

---

* £18,000 is roughly £160,000 in 2021.

they will also receive a very large sum in surtax from her. Then she has to pay agent's commission, the Director's fees, £1000, her solicitor's and accountant's charges – by the time that all these have reaped their harvest, there will not be much left for Miss Mills.'

'Yes! Yes!!' I thought, my heart thrashing and the baby starting to kick. 'Finally! Someone who gets it!'

'It is obvious to me that if Miss Hayley Mills is bound to pay the surtax now claimed by the Revenue . . . the whole of these arrangements were not made for her benefit *in the least*. They ought never to have been entered into by her father, nor anyone advising him – or her. They could only be justified if they resulted in a substantial saving of surtax.'

I can quote Lord Denning verbatim since all the details of the hearing were written down and one can still read his summation online today. He went on to say that at the age of fourteen I could not be treated as having made the settlements myself as I did not have 'the understanding or discretion'.

Concluding, he said, 'In my opinion, the "settlor" in this case was the father, John Mills himself. It was he who made the settlements and each of them. It was not his daughter Hayley Mills. She ought not to be held a "settlor" nor should the income from the shares [paid to the trustees] be regarded as her income.'

As Lord Denning's gavel struck, his words slowly sank in. I couldn't believe it. After five years . . . I'd won!

If I could have, I would have flung my arms around his Lordship's neck!

I wandered out of the court, just as I had on my twenty-first birthday meeting with Stanley, numb with shock, but this time it was because I was ecstatically, deliriously happy.

Crispian was born in Queen Charlotte's Hospital on 18 January 1973.

Roy chose his name; he was Roy's seventh son. My parents came with smiles and hugs and gazed delightedly at the baby. Friends and family came with little gifts and the room was soon filled with the scent of so many flowers. I felt as if nobody had ever managed to have a baby before!

After everyone had finally gone and the room was silent, I remember standing with my baby in my arms, looking out of the window, down to the road. Life was carrying on as normal. And yet it was a new world. Everything felt different because ... I was different. The baby changed everything. I was a woman now, a mother holding the baby she thought she'd never be able to have. And I felt attuned to a truth so simple, so obvious and yet so profound, that every person I saw below, walking along the street, had all been somebody's baby too, had all been welcomed into the world with smiles and tears of joy. All had mothers who would be bound to them for the rest of their lives, whatever trials and tribulations they would experience. And I realised in that peaceful silence, not only was I no longer a child, but I had finally joined the human race. It was a fleeting moment of clarity, but something I will always remember. I no longer felt alone, because I really wasn't. And I felt imbued with a deep connection and compassion for all life.

As the saying goes, 'what goes up must come down'. Shortly afterwards I was informed that the Revenue's Commissioners of Tax had invoked their right to appeal to the House of Lords. They had the scent of blood and were determined not to let me get away – they were going to fight me to the last ditch.

In November 1973, the Crown took my case before the House of Lords and after a few more protracted months of torture, the judgement was finally given – unanimously.

In favour of the Crown.

And with costs.

Those Lordly Ones held that the Commissioners were correct

and I was liable to pay surtax of £106,598 – in today's value, over two million pounds.

The state plundered my trust like a horde of pirates, which is really what they were. It was all over. Seven years of battle, seven years of uncertainty, the highs and lows, not to mention seven years of paying my solicitors to challenge the case – the whole debacle had left me emotionally and financially exhausted.

Apart from the villa in the South of France there wasn't much left. I wasn't living on the streets but I was far from being the financially solvent young woman that I had expected to be, and instead of enjoying the fruits of my child labour, I would have to continue to work, like everyone else, for the rest of my life.

Of course, I mourned the loss of the freedom my small fortune might have given me – but not the money itself. After all, how can you miss something that you never had? The trust money was never a reality. I had never got to see it, to spend it, it was just the knowledge that there was a golden nest egg 'out there' somewhere, waiting for me. And then it was gone. It was never any more substantial than a ghost.

I wonder sometimes, if I had been able to keep the money, which I had worked so hard for as a child, how much difference would it actually have made to my life? I would have been able to buy a bigger house, and not have to worry about paying school fees. But one thing I do know, it would have given me freedom, especially the freedom to say no to a job that meant having to go away and leave my children. That is the only regret I have about losing the money I had earned during those years – losing the freedom to say no.

Aside from the Crown, one person who was considerably richer from my case was Stanley Passmore whose firm did very well to line their pockets. Yes, I still could have 'sued the bastards' but by the time my case was lost Stanley was a very old man, retired and in ill health, and I didn't know if I could risk losing again, this time in a fight against my old solicitors. It is very doubtful he would have been able to pay me back the money anyway. It felt like the moment had passed. If it was to be done, I should have done it right at the beginning. I allowed myself a grim chuckle, for the punchline to this black comedy was that both Jack Hawkins' trust and my own were set up by the same firm: solicitors JD Langton and Passmore.

It was also Stanley who had advised my father to fight the Revenue over their surtax claim on his Rank Organisation bonus. Not only had he lost that case, he'd also had to pay costs. So one way or another, 'Stanley & Elsie', of little white mice fame, cost my family an enormous amount of our hard-earned money.

I wonder if Stanley's conscience bothered him as he spent his declining years living on pale, saltless meals and drinking water, sitting old and alone in the wintry sun of the South of France.

I very much doubt it.

My consolation was the happiness I experienced as a mother. The bond I felt with this tiny being was so powerful, I could always tell his cry from among the cries of all the other babies in the hospital crèche. At that moment, all my own troubles and struggles slipped away; here was something much more important. This child was my sunshine, his smiles, his rages, his laughter enchanted me; from the very beginning he was single-minded and would go his own way; startlingly wise, headstrong and fearless he leapt into life – and I was reminded of that miraculous place of pure loving existence from which we are all born.

Perhaps it was the shock of losing all my money, perhaps it was the joy of becoming a mother, but the combined effect shook me at a profound level and one day, I finally came to accept the hard truth: my marriage to Roy was over. By the end, we had drifted so far apart, neither of us communicated enough to really know each other. Roy responded by becoming more and more controlling, questioning my every move, censoring my friends. He wouldn't even like it if I wanted to go out with the company or to the pub after the curtain came down. And the more he pulled me back, the more I pulled away. 'Let me have my freedom,' I tried to explain. 'Don't keep me on such a short lead and I will always come back to you.' I didn't mean freedom to have other relationships, just the freedom to be young and have friendships with other young people. But he was fearful. He tightened his hold and shortened the lead.

One day, I just walked out the door. I walked away and took nothing but my baby.

I left with the callousness of youth and driven by a primitive need to survive, to start a new life. I left behind everything – the house in London, the windmill that we never finished and would never become our family home, standing there sadly waving its wooden arms at us from the top of the hill.

I was twenty-eight and I knew that life ahead would probably be full of many more mistakes and failures, but at least these would now be solely my responsibility. For better or for worse, they were my choices now. I wasn't going to have to ask anyone's permission, nor would I be able to blame anyone when things went wrong.

I didn't want to feel any bitterness about all the things that had happened. Not towards my parents, not even to Stanley. I did regret the pain I caused Roy, but my marriage had become like a life in retirement, and I was too young to disappear from the world. When the sword finally cut, I offered to give him the villa but, generous to the end, he would not take it. So I arranged for it to be sold – it had too much history for us.

I moved on and began a new life. I had another baby; a sweet, gentle, loving and thoughtful little boy with a wonderful sense of humour who loved animals and nature and watched over everything with a concern and a wisdom beyond his years. Ace had arrived in my life and I was twice blessed. Eventually I bought an old coach house near the Thames at Hampton, where my little boys would grow up. As I watched my children grow and evolve, seeing their own horizons open up before them, it naturally made me reflect on my own childhood. I was reminded of the nagging confusions and guilt I had felt about my extraordinary luck and good fortune. But, at the same time, I also began to see that there was a price attached and, somehow, somewhere, although it may be years in the future, the results of our actions come back to us like homing pigeons.

At a certain point I realised that either one believes life is purely random and chaotic, or you have faith that there's also a higher order – a loving, meaningful purpose, which connects us all. For me, the Law of Karma made perfect sense of this, cause and effect; it seems irrefutable and I believe it absolutely – literally and spiritually. I remember the first time a Krishna devotee carefully and clearly explained to me about karma, and it was like a light going on. We are all 'spiritual beings on a human journey' – so many things happening to us, sometimes good, sometimes bad, but all of it is temporary; the eternal soul, the same spirit within all life, is unchanged and untouched. For my whole life I had struggled with this guilt about my success, but this new perspective helped me to accept that my luck wasn't some terrible cosmic mistake – it was simply my karma. My story. And there's more to come. We are, all of us, still creating our story, our karma, making our choices, consciously or unconsciously, in the here and now – which is a cautionary thought.

Both my boys have children of their own now and I find myself enjoying maternal happiness all over again. Being a grandmother is one of the best gigs in the world. You pick them up, spoil them rotten, stuff them with ice cream and pasta and then just hand them back to the tired parents when they start being sick.

When it comes to being parents, I hope my boys learn from my mistakes. But did I learn from my parents? My mother battled with alcohol her whole life. She never really got the better of it and she paid the price. My father never stopped loving her, nor she him, but their struggle served as a warning. Not necessarily of the perils of drink, but the dangers of failing to face one's demons. So perhaps her battle had a positive outcome after all. Maybe that sounds a bit Pollyanna . . .

There's no doubt that playing that character at such an early age had a lasting influence on me. It made me aware of the importance of seeing the positive. It's not always easy. We all face the struggle to know ourselves and to find the courage to truly be ourselves. When you learn who you are, you learn self-respect, and with that comes the potential for real love. I suppose that's living in Truth.

It was my father's creed and one he always strove to live by. He chose, as our family motto, a line from Polonius's advice to his son Laertes in *Hamlet*. I've heard it said that Shakespeare intended this profound speech as comic relief – but I think that's part of the joke.

Life is half tragedy and half comedy, after all.

To thine own self be true.
Then it shall follow, as night the day,
thou can'st not then be false to any man.

Epilogue

The house I bought in Hampton was a seventeenth-century coaching inn. It had quite a history. Charles Dickens had once stayed there and alluded to it in *Oliver Twist*. The house had a wonky roof and the porch, covered by japonica, listed to one side. It was a very romantic house. Through the glass-panelled front door, you could see straight out to the garden and a rose-covered archway, and beyond that, dominating everything, was a great oak tree that spread its strong limbs like a sentinel across the whole width of the lawn. There were three historic little pear trees that had been planted by Queen Victoria's grandchildren, and over a crumbling red-brick wall was an orchard full of apple trees. In the summer the long grass, full of cow parsley, made wonderful hiding places for hedgehogs and rabbits, and two white-haired little boys.

One evening, I stood outside on the drive and looked back at the dear old house; the lights were all on, I looked up at the two small windows of my boys' bedrooms under the eaves, and the thought came to me that one day they wouldn't be there, they would have grown up and they would have gone. A sudden chill crept into my heart. For a second I stepped outside of Time. The past, the present and the future all seemed part of one singular moment: flashes of my room at The Wick; the view from the top of Richmond Hill; Soxie's smiling face; the rain pounding on the roof of the Dutch barn; my first day filming in Cardiff; the sound of Walt's laughter and that day on the sunny hill with Daddy. All my childhood memories were still alive, as were those of my own mother, fearlessly galloping her pony bareback across the sands in Macau, the wind in her fiery hair – and with this glimpse of undying youth, a realisation that all things must pass.

I shivered and walked quickly back into the light and the warmth, so grateful to be able to rejoin the present when my boys were both still so young, and we were together.

Acknowledgements

It was my son Crispian who, from the first, encouraged me to write this book. He was my creative collaborator, who helped guide me through the labyrinth of my weird childhood. When I expressed doubts as to my ability to write a book, he simply said 'I will help you.' And he did. We sat down together and talked for hours; it was an education! As a working screenwriter, film director and a recording artist with an extremely boisterous young family, he had his hands full, but he explained the vital importance of narrative structure, bringing me back to 'the story' again and again – despite the chaotic events of my early life. Constantly pressing me to go deeper and re-examine past events, asking 'But what did you think? How did it make you feel?', endlessly patient and encouraging; his great insight and marvellous sense of humour helped to keep me on track and not lose the plot entirely! Thank you, darling Crisp, for the absolute joy of working with you on this book. It would simply not exist without you.

A huge thank you must also go to Howard Green, Vice President of Communications at Disney Studios in Burbank, California, for his tremendous generosity and help. And for introducing me to Rebecca Cline, Director of Walt Disney Archives, who gave me unlimited access to the department, which fired my imagination.

Thank you to Kate Staddon, my agent at Curtis Brown, who led me across the office to meet the excellent Gordon Wise, who suddenly, to my astonishment, became my literary agent! Believe me, I am aware how lucky that was. Gordon whirled me around London one day in search of the perfect publisher, who materialised in the shape of Alan Samson of Weidenfeld & Nicolson, of the Orion Publishing Group; a man of excellent taste and judgement. And the rest of the great team: dear Georgia Goodall, Project Editor; Elizabeth Allen, in charge of publicity; and Niall Harman at Curtis Brown.

I am hugely appreciative for the research work of Dennis Lanahan, who helped me immeasurably to understand my deep connection with America, through my ancestors.

Special thanks to my dear cousin Susie Blake, who discovered her grandmother's (my aunty, Annette Mills) old folder of fabulous photographs. And to my cousin Shirley Steel, who typed out the first chapter and got the ball rolling! My entire family has been tremendously encouraging and supportive; none more so than my darling, long-suffering partner of twenty-five years, Firdous Bamji. An actor and fellow writer, in a heartbeat he took over all the daily maintenance of life – keeping body and soul together with superb meals, love and understanding, and patience in the face of my endless meltdowns over the computer! And to my beautiful flame-haired daughter-in-law, Jo, Crisp's wife, for her huge enthusiasm and expertise with Instagram; which I still struggle with.

All my love to Ace, my son, who cheered me on with flowers and calm words of advice as more than once I hit a brick wall. And to my sister, Juliet; loving, positive and generous to a fault and keeping me constantly supplied with some of life's necessities all the way from California! My brother, Jonathan, even though he was on the other side of the world, a rock to lean on.

Special love and thanks to my friend and secretary down the years, Susie Nollet, who made sure that life stayed on course and the bills were paid. To dear Rupert Boulting, for excavating some painful memories and delivering a trove of old letters. Nanette

Newman Forbes, for her wise words and generous advice; bless you, Nan. To John 'Worthy' Watts, a precious and constant source of laughter and positivity. And treasured friend Hazel Graeme Appleyard. And to Andrew Birkin, thank you for letters, photographs and friendship that has endured a lifetime.

I have been blessed with friends who, in no small way, have all contributed to keeping the fire going and the pot boiling: Jane Alexander Millet and Elizabeth de Grunwald Walford, still miraculously in my life; Vanessa Forsyth, a faithful friend through thick and thin; Michael Giaimo, a dear new friend; and Arlene Ludwig, a dear old friend. Thanks to Michael Attenborough for his help and support. And a special thank you to Bee Gilbert, who has consistently taken the best photographs of me – one of which has been used as the author headshot for this book.

One of the gifts of writing this book is that it has brought some special people back into my life: Michael Anderson Jnr and Keith Hampshire, and Susan Henning Schutte, my lovely long-legged photographic double from *The Parent Trap*.

Crispian and I would also like to express our huge thanks and gratitude to Gretchen Young at Grand Central, Hachette Book Group in America, and her team, Staci Burt and Alana Spendley. And my dynamic agent in New York at Don Buchwald, Joanne Nicci.

And last, but by no means least, I want to acknowledge and thank from the bottom of my heart all the amazing people who have continued to support me throughout my entire life – my fans, many of them my friends. You will never know how much your support has meant to me and kept me going for so many years.

With love and gratitude,
Hayley

Index

About the Author

Hayley Mills began her acting career as a child and won a BAFTA award for her performance in the British crime drama *Tiger Bay*. Her seven-picture deal with Walt Disney made her an international star and included her dual role as the twins Sharon and Susan in *The Parent Trap*. She won a special Academy Award at the age of fourteen for *Pollyanna*. For her success with Disney, she received the Disney Legends Award.

Hayley's role in *Whistle Down the Wind*, a 1961 adaptation of the novel written by her mother Mary Hayley Bell, secured her a nomination for the BAFTA award for Best British Actress. She has continued to make films and TV drama, among them *The Flame Trees of Thika*, and featured as Miss Bliss in *Good Morning, Miss Bliss*, and as Caroline in *Wild at Heart* on ITV. She lives in south-west London.